TOXIC LOOPHOLES
Failures and Future Prospects
for Environmental Law

The EPA was established to enforce the environmental laws Congress enacted during the 1970s. Yet today lethal toxins still permeate our environment, causing widespread illness and even death. *Toxic Loopholes* investigates these laws, and the agency charged with their enforcement, to explain why they have failed to arrest the nation's rising environmental crime wave and clean up the country's land, air and water.

This book demonstrates how weak laws, legal loopholes and regulatory negligence harm everyday people struggling to clean up their communities. It concludes that our current system of environmental protection pacifies the public with a false sense of security, dampens environmental activism and erects legal barricades and bureaucratic barriers to shield powerful polluters from the wrath of their victims.

After examining the corrosive economic and political forces undermining environmental lawmaking and law enforcement, the final chapters assess the potential for real improvement and the possibility of building cooperative international agreements to confront the rising tide of ecological perils threatening the entire planet.

Dr. Craig Collins has authored articles on climate negotiations for *AMBIO* and the Clinton administration's environmental policies for *Mother Jones*. After teaching at Sonoma State University and the University of California, Davis, in the early 1990s, he became part of the faculty at California State University East Bay, where he continues to teach environmental law and policy-making, Latin American politics, global political economy, U.S. foreign policy and several other courses. As visiting faculty for the University of Pittsburgh's Semester at Sea program, Collins has lectured on world affairs, climate change negotiations, U.S. foreign policy and Latin American politics aboard ship on the program's world tour and its tour of the Caribbean basin.

TOXIC LOOPHOLES

FAILURES AND FUTURE PROSPECTS
FOR ENVIRONMENTAL LAW

CRAIG COLLINS, Ph.D.

Department of Political Science,
California State University East Bay

CAMBRIDGE
UNIVERSITY PRESS

CAMBRIDGE UNIVERSITY PRESS
Cambridge, New York, Melbourne, Madrid, Cape Town, Singapore,
São Paulo, Delhi, Dubai, Tokyo

Cambridge University Press
32 Avenue of the Americas, New York, NY 10013-2473, USA

www.cambridge.org
Information on this title: www.cambridge.org/9780521143028

First published 2010

Printed in the United States of America

A catalogue record for this publication is available from the British Library.

Library of Congress Cataloguing in Publication data
Collins, Craig.
Toxic loopholes : failures and future prospects for environmental law / Craig Collins.
p.   cm.
Includes bibliographical references and index.
ISBN 978-0-521-76085-0 – ISBN 978-0-521-14302-8
1. Environmental law – United States.   I. Title.
KF3775.C65   2010
344.73′046–dc22   2009046268

ISBN 978-0-521-76085-0 Hardback
ISBN 978-0-521-14302-8 Paperback

Contents

This book is dedicated to
Barbara, Kyla and Gerti,
the most wonderful Earthlings I know.

INTRODUCTION

Crime Without Punishment

Common criminals – such as burglars, drug dealers, kidnappers and bank robbers – frequently find themselves behind bars for their crimes. But one group of lawbreakers – corporate polluters – rarely see the inside of a prison cell, although their crimes pose a greater threat to American lives, health and property than all the rest. Why? Because unlike ordinary criminals, mega-polluters have the wealth and political clout to elect the following:

- Presidents who appoint polluter-friendly administrators to head up the country's pollution control agencies;
- District attorneys who rarely prosecute them for their crimes;
- Sympathetic judges who give them little more than "a slap on the wrist"; and
- Lawmakers who will craft loopholes to make most of their offenses legal.

These powerful polluters routinely disgorge deadly toxins into our air, water and land. Every year their poisons kill more Americans than all murderers combined.[1] Yet these corporate criminals are seldom prosecuted, rarely fined and almost never jailed. For example:

- Air pollution claims at least 70,000 American lives annually – as many as breast and prostate cancer combined – 30,000 more than all traffic fatalities and 54,000 more than all homicides.[2]
- Based on EPA data, every year between 5,500 and 9,000 Americans have their lives shortened by air pollution from power plants that the Department of Justice has taken to court for violating the Clean Air

---

[1] In a typical year, more than 10,000 murders are committed in the United States. In 2001, 15,980 Americans were murdered. Air pollution alone claims about 70,000 American lives annually. *International Encyclopedia of Justice Studies: Chapter 4 – Survey of Criminal Justice*. http://www.iejs.com/Survey_of_CJ/CH04.htm. Fischlowitz-Roberts, Bernie. *Air Pollution Fatalities Now Exceed Traffic Fatalities by 3 to 1*, Earth Policy Institute (September 17, 2002). http://www.earthpolicy.org/Updates/Update17.htm.

[2] Fischlowitz-Roberts, Bernie (September 17, 2002).

Act. These plants trigger between 107,000 and 170,000 asthma attacks annually.[3]
- Yet, according to the EPA's own records, dozens of the country's biggest corporate air polluters – including Ford, General Motors, Shell and Exxon – habitually violate the Clean Air Act by spewing tons of toxins into the air without paying a single penny in fines.[4]

After teaching environmental law for nearly two decades, I have come to realize that there are some serious omissions in the available textbooks on this subject. Generally, environmental law texts do a fine job of presenting the major federal environmental statutes. Some do a decent job of describing the nature and seriousness of the environmental problems these laws are meant to address. However, even the best texts rarely focus on the actual enforcement and effectiveness of our environmental laws, and none have carefully addressed the questions:

- How well are our major environmental laws working?
- What prevents them from achieving their stated goals?

These two questions cannot be answered without exposing the reader to the seamy backstage drama of influence peddling, double-dealing, institutional corruption and public deception that undermines our environmental laws and endangers the health of the people and the planet they are supposed to protect. Yet even the best texts either ignore this pernicious political drama or minimize its insidious impact by sanitizing it under the innocuous label of "policy-making."

To improve our country's environmental law enforcement system, these two questions must be answered. In addition, these questions raise an even more vexing question regarding the possible futility of fundamentally "improving" this system. *Can any government, even one as wealthy and powerful as the United States, hope to bring our fossil fuel-powered, growth- and profit-driven, increasingly globalized economy into a sustainable, healthy relationship with the people, creatures and ecosystems of our planet?*

As we examine each of the major environmental statutes in the following chapters, the astute reader will notice an emerging pattern. All of these laws are under constant assault – directly and indirectly, openly and covertly – by the most powerful polluters they attempt to regulate. This ambush begins "in the womb," when these embryonic laws are still bills passing through Congress. Here, before they were born, even our most promising environmental bills were deformed and crippled by toxic loopholes created by politicians seeking to please the powerful polluting industries that lavish them with favors and fund their campaigns.

---

[3] Clean Air Task Force. *The Power to Kill: Death & Disease from Power Plants Charged with Violating the Clean Air Act* (July 2001). http://cta.policy.net/proactive/newsroom/release.vtml?id=20720.

[4] Coequyt, John, Richard Wiles, & Christopher Campbell. *Above the Law: How the Government Lets Major Air Polluters off the Hook.* (Environmental Working Group: May 1999).

Once born, these weakened laws are rendered into even weaker rules and regulations by a government agency whose mission of environmental protection is seriously compromised by its illicit relationship with the very polluting industries that lobbied against these laws in Congress. Industry lawyers intensively lobby the EPA to further dilute and delay the rule-making process. Often, they receive a sympathetic hearing from EPA officials who hope to one day become high-paid executives for the very polluting firms they now regulate. This "revolving door" has become so incestuous that some environmental groups have had to specialize in suing the EPA to secure court-imposed deadlines that will force the agency to promulgate and enforce its own regulations. Yet, despite this legal pressure to uphold the law, the EPA's history of enforcement remains shamefully defective.

Success in the courts requires a judicial system not predisposed to favor corporate property rights over environmental protection. Unfortunately, because property law has a long and prominent place in American jurisprudence and environmental laws are relatively new, it has been a steep uphill battle to persuade judges to take environmental laws seriously. To make matters worse, because most states elect their judges, candidates for the bench often find themselves taking large campaign contributions from the same polluting firms they face in court. In fact, many of the worst polluters have made it part of their overall strategy to gain as much influence over the courts as possible to avoid taking responsibility for their crimes. In the words of one pro-business lobbyist:

> The business community woke up in the late 1980s and realized that there are three legs to the government stool – the executive branch, the judicial branch and the legislative branch. We were playing quite well for over a decade in two of those three and decided that the judicial branch are the arbitrators of the final interpretation of all rules and regulations that are passed by the legislature. Consequently, from '89 to the present, [we] got involved in statewide appellate court races, most of those being supreme court races … the whole idea … is it's easier to lobby your friends than your enemies.[5]

The arduous process of environmental lawmaking, enforcement and adjudication could be dramatically improved by a presidential administration seriously committed to cracking down on criminal polluters and protecting our natural resources. A president of this caliber could champion a green legislative agenda, steadfastly oppose efforts to insert toxic loopholes, increase the budget of the EPA, eliminate its "revolving door" with industry and appoint agency chiefs and federal judges committed to strictly enforcing our environmental laws. But this has never been the case. Those presidents who have advocated mildly pro-environmental policies have found themselves pilloried by the corporate media, industry and their political rivals as big government liberals whose anti-business policies will ruin the economy. Thus, no

---

[5] *Frontline.* "Justice for Sale." (PBS: November 23, 1999). Read Bill Moyers' interview with Bill Cook, President of Pennsylvanians for Effective Government, a business lobby that raises money for judicial candidates. http://www.pbs.org/wgbh/pages/frontline/shows/justice/etc/script.html, http://www.pbs.org/wgbh/pages/frontline/shows/justice/interviews/cook.html.

administration – no matter how green its rhetoric – has ever made environmental protection a top priority.

Given the relatively low level of public knowledge, concern and activism around the environment, it would be political suicide for any president to directly confront the nation's major polluters. Only large numbers of active, concerned citizens can combat the power of money to pollute democracy. Without this broad base of organized popular support, the ultimate fate of any dedicated green politician is media invisibility coupled with ridicule and character assassination by his or her well-heeled adversaries.

This brings us back to the two questions consistently ignored by environmental policy and law texts. To transform public ignorance and apathy into the kind of citizen movement necessary to make politicians crack down on this mounting toxic crime wave, these two questions must be confronted:

- How well are our major environmental laws working?
- What prevents them from achieving their stated goals?

It is not the intent of this book to examine the effectiveness of every environmental statute on the books. Instead, attention will be focused on the central flaws in our nation's most renowned air, water, toxic control and hazardous waste cleanup statutes and the EPA's nominal record of enforcement. Because the EPA is not the only government agency charged with environmental protection, one chapter will examine the Department of Interior's effort to implement the Endangered Species Act. In doing so, it will become obvious that the nation's failure to protect the environment cannot be attributed to the EPA alone. Global environmental protection will be examined in Chapter 7. By comparing the international community's successful ratification of an ozone treaty with the faltering effort to craft an effective climate agreement, this chapter highlights the three major obstacles to negotiating environmental treaties and assesses the veracity of four rival theories of global cooperation.

Finally, the conclusion assesses the prospects for using laws and international treaties to achieve environmental protection and ecological sustainability within the confines of a factious domestic and global political economy dedicated to maximize economic growth and national power.

I

The EPA – Policing or Protecting Polluters?

Before 1970, America's few environmental laws were hardly worth the trees sacrificed to write them, and no single agency was charged with their enforcement. Over the ensuing decade, this situation changed. Congress passed 27 major environmental laws, and President Nixon created a single federal agency – the Environmental Protection Agency (EPA) – whose sole mission was environmental protection. This dramatic government action was a direct response to widespread public concern and unrelenting, intrepid grassroots activism.

Ignited by media coverage of several sensational environmental calamities and the obviously deteriorating condition of the country's land, air and water, public alarm was adeptly mobilized by a growing army of environmental activists schooled in the civil rights, women's liberation and anti-war movements. Groups such as Greenpeace, Friends of the Earth and the Sierra Club channeled public concern into a powerful ecology movement that compelled politicians to elevate environmental protection to a front-burner issue for the first time in American history.

The ecology movement insisted that the federal government must shoulder responsibility for defending the environment. Environmentalists argued that because pollution ignored state boundaries, and individual states lacked the resources and political will to confront powerful polluters, it was primarily Washington's job to police the polluters and set nationwide goals and standards for all states to follow. In addition, they believed that national standards would prevent a "race-to-the-bottom" between states hoping to attract business by offering the most lax environmental standards.

Once the EPA was established, and tough-sounding laws were passed, many Americans let down their guard. While environmental concern remained high, people figured they could rest easy now that the federal pollution police were watching out for their safety. So when industry continued to discreetly discharge noxious toxins into communities around the country, most folks barely noticed. They figured *if it were dangerous, the government wouldn't allow it*. The environmental movement lost steam. The established environmental organizations became content with beltway lobbying and direct mail memberships. Many people stopped asking questions, speaking out or taking action.

But their complacency proved to be premature. Soon communities, towns and neighborhoods across the country, from Anniston (Alabama) and Times Beach

(Missouri) to Calvert City (Kentucky) and Overland Park (Colorado), discovered that industrial polluters, hazardous waste dumps and toxic waste incinerators had poisoned them. Their faith in government was shaken. However, once the truth was out, they figured the EPA would come to their defense, put a stop to the pollution, clean up their neighborhoods and bring the polluters to justice.

To their shock and dismay, EPA officials were either condescending and indifferent or openly antagonistic to their pleas for help and justice. Neighborhood associations that believed they could count on the EPA to investigate and prosecute criminal polluters were stunned to realize they had to gather their own health and environmental data and hire their own experts, while agency officials concealed or denied them access to the same information collected at taxpayers' expense.

Often, community groups had to raise money and hire lawyers to sue the EPA into action. Once in court, they found themselves up against a battery of government attorneys paid for with their tax dollars. Even when compelled into action by judges or bad publicity, it was very unusual for the EPA to crack down on environmental lawbreakers. Stiff punishments were seldom imposed on corporate polluters, and they were rarely forced to adequately decontaminate the communities they poisoned or redress the suffering they caused.

The aftermath of their harrowing ordeal left many victims of environmental crime disillusioned, outraged and baffled. Why had the agency whose mission is environmental protection treated *them* like adversaries instead of the polluters? Whose side was the law on, anyway? A brief review of the EPA's history sheds a revealing light on these questions.

By the end of the 1970s, the environmental movement was dizzy with success. Ecology activists were elated; finally, the federal government had assumed primary responsibility for the condition of the country's environment. President Nixon and Congress had empowered a specific agency with the authority to enforce a new and growing arsenal of tough-talking environmental laws for the first time in history. This groundbreaking achievement fundamentally elevated the status and political nexus of environmental policy-making. The country's environmental powers were now amassed under a single agency instead of being diluted and dispersed across 50 states and a gaggle of disparate bureaucracies.[1]

Did Nixon's historic decision to consolidate environmental authority under a single agency mean he was a champion of the environment? Hardly. For Nixon, creating the EPA was little more than a political makeover devised by his chief

---

[1] The EPA was cobbled together from programs previously administered by three departments, three bureaus, three agencies, two councils, one commission, one service and several small offices. The Federal Water Quality Administration and all of its pesticide programs were moved from the Interior Department to the EPA. From the Department of Health Education and Welfare, the EPA assumed control over the National Air Pollution Control Administration, the Food & Drug Administration's pesticide research, the Bureau of Solid Waste Management, the Bureau of Water Hygiene and parts of the Bureau of Radiological Health. The Department of Agriculture's Research Service relinquished its pesticide activities to the EPA, while the Atomic Energy Commission and the Federal Radiation Council gave up their radiation criteria and standards programs. Also, the Council on Environmental Quality, created early in 1970, transferred its ecological research to the new agency.

domestic advisor, John Erlichman, to lift his sagging environmental reputation before the upcoming election. By 1970, protecting nature had become a make-or-break "hot button" issue. In April, 20 million people participated in the first Earth Day; *Time* magazine named the environment "Issue of the Year"; and its sister publication, *Life*, designated the 1970s "The Environmental Decade."

At the time, Nixon's primary rival was the front-running Democratic contender for the presidential nomination, Senator Edmond Muskie from Maine. An enthusiastic proponent of Earth Day, Muskie was known on the hill as "Mr. Clean" for his strong environmental record. As chairman of the Senate Public Works Committee on Air and Water Pollution, Muskie sponsored some of nation's toughest new environmental laws, including the newly revised Clean Air Act (CAA).

Erlichman warned Nixon that unless he quickly revamped his dreary environmental image, the issue could sink any prospects for reelection. Referring to recommendations offered by a recent presidential report,[2] Erlichman told the president:

> You know, there's this idea in it. Pretty easy, sounds like. You take a bunch of water pollution stuff that's currently housed over in the Department of Interior; some air pollution stuff that's in Health, Education and Welfare; some radiation stuff over in the Atomic Energy Commission ... Lump them all together, call it the Environmental Protection Agency. Won't cost a cent because we're already doing all this stuff. You just lump it all together and suddenly you're a player.[3]

Although creating the EPA was politically expedient, Nixon was never enthused about the mission of the agency he sired. Immediately after his reelection, Nixon held the first of the few conversations he ever had with his newly appointed EPA chief, William Ruckelshaus. Ruckelshaus recalled that he had just begun to brief the president on his plans for the new agency when Nixon interrupted him saying, "You better watch out for those crazy enviros, Bill! They're a bunch of commie pinko queers!"[4]

Thus, from its inception, the primary purpose of the EPA was never environmental protection. Instead, the EPA was, first and foremost, a political vehicle – the president's way of demonstrating his supposed concern for the environment. Unfortunately, this is the way presidents have used the EPA ever since.

Every presidential administration favors a handful of "front-burner issues," which are usually national security and foreign affairs, the economy and the budget and perhaps one or two others. These top-drawer issues are the ones he plans to act on. Barring any unforeseen crises, they are expected to dominate the administration's political focus and become the center of national attention. Then there are "back-burner issues." On these issues, the president does not expect action and performance – he wants peace and quiet. Instead of being at the center of national attention,

---

[2] The President's Advisory Council on Executive Organization headed by Roy Ash made the recommendation.

[3] Quoted in: Hayes, Dennis. "Earth Day 2000: End Global Warming," *TIMELINE No. 50* (March/April 2000 – email edition). http://www.globalcommunity.org/cgpub/50/50.htm.

[4] Quoted in: Davis, Derva. *When Smoke Ran Like Water*. (NY: Basic Books), 2002: 95.

these issues are supposed to stay off the evening news and fade quietly into the background.

Regardless of party affiliation, presidents prefer the environment to remain a back-burner issue. They bring environmental issues up to the front burner only when they have little choice. The crises at Three Mile Island and Love Canal forced President Carter to put the environment on the front burner. But even then, the goal was to handle each crisis as quickly as possible in order to return it to the back burner where it belonged.

Presidents avoid appointing activist EPA chiefs – administrators who will increase awareness of the ominous environmental crises confronting us and lead the effort to overcome them. Why? Because there is little the EPA can do about these crises without stepping on some very influential toes.

No president has encouraged the EPA to write stiff regulations to prevent global warming and improve air quality because the powerful oil, coal and auto industries would line up against him claiming his policies will cause an energy crisis and economic recession. No president wants the EPA to dramatically reduce the level of toxins and carcinogens in our nation's waterways or carefully test and restrict the use of pesticides and other dangerous chemicals because powerful chemical companies and agribusiness interests would go on the warpath against "heavy-handed government over-regulation."

Presidents and presidential candidates who dare to pay more than lip service to environmental protection find powerful polluters lining up to support their rivals. For example, Al Gore's light green image was not appreciated by the major chemical, oil, coal, timber and mining industries. They favored the toxic Texan with more than 90 percent of their campaign contributions. This allowed the Bush campaign to outspend Gore 10 to 1.[5]

Presidents who don't wish to court political suicide are careful not to become too serious about their efforts to protect the environment. Instead, they appoint EPA chiefs who know how to avoid stepping on powerful toes while keeping serious environmental problems off the front pages and milking any small efforts on behalf of Mother Nature for as much positive press as possible.

It is hard to exaggerate the impact of presidential leadership over the agency's enthusiasm for fighting environmental crime. The EPA's enforcement record is heavily influenced by the messages it receives from the top. David A. Ullrich, an experienced and respected former EPA regional manager, explained:

> The people [at EPA] who work on enforcement are very, very sensitive to signals about what they are doing. Because enforcement has always been, and will always be, controversial and contentious, it is very critical that the people working on it have entirely clear signals that enforcement is important, that compliance with

---

[5] PEER. "Polluters Get Big on Bush on the Campaign Money Trail," *The Toxic Texas Tour* (November 1995). http://www.txpeer.org/Bush/Polluters_Bet_On_Bush.html; Case, David. "Grumbling About Gore," TomPaine.com. http://www.tompaine.com/feature2.cfm/ID/3845.

environmental laws is important and that the people who do the work will be supported. Those signals have to come from the top.[6]

Yet, according to veteran EPA officer, William Sanjour, the consistent message from the top is this: *keep the environment on the back burner – don't make waves!* Sanjour believes this directive, set by every president and his appointed EPA chiefs, fosters a bureaucratic culture of "procrastination, obfuscation and coming up with super-ficially plausible reasons for accomplishing nothing."[7]

Does this mean that the EPA is a monolithic government agency staffed from top to bottom by "do-little" bureaucrats motivated only by narrow self-promotion? On the contrary, some EPA officials joined the agency with the idealistic goal of devoting their careers to improving the environment. Indeed, this dwindling number of agency "enviros" has been the EPA's conscience over the years. William Sanjour was one of these endangered species of enviros who worked tirelessly to compel the EPA to reform itself and fulfill its mission. By building alliances with environmental organizations, community activists, sympathetic politicians and journalists, enviros have blown the whistle on agency conflicts of interest, corruption and deceit, and have championed the ongoing struggle to make the EPA do its job.

However, instead of being rewarded for their efforts, EPA whistleblowers have been demoted, fired, harassed, threatened and even put under surveillance by their bosses. For example, Reagan's EPA chief, Anne Burford, tried to silence agency whistleblower, Hugh Kaufman, with surveillance photos of him entering a hotel room accompanied by a brunette. The effort backfired when the brunette turned out to be his wife.[8]

Unlike the shrinking faction of enviros and whistleblowers within the EPA, most agency employees are either apathetic get-alongs or ambitious careerists. Careerists know that maintaining a tranquil, nonconfrontational relationship with the polluting industries they regulate is the key to pleasing their superiors and advancing their careers. This polluter-friendly orientation helps many EPA regulators land lucrative industry jobs when they leave the agency. In addition, a polluter-tolerant attitude facilitates promotion within a bureaucratic hierarchy run by presidential appointees whose job security depends on keeping the environment out of the spotlight and avoiding confrontations with powerful polluters.

At the top of agency's careerist hierarchy are the program honchos ensconced in the EPA's Washington, DC headquarters. Many of these top-level politicos are presidential appointees. The regulations and programs they promulgate must fall within the parameters of the law, stand up to judicial review, weather Congressional oversight and satisfy the White House. In addition, program honchos are subject to

---

[6] Mintz, Joel A. "Treading Water: A Preliminary Assessment of EPA Enforcement During the Bush II Administration," *Environmental Law Review* (October 2004): 34.

[7] Sanjour, William. "In Name Only," *Sierra Magazine* (September/October 1992). http://pwp.lincs. net/sanjour/Sierra.htm#hammer.

[8] "EPA Chief Harassing Whistleblowers," *Rachel's Hazardous Waste News* #254 (October 9, 1991). http://www.ejnet.org/rachel/rhwn254.htm.

unrelenting, direct and indirect lobbying pressure to go easy on the powerful polluting interests their policies will affect.

Of course, the nation's major environmental groups seek to influence the program honchos' policy-making process as well. But a sense of perspective is important here. The combined lobbying power of all major environmental organizations on Capitol Hill is approximately 80 lobbyists. The nine largest polluting industries have more than 80 lobbyists apiece.[9] Thus, unless these environmental groups can muster vast public support and garner sympathetic media attention for their cause, any behind-the-scenes lobbying effort will be dominated by powerful polluters.

Program honchos are continually courted and seduced by the promise of lucrative future positions with the polluting corporations they regulate. For example, after stepping down from his position as the EPA's second chief administrator, Russell Train took a position on the board of directors of Union Carbide; Lee Thomas, EPA chief from 1985 to 1989, became executive vice president of Georgia Pacific; and DuPont put William Reilly on its board of directors after he resigned as head of the agency in 1993.[10]

The EPA's first boss, William Ruckelshaus, was the quintessential master of the agency's revolving door with industry. After leaving the EPA in 1973, Ruckelshaus became senior vice president and director of Weyerhaeuser – the giant timber and paper products corporation. Meanwhile, his law firm (Ruckelshaus, Beveridge Fairbanks & Diamond) was hired by the Society of the Plastics Industry (SPI) to defend dangerous chemicals like vinyl chloride from adverse publicity and the increasing regulatory initiatives of Congress, EPA, Occupational Safety and Health Administration (OSHA) and the Food and Drug Administration (FDA).[11]

In the mid-1970s, the chemical and plastics industry was aggressively defending itself from mounting scientific evidence that vinyl chloride was responsible for causing angiosarcoma. Consumer groups were calling for a ban on vinyl chloride as a spray can propellant; Clairol pulled 100,000 cans of hair spray from store shelves and the EPA issued a rare "Emergency Suspension Order" for all pesticide sprays containing vinyl chloride for use in homes and other enclosed areas.[12] With Ruckelshaus's experience, reputation and high-level contacts inside the White

---

[9] Atmosphere Alliance. *Life Support: A Citizens' Guide to Solving the Atmosphere Crisis.* (Olympia, WA: Earth Island Institute), 1995: 19. See also: "Tools for the Rollback – $$ and Lobbyists," *US-PIRG.* http://www.pirg.org/reports/enviro/super25/page4.htm.

[10] A more extensive analysis of the EPA's revolving door can be found at: http://www.sourcewatch.org/index.php?title=EPA%27s_Revolving_Door. For a more detailed list of EPA program honchos who have taken lucrative positions in the waste management industry see: "EPA's Revolving Door," by William Sanjour. http://pwp.lincs.net/sanjour/Revolving.htm. Finally, the report, *From Bureaucrats to Fat Cats* by the Environmental Working Group provides information on the revolving door between the pesticide industry and the program honchos in the EPA's pesticide program. http://www.ewg.org/reports/fatcats/fatcats.html.

[11] Markowitz, Gerald & David Rosner. *Deceit and Denial: The Deadly Politics of Industrial Pollution.* (Berkeley, CA: University of California Press), 2002: 210.

[12] Markowitz, Gerald & David Rosner, 2002: 208–9.

House and the EPA, his law firm was the ideal defender of vinyl chloride from agency regulators who were in the midst of deciding whether to impose stiffer air quality standards on the chemical.[13]

After helping Weyerhaeuser, the chemical industry and other clients finesse EPA regulations and outmaneuver environmental and consumer groups, Ruckelshaus returned to head up the agency under Ronald Reagan from 1983 to 1985. Between and after his two terms, Ruckelshaus was a director of several corporations concerned with EPA regulations including Monsanto and the American Paper Institute.

After his second stint with the EPA, Ruckelshaus formed a consulting firm that was hired by The Coalition on Superfund. Composed of some of the nation's worst polluters – such as Monsanto, Occidental Petroleum, Alcoa, Dow Chemical, AT&T, DuPont and Union Carbide – this coalition sought Ruckelshaus's influence to help weaken the Superfund law and absolve them of strict liability for cleaning up their toxic waste dumps. To assist him in this cause, Ruckelshaus sought the assistance of two former EPA chiefs: William Reilly and Lee Thomas.[14]

Later, Ruckelshaus became CEO of Browning-Ferris (BFI), the country's second largest waste management company. BFI was a notorious environmental criminal with known underworld connections and a long rap-sheet that had cost the corporation millions in fines.[15] Ruckelshaus's appointment as a Browning-Ferris director in June 1987 came roughly one month after the EPA filed a $70 million lawsuit alleging thousands of violations by the company at a Louisiana landfill. Several months later, Ruckelshaus became George H. W. Bush's environmental advisor while Bush ran for president in 1988. When Bush won the election, Ruckelshaus used his influence to install his friend and protégé, William Reilly, as EPA chief, and his former employee (in his consulting firm), Henry Habicht, as deputy EPA administrator.

Thus, Ruckelshaus – the CEO of a major corporate polluter being sued by the EPA – was able to successfully place two close associates in the top two positions within the EPA.[16] In August 1988, Browning-Ferris and the EPA agreed to settle the $70 million suit for a controversial $1.1 million; the next month, *Industry Week* reported that Ruckelshaus was named president and CEO of BFI at a salary exceeding $1 million.[17]

[13] CMA (Special Programs Advisory Group). "Record of Meeting," *MCA Papers* (April 21, 1981); Markowitz, Gerald & David Rosner, 2002: 208–9.
[14] Sanjour, William (September/October 1992).
[15] For more information to BFI's organized crime connections see: Lipset, Brian. "BFI: The Sludge of the Waste Industry," *Multinational Monitor*, v. 11, n. 6 (June 1990). http://multinationalmonitor.org/hyper/issues/1990/06/lipset.html.
[16] Sanjour, William (September/October 1992).
[17] Ballenger, Josey. "EPA's Industry Tilt," *Garden State EnviroNet* (February 21, 2001). http://www.gsenet.org/library/10gov/epa-whit.php.

COULD WE FIX THE EPA BY ELECTING A DEMOCRATIC PRESIDENT, LIKE AL GORE OR BARAK OBAMA, KNOWN FOR THEIR ENVIRONMENTALIST CONVICTIONS?

Most liberal environmentalists believe there are *major* differences between Republican and Democratic presidents when it comes to environmental protection. On the surface, they appear to be right. Democratic presidents have a somewhat greener environmental record than Republicans. Why? Because the coalition of powerful interests that backs Republican presidents reads like a "Who's Who" of the nation's worst polluters.

Nevertheless, this doesn't mean Democratic presidential candidates turn down campaign contributions from corporate polluters. In fact, many of the country's largest polluters contribute to both parties.[18] This gives them access to, and influence over, whoever is elected. However, in addition to industrial polluters, Democratic presidents must heed environmentalists as well because the coalition of interests that supports Democratic candidates includes most of America's prominent environmental organizations.

Unfortunately, these environmental groups lack the resources to be major campaign donors. Studies by Greenpeace and the Center for Responsive Politics showed that, from 1991 through 1994, environmental political action committees (PACs) donated a grand total of $1.7 million to political candidates.[19] Whereas, in the 1992 elections alone, polluter PACs from the coal and oil industries, electric utilities, automobile manufacturers and chemical companies gave $23 million to Republican and Democratic candidates.[20] Thus, in broad terms, major polluters contributed about 98 percent more campaign cash than environmentalists.[21]

Although the meager sums environmental groups donate pale in comparison to the financial backing the country's major polluters can offer favored candidates, some argue that environmentalists still have substantial leverage over Democratic politicians because of their sway over voters with strong ecological concerns. However, this influence may not generate the political clout one would expect. Why? Because in our winner-take-all electoral system dominated by two parties, Democratic politicians know that environmentally concerned voters won't abandon them for their Republican rivals. With the environmental vote "in-the-bag," Democratic politicians frequently betray this constituency to curry favor with wealthy corporate polluters.

[18] Greenpeace Report. *Oiling the Machine: Fossil Fuel Dollars Funneled into the US Political Process* (October 20, 1997). http://archive.greenpeace.org/climate/kindustry/government/machine.html.
[19] Atmosphere Alliance. *Life Support: A Citizen's Guide to Solving the Atmospheric Crisis.* (Olympia, WA: Earth Island Institute): 19; Greenpeace Report. *Oiling the Machine: Fossil Fuel Dollars Funneled into the US Political Process.* http://archive.greenpeace.org/climate/kindustry/government/machine.html.
[20] Center for Responsive Politics. *PACs in Profile: Spending Patterns in 1992 Elections.* (Washington, DC: CRP), 1993.
[21] This figure is quite conservative because it does not include contributions from many other anti-environmental interests – like waste management, timber, mining and agri-business – that made substantial campaign contributions.

Case in point: Immediately before and after the 1992 presidential election, Vice President-elect Al Gore assured the residents of East Liverpool, Ohio that the Clinton/Gore administration would not permit the infamous Waste Technologies Industries (WTI) toxic waste incinerator to continue poisoning their community. After a 10-year battle to shut down the incinerator, East Liverpool residents were overjoyed. Located just 400 yards from a school and 320 feet from the nearest home, this incinerator – the largest in the nation – released at least 3.5 million pounds of highly toxic substances into the air each year even when operating at maximum efficiency.[22]

But after 8 years in office, the Clinton/Gore administration never moved to shut down the WTI toxic waste incinerator, despite continuing public protest and more than 130 violations of WTI's operating permit.[23] In 1993, when the *Cleveland Plain Dealer* asked EPA whistleblower, Hugh Kaufman, "Why would this ostensibly pro-environmentalist Democratic administration break its promise to shut down the WTI incinerator?" His response was, "The best way to understand what happens in Washington is to follow the money … With WTI, all money roads lead to Jack Stephens."[24] Indeed, a host of investigative articles revealed that Gore's betrayal was probably linked to Jackson Stephens, the chairman of Stephens Inc., the nation's largest investment bank off Wall Street (located in Little Rock, Arkansas).[25]

Jackson Stephens was the biggest single financial backer of the Clinton/Gore campaign and the original lead investor in the WTI incinerator. This Little Rock billionaire had supported Clinton in each of his campaigns for governor; raised $100,000 in contributions for the 1992 Clinton-Gore campaign and extended a $3.5 million line of credit to the campaign through his bank.[26] According to investigative reporters, Peter Truell and Larry Gurwin, no group raised more money for the Clinton presidential campaign than the Stephens Group.[27]

Stephens was well placed to make sure the WTI incinerator continued to operate, no matter who became president. He kept strong ties to many former presidents – from Jimmy Carter to George Bush, Senior – and to both political parties. In 1991, Stephens's wife was the Arkansas cochair of Bush senior's presidential campaign and Stephens

[22] Maximum efficiency, according to the EPA's own records, was almost never accomplished.
[23] Sierra Club, Greenpeace, Tri-State Environmental Council, Ohio PIRG, et.al. "Letter to President Clinton with Concerns about WTI," *Greenlink* (December 6, 2000). http://www. greenlink.org/public/hotissues/wtipres.html.
[24] Jake Tapper. "The Town That Haunts Al Gore," Salon.com (April 26, 2000). http://archive.salon. com/politics2000/feature/2000/04/26/gore/index3.html.
[25] Stephens Inc. was listed as one of the biggest institutional shareholders in 30 large multinationals including the Arkansas-based firms Tyson Food and Wal-Mart. It was Stephens who staked Sam Walton when he started Wal-Mart in 1970, and financed Tyson's takeover of Holly Farms in 1988. See: Lipsett, Brian & Ellen Connett. "Jackson Stephens – Father of WTI," *Free Republic.com a Conservative News Forum.* http://www.freerepublic.com/forum/a37d95a0809ce.htm.
[26] O'Donnell, Jennifer. "Gore & Bush Tied to WTI Incinerator," *Ohio Citizen Action* (Fall/Winter 1999–2000). http://www.ohiocitizen.org/campaigns/prevention/wti/jennl.html.
[27] Truell, Peter & Larry Gurwin. *False Profits: The Inside Story of BCCI, the World's Most Corrupt Financial Empire.* (NY: Houghton-Mifflin), 1992.

himself contributed $100,000 to the Republican Party.[28] In that same year, according to *The Wall Street Journal*, Stephens arranged to bail out a small Texas oil company on the verge of bankruptcy. One of the company's directors and major stockholders was George W. Bush.[29]

The outgoing Clinton-Gore administration retaliated against EPA whistleblower, Hugh Kaufman, for helping the citizens of East Liverpool keep the WTI incinerator and the administration's broken promises in the media spotlight. They blamed Kaufman for keeping this issue on the front burner and exposing damaging information that harmed Gore's bid for president in Ohio and Florida. Kaufman was relieved of his duties by Clinton appointee, EPA administrator Tim Fields, in the final days of Clinton's term in office.[30]

Hugh Kaufman had worked as chief investigator in the Ombudsman's Office – a tiny, understaffed watchdog unit within the EPA responsible for investigating citizen and Congressional complaints leveled against the agency. In this capacity, Kaufman investigated three cases that all became major thorns in the side of Clinton's EPA chief, Carol Browner, by exposing a host of flawed cleanup plans and a rash of government-polluter collusion.

Two of these three high-profile, politically damaging cases were in Florida. The third was the WTI incinerator in Ohio. Ohio and Florida were both states Gore narrowly lost in the presidential election. Just days before the 2000 election, an ombudsman's investigation revealed that Gore had passed up an opportunity to scuttle the WTI incinerator's trial burn permit in the weeks between the 1992 election and the 1993 inauguration. Yet, Gore had encouraged outgoing EPA Administrator, William Reilly, to approve the incinerator's trial burn permit *before* he and Clinton assumed power. A month after this story hit the media, and the day after Gore conceded the election, Kaufman lost his job.[31]

Hugh Kaufman, a 30-year EPA veteran, called the move, "politically motivated revenge … It's revenge of the EPA bureaucracy and revenge of the politicos who wanted Gore elected," Kaufman told the Environmental News Service. "After Gore conceded, there was a confluence of revenge from the politicos and the entrenched bureaucracy to cripple the ombudsman's office."[32]

Unlike Republicans, Democratic presidents usually talk green, and sometimes they want to demonstrate their concern for nature by appointing moderate environmentalists to head up key government agencies and prosecute a few high-profile

---

[28] Lipsett, Brian & Ellen Connett. "Jackson Stephens – Father of WTI," *Free Republic.com a Conservative News Forum* (June 1990). http://www.freerepublic.com/forum/a37d95a0809ce.htm.

[29] See: *The American Spectator* (October 1992); O'Donnell, Jennifer. "Gore & Bush Tied to WTI Incinerator," *Ohio Citizen Action* (Fall/Winter 1999–2000). http://www.ohiocitizen.org/campaigns/prevention/wti/jennl.html.

[30] St. Clair, Jeffrey & Alexander Cockburn. "Nature and Politics," *Eat the State*, v. 5, n. 10 (January 2001). http://eatthestate.org/05-10/NaturePolitics.htm.

[31] Hansen, Brian. "Removal of EPA Investigator Called Political Revenge: Why Gore Really Lost Ohio," *Environmental News Service* (December 18, 2000). http://www.mapcruzin.com/news/news121900a.htm.

[32] Hansen, Brian (December 18, 2000).

environmental crimes. However, like their Republican counterparts, they prefer environmental issues to remain on the back burner and they are still quite willing to soft-pedal enforcement, sell out to wealthy polluters; ignore agency corruption; and retaliate against those who expose their double-dealing, broken promises and cover-ups to the public.

CAN THE SYSTEM BE REFORMED?

The most effective, courageous and dedicated community leader to emerge from the struggle to shut down the WTI incinerator was Terri Swearingen. A nurse and mother from the Ohio Valley, Terri earned national renown for her tireless activism and was awarded the Goldman Environmental Prize for North America in 1997. In her acceptance speech, Terri summarized the lessons she learned about the EPA and our political system. Her insights merit extensive quoting:

> One of the main lessons I have learned from the WTI experience is that we are losing our democracy. How have I come to this sad realization? Democracy is defined by Merriam Webster as "government by the people, especially rule of the majority," and "the common people constituting the source of political authority." This definition of democracy no longer fits with the reality of what is happening in East Liverpool, Ohio.
>
> For one thing, it is on the record that the majority of people in the Ohio Valley do not want the WTI hazardous waste incinerator in their area, and they have been opposed to the project from its inception. Some of our elected officials have tried to help us, but the forces arrayed against us have been stronger than we or they had imagined. Public concerns and protests have been smothered with meaningless public hearings, voodoo risk assessment and slick legal maneuvering. *Government agencies that were set up to protect public health and the environment only do their job if it does not conflict with corporate interests.* Our current reality is that we live in a "wealthocracy" – big money simply gets what it wants. In this wealthocracy, we see three dynamics at play: corporations versus the planet, the government versus the people, and corporate consultants or "experts" versus common sense. In the case of WTI, we have seen all three.
>
> *The second lesson I have learned ties directly to the first, and that is that corporations can control the highest office in the land.* When Bill Clinton and Al Gore came to the Ohio Valley, they called the siting of the WTI hazardous waste incinerator – next door to a 400-student elementary school, in the middle of an impoverished Appalachian neighborhood, immediately on the bank of the Ohio River in a flood plain – an "UNBELIEVABLE IDEA." They said we ought to have control over where these things are located. They even went so far as to say they would stop it. But then they didn't! What has been revealed in all this is that there are forces running this country that are far more powerful than the President and the Vice President. This country trumpets to the world how democratic it is, but it's funny that I come from a community that our President dare not visit because he cannot witness first hand the injustice which he has allowed in the interest of a

multinational corporations – Von Roll of Switzerland; the Union Bank of Switzerland; and Jackson Stephens, a private investment banker from Arkansas. These forces are far more relevant to our little town than the President of the United States![33]

The lessons drawn by Terri Swearingen demonstrate that citizens must demand fundamental reforms of the EPA in particular, and the political system in general, to make them responsive and accountable to communities and citizens, not corporate polluters. The EPA cannot be effective unless both the president and Congress want effectiveness.

However, the current system of campaign finance allows polluters to purchase influence over our political representatives, and even presidents, from both major political parties. Without basic campaign finance reforms, this problem will continue. In addition, Democratic politicians will continue to betray environmentalists and take the green vote for granted as long as they think they have a lock on it. To dismantle these two roadblocks to democracy, at least two reforms are essential:

(1) Campaign finance reform that effectively deprives corporate polluters of their leverage over politicians and election outcomes; and

(2) A strong, citizen-based Green Party alternative to the Republican and Democratic parties' duopoly over our electoral system.[34]

With these reforms in place, voters would dramatically improve their chances of electing a President and a Congress committed to making the EPA favor the public over the polluters. Three ways to do this are as follows:

(1) Protect and reward whistleblowers for calling attention to waste, graft, corruption, fraud and conflicts of interest that prevent regulators from protecting the environment and the public.

(2) Eliminate the revolving door between the EPA and the industries it regulates.

(3) Pass strict bad-boy laws to deter chronic polluters.

Bad-boy laws are used in several states. They ban chronic environmental lawbreakers from doing business with state governments. Unfortunately, existing bad-boy laws are too discretionary and seldom invoked. Many of the nation's worst polluters are hazardous waste disposal facilities, such as the WTI incinerator in East Liverpool. All these facilities must obtain federal licenses and most have contracts with some combination of local, state and federal government. William Sanjour, veteran EPA official with extensive experience in the area of hazardous waste disposal, contends

---

[33] Swearingen, Terri. *Goldman Environmental Prize Acceptance Speech* (1997). (Greenpeace Website). http://www.greenpeaceusa.org/wti/terry.htm.

[34] Maximizing the influence of an alternative party like the Greens would require implementing some other basic democratic electoral reforms like: (1) proportional (or full) representation and (2) instant run-off voting. For further information see: *The Center for Voting Democracy*: http://www.fairvote.org/.

that a mandatory federal bad-boy law applied to the licensing of hazardous waste disposal sites would force these facilities to obey the law or cease operation.[35]

Because many of the nation's worst polluters contract with the government, require government licenses and permits, or lease government land, bad-boy laws could be used far more extensively against polluters. Why should citizens allow the government to award contracts and tax dollars to environmental criminals with extensive records of poisoning the public? Instead of rewarding incorrigible polluters with lucrative government contracts, shouldn't these serial criminals face stiff penalties or prison sentences?

The revolving door has already been discussed. It should be obvious that regulatory officials who view their jobs as stepping stones to better ones with the industries they regulate cannot be relied on to serve the public interest faithfully. Yet revolving doors can be found between almost all government agencies and the businesses they regulate. And everywhere they exist, they foster conflicts of interest that compromise the agency's capability to serve the public. Revolving doors should be slammed shut and locked. The law should forbid political appointees and senior government employees from accepting any form of employment, fee or other form of compensation from any person or corporation regulated by their agency for a period of at least 5 years after leaving government office. Unfortunately, Congress has never passed a law prohibiting regulatory officials from going to work for companies their agency regulates.[36]

Opponents of such laws generally argue that they would prevent good people from entering government. However, the opposite effect seems more likely. A strong revolving door prohibition would repel the self-serving careerists who now permeate the EPA (and other government agencies) and attract people with a genuine desire to protect the environment and the public.

Whistleblowers keep government agencies honest. However, as the cases of Hugh Kaufman and William Sanjour demonstrate, EPA officials who expose high-level agency corruption and collusion with corporate polluters can expect to be investigated, harassed, threatened, isolated and even demoted or fired.[37] The EPA will never improve by persecuting whistleblowers. Congress must make sure whistleblowers are legally protected and even rewarded when their charges are proven correct. This would increase the number of whistleblowers and send a potent warning to those in the agency who would abuse their power and position.[38]

---

[35] Sanjour, William (September/October 1992).

[36] President Clinton made a half-hearted effort to control the revolving door between government regulators and the industries they regulate when he issued Executive Order 12834. It required all executive branch political appointees above a Level V pay grade to take a binding and legally enforceable pledge that they would not lobby any officer or employee of that agency within 5 years after leaving their appointment. However, he rescinded this order before leaving office.

[37] For more case studies see: National Whistleblower Center. "Political Science Prevails Over Sound Science at EPA" (1992). http://www.whistleblowers.org/epawhistleblowers.htm.

[38] For more information on Whistleblowing and the law visit *The National Whistleblower Center.* http://www.whistleblowers.org/.

One final way to compel the EPA to put the public interest over the polluters is to empower the Ombudsman's Office within the EPA by increasing its legal mandate, independence, staff and operating budget. A strong, independent Ombudsman's Office is essential for keeping the EPA honest, accountable and responsive to the citizens and communities it is supposed to protect. After coming under the direction of chief ombudsman Robert Martin, the EPA's Ombudsman's Office earned the respect and trust of grassroots environmental groups around the country struggling to get the EPA to listen to their problems and detoxify their neighborhoods. Time after time, Martin's office provided these groups with the only avenue for voicing their concerns, airing their grievances and improving the undemocratic, dangerous industry-friendly cleanup methods so often employed by EPA bureaucrats.

Although the ombudsman has no formal power, he can order investigations and make recommendations for change that have real clout. Martin and his chief investigator, Hugh Kaufman, conduct hearings with dissatisfied communities and occasionally go door to door to talk with neighbors living closest to the EPA's most controversial cleanups. The Ombudsman's Office has launched investigations into agency cover-ups, the falsification of scientific data, the suppression of unwanted studies, graft and collusion with industry. At times, ombudsman investigations have led to peace talks between the EPA and angry taxpayers; often, they have exposed possible criminal chicanery requiring FBI involvement.

While none of this endeared the Ombudsman's Office to the EPA's top brass, it earned Martin and Kaufman the enduring gratitude of the communities they have gone to bat for. For example, EPA officials continually ignored citizen activist, Marie Flickinger, and her neighbors in the South Belt suburb of Huston. For years, they urged the agency to look into the sick pets, tumor-laden dogs and the black goo that seeped up from beneath their driveways and homes. In one year, 11 of the 13 babies born in their Huston subdivision suffered from severe birth defects.

Finally, with the ombudsman's help, the site was examined. They discovered that the toxic soup saturating this community had been dumped by Monsanto and other chemical companies for years. When regional EPA officials decided to dredge up and incinerate the 245,000 tons of toxic sludge at a site within their community, Marie Flickinger sought the ombudsman's help again. But the EPA top brass refused to pay for Robert Martin's airfare to Texas. In desperation, Flickinger offered to pay his airfare out of her own pocket.

Eventually, the Ombudsman's Office got involved. Martin's investigation revealed that Monsanto's wastes contained high levels of mercury that cannot be destroyed by incineration. This finding finally convinced the EPA to scrap the toxic incinerator only ten days before burning was scheduled to begin.[39] Instead, the EPA decided to contain the toxic sludge in a 50-foot-deep pit, surrounded by a concrete wall, covered with a gas containment layer, and studded with air-monitoring devices. Standing water is pumped and treated in an attempt to lower the volume of contaminants in the bodies of fish caught in nearby Clear Creek, which already had the

---

[39] Dubose, Louis. "Whacked by Whitman," *The Texas Observer* (May 24, 2002). http://www.texasobserver.org/article.php?aid=740.

highest trace amounts of toxic substances ever detected in fish tested in the United States. A toxic elementary school and 677 contaminated homes had to be razed by the developer and dumped in this landfill.[40]

According to Marie Flickinger, the ombudsman's office is " ... the only hope in the system. There is no one else. Where Bob Martin's concerned, he is the purest-hearted person I have ever met in my life besides my father. You cannot have a stronger advocate than that man."[41]

This was Robert Martin's first case as ombudsman and it set a pattern that would repeat itself many times. Martin's office earned the respect and trust of community groups from the pesticide-laden waste dumps of McFarland, California and the dioxin-drenched community of Times Beach, Missouri to Denver's Rocky Mountain Arsenal where the U.S. Army and Shell Oil left a 27-square-mile wilderness saturated with the toxic contaminants of chemical and biological weapons production.[42] Martin's integrity and the ombudsman's ability to dig through confidential files and summon witnesses from the deepest reaches of the EPA encouraged citizens groups not to give up the fight to detoxify their communities.[43]

According to Martin, "The classical model of ombudsman goes back three, four hundred years ago in Sweden, where you had an official who literally would stand between the king and the governed." According to that model, the ombudsman "can investigate any complaint that a person brings to them," says Martin. "I have tried to follow that model as much as possible ... A true ombudsman has to be independent. He can't be told not to look into something – not to think this, or say that – because that stifles the function. That's really the first hallmark of a classical ombudsman: independence from the entity you've been charged to look at."[44]

Congress established the Ombudsman's Office in 1986 as part of the Resource Conservation and Recovery Act (RCRA) – the major federal law governing the legal disposal of hazardous wastes. Unfortunately, the Ombudsman's Office was never given the complete independence or sufficient resources necessary to adequately investigate community complaints or suggest remedies regarding the EPA's handling of environmental problems.[45]

---

[40] Dubose, Louis (May 24, 2002).

[41] Worland, Gayle. "Mr. Clean: Superfund Ombudsman is Either a White Knight or an EPA Whitewash," *The Denver Westword* (April 1, 1999). http://www.westword.com/issues/1999-04-01/feature2.html/1/index.html.

[42] The Sierra Club. "The Real Truth About the Rocky Mountain Arsenal" (July 1999). http://www.rmc.sierraclub.org/emg/RMA.html.

[43] *Written Testimony of William A. Smedley for the Senate Environment and Public Works Committee Hearing Regarding the EPA National Ombudsman Office* [submitted on behalf of three nonprofit organizations: GreenWatch, The Pennsylvania Environmental Network (PEN) and Arrest the Incinerator Remediation (AIR)] (July 15, 2002). http://www.senate.gov/~epw/107th/Smedley_062502.htm.

[44] Worland, Gayle (April 1, 1999).

[45] Project on Government Oversight. Comments on the "Draft Guidance for the National Hazardous Waste and Superfund Ombudsman and Regional Superfund Ombudsmen Program," *Federal Register*, v. 66, n. 2 (January 3, 2001). http://www.pogo.org/p/environment/eo-010112-epa.htm.

In fact, the EPA's top brass tried to keep the Ombudsman's Office unpublicized and unknown. For example, on the EPA website, the Ombudsman's Office was not included in the EPA organizational chart.[46] Environmental lawyer, Sandra Jaquith, fought EPA intransigence and industry collusion around the cleanup of the Rocky Mountain Arsenal for many years without knowing the Ombudsman's Office even existed. "It's the best-kept secret in the federal government," she told The Denver Westword, and added that most of her citizen-activist contacts around the country had never heard of the ombudsman. "I suspect it's because he's effective."[47]

Despite the ombudsman's puny resources, small size and relative obscurity, Robert Martin and his skeletal staff (one full-time investigator and three office staff) valiantly strove to handle the 4,000-plus complaints that came in on their toll-free line every year. In addition, they read mailbags of letters asking them to look into conflicts with the EPA's toxic cleanup programs. Unfortunately, many of these problems went uninvestigated because the office's meager staff and paltry annual budget ($100,000) could not possibly handle them.[48]

The Ombudsman's Office was designed to field problems within the EPA's hazardous-waste disposal program; consequently, its purview was limited primarily to only two of the many laws the EPA is mandated to enforce.[49] In addition, the operational scope and independence of the ombudsman were sharply restricted by the fact that its budget was not separate from the agency, and the president's EPA chief could determine the cases the ombudsman was allowed to investigate.

In 2001 and 2002, Congress's investigatory arm, the General Accounting Office (GAO), released reports recommending that the EPA "provide [its] ombudsman with a separate budget and ... the authority to hire, fire and supervise his own staff." It concluded that "If both the ombudsman's budget and workload are outside his or her control, then the ombudsman will be unable to ensure that the resources for implementing its function are adequate."[50]

The EPA's top brass never embraced the GAO's recommendations. Instead, throughout the Clinton and George W. Bush presidencies, successive EPA chiefs have sought to weaken the ombudsman's powers and even eliminate the office completely. Carol Browner, Clinton's EPA chief, tried unsuccessfully to force citizens to go through hastily contrived "regional ombudsmen" who would then contact EPA top brass who would decide whether or not to involve Martin's office. In one of her last acts, Browner fired Hugh Kaufman as Martin's chief investigator, but a public outcry that gained bipartisan support restored Kaufman to his job.

If hostility characterized the ombudsman's relationship with Clinton's EPA boss, "total war" is the only way to describe the relationship between the Ombudsman's

---

[46] *EPA Organizational Structure* (November 10, 2009). http://www.epa.gov/epapages/epahome/organization.htm.

[47] Worland, Gayle (April 1, 1999).

[48] Worland, Gayle (April 1, 1999).

[49] These two laws are RCRA (the Resource Conservation and Recovery Act) and CERCLA (the Comprehensive Environmental Response, Compensation and Liability Act), better known as Superfund.

[50] GAO. *Issues Raised by the Reorganization of EPA's Ombudsman Function* (October 31, 2002).

Office and Bush's first EPA boss, Christie Todd Whitman. This war took place on a several fronts and began with a battle over a superfund cleanup in Denver.

The Shattuck Chemical Company, located in Denver's working class neighborhood of Overland Park, had been listed as a superfund site since 1983. After years of pushing the EPA to remove the tons of radioactive waste located at the site, the EPA finally agreed that removal was the only remedy that would adequately ensure the health and safety of the community.

But suddenly, without explanation or consultation with the residents of Overland Park, the EPA reversed itself and announced a new plan. Labeled the "mound-and-cap" method, this plan consisted of piling half a million cubic yards of radioactive waste inside a concrete block and sealing it with a clay cap. The result would be a giant 17-foot high monolith filled with radioactive waste right in the middle of Overland Park.

Overland Park residents felt betrayed and outraged. The plan was angrily opposed by the neighborhood, the mayor of Denver, the Governor of Colorado and Republican Senator Wayne Allard. Allard encouraged citizens to contact the Ombudsman's Office.

In 1999, Martin and Kaufman initiated their investigation and concluded that the "mound-and-cap" plan was faulty, dangerous and not the normal procedure for dealing with this type of problem. Then they launched an inquiry into why the EPA had abruptly reneged on its removal agreement.

They found that EPA's reversal came after a series of secret meetings between high-level EPA officials and the attorneys representing Shattuck Chemical Company, the party liable for cleaning the site. In addition, the ombudsman's investigation forced EPA officials to concede that they purposely misled the public about the safety and stability of the concrete container that would degenerate and leak radioactive waste much sooner than they originally claimed.[51] Public outrage prompted the agency to scrap the "mound-and-cap" plan and restore the removal policy.

Removing the radioactive soil and hauling it to a hazardous waste disposal site was a much more expensive remedy. So Shattuck Chemical and its parent company, Citigroup, pressured the EPA to reduce their cleanup liability and use taxpayer dollars to make up the difference. Before these negotiations were finalized, President Bush appointed Christie Todd Whitman to head up the EPA.

Citigroup was the very first firm listed on Whitman's "Public Finance Disclosure Form." She and her husband owned about $250,000 of Citigroup stock. In addition, Whitman's husband, who worked for Citigroup for 15 years, had recently become managing partner in a venture capital firm (Sycamore Ventures) in which Citigroup was a principle investor.[52] Clearly, any involvement by Whitman in the negotiations between EPA and Citigroup-Shattuck would be a serious conflict of interest.

---

[51] Hansen, Brian. "Critics Say EPA Needs Independent Oversight," *Environmental News Service* (September 25, 2002). http://www.agrnews.org/issues/90/environment.html.
[52] Hertsgaard, Mark. "Conflict of Interest for Christie Todd Whitman?," Salon.com (January 14, 2002). http://www.salon.com/politics/feature/2002/01/14/whitman/print.html.

A federal criminal statute (18 U.S.C. 208) prohibits federal officials from participating personally and substantially in matters that would affect their financial interests. As required upon assuming office, Whitman filed a written ethics agreement promising to recuse herself from participating personally and substantially "in any particular matter in which I have, or any person or organization whose interests are imputed to me has, a financial interest, if the particular matter will have a direct and predictable effect on their financial interest."[53] However, Whitman never formally recused herself from the Shattuck negotiations.

Citigroup faired exceptionally well in the final agreement. The EPA agreed to limit Citigroup's liability to $7.2 million while Martin and Kaufman estimated that the total bill for the cleanup could easily reach $100 million.[54] Thus, the EPA negotiated an agreement that might have allowed Citigroup to stiff taxpayers for more than $90 million in cleanup costs.[55] Martin and Kaufman exposed this taxpayer rip-off, initiated a probe into Whitman's role in this sweetheart deal and began to organize public hearings in Denver to oppose the agreement and present their findings to a Colorado judge.

In the midst of this controversy, another battlefront opened up between Whitman and the Ombudsman's Office. Once again, it involved Christie Todd Whitman's Citigroup connections and a lead-contaminated superfund site in Scranton, Pennsylvania. Local residents wanted a thorough cleanup and removal that would have cost about $85 million. However, the owners of the contaminated Marjol Battery site, Gould Electronics – Citigroup's partner in a $1.5 billion joint venture – favored a $10–24 million partial cleanup that would leave most of the contamination buried in the neighborhood under an impermeable cap. In a virtual replay of the situation in Overland Park, EPA officials under Whitman's authority came out in favor of the cheaper solution, saving Citigroup's business partner about $70 million. The Ombudsman's Office exposed Whitman's conflict of interest and came out in favor of the more thorough cleanup plan.

Neither of these battles gained much national publicity until yet another conflict erupted between EPA chief Whitman and Martin's office. This conflict was destined to gain media attention because it involved the cleanup of the World Trade Center (WTC) after 9–11.

It was the EPA's duty to investigate the possible environmental threats created by 9–11; keep the public informed about how to protect themselves and oversee the process of cleaning up any toxic hazards created by the disaster. Instead, the cover-up and high-level mismanagement began almost immediately. Only three days after 9–11, Christie Todd Whitman personally assured New Yorkers that the dust-filled air around Ground Zero was "not a health problem." Four days later, Whitman told reporters, "I am glad to reassure the people of New York . . . that their air is safe to

---

[53] Cherry, Sheila R. "Uproar at EPA," *Insight on the News* (May 6, 2002). http://www.insightmag. com/main.cfm/include/detail/storyid/249993.html.

[54] EPA officials estimate $22 million. Hertsgaard, Mark (January 14, 2002).

[55] Hertsgaard, Mark (January 14, 2002).

breathe and their water is safe to drink."[56] On September 21, the EPA's website claimed, "City residents are not being exposed to dangerous contaminants."[57] These public announcements were made despite the fact that the EPA was well aware that the two towers contained enormous amounts of asbestos and other life-threatening substances.

Unbeknownst to the public, Whitman's false reassurances were made under direct pressure from the White House and without any scientific evidence to support them. Later investigations revealed that the White House had compelled the EPA to add language to a press release announcing that "our tests show that it is safe for New Yorkers to go back to work in New York's financial district" even though EPA tests were showing levels of asbestos 200–300 times above the level considered safe by the agency.[58] In the weeks and months that followed, the White House continued to pressure the EPA to downplay and ignore the serious indoor and outdoor threats posed by WTC dust and debris, and to omit from their press releases any guidance about safe indoor cleanup procedures for residents and businesses.[59]

Those responsible for this cover-up of 9–11's toxic fallout have yet to be named. It is clear that they were members of Bush's National Security Council and the Council on Environmental Quality (CEQ). The CEQ is chaired by James Connaughton, a lawyer who formerly represented the asbestos industry. However, President Bush stonewalled all efforts to investigate the matter further.

In the weeks after 9–11, Robert Martin's Ombudsman's Office began to receive questions and complaints from New Yorkers whose knowledge and experiences told them the EPA was ignoring and whitewashing the serious environmental threats posed by the collapse of the two towers. Unfortunately, EPA chief Whitman would not allow the Ombudsman's Office to become officially involved until a groundswell of protest led by New York Congressman Jerrold Nadler's "Ground Zero Elected Officials Task Force" compelled her to relent.

Four months after 9–11, the Ombudsman's Office finally arrived in New York and began its investigation. Quickly it became obvious that the evidence of a cover-up was overwhelming. Congressman Nadler was furious: "EPA officials lied when they initially were telling people that the air was safe!" He suggested that the White House had allowed economic concerns, such as the desire to reopen Wall Street, to take precedence over public health.[60] Nadler praised the Ombudsman's Office and said Martin's and Kaufman's involvement initiated a "sea change" in the

---

[56] Gonzalez, Juan. *Fallout: The Environmental Consequences of the World Trade Center Collapse.* (NY: The New Press), 2002.

[57] Newman, David. NYCOSH *Testimony at the EPA Ombudsman Investigative Hearing on the Environmental & Public Health Impact of the WTC Attack* (February 23, 2003). http://911digital archive.org/webcontent/nycosh/UPDATES/EPAOmbudsHearingFeb23.html.

[58] Kennedy, Robert F. Jr. *Crimes Against Nature*. (NY: Harper/Collins), 2004: 81.

[59] Lee, Jennifer. "White House Sway is Seen in EPA Response to 9–11," *New York Times* (August 8, 2003). http://www.732-2m2m.com/tt/2003-05_articles.htm.

[60] Shogren, Elizabeth. "EPA Accused of Softpedaling 9–11 Data," *LA Times* (August 23, 2003).

relationship between the EPA and the worried, frustrated and angry residents of New York.[61]

But despite the mounting evidence collected by Martin and Kaufman, EPA chief Whitman continued to stonewall and side-step all the hard questions being asked by the residents near Ground Zero and Congressman Nadler's task force. How dangerous was the air around Ground Zero? Were evacuations necessary? Was it safe to breathe the air indoors? What was causing all the adverse health effects being experienced by rescue workers and residents of New York? Was the fine dust and debris that blanketed the city toxic? What precautions should be taken when cleaning it up? Will the government clean up indoor areas? Who will pay for these cleanups? What are the long-term health threats to the residents around Ground Zero who are continually exposed to the dust and debris of the WTC?

When presented with these vital questions and concerns, the EPA top brass either maintained that everything was safe or claimed that the city of New York was in charge of indoor environments and that EPA had no authority for ensuring indoor air quality. Neither of these responses was the truth. Yet the agency stubbornly held to its position that the air around Ground Zero was safe even after being presented with independent test results, conducted by long-time EPA contractors, which showed hazardous particulate concentrations "never before seen" and dangerously elevated levels of extremely toxic materials – asbestos, heavy metals, PCBs and dioxin – inside downtown apartments.[62]

With conflicting information flying about, nobody knew whom to believe. The rescue workers and residents, who trusted EPA chief Whitman as head of the government's expert agency on environmental health problems, went about their business without taking the necessary health precautions. This was a decision many now regret. A Mount Sinai Medical Center Study found that 78 percent of the rescue workers suffered lung ailments, and 88 percent had ear, nose and throat problems in the months following the attack. Ten months later, lung and respiratory problems persisted for half of them.[63]

However, lacking expert investigation and guidance, even the skeptical were left in the dark about what precautions to take. Should they evacuate their homes? For how long? If they stayed, should they wear masks that filter dust? How effective was this? Should masks be worn indoors and outdoors? For how long? If the indoor dust is as hazardous as some say, how do you get it out of your homes safely? With the lead government agency refusing to acknowledge the dangers or plan a cleanup of highly contaminated indoor spaces, confused residents and businesses were left to fend for themselves.

When the ombudsman's team finally arrived at Ground Zero, it held public hearings and gathered and disseminated as much information regarding these

---

[61] Press Release. Representative Jerrold Nadler. *Rep. Nadler Offers Assessment of Federal Response to 9–11 in Front of National Commission* (May 22, 2003). http://www.house.gov/nadler/9–11commission_052203.htm.

[62] Kennedy, Robert F. Jr., 2004: 82; Press Release. Representative Jerrold Nadler (May 22, 2003).

[63] Kennedy, Robert F. Jr., 2004: 82.

questions as possible. Martin and Kaufman were able to tell the city's residents what the EPA should have done, could have done and has done at other hazardous sites around the country. According to Congressman Nadler:

> ... most importantly, the Ombudsman process provided a forum to communicate with my constituents, listen to their complaints and concerns, issue requests for the production of documents and interrogatories, hold public hearings, bring in experts from around the country to help the citizens understand the full magnitude of the issues, make recommendations for corrective action, and truly get to the bottom of what EPA did and did not do. Through these activities, the Ombudsman process documented areas where the EPA was not following the law and standard procedures in the World Trade Center case, and recommended corrective action to protect the public.
>
> The key to all of this is that it was a public and transparent process. We held two eleven-hour hearings that were open to the public, documented with a court reporter, the transcripts of which are available to anyone. We heard from residents, workers, business owners, city and state elected officials, firefighters, police officers, parents and the NYC Board of Education.[64]

New Yorkers and Nadler's task force would have liked Whitman and the other EPA officials in charge to participate in the hearings as well, but – except for Martin and Kaufman – the agency refused to participate. A spokesperson for Christie Todd Whitman said the agency did "not believe ... hearings on this issue [would] be productive" and dismissed the ombudsman's hearings as "pure theater."[65] An outraged Congressman Nadler replied:

> Except for the Ombudsman, the EPA has yet to engage in a public and transparent process regarding the cleanup of the World Trade Center. If anything, it has done just the opposite. Questions have gone unanswered, and information obtained only through the Freedom of Information Act, if at all. Trying to get the agency to act has been a lengthy, arduous and often unsuccessful process. The Ombudsman process was essential to address citizen complaints and focus public pressure on the agency to resolve those complaints.[66]

Although Congressman Nadler and the residents of New York appreciated the ombudsman's hearings and investigations, they drew media attention to the EPA cover-up and generated a hornets' nest of negative publicity for Christie Todd Whitman. By early 2002, the public anger generated by the EPA's whitewash and mishandling of the 9–11 cleanup had become a serious political liability for Bush's EPA chief.

To provide legal cover for the EPA and the White House, the president gave Whitman the power to bury embarrassing documents by classifying them "secret." "I hereby designate the Administrator of the Environmental Protection Agency to

---

[64] Representative Jerrold Nadler (May 22, 2003).
[65] Cottin, Heather. "EPA and City Ignore Dangers," *Workers' World News* (March 7, 2002). Quoted from *NY Times* (February 24, 2002).
[66] Representative Jerrold Nadler (May 22, 2003).

classify information originally as 'Secret,'" states the executive order signed by President Bush on May 6, 2002.[67] Bush's explanation for the directive was to keep "national security information" from falling into enemy hands. However, advocates for thousands of ailing Ground Zero heroes suspect a more sinister motive. "I think the rationale behind this was to not let people know what they were potentially exposed to," said Joel Kupferman of the New York Environmental Law and Justice Project. "They're using the secrecy thing to cover up their malfeasance and past deceptions."[68]

While covering her tracks, Whitman searched for a way to silence the ombudsman without appearing that she was trying to eliminate her critics. In November 2001, Whitman tried to subordinate the Ombudsman's Office to the authority of the EPA's Inspector General (IG). She insisted that the move was designed to give the ombudsman more independence because of the IG's watchdog function. But to those who understood the internal politics of the EPA, Whitman's real intentions were transparent.

The Inspector General's Office (IGO) was anything but a friendly, or even neutral, location to move the ombudsman. The IGO itself was the target of an ombudsman probe to see whether it had purposely disregarded health risks stemming from toxic gases leaking into homes around Overland Park and other Colorado superfund sites. With the bipartisan support of 26 members of Congress, the General Accountability Project (GAP) and community activists around the country, Martin resisted Whitman's effort to move and muzzle his office.[69]

Lawyers from the Government Accountability Project (GAP) – a nonprofit, public interest law firm that defends whistleblowers – volunteered to help Martin defend the independence of his office in court. GAP lawyer, Jack Sheridan, told the press, "[Whitman] is cutting sweetheart deals and getting rid of people who can raise questions about it."[70] In January 2002, Martin scored a preliminary victory when a U.S. District Court judge granted a temporary restraining order against Whitman's attempt to relocate the Ombudsman's Office.

Whitman scrambled to counter Martin's charges that her actions were a retaliatory effort designed to cripple the Ombudsman's Office and shut down their investigations into the agency's 9–11 cover-up and her covert involvement in sweetheart deals the EPA had negotiated with Citigroup and its partners in the Denver and Scranton superfund cleanups.

When questioned by the press, Whitman first insisted that she had recused herself from the Denver case. But when she could produce no document to verify her statement, she changed her position, insisting that she didn't have to formally recuse herself because she was never involved in these cases.

---

[67] "EPA's 9–11 'Secret' '02 Exec Order Let Agency Bury Info on Air Hazards," *New York Daily News* (July 28, 2006).

[68] "EPA's 9–11 'Secret' '02 Exec Order Let Agency Bury Info on Air Hazards" (July 28, 2006).

[69] *Statement of Robert J. Martin Before the US Senate Committee on Environment and Public Works* (June 25, 2002).

[70] Soraghan, Mike. "Ties to Shattuck's Owner Hike Scrutiny of EPA Chief," *The Denver Post* (January 21, 2002). http://www.denverpost.com.

While EPA chief Whitman impatiently waited out her temporary restraining order,[71] Martin and Kaufman's investigation of the 9–11 cover-up revealed yet another conflict of interest involving the EPA chief and her husband's financial ties to Citigroup. Hugh Kaufman's conflict of interest probe revealed that Citigroup – a giant insurance and banking conglomerate – stood to lose many millions of dollars if the EPA applied more stringent cleanup standards to the contaminated area of lower Manhattan where environmental scientists were finding levels of outdoor and indoor toxins higher than many superfund sites.

In fact, just one of Citigroup's insurance companies – Travelers Insurance – was probably the largest underwriter of commercial property and business-interruption insurance in New York.[72] According to Kaufman, if the hazard zone at Ground Zero were widened to include lower Manhattan, as he believes it should have been from the start, the costs to insurers, the largest of which is Travelers, would skyrocket.

Kaufman asked the Department of Justice (DoJ) and the FBI to investigate further. In a memorandum sent to the DoJ, Kaufman charged Whitman with providing false information to the public on the air quality surrounding the World Trade Center. "We have on the record that insurance companies saved millions of dollars by relying on Whitman's false statements in sending residents of Lower Manhattan back into unsafe conditions," he said.[73]

On April 12, Martin's temporary restraining order (TRO) against Whitman was lifted after EPA attorneys assured the judge that Martin's concerns about reassignment would be addressed within the EPA's established administrative remedies. But this was not to be. As soon as the TRO was lifted, Whitman ordered the ombudsman's immediate reassignment.

On Earth Day, April 22, while Martin was out of town, Whitman sent EPA officials to raid the Ombudsman's Office. The Inspector General seized Martin's files and computers, removed all telephones from the office and changed the lock on the office door. Martin and Kaufman labeled Whitman's act a criminal cover-up. Martin informed reporters that Whitman and her husband had financial holdings in most of the 24 pending cleanup disputes under investigation when she abolished his office and seized his files.[74]

After the raid, Robert Martin resigned. In part, Martin's letter of resignation to Whitman said:

"I hope you find it in yourself to recognize that by obliterating the independent Ombudsman function, you have deprived the American people and the Congress of

---

[71] In late January, Whitman sent five EPA officials to Martin's office and attempted to confiscate his files. See: Beaudry, Kendall. "EPA Ombudsman Fights for His Job," *Environmental News Network* (March 15, 2002). http://www.enn.com/news/enn-stories/2002/03/03152002/s_46676.asp.

[72] Cherry, Sheila R. "Uproar at EPA," *Insight on the News* (May 6, 2002). http://www.insightmag.com/main.cfm/include/detail/storyid/249993.html.

[73] Beaudry, Kendall (March 15, 2002).

[74] Press Release. "Whistleblower Group Calls for Congressional Probe of EPA Leadership: GAO Exposes False Statements in Court," *Government Accountability Project* (November 14, 2002). http://www.whistleblower.org/article.php?did=173&scid=108.

a valuable means with [which] to keep the EPA true to its mission of protecting human health and the environment and to be accountable to American communities.

I cannot recognize in principle and conscience ... the seizure of my files and planned transfer to the Office of Inspector General where I will not continue to serve as an independent Ombudsman, but will merely answer a telephone. Moreover, your communication to the inspector general to seize my files, change my locks and transfer me immediately to the Office of Inspector General underscores the fact that the inspector general had no actual independence if they proceeded to act at your discretion.

... It was wrong of you to unilaterally decide this matter while ignoring the pleas of dozens of Members of Congress, both Republicans and Democrats ... The American people deserve nothing less than a truly independent Ombudsman, especially those facing threats to their health by uncontrolled hazardous and toxic waste sites across the Nation, most recently at Ground Zero in New York City ..."[75]

Whitman's raid on the Ombudsman's Office and the resignation of Martin angered, shocked and dismayed all the people who had come to respect and rely on the Ombudsman's Office to come to their assistance when faced with collusion between a callous, intransigent bureaucracy and the polluters who had poisoned their communities. Around the country, environmental activists and community leaders denounced the raid and called for Congress to create a truly independent Ombudsman's Office.[76]

The residents of Lower Manhattan were especially frustrated and angered by the loss of the ombudsman. The leaders of one neighborhood group said,

Without Martin's hearings, our concerns and the independent tests which prove the existence of hazardous substances in this and surrounding neighborhoods, would not be a matter of public record ...

As a result of the EPA's negligence, numerous residents have been ill since 9/11/01, unable to resume their lives, despite being relocated. Numerous residents have upper respiratory complications, decreased pulmonary function, reactive airway disease and spontaneous nosebleeds. Specific residents have been advised by their pulmonologists and environmental physicians that they should not return to their homes until the EPA comprehensively remediates all contaminated zones and enforces mandatory remediation of exteriors, interiors and HVAC systems for asbestos, cadmium, dioxin, fiberglass, mercury, PCBs, silica, etc. According to our physicians any exposure is significant in terms of health consequences. Without an

---

[75] The full text of Robert Martin's letter can be found at the *Grist Magazine* website: http://www. gristmagazine.com/muck/muck042302.asp.

[76] For a collection of statements by leaders from community groups around the country denouncing the raid, testifying to the value of Martin's Ombudsman Office and calling for Congress to create a new independent Ombudsman's Office see: Project on Government Oversight (POGO). *Written Statements of Community Members Participating in the Citizens' Briefing on the EPA Ombudsman Issue* (January 14, 2003). http://www.pogo.org/p/environment/eo-030101b-epa.html.

independent ombudsman as an advocate for those affected by the EPA's dissimulation and inaction, we are deprived of our health, our homes, our work, our neighborhoods.[77]

Getting rid of Robert Martin made Christie Todd Whitman very unpopular – especially in New York. So the following month, the EPA chief decided to give her tarnished reputation a facelift. In May, 2002 – four months after the Ombudsman's Office began holding hearings and eight months after the collapse of the World Trade Center – Whitman finally reversed herself and agreed to begin some limited level of indoor residential cleanup around Ground Zero.

It was too little, too late. Congressman Nadler's task force and most independent experts considered this new cleanup policy woefully inadequate. For example:

(1) The EPA will clean apartments only on request, ignoring the threat of cross- and recontamination from uncleaned apartments and from building HVAC systems.

(2) The EPA will test for asbestos only in the air, and will not assess dust or hard surfaces that are also pathways of exposure.

(3) The EPA will not test for any of the other contaminants that were present in World Trade Center debris, such as lead, mercury, dioxin and fine particulate matter.

(4) The cleanup plan is available only south of an arbitrary boundary at Canal Street, cutting off other areas covered by the debris cloud, including parts of Brooklyn, Chinatown and the Lower East Side. Besides not dealing with many potentially contaminated areas, this presents an environmental justice problem.

(5) The EPA will not clean commercial spaces, fire stations[78] and schools.

(6) The workers will not be wearing protective gear, which would seem to be a clear violation of OSHA regulations.[79]

In Nadler's opinion, the EPA would not have made even this limited concession "... without the Ombudsman process, and the expertise and hard work of Mr. Martin, his Chief Investigator Hugh Kaufman and the people who worked with them to use the Ombudsman process so effectively."[80]

Even after his resignation, Martin continued to work unofficially with Nadler's task force and encouraged the citizens of New York to demand that the EPA establish a

---

[77] *Citizens' Briefing on the Ombudsman Issue.* Written Statement of Environmental Watch, submitted by Carla Breeze, Wayne Decker, Tina & Adrian Panaro, George & Wendy Tabb, Miriam & Louis Songster, B. L. Ochman, Kate Bernstein, M. D. Miriam Nunberg, Esq., Linda Burdick, Barbara Einzig, Ban Leow, Caroline Martin – Treasurer of Family Association of Tribeca East (not displaced), Diane Dreyfus (January 14, 2003). http://www.pogo.org/p/environment/eo-03010rb-epa.html.

[78] Press Release. *Nadler Blasts EPA on Firefighter Snub, Demands Answers* (March 13, 2003).

[79] Representative Jerrold Nadler (May 22, 2003).

[80] Representative Jerrold Nadler (May 22, 2003).

Citizen's Advisory Group, hold public hearings, establish an administrative record accessible to the public and create a more comprehensive cleanup process that complies with the laws governing the treatment of this type of hazardous environment.[81]

On Earth Day 2003, President Bush sent EPA chief Whitman to New York to defend and praise his environmental record. Congressman Nadler, who was named public official of the year for his tireless work on behalf of the residents of New York, was furious. He blasted Whitman in the press:

> Without a doubt, Administrator Whitman has led an agency that has done more harm to New Yorkers than perhaps all of the previous Administrations combined. For her to come to New York on Earth Day and pretend she is a friend to New York and its environment is a complete sham.
>
> Under Administrator Whitman, the EPA bucked its responsibility under Federal law to clean up interior spaces of New York City that were – and continue to be – contaminated with hazardous materials released by the collapse of the World Trade Center ...
>
> In ten years or so, this City will see an explosion in cases of cancer, mesothelioma and other respiratory diseases that will dwarf the problems many New Yorkers already have faced because of contaminated interiors. We will look back at this Earth Day, when she pretends to be helping New Yorkers, and wonder how anyone could perpetrate such a farce.[82]

One month after her visit to New York, Christie Todd Whitman resigned her post as head of the EPA and Congress dropped its investigation of her role in the 9–11 cover-up.

However, in June of 2007 a new Congress took up the issue again. By this time, a class action lawsuit had been filed on behalf of the residents, office workers and students from Lower Manhattan and Brooklyn. In court, Whitman was steadfastly unapologetic for her false reassurances after 9–11. She expressed "outrage" that the suit was filed and called the plaintiffs' claims "off-base." "Every action taken by the EPA during this horrific event," she said, "was designed to provide the most comprehensive protection and most accurate information to the residents of Manhattan."[83]

However, U.S. District Court Judge Deborah Batts disagreed. In a pretrial ruling she blasted the EPA for its response to 9–11, denied the agency's motion to dismiss the case and refused to grant Whitman immunity. In her ruling she publicly scolded Whitman, declaring her statements so "deliberate and misleading" they "shock the conscience." Batts concluded:

[81] Hugh Kaufman stayed on with the EPA, but in a different capacity since the Ombudsman's Office was closed.
[82] Press Release. *EPA's Earth Day Sham.* Congressman Jerold Nadler and the NRDC (April 22, 2003).
[83] Lombardi, Kristen. "Sick of Being Lied to by the EPA, 9–11 Plaintiffs Use the Courts to Force the Answers They Seek," *The Village Voice* (February 21, 2006). http://www.villagevoice.com/2006–02–14/news/truth-out/.

No argument can be made that Whitman could not have understood from existing law that her conduct was unlawful ... No reasonable person would have thought that telling thousands of people that it was safe to return to Lower Manhattan, while knowing that such return could pose long-term health risks and other dire consequences, was conduct sanctioned by our laws.[84]

Unmoved by the judge's opinion, ex-EPA chief Whitman continued to defend her actions before Congress in June 2007.

The future of the Ombudsman's Office was determined by the fate of Senate Bill 606 – the "Ombudsman Reauthorization Act" – that would have established an independent Office of the Ombudsman within the EPA. In November 2002, the Senate passed S. 606 and sent it to the House for action, but the bill made it no farther than the House Energy and Commerce Committee before the 107th Congress adjourned.[85]

In half the time of Congressman Nadler's prediction, New York began seeing "an explosion of ... respiratory diseases" linked to 9–11. On September 4, 2006, the Mount Sinai Medical Center released its study based on detailed exams of 9,442 of the estimated 40,000 Ground Zero rescue and recovery workers between July 2002 and April 2004. Dr. Robin Herbert, codirector of a Mount Sinai medical team, reported that nearly 70 percent of those examined suffered new or worsened lung problems after 9–11 and many are not getting better. Among nonsmokers, 28 percent of responders had abnormal lung function tests – twice as many as in the general population.[86]

"This study, I hope, puts to rest any doubt about what happened to those who were exposed," said then-Senator Hillary Clinton (D-NY). Clinton added that the new research proves that EPA chief Whitman and other government officials were too hasty in reassuring New Yorkers about air quality in lower Manhattan immediately after 9–11. "We quickly learned," she said, "our government was not telling us the truth. The air was not safe to breathe."[87]

The battle between the Ombudsman's Office and the presidential appointees of the Clinton and Bush administrations highlights the underlying similarities and obvious differences between the ways these two administrations executed environmental law. Both administrations preferred to keep the EPA on a tight leash and environmental problems on the back burner unless they could garner positive press without stepping on influential toes. Thus, neither administration was willing to seriously confront environmental crime. But while the Clinton administration was

---

[84] Batts, Deborah A. United States District Judge. "Opinion Against Defendants Christine Todd Whitman, Marianne L. Horinko, Michael Leavitt and The United States Environmental Protection Agency in United States District Court Southern District of New York" (February 2, 2006). 04Civ1888.pdf (found at: http://www.nyenvirolaw.org/nyeljp-benzman.html).

[85] Ballard, Tanya N. "Bill To Liberate EPA Ombudsman Languishes," *Gov. Exec.com Daily Briefing* (November 26, 2006). http://www.govexec.com/dailyfed/1102/112602t1.htm.

[86] Shin, Paul. "Health of 9–11 Heroes at Risk," *New York Daily News* (September 5, 2006). http://www.nydailynews.com/news/local/story/449817p-378596c.html.

[87] Shin, Paul (September 5, 2006).

seldom willing to seriously provoke polluters; the Bush administration actively sought ways to circumvent environmental regulation and eviscerate enforcement in order to foster its tight relationship with major polluting industries. Meanwhile, it disingenuously camouflaged its policies in green verbiage to make them palatable for public consumption.

Environmentally hostile even by Republican standards, Bush administration policies had a chilling impact on EPA enforcers. Interviews with members of the agency's career enforcement staff elicited comments like: "We are hunkered down." "People are nervous. They are trying to keep a low profile." "The situation is very depressing." "I just try to push out of my mind all of the changes I see happening now … The situation is dire."[88]

The enforcement debacle under Bush was exaggerated further after 9–11. Many EPA investigators were reassigned to focus on security for public water supplies, chemical manufacturing facilities and pipelines. Others were diverted to work as personal security for high-level officials such as Christie Todd Whitman.[89] After 9–11, the Bush environmental enforcement record remained in a constant state of free fall. According to DoJ figures released in September 2006, the enforcement of antipollution laws by the federal government declined steadily and substantially after George W. Bush became president. Requests by federal agencies for criminal prosecution dropped by more than half after 2000 while such referrals for civil prosecution declined by more than one-third.[90]

The EPA's enforcement record under Bush has been carefully scrutinized by the Environmental Integrity Project (EIP). Eric Schaeffer, the EPA's former chief enforcer who resigned over the Bush administration's refusal to enforce the CAA, leads this nonprofit watchdog group.[91] In mid-2007, an EIP report entitled, *Paying Less to Pollute: Environmental Enforcement Under the Bush Administration*, examined the track record of 10 years of EPA enforcement by comparing the EPA's record under Bush from fiscal years 2002–2006 to fiscal years 1996–2000 under Clinton. It concluded that under Bush, EPA enforcement declined 25 percent on four out of five key fronts: court filings, criminal investigations, civil fines and criminal penalties. According to Schaeffer, "The bad news here is that it now costs less to pollute. Over the past 5 years under the Bush Administration's EPA and Department of Justice, environmental violators have been less likely to face court actions, be subject to criminal investigation, or pay civil or criminal penalties."[92]

---

[88] Quotes taken from interviews found in: Mintz, Joel A (October 2004): 10933–53.

[89] Mintz, Joel A (October 2004): 10933–53.

[90] PEER. *Environmental Enforcement Continues Decline Under Bush* (September 6, 2006). http://www. peer.org/news/news_id.php?row_id=744.

[91] See Chapter 2 on the Clean Air Act.

[92] Environmental Integrity Project (U.S. Newswire press release). "EIP Data: Pollution Enforcement Efforts Under Bush Administration's EPA Drop on Four Out of Five Key Fronts," Washington, DC (May 23, 2007).

A similar analysis of the Bush enforcement record in 2006 by Public Employees for Environmental Responsibility (PEER)[93] revealed that:

- Referrals for new environmental criminal prosecutions government-wide dropped by more than half (54 percent) from 2000 to 2005. In the EPA, such requests for prosecution fell 33 percent during that same 5-year period;
- Referrals for new civil prosecutions of environmental offenses declined by more than one-third (34 percent) between 2000 and 2003 (the last year for which statistics were available). New federal civil court complaints against polluters dropped even more, with a government-wide decline of 37 percent in new cases filed. EPA civil filings fell by 44 percent in this same period; and
- The number of federal criminal environmental prosecutions filed in 2005 decreased 14 percent since 2000 and the number of convictions obtained went down 13 percent. During the same period, criminal prosecutions filed on EPA cases declined by 18 percent while convictions dropped 6 percent.[94]

Bush's enforcement numbers were far lower than Clinton's and, in many cases, well below those of his father's presidency. "This Bush administration can make no claim to law and order credentials when it comes to pollution," declared PEER's Executive Director, Jeff Ruch. "Corporate transgressors have growing reason for confidence that environmental violations will not trigger federal prosecution."[95]

While the EPA's performance under George W. Bush could be considered among the most corrupt and ineffective in its history, its initial performance under Barak Obama appears to lean toward the other side of the spectrum. President Obama's 2010 EPA budget is $10.5 billion – a 34 percent increase over the 2009 budget. This includes $3.9 billion for EPA's operating budget, which includes enforcement.[96] Only time will tell whether this increased budget will translate into a firmer commitment to environmental protection throughout Obama's time in office.

Viewed over the entirety of its institutional lifespan, the EPA has utterly failed to live up to its name. Instead, its performance has never veered far from the intended purpose of its founder, Richard Nixon, who used the agency as a political vehicle to green his presidential image without seriously interfering with business as usual. This doesn't mean the EPA has never been at odds with the White House. Like all executive agencies, it functions under the direction of the president; but according to the legal parameters established by Congress, as interpreted by the courts; and within the swirling currents of national and state politics. Therefore, the EPA is

[93] Public Employees for Environmental Responsibility. PEER's analysis was based on Syracuse University's Transactional Records Access Clearinghouse (TRAC) database compiled by the Executive Office of U.S. Attorneys.
[94] PEER (September 6, 2006).
[95] PEER (September 6, 2006).
[96] "Enviro Enforcement Under Obama," Enviro BLR.com (July 14, 2009). http://enviro.blr.com/news.aspx?id=106318.

buffeted by a host of forces. Sadly, none of these forces is intent upon making sure the agency prioritizes environmental protection.

Presidents and Congressional representatives are driven by their ambitions: advancing their political influence and careers, appeasing campaign contributors and powerful lobbyists, and maintaining a positive image among the voters. Protecting the environment may or may not become a significant factor in their policymaking calculus, depending upon how it plays in relation to these overriding priorities. More often than not, advancing their careers and pleasing wealthy campaign contributors conflicts with a steadfast commitment to environmental protection.

The same powerful corporate interests that discourage presidents and politicians from adopting strong environmental policies also exercise substantial influence over the regulatory and enforcement determinations within the EPA itself. More often than not, the direct lobbying efforts of powerful polluters gain a receptive hearing at the highest levels of the agency. Yet not all presidents have followed the Reagan and Bush example of appointing enthusiastically pro-polluter candidates to head up and hobble the agency. On rare occasions, some EPA chiefs have even put themselves at odds with the White House by taking their environmental mission a bit too seriously. But by and large, EPA administrators try to operate within the parameters set by the political posture of the president, which rarely involves cracking down on influential polluters.

As the fate of the Ombudsman's Office demonstrates, the agency actively discourages whistleblowers and dedicated environmental defenders, even under Democratic administrations. Over time, most agency officials have learned not to rock the bureaucratic boat and to appreciate the benefits of the revolving door that leads to lucrative positions with the industries they regulate. Further, legal loopholes and budgetary limits often force the EPA to rely on industry to assess the dangers of its chemical products and wastes, and to monitor and self-report its own violations.

Ultimately, the EPA is hardly different from the other federal agencies whose nominal mission has been subordinated to, and subverted by, the dictates and constraints of the political and economic status quo. These debilitating conditions drive government agencies to put political expedience and corporate profits over environmental protection; our rights as consumers and workers; the security of our savings and pensions; the health and safety of our food, drugs and working conditions; and the preservation of our public lands, national forests and wilderness areas. This pervasive situation raises grave questions about the potential for government to truly protect, preserve and defend the public interest in a society dominated by powerful corporations and dedicated to private enterprise and the pursuit of profit above all else.

2

The Clean Air Act – Gasping for Breath

To be deadly, the air you breathe doesn't have to be brown and smelly or sting your eyes. Sure, some airborne contaminants, such as the brownish-gray smog caused by ground-level ozone, can be seen and smelled. But others, such as carbon monoxide, radon and BPA (Bisphenol-A),[1] fly under the radar of our senses. In fact, the most noxious types of airborne toxins are so virulent they can cause illness, disability, cancer, reproductive problems and even death at levels difficult to detect by even the most advanced technologies.

Air pollution was the first type chosen by Congress for federal regulation. Airborne contaminants are especially dangerous because the lungs provide them with direct access to our bloodstream. The average adult breathes about 3,400 gallons of air every day.[2] At this great volume, even unimaginably minute concentrations of some airborne toxins can do grave damage to our bodies.[3]

Most of us underrate the menace of airborne pollutants. The number one killer in America is heart disease; lung cancer is the number one cancer killer and asthma is the number one chronic disease in children. These diseases have a frightening commonality – air pollution makes all of them worse.[4] In the United States, traffic fatalities total just over 40,000 per year, while air pollution claims at least 70,000 lives annually – as many as breast and prostate cancer combined. The EPA and the

---

[1] For more information see: *Our Stolen Future*. http://www.ourstolenfuture.org/NewScience/oncompounds/bisphenola/bpauses.htm.

[2] EPA. *Air Quality Planning & Standards: Introduction*. http://www.epa.gov/oar/oaqps/airtrans/intro.html.

[3] An explosion of laboratory studies since 2000 have demonstrated that BPA (Bisphenol-A) at parts per *trillion* alters the development of cells in some of the major physiological systems critical for normal function, such as the brain, prostate, mammary gland and pancreas. While there may be no "safe" level of exposure to some chemicals, the EPA has set unsafe levels of exposure to extremely potent toxins like dioxin at 60 parts per billion. See: World Wildlife Fund. *Exposing Hormone Disrupting Chemicals* (February 25, 2005). http://www.panda.org/about_our_earth/teacher_resources/webfieldtrips/toxics/news/?18830.

[4] CNN.com Health. "Studies Confirm Dirty Air May Cause Disease" (March 6, 2002). http://www.cnn.com/2002/HEALTH/03/05/pollution.dangers/.

National Resources Defense Council (NRDC) estimate that 64,000 deaths are caused each year by just one type of air pollutant: particulate matter (PM-10).[5]

"The dangerous thing about these fine particles is that they are tiny enough to penetrate the body's natural defense systems," says Norman H. Edelman, MD, the American Lung Association's consultant for scientific affairs. "This means when you inhale these particles, they embed themselves deep in the lungs. Some may even pass through the lungs to the blood." Edelman compares particle pollution to an invisible army, "wreaking havoc on your body through complicated mechanisms we're still sorting out ... Studies link particle pollution to increased risk of asthma attacks, heart attacks and strokes, lung cancer and premature death, to name just a few of the ways this tiny army attacks."[6] Currently, these chronic heart and lung diseases cripple more than 30 million Americans[7] – more than all the people living in Arizona, Iowa, Hawaii, Connecticut and Florida combined.[8]

Air pollution affects everyone, but not equally. It is most devastating to infants, children, the elderly and those with weakened immune systems. Throughout childhood, the impact of breathing polluted air is magnified because

- Children's lungs are still developing. As a "work in progress," they are much more likely to be damaged by airborne pollutants.
- Children need more oxygen for their body weight than adults and, as a result, breathe at a faster rate. Breathing faster means that they take in proportionally more air and pollutants.
- Children spend more time outdoors and are more active than adults. This increases their exposure to pollutants, especially if they play in parks and school playgrounds close to high traffic and industrial areas.
- Children's smaller size and their tendency to play on or nearer the ground make them more likely to come into contact with pollutants that are found closer to ground level.[9]

Lung disease (and other breathing problems) is the number one killer of babies younger than one year old.[10] In Los Angeles, the air is so toxic that after just 12 days of life an infant will inhale more cancer-causing pollutants than the EPA considers safe for an entire lifetime.[11] In San Francisco, it takes nineteen days for an

[5] For estimates of PM-10 caused deaths in your part of the country see: Natural Resources Defense Council (NRDC). *Breath-Taking Premature Mortality Due to Particulate Air Pollution in 239 American Cities* (May 1996). http://www.nrdc.org/air/pollution/bt/btinx.asp.

[6] *American Lung Association State of the Air: 2004 Report Ranks Cities and Counties Threatened by Dirty Air* (April 29, 2004). http://www.lungusa.org/site/apps/nl/content3.asp?c=dvLUK9OoE&b=40676&ct=66972&notoc=1.

[7] *State of the Air 2003*. American Lung Association (April 2004). http://www.lungusa.org/diseases/.

[8] U.S. population by State (July 2002). http://www.infoplease.com/ipa/A0004986.html.

[9] Canadian Institute of Child Health. *Climate Change and Your Child's Health: Fact Sheet on Air Pollution* (April 30, 2003). http://www.cich.ca/EnvironmentHealth_ClimateFactSheets.html.

[10] *State of the Air 2003*. American Lung Association (April 2004).

[11] Reuters. "L. A. Babies Get Lifetime's Toxic Air in 2 Weeks, Says Study" (September 17, 2002). http://www.enn.com/news/wire-stories/2002/09/09172002/reu_48435.asp. The Executive Summary of the

infant to breathe its "safe" lifetime limit. Recently, federal researchers discovered that infants living in areas with higher levels of industrial soot and smog were 40 percent more likely to die from respiratory failure and 26 percent more likely to die from SIDS than babies living in areas with relatively clean air. In addition, they found that increased mortality occurred even in cities that met the EPA's so-called clean air standards.[12]

Because air pollution is most concentrated in neighborhoods where the atmosphere is laden with the toxins spewed by cars, trucks, heavy equipment and factories, it poses a disproportional threat to the poor, working class and minority communities of the inner cities. For healthy adults, long-term exposure to big city air pollution increases the risk of cancer to the same degree as living with a chain smoker.[13] Of course, the risks are magnified for the most vulnerable members of the urban population. Pregnant women living in areas with the highest levels of carbon monoxide and ground-level ozone triple their risk of delivering a child with certain heart malformations and valve defects compared to mothers living in the least noxious neighborhoods.[14]

HAS THE CLEAN AIR ACT MADE A DIFFERENCE?

Although air pollution continues to kill, incapacitate and shorten the lifespan of millions of Americans, things could be much worse. Despite its gaping loopholes and serious flaws, the Clean Air Act (CAA) has dramatically reduced the lethal ravages of air pollution. One EPA study used a sophisticated array of computer models to estimate the benefits and costs of the CAA's pollution-control programs and compare them with the costs and benefits of a hypothetical America without air pollution controls. The study found that, by 1990 – after 20 years of CAA regulations – the differences between the two scenarios were so great that, under the so-called "no air pollution control case," an additional 205,000 Americans would have died prematurely and millions more would have suffered illnesses ranging from mild respiratory symptoms to heart disease, chronic bronchitis, asthma attacks and other severe respiratory problems. In addition, the lack of CAA controls on the use of leaded gasoline would have resulted in major drops in child IQ and sharp increases in adult hypertension, heart disease and stroke.[15] The study concluded that:

study, *Toxic Beginnings*, put out by the National Environmental Trust can be read at: http://www.mindfully.org/Air/2002/Cancer-Risks-Children-CA-AirSep02.htm.

[12] *Doctors' Guide*. "Air Pollution Linked to Infant Death, Including SIDs, New Study Reports" (June 1997). http://www.pslgroup.com/dg/2c4b2.htm.

[13] CNN.com Health. "New Evidence of Pollution Dangers" (December 15, 2000). http://www.cnn.com/2000/HEALTH/mayo/12/15/pollution.dangers/.

[14] Selim, Jocelyn. "Fetuses Take Air Pollution to Heart," *Discover* (April 2002). http://www.discover.com/apr_02/breakair.html.

[15] *Benefits & Costs of Clean Air Act: Study Design & Summary of Results* (March 6, 2007). http://www.epa.gov/air/sect812/design.html.

Other benefits which could be quantified and expressed in dollar terms included visibility improvements, improvements in yields of some agricultural crops, improved worker attendance and productivity, and reduced household soiling damage.

When the human health, human welfare and environmental effects which could be expressed in dollar terms were added up for the entire 20-year period, the total benefits of Clean Air Act programs were estimated to range from about $6 trillion to about $50 trillion, with a mean estimate of about $22 trillion. These estimated benefits represent the estimated value Americans place on avoiding the dire air quality conditions and dramatic increases in illness and premature death which would have prevailed without the 1970 and 1977 Clean Air Act and its associated state and local programs. By comparison, the actual costs of achieving the pollution reductions observed over the 20-year period were $523 billion, a small fraction of the estimated monetary benefits.[16]

Every car-driving American has some experience with CAA regulations. No one enjoys the time and expense involved in getting smog tests and certificates. The process becomes even less enjoyable if your car flunks the test and you must pay the extra expense of getting it fixed. But we do it anyway for two reasons. First, it reduces air pollution. Imagine how poisonous our air would be without smog control devices! Second, it's the law; stiff fines are imposed for continuing to drive after skipping or failing a required emissions inspection.

Yet, our individual cars emit a tiny fraction of the pollution spewed by the nation's biggest air polluters: coal–burning power plants, oil refineries, chemical plants and toxic waste incinerators. Therefore, it seems only fair, expedient and logical that the regulations imposed on these mega-polluters would be applied just as strictly as they are on our cars. Unfortunately, this is not the case.

AMERICA'S MOST WANTED AIR POLLUTION OUTLAWS

Government inspectors have found that hundreds of America's worst industrial polluters openly violate the CAA on a daily basis, on a massive scale, year after year, and get off scot-free. According to the EPA's own investigations, dozens of the country's biggest, wealthiest air polluters – including Ford, General Motors, Shell and Exxon – make a habit of breaking the CAA without paying a single penny in fines.[17] Other major air polluters are given such small fines (compared with the cost of complying with the law) that they simply pay these paltry penalties and go on polluting. For America's corporate polluters, getting off the hook for violating clean air laws is just part of doing business.

According to the EPA's own figures, 41 percent of the nation's oil refineries and roughly one-third of the country's iron and steel plants are significant violators of America's clean air laws.[18] The 1990 Clean Air Act requires such facilities to obtain a pollution permit that sets a legal limit to the levels of air pollution they are allowed to emit. The EPA can fine companies that significantly exceed their permit limits as

---

[16] *Benefits & Costs of Clean Air Act: Study Design & Summary of Results* (March 6, 2007).

[17] Coequyt, John, Richard Wiles & Christopher Campbell. *Above the Law: How the Government Lets Major Air Polluters off the Hook* (Environmental Working Group: May 1999).

[18] Coequyt, John, Richard Wiles & Christopher Campbell (May 1999).

much as $25,000 per day (with a total limit of $200,000). State officials can set fines well over this limit if they choose. However, most of the time, no fines are levied at all.

An analysis of EPA data for 1997–1998 by the Environmental Working Group (EWG) found that 53 of the country's major polluters were *significantly violating* their CAA permits every single quarter of both years, but only 20 of them paid any fines.[19] Over this two-year period, 39 percent (227 of 575) of all major industrial polluters violated the CAA – and not just once. On average, they violated it about four of the eight quarters. Federal or state regulators fined only 36 percent of these 227 violators.[20] While a small group of firms accounted for most of the larger penalties, in general, the EWG found that when fines were levied they were generally "too small to have a deterrent effect."[21]

Although unpunished permit violations are a serious problem, they are only the tip of the iceberg. It is an open secret within the EPA that many industrial polluters continue to operate without any permit whatsoever. Officially, the 1990 CAA required all "new or modified major stationary sources"[22] of air pollution to obtain a permit and satisfy stringent regulatory conditions before operation. However, 13 years later, one-third of the country's factories, power plants and other major polluters were still operating without a Title 5 permit.[23]

In 1997, a statutory permit deadline came and went. Four years later, an unpublished report from the EPA's Inspector General's Office (IGO) stated the obvious – the absence of operating permits undermines monitoring, enforcement and pollution prevention – all the essentials of an effective clean air program.[24] Worse yet, several of the eastern industrial states with the worst air pollution have the lowest rates of permit issuance.[25]

---

[19] These were not mere paperwork violations. They all involved serious illegal releases of air pollution. Coequyt, John, Richard Wiles & Christopher Campbell (May 1999).

[20] These statistics are drastic underestimations of total air pollution violations because state officials rarely inspect these facilities. Thus, countless violations go undetected and unreported. Also, the EPA data used in the EWG Report included only federal quarterly violations. Thus, monthly federal infractions and all state violations were omitted from this analysis. Coequyt, John, Richard Wiles & Christopher Campbell (May 1999): 17.

[21] The average fine for the significant violator was $318,290. The average corporate earnings for these major industrial polluters were $24.2 billion in 1998. Coequyt, John, Richard Wiles & Christopher Campbell. *Above the Law: How the Government Lets Major Air Polluters Off The Hook.* Online Executive Summary (Environmental Working Group: May 1999). http://www.ewg.org/pub/home/reports/abovethelaw/abovethelawes.html.

[22] The 1990 CAA defines a "major source" as one that has the potential to emit ten tons per year (TPY) of any single hazardous air pollutant (HAP); 25 TPY of any combination of HAPs; or 100 TPY of lead, sulfur dioxide, nitrogen oxides, carbon monoxide, particulate matter, volatile organic compounds or other regulated pollutants.

[23] Press Release. Public Employees for Environmental Responsibility (PEER). "One-Third of Major US Air Polluters Still Lack Pollution Permits" (March 11, 2002). http://www.peer.org/press/217.html.

[24] EPA Office of Inspector General. *AIR: EPA & State Progress in Issuing Title V Permits* (March 29, 2002). http://www.epa.gov/oar/oaqps/permits/pdfs/oig-titlev.pdf.

[25] EPA Office of Inspector General. *Draft Report: EPA & State Progress in Issuing Title V Permits* (October 5, 2001). Available in pdf form online at: EPA Office of Inspector General (March 29, 2002).

According to Jeffrey Holmstead, head of the EPA's Air Office, "We're more than 10 years into the Title 5 program, yet only about two-thirds of the major sources in the country have received their Title 5 permits. And most of the largest, most complex – and most important – sources remain un-permitted and are operating under the so-called application shield."[26] This application shield loophole allows polluters to continue operating and prohibits any enforcement action against them if they have *begun* to apply for a permit, a process that the EPA Inspector General (IG) estimates takes between three and four years.[27]

Why has enforcement of the CAA's Title 5 permit program been so abysmal? Principally because the law gives primary responsibility for enforcement to the states, and most states have neither the resources nor the political will to take this responsibility seriously. As a general rule, state governors, legislators and regulatory agencies are even more heavily swayed by the lobbying power and campaign cash of the major polluting industries than federal officials. Consequently, state EPAs (SEPAs) are usually even less enthusiastic pollution police than their federal counterpart.

In many states, such as Wisconsin, Illinois and New Jersey, the percentage of major un-permitted polluting facilities hovers above 40 percent.[28] But even for facilities with permits, the quality of enforcement varies greatly, not only from state to state, but also within a state, from one air quality district to another.

For example, in California, where air pollution causes more deaths than AIDs, murder and car accidents combined,[29] the EWG study found that there were major disparities in the Title 5 enforcement efforts between Los Angeles and the San Francisco Bay Area.[30] Bay Area refineries committed eight times more violations than refineries in Los Angeles County. Why? Because LA's South Coast Air Quality District assessed average fines per violation that were 28 times higher than the Bay Area air district. From 1996–1999, the top three Bay Area polluters – Shell, Tosco and Exxon – committed more violations than all other companies in the California database combined. However, their fines averaged a meager $699.[31]

"If the typical Bay Area resident were assessed a smog-violation fine comparable to what Shell or Tosco get away with, it would be a tiny fraction of one cent," said Bill Walker, California director of EWG. "This double standard for polluters and the public isn't fair and it isn't working: Major polluters repeatedly violate the law, get

---

[26] Press Release. Public Employees for Environmental Responsibility (PEER) (March 11, 2002).

[27] *Georgia Tech Research News*. "The Cost of Cleaning the Air: Study Shows Permit Application Costs Lower Than Expected – with Key Benefits to Industry" (September 21, 1999). http://gtresearchnews.gatech.edu/newsrelease/TITLEV.html; Press Release. Public Employees for Environmental Responsibility (PEER) (March 11, 2002).

[28] Wisconsin is the worst at 46 percent. Sierra Club Press Release. "Wisconsin: Worst in the Nation When it Comes to Issuing Air Permits" (December 16, 2002).

[29] Coalition for Clean Air, *What Every Californian Should Know About Air Pollution and Health* (2006). http://www.coalitionforcleanair.org/air-pollution-10facts.html.

[30] Environmental Working Group. *Above the Law: How California's Major Polluters Get Away with it* (July 28, 1999). http://www.ewg.org/reports/ca_abovethelaw/AboveTheLawCa.html.

[31] Environmental Working Group (July 28, 1999).

slapped on the wrist with fines that are a ridiculously small fraction of their multibillion dollar profits, and keep polluting."[32]

In sum, Title 5 of the CAA is constantly violated because many major criminal polluters continue to operate without permits while the remainder are seldom deterred by the rare inspections and small fines imposed by state agencies with neither the resources nor the political will to do a better job of policing polluters. Although the law requires the EPA to step in when states are not doing an adequate job of enforcing the law, the agency has essentially ignored this statutory requirement.[33]

As a last recourse, environmental groups in some states have sued regional air boards, SEPAs and the EPA in hopes that the courts will require government action. These expensive and time-consuming tactics have been somewhat successful. In May 2003, Bay Area activists announced a settlement with their Air Quality Management District that achieved a commitment to issue all outstanding Title 5 operating permits by the end of 2003.[34] Similar successes have been registered in Tennessee and New York and this tactic is slowly spreading to other states.

Although lax enforcement has seriously undermined the CAA's effectiveness, there is no doubt that we are far better off with it than without it. Over the last 30 years of CAA regulation, considerable progress has been made toward reducing *some* of the country's most damaging air pollutants.

National Emissions of Common Air Pollutants[35] 1970–1998 (Thousands of Short Tons). But this progress came primarily in the first ten years of the law's implementation.[36] As major polluters learned to take advantage of lax enforcement and exploit legal loopholes, advances in air quality stagnated and some types of air pollution and some areas of the country have become substantially worse.

---

[32] Environmental Working Group (July 28, 1999).

[33] When a state fails to adequately enforce its Title 5 program, the EPA is supposed to step in and remedy the situation by issuing a notice of deficiency that gives the state a deadline for remedying the problem(s). If the state fails, EPA is obligated (after 18 months) to impose sanctions, including withholding federal transportation funding. If the deficiency is still not resolved two years after giving notice, the EPA is required to step in and administer the program itself. This has never been done.

[34] InsideEPA.com "Activists' Suits Successfully Target States' Title 5 Permit Delays," *Clean Air Report* (May 23, 2002). http://www.ocefoundation.org/completed.html#bayarea. In the San Francisco area settlement, the air district must act on more than 20 outstanding permits including those for several oil refineries. The December 1, 2003, deadline, which was listed as the latest target by the air district, is now federally enforceable after the district missed the previous deadline.

[35] Clean Air Act Performance Statistics. Patricia Michaels. http://greennature.com/article247.html.

[36] Easterblogg. "Another Overstated NY Times Magazine Story" (April 5, 2004). http://www.tnr.com/easterbrook.mhtml?pid=1529.

Pollutant	1970	1998	% Change
CO	129,444	89,454	−30.9%
NOx	20,928	24,454	+16.8%
VOC	30,982	17,917	−42.2%
SO₂	31,161	19,647	−36.9%
Lead	220,869	3,973	−98.2%
PM – 10	13,042	34,741	+266.4%

A prime example of this stagnation and backsliding can be seen in the controversy over the George W. Bush administration's efforts to eliminate most of the major pollution controls of the CAA and replace them with a less stringent set of provisions the White House called "The Clear Skies Initiative."

CLINTON'S HALF-HEARTED EFFORT TO ENFORCE THE CAA

Despite the life-preserving benefits all Americans derive from the CAA (even when only partially enforced), the major polluting industries have always viewed the CAA as a thorn in their side. When President Clinton mounted a half-hearted effort, near the end of his term, to enforce the law and punish major violators, this thorn began to fester. In response, the nation's largest criminal polluters decided it was time to rid themselves of this annoying law once and for all, especially its most troublesome provision: New Source Review (NSR).

Ironically, NSR was something the dirtiest power plants had lobbied for back in 1977 when the CAA was first amended. Back then, the nation's energy companies insisted that Congress should exempt more than 17,000 of their dirtiest, oldest oil refineries and power plants from stiff CAA pollution controls on the premise that these dinosaur facilities would soon be phased out and shut down. Congress granted them exemptions *with conditions* – this part of the CAA was called New Source Review.

Under NSR, old, dirty plants were not allowed to make major technological renovations (that would increase their levels of pollution by extending their longevity or expanding their generating capacity) without losing their exemption. Major renovations to any old plant would trigger the legal requirement to obtain CAA permits and adopt expensive, state-of-the-art, air pollution controls – just like new facilities.

However, as the years passed, many utilities quietly revamped their aging plants on the sly, without adopting new pollution controls or obtaining the required permits. By calling these major overhauls "routine maintenance," 363 of the country's dirtiest power plants fraudulently increased their longevity, coal use, energy generation and pollution levels by holding on to these bogus exemptions.

The owners of these old, pollution-puffing power plants found their bogus "pollution passes" even more lucrative after 1992 when Congress deregulated wholesale electricity prices. With deregulation, exempt plants became cash cows because they were competing with newer plants that had to install and maintain expensive pollution control equipment. Their unfair advantage paid off; NSR-exempt plants pocketed about $3.6 billion in annual savings.[37] Consequently, these dirty utilities lobbied intensely to keep their illicit exemptions and insisted that every major upgrade was just "routine maintenance."

For most of her time in office, Carol Browner, Clinton's pollution police chief, coddled these chronic criminals. Under her watch, the EPA bent over backward to find ways to make NSR requirements more appetizing to these mega-polluters without allowing them to completely ignore the law and the public health. The power companies were willing to negotiate, but they really wanted nothing less than permanent exemptions: the total elimination of all legal requirements to adopt new emission controls.

Browner balked at bending over that far. But because the EPA wasn't requiring pollution controls or prosecuting NSR violations while negotiations dragged on, the utilities found it far cheaper to engage in endless discussions while ignoring the law instead of accepting any of Browner's proposed modifications.

In the last years of the Clinton administration, things changed. Public pressure to reduce air pollution became irresistible. Throughout the 1990s, a growing body of scientific evidence demonstrated that prevailing levels of air pollution across the nation were far more dangerous than previously believed. Then, in the late 1990s, an Environmental Working Group (EWG) report seriously tarnished the administration's fading green patina. The report, *Above the Law: How the Government Lets Major Air Polluters off the Hook*, exposed the EPA's undisclosed internal investigation which admitted that, under Clinton's watch, the agency had chosen to ignore a persistent, ongoing, 20-year record of criminal violations of the CAA at the expense of public health.[38] In addition, the EPA's investigation revealed that approximately 70 percent of the coal-fired electricity generating plants in the country were chronic violators of NSR standards.[39]

The bad press and public outcry over EPA's appalling enforcement record forced Browner to get tough in order to avoid charges of criminal negligence. In November 1999, the agency announced it was taking some of the nation's major polluters to court.[40] On behalf of the EPA, the Department of Justice (DoJ) filed lawsuits against only 32 plants, owned by seven electric utility and energy companies and accounting for 40 percent of the nation's mega-wattage. They were charged with violating the conditions of their NSR exemptions and illegally releasing enormous amounts of air pollution; in some cases, for over two decades.[41]

---

[37] Pope, Carl. *Strategic Ignorance.* (San Francisco, CA: Sierra Club Books), 2004: 84.

[38] Coequyt, John, Richard Wiles & Christopher Campbell (May 1999).

[39] Mintz, Joel A. "Treading Water: A Preliminary Assessment of EPA Enforcement During the Bush II Administration," *Environmental Law Review* (October 2004): 34.

[40] For a full list go to: EWG. "Power Plants Caught Cheating" (November 3, 1999). http://www.ewg.org/reports/powerplants/powerplants.html.

[41] These companies included: First Energy, American Electric Power, Cinergy, Southern Indiana Gas & Electric, Illinois Power, Tampa Electric and Alabama & Georgia Power (subsidiaries of the Southern Company). DoJ Press Release. *U.S. Sues Electric Utilities in Unprecedented Action to Enforce the Clean Air Act: Complaints Filed After One of the Largest Enforcement Investigations in EPA History* (November 3, 1999). http://www.usdoj.gov/opa/pr/1999/November/524enr.htm.

In just six years (from 1992 to 1998), EWG estimated that the industries being sued had illegally emitted more air pollution than 6.8 million cars.[42] The EPA then put a number of other utilities and energy companies on notice that, if they didn't clean up their acts, the DoJ would be after them next. By 2000, Browner told *The New York Times* that all efforts to find a compromise with these polluting industries "were essentially dead."[43]

Finally, it appeared that at least 32 of the 363 worst air polluters in the country, whose aggregate poisonous emissions had lead to the deaths of thousands Americans every year,[44] would be brought to justice and forced to comply with the law. The potential costs of penalties and compliance were substantial. Fines could run as high as $27,500 for each day a plant was in violation of the law. Because many plants began violating the law back in the 1970s, potential penalties could run into the tens of millions.

However, this was a pittance compared with the actual damages their power plant pollution had imposed on public health and the environment for 20 years. While lives are priceless, using the accepted valuation methods employed by the EPA, ABT Associates found that the total monetized health costs of U.S. power plant pollution is $167.3 billion annually – this adds up to about $3.35 trillion over the 20-year period power plants have violated the CAA![45]

In addition to penalties, guilty industries would be required to comply with the law. This meant implementing the best available technologies for reducing air pollution and/or reconfiguring their plants to run on natural gas instead of coal. Estimated costs per plant were in the hundreds of millions, but the potential health and environmental benefits were far higher. Thirty thousand deaths per year are attributable solely to power plant pollution – nearly ten times more deaths than occurred on 9–11.[46] And, while penalties and compliance costs were large, they were small change stacked against the industry's annual profits. In 1999 alone, Southern Company reported $1.3 billion in profits.[47]

The newspapers were full of stories about Browner's crackdown on industry. The impression fostered by industry and often echoed in the press and was of an over-zealous agency hell-bent on forcing these rigid standards on the country regardless of

---

[42] EWG (November 3, 1999). Barcott, Bruce. "Changing the Rules," *New York Times Magazine* (April 4, 2004): 43.

[43] Barcott (April 4, 2004): 42.

[44] See: Clean Air Task Force. *Death, Disease and Dirty Power: Mortality and Health Disease Due to Air Pollution from Power Plants* (October 2000). http://www.cleartheair.org/fact/mortality/mortalitylowres. pdf; The Clean Air Task Force. *Dirty Air, Dirty Power* (2004). http://www.catf.us/publications/view/24. The EPA estimates that more protective health standards for fine particles could save 15,000 lives per year. Pollution from power plants cuts short the lives of nearly 24,000 Americans nationwide every year. Those 24,000 Americans die an average of 14 years early because of exposure to power plant pollution; 2,800 of those deaths are from lung cancer. Power plant pollution is responsible for 38,200 non-fatal heart attacks per year.

[45] The Clean Air Task Force (2004); *Technical Addendum: Methodologies for the Benefit Analysis of the Clear Skies Act of 2003.* http://www.epa.gov/air/clearskies/tech_addendum.pdf.

[46] Pope, Carl, 2004: 83.

[47] Barcott, Bruce (April 4, 2004): 43.

the consequences. Left unmentioned was the fact that Browner took action only after bad press and an American Lung Association lawsuit compelled the agency to write the minimal standards it thought it could get away with and fine a few of the biggest polluters in the country.

Faced with mounting fines, some utilities struck deals with the federal government. Tampa Electric's deal took 123,000 tons of pollution out of the air annually by requiring $1 billion to be invested in pollution controls. In addition, the DoJ imposed $3.5 million in civil penalties – less than 2 percent of the company's annual profits.[48]

THE ENERGY EMPIRE STRIKES BACK

However, many other energy companies refused to reach any settlement with federal prosecutors. Instead, they opted for a more portentous strategy. They redoubled their efforts to install a friend in the White House – someone who might use his power to get them completely off the hook. While dragging out their court cases, they bankrolled George W. Bush's bid for president with stacks of campaign cash.

Reliant Resources' CEO, Steve Letbetter; its chairman, Don Jordan; and First Energy's president, Anthony Alexander all became "Pioneers" – the special title the Bush campaign bestowed on those who raised more than $100,000 to secure his grab for the White House. Six other lawyers and lobbyists for power companies under investigation or litigation also became Pioneers. Not to be outdone, the Southern Company's[49] executive vice president, Dwight Evans, became a Republican "Ranger" – an elite group of donors who raised more than $200,000 to put Bush in power.[50] In the 2000 election, 41 of Bush's Pioneers were from the oil and gas industry; as a group, the industry donated more than $1.8 million, while the electric utilities contributed another $4 million to elect the "toxic Texan."[51] Their total contribution to the Bush campaign was larger than any other industry.[52]

After Bush's inauguration, *Coal Age* (the coal companies' trade magazine) touted the energy industry's "high-level access to policymakers in the new administration."[53] It focused its efforts to dismantle the CAA on Vice President Cheney's *Energy Policy Development Group*. At the top of the hit list was the CAA's NSR.[54] In 2001, Cheney's energy task force conferred with at least three large utilities facing NSR lawsuits and with lobbyists representing all nine energy companies facing NSR litigation. Internal documents revealed that the task force met with representatives of Southern Co. at

---

[48] Barcott, Bruce (April 4, 2004): 43.
[49] The Southern Company was making about $852 million annually from the exemptions from its dirty plants. Pope, Carl, 2004: 84.
[50] Barcott, Bruce (April 4, 2004): 43.
[51] That total included $1.85 million from the four electric utilities facing the largest NSR lawsuits and the leading industry trade association. Another five utilities also facing NSR lawsuits gave an additional $424,700. Public Citizen. *Bush Appointees Gut Air Quality Rule and Give Congress False Information About the Consequence* http://baltimorechronicle.com/nov03_choke-on-it.html; Citizen Works. "Why Are We Going to War? A Fact Sheet." http://www.targetoil.com/downloads/oilandwarv128.pdf.
[52] Mintz, Joel A (October 2004): 34.
[53] Barcott, Bruce (April 4, 2004): 44.
[54] Barcott, Bruce (April 4, 2004): 66, 73.

least seven times and with the industry's trade association, the Edison Electric Institute (EEI), at least 14 times. In May 2001, the task force called for reevaluations of NSR by the DoJ and the EPA.[55]

Savvy public interest advocates soon realized that these big-time outlaw polluters were pursuing the devious strategy of trying to eradicate the laws they had violated. Public Citizen's *Congress Watch* Director, Frank Clemente, was one of many to recognize the pattern:

> This is a classic Washington 'follow the money' story. When the electric utility industry faced strong government attempts to clean up many of its aging coal-fired power plants, ... [They] began an intensive campaign to derail the effort. Their strategy: help elect an industry-friendly president, fill federal regulatory posts with former utility executives and lobbyists, and hire a small army of lobbyists and lawyers connected to the new president to engineer regulatory changes that would undermine the EPA's Clean Air Act enforcement cases and weaken rules that already were in the pipeline.[56]

THE CLEAN AIR ACT VERSUS THE TOXIC TEXAN

By early 2002, Cheney's energy task force had developed a two-pronged attack on the CAA and NSR. The first prong was the more overt public effort to weaken the nation's air pollution laws. The Bush White House had learned from the public outcry against President Reagan's blatant efforts to cripple environmental protections that it is not wise to openly oppose environmental laws. A 2001 Gallup poll found that 81 percent of Americans supported stronger environmental standards for industry.[57] Therefore, they camouflaged their overt assault on the CAA to mask its real purpose. Their overt effort to undermine the CAA was given a nice "green" disguise – The Clear Skies Initiative – and sold to the public as a major improvement.

Bush told the press that his Clear Skies Initiative "will cut sulfur dioxide emissions by 72 percent ... nitrogen oxide emissions by 67 percent. And, for the first time ever, we will cap emissions of mercury, cutting them by 69 percent."[58] But in fact, these numbers represented a significant retreat from the stricter requirements of the CAA (see the following chart). In truth, Bush was touting his proposed emission cuts as an advance – not over the CAA itself – but over "current levels" of air pollution being generated by all the dirty power plants being allowed to evade NSR and shun the emission controls triggered by losing their exemptions.

---

[55] Public Citizen. *Bush Appointees Gut Air Quality Rule and Give Congress False Information About the Consequence* (November 3, 2003). http://baltimorechronicle.com/nov03_choke-on-it.html.

[56] *Study: Top U.S. Air Polluters Are Closely Tied to Bush Fundraising, Pollution Policymaking Process* (May 5, 2004). http://www.citizen.org/pressroom/release.cfm?ID=1706.

[57] Barcott, Bruce (April 4, 2004): 44.

[58] The White House Homepage. *Executive Summary – The Clear Skies Initiative* (February 2002). http://www.whitehouse.gov/news/releases/2002/02/clearskies.html; EPA Newsroom. "President Bush Announces Clear Skies & Global Climate Change Initiatives" (February 14, 2002). http://www.epa.gov/epahome/headline2_021402.htm. see also: Pope, Carl, 2004: 85.

As for Bush's proposed mercury cuts, a court had already issued a consent decree requiring power plants to cut up to 90 percent of their mercury emissions by December 2007.[59] The Clear Skies Initiative did not require any mercury reductions until 2010. By 2018, "Clear Skies" would permit more mercury in the air than the CAA would allow by 2007.[60] The following chart provides a more thorough comparison.

Comparison of Bush Administration's Clear Skies Initiative with Existing Clean Air Act Programs[61]

	Sulfur dioxide (SO_2)	Nitrogen oxides (NOx)	Mercury (Hg)
Clean Air Act (implementation of existing law)	2 million ton cap by 2012	1.25 million ton cap by 2010	5 tons per year by 2008
Bush Administration Clear Skies Initiative	1st Step: 4.5 million ton cap by 2010 2nd Step: 3 million ton cap by 2018	1st Step: 2.1 million ton cap by 2008 2nd Step: 1.7 million ton cap by 2018	1st Step: 26 tons per year by 2010 2nd Step: 15 tons per year by 2018
Increase allowed by Bush Plan over Clean Air Act existing programs	2010–2018: 2.5 million tons/ yr more SO_2 After 2018: 1 million tons/yr more SO_2	2010–2018: 850,000 tons/yr more NOx After 2018: 450,000 tons/yr more NOx	2010–2018: 21 tons/yr more mercury After 2018: 10 tons/yr more mercury
% Increase allowed by Bush Plan over Clean Air Act's existing programs	**2010–2018**: 225% as much SO_2 **After 2018**: 150% as much SO_2	**2010–2018**: 168% as much NOx **After 2018**: 136% as much NOx	**2010–2018**: 520% as much mercury **After 2018**: 300% as much mercury
Delay allowed by Bush Plan over Clean Air Act's existing programs	Up to 6 years delay	Up to 8 years delay	Up to 10 years delay

[59] Pope, Carl, 2004: 85.
[60] Pope, Carl, 2004: 85–6.
[61] NRDC Backgrounder (in collaboration with: American Lung Association, Clean Air Task Force, Clean Water Action, Clear the Air, League of Conservation Voters, National Environmental Trust, National Parks Conservation Association, National Wildlife Federation, Natural Resources Defense Council, Physicians for Social Responsibility, Environmental Integrity Project, Sierra Club, Union of Concerned Scientists, U.S. Public Interest Research Group, World Wildlife Federation). *The Bush Administration's Air Pollution Plan Hurts Public Health, Helps Big Polluters, Worsens Global Warming*. http://www.uwmc.uwc.edu/geography/350/clear-skies-NDRC%20analysis.htm.

Knowing the Clear Skies Initiative might languish in Congress, the vice president's energy task force quietly began pushing the second, more covert, tactic behind its strategy to cripple the CAA and NSR. The White House and many of the president's political appointees in the EPA (in collaboration with Bush appointees in the Office of Management and Budget (OMB), and the departments of Interior, Energy and Agriculture) began clandestinely dismantling the CAA – through closed-door legal settlements and obscure rule changes – without Congressional approval.

DISSENTION IN THE RANKS

This covert assault on the CAA and NSR did not sit well with everyone in the administration. Behind the scenes, EPA chief Whitman was having a hard time being a "team player" if it meant scrapping the law she had used, as governor of New Jersey, to make Ohio-based American Electric Power clean up the coal-fired power plants that were contaminating her state's air. Now she was being asked, as a member of the VP's energy task force, to side with American Electric and the other power plants who wanted to gut NSR.

Whitman, her associate EPA administrator Tom Gibson, and EPA's head of civil enforcement Eric Schaeffer all voiced their concerns about weakening the CAA by eliminating NSR. They knew this policy jeopardized all the EPA's ongoing litigation against the mega-polluters that had been violating NSR pollution controls for decades. In a memo to Vice President Cheney, two weeks before the task force released its policy recommendations, Whitman said, "As we discussed, the real issue for industry is the enforcement cases. We will pay a terrible political price if we undercut or walk away from the enforcement cases; it will be hard to refute the charge that we are deciding not to enforce the Clean Air Act."[62]

Whitman's concerns fell on deaf ears. After one task force meeting, she told sympathetic Treasury Secretary Paul O'Neill, "This is a slaughter. It's 10 on 2, not counting White House people and all the advisors to the group from the various industries."[63] As expected, when Cheney's task force released Bush's National Energy Policy, it recommended replacing tough CAA rules – including NSR – with an industry-backed pollution trading system.

NSR was first on the chopping block. The White House immediately directed the DoJ to review its NSR cases to see whether the suits against the Southern Company, American Electric and all the others might be dropped. The DoJ said no, the legal cases were too strong. Then the White House appointed a former energy industry lobbyist, Jeffrey Holmstead, to the job of EPA assistant administrator for air and radiation.[64] Holmstead's top priority was to rewrite CAA rules and gut NSR.

---

[62] Barcott, Bruce (April 4, 2004): 73.

[63] Suskind, Ron. *The Price of Loyalty.* (NY: Simon & Schuster), 2004; Barcott, Bruce (April 4, 2004): 73.

[64] The Clean Air Trust. Clean Air Villain of the Month (March 2002). http://www.cleanairtrust.org/villain.0302.html. Jeffrey Holmstead's former boss and political mentor, former White House Counsel C. Boyden Gray, had lobbied to get his clients, Southern Company, and other major electric power companies, off the hook for alleged violations of new source review.

Over the summer of 2002, the EPA went through the legal formality of holding hearings on the proposed rule changes; meanwhile, Whitman was already collaborating with the Department of Energy to finalize industry-friendly replacements for NSR. Holmstead testified before Congress that the proposed rule changes would not have any negative impact on the EPA's pending lawsuits against NSR violators even though his key aides in charge of prosecuting the cases had told him the opposite.[65] They were right.

When the task force's plans to undermine NSR hit the press, it completely undermined the EPA's legal leverage. In the courtroom, things were becoming impossible for the agency's enforcement officials in charge of prosecuting NSR cases. Energy industry attorneys – secure in the knowledge that their friends in the White House were drafting rules to eviscerate NSR and cripple the CAA – lost all incentive to compromise or cut deals.

In complete frustration, Eric Schaeffer, EPA's head of civil enforcement, resigned his position and denounced the president's entire Clear Skies Initiative on ABC's *This Week*. He told NRDC lawyer, Robert Kennedy, "The EPA is no longer a public health agency. It's become a country club for America's polluters."[66]

Schaeffer had been the man in charge of NSR lawsuits from their inception. His letter of resignation said he was tired of "fighting a White House that seems determined to weaken the rules we are trying to enforce."[67] He continued:

> The companies named in our lawsuits emit an incredible 5 million tons of sulfur dioxide every year (a quarter of the emissions in the entire country) as well as 2 million tons of nitrogen oxide. As the scale of pollution from these coal-fired smokestacks is immense, so is the damage to public health. Data supplied to the Senate Environment Committee by EPA last year estimate the annual health bill from 7 million tons of SO_2 and NO_2: more than 10,800 premature deaths; at least 5,400 incidents of chronic bronchitis; more than 5,100 hospital emergency visits; and over 1.5 million lost work days. Add to that severe damage to our natural resources, as acid rain attacks soils and plants and deposits nitrogen in the Chesapeake Bay and other critical bodies of water …
>
> It is no longer possible to pretend that the ongoing debate with the White House and Department of Energy is not affecting our ability to negotiate settlements. Cinergy and Vepco have refused to sign the consent decrees they agreed to 15 months ago, hedging their bets while waiting for the Administration's Clean Air Act reform proposals. Other companies with whom we were close to settlement have walked away from the table. The momentum we obtained with agreements announced earlier has stopped, and we have filed no new lawsuits against utility companies since this Administration took office. We obviously cannot settle cases with defendants who think we are still rewriting the law.[68]

[65] Eric Pianin (Washington Post). "Ex-EPA Officials Question Lawsuits," *MSNBC News.* http://www.msnbc.com/news/978484.asp.

[66] Kennedy, Robert F. Jr. *Crimes Against Nature.* (NY: Harper/Collins), 2004: 34.

[67] Barcott, Bruce (April 4, 2004): 73.

[68] *Letter of Resignation from Eric Schaeffer* (2004). http://ohio.sierraclub.org/tecumseh/EPAresignfeb02.htm.

The White House and the EPA sought to avoid publicity when it finally revealed its completed NSR overhaul. The announcement was made on a late Friday afternoon around Thanksgiving. Neither the president nor the EPA chief attended the event, and no cameras were allowed.

Industry was thrilled with the result. The National Petrochemical & Refiners Association said, "We believe that these NSR reforms represent an important and well-considered step which will help maintain a healthy and diverse U.S. refining and petrochemical industry."[69] But the American Lung Association retorted, "EPA policy should be based on protecting public health, not bolstering industry profits."[70] A coalition of environmental groups headed by the Lung Association labeled the NSR overhaul, "the most harmful and unlawful air pollution initiative ever undertaken by the federal government."[71]

When the administration finished working over NSR, it was weakened in several ways.[72] The most damaging weakness was the dramatically expanded definition of "routine maintenance." The new definition enabled old plants to undertake major renovations (amounting to tens of millions of dollars and significantly increasing pollution levels) without losing their exemption from installing modern emission control technologies.[73] Plants were allowed to spend 20 percent of their replacement cost on annual "routine maintenance" before losing their exemption. For those in the EPA who knew the costs of power plant maintenance, this figure was ridiculous. Most plants spend considerably less than 5 percent of their replacement value on annual maintenance. According to Eric Schaeffer, "What I don't understand is why they were so greedy . . . Five percent would have been too high, but 20! I don't think industry expected that in its wildest dreams."[74]

The American Lung Association estimated that, compared to the old NSR, the new rules would produce seven million more tons of SO_2 and 2.4 million more tons of NOx per year by 2020.[75] In fact, if the new NSR had been the original NSR, all of the NSR violations the EPA and DoJ had sued industry for would have been perfectly legal.

After Eric Schaeffer resigned, Bush appointed J. P. Suarez to the job of assistant administrator of enforcement. Suarez, who had no experience in environmental

---

[69] Mother Jones. "Clean Air Axed" (August 29, 2003). http://www.motherjones.com/news/dailymojo/2003/08/we_536_05a.htm.

[70] Mother Jones (August 29, 2003).

[71] Barcott, Bruce (April 4, 2004): 76.

[72] *Example 1*: A facility was allowed to increase its emissions as long as it didn't emit more than it did during its dirtiest year out of the previous ten years, thereby enshrining a facility's worst emissions as the status quo. *Example 2*: One exemption allowed facilities that installed pollution controls in the past 10 years a blanket exemption for all emissions increases 15 years into the future. *Example 3*: Polluters would be exempt from adopting pollution controls if they agreed to put a cap on their air pollution. The cap could be set far higher than the plant's current emissions, allowing pollution to increase. Earthjustice. "Stopping the Rollback of New Source Review." http://www.earthjustice.org/policy/rider/display.html?ID=12#one.

[73] Earthjustice. "Stopping the Rollback of New Source Review" (July 21, 2006). http://www.earthjustice.org/policy/rider/display.html?ID=12#one.

[74] Barcott, Bruce (April 4, 2004): 77.

[75] Barcott, Bruce (April 4, 2004): 77.

enforcement, informed his staffers that the agency would not pursue its ongoing NSR investigations. Except for those cases already in court, investigations into 70 companies suspected of major CAA violations were simply dropped.

Following Suarez's announcement, two more EPA career enforcement officials resigned: Bruce C. Buckheit, head of the enforcement office's air division, with 15 years of federal prosecutorial experience, and Richard Biondi, enforcement office associate director, with 30 years at EPA. They both blamed the Bush administration's reluctance to enforce environmental laws as their reason for resigning. According to Biondi, who joined the EPA back in 1971, the administration's decision to abandon its NSR suits was the last straw because it "excused decades of violations … We worked 30 years to develop a clean air program that is finally achieving our goals. It was frustrating to see some of our significant advances taken away. I left because I wanted to make a difference and it became clear that that was going to be difficult at EPA."[76]

By this time, the EPA's enforcement staff had fallen to its lowest level since the agency was established. It had declined from 528 to 464 since Bush took office.[77] According to a former EPA employee who spoke to *Grist Magazine* on condition of anonymity, the Bush administration was pursuing a master plan to quietly remove the senior career staff at EPA. The plan was carried out through two tactics: (1) demoralization by undermining their regulatory and enforcement powers; and (2) incentives for early retirement. "I've heard that they are offering a financial incentive of $25,000 in addition to their retirement plans to get out," said the former official. "The Bush administration is the first ever to offer such a plan to senior officials at EPA."[78]

This was rumored to be precisely the tactics that removed Buckheit and Biondi – after making their jobs redundant, the administration offered them a buyout. Given their tremendous frustration, they took it. Once their boss, J. P. Suarez, had dismantled NSR enforcement and litigation (and Buckheit and Biondi were gone), Suarez quit to take a position with Wal-Mart.[79]

Frank Clemente and Joan Claybrook, leaders of the public interest watchdog group Public Citizen, summed up the Bush administration's approach to clean air policy:

> The Bush administration's approach … is to change the laws in exchange for millions in contributions from the violators. This administration's willingness to sacrifice public health by exchanging environmental policy revisions for cash is so extreme that they are now changing the enforcement of those rules retroactively.
>
> This is a prime example of big campaign donors getting huge paybacks … These electric utilities were rewarded with positions on the Department of Energy's

---

[76] Barcott, Bruce (April 4, 2004): 78.
[77] Griscom, Amanda (Grist Magazine). "Jumping Ship at the EPA," *AlterNet* (January 7, 2004). http://www.alternet.org/story/17518/.
[78] Griscom, Amanda (Grist Magazine) (January 2004).
[79] Johnson, Jeff. "EPA's Top Cops Resign," *Chemical & Engineering News* (January 12, 2004). http://pubs.acs.org/cen/topstory/8202/8202notw6.html.

transition team and with free access to Vice President Cheney's secret energy task force. Now, a crucial air quality rule has been watered down as Cheney's task force recommended.[80]

However, the battle over clean air enforcement was not over. Forty-eight hours before the weakened NSR rules were to take effect, a federal appeals court halted their implementation. The judge found the EPA's new NSR rules to be so damaging and legally ineffective that the court issued a rare stay, immediately blocking the new rules from taking effect. The judge ruled that the new regulations could not go into effect until a lawsuit brought by New York State Attorney General Eliot Spitzer (and 14 more attorneys general) was heard.

The NSR lawsuit charged the Bush administration and the EPA with exceeding their authority by enacting rules that weaken the CAA. "The Bush Administration is attacking the Clean Air Act, which has been a cornerstone of our national commitment to environmental cleanup for two generations," said Attorney General Spitzer. "The Bush Administration is again putting the financial interests of the oil, gas and coal companies above the public's right to breathe clean air. It is incumbent on the states to take action to ensure that the public health and environment are protected."[81] The court's ruling meant that the watered-down NSR rules would be tied up in court for at least a year.

CLINTON AND BUSH: A DIME'S WORTH OF DIFFERENCE?

As the NSR example clearly demonstrates, no president – Republican or Democrat – has made any serious, consistent effort to enforce our clean air laws against the nation's most incorrigible criminal polluters. NSR is typical, not unique. Decade after decade, in case after case, the basic pattern repeats itself from the EPA's lax effort to regulate airborne toxins to their refusal to reduce the emissions of major climate disruptors such as methyl bromide and carbon dioxide. Unless public outrage threatens their political position, presidents seldom enforce the law against wealthy, influential corporations, especially if they are major financial backers.

Even in the face of highly negative publicity, Clinton refused to shut down the infamous Waste Technologies Industries (WTI) incinerator because of his "special relationship" with the incinerator's major financial backer. And, until their 20-year crime spree was exposed and became a political liability on his watch, Clinton's EPA refused to file suit against hundreds of the country's dirtiest power plants for poisoning the American people and violating the Clean Air Act. However, there are some notable differences between Clinton's Democratic administration and the

---

[80] Public Citizen. *Bush Appointees Gut Air Quality Rule and Give Congress False Information About the Consequence* (November 3, 2003). http://baltimorechronicle.com/novo3_choke-on-it. html.

[81] Press Release, NY State Attorney General. *Spitzer to Sue Bush Administration for Gutting Clean Air Act* (November 22, 2002). http://www.oag.state.ny.us/press/2002/nov/nov22b_02.html.

Republican administration of George W. Bush. While the Clinton administration's clean air enforcement record could be characterized as weak and ineffective, the Bush record has been aggressively hostile. Like the Reagan administration, the Bush White House stands out for its thinly veiled hostility to science and environmental regulation and its willingness to pursue strategies to gut the law and undermine enforcement against its polluting patrons. Thus, the basic difference between Clinton and Bush is the difference between a cop who is asleep on the beat and one that is aiding and abetting criminal activity.

While it is far too soon to say anything definitive about the EPA's commitment to clean air under President Barack Obama, there is some indication that his new EPA chief, Lisa Jackson, will be less tolerant of polluters than either Bush or Clinton. Within the first half year under her direction:

- Two petroleum refiners have agreed in separate settlements to spend a total of more than $141 million in new air pollution controls at three refineries in Kansas and Wyoming.
- BP Products agreed to pay nearly $180 million to settle clean air violations at its Texas City refinery.
- The United States filed a CAA lawsuit against Louisiana Generating for not installing and operating modern pollution control equipment after the generating units had undergone major modifications.
- Kentucky Utilities, a coal-fired electric utility, has agreed to pay a $1.4 million civil penalty and spend approximately $135 million on pollution controls to resolve violations of the CAA.[82]

---

[82] "Enviro Enforcement Under Obama," Enviro BLR.com (July 14, 2009). http://enviro.blr.com/news.aspx?id=106318.

3

The Clean Water Act – Up Sh*t Creek

Humans derive great spiritual and practical value from water. Throughout the ages, water has been a symbol of purity and renewal whose powers were often considered miraculous. We admire water's splendor in many forms: from shimmering icicles and cascading waterfalls to turbulent rivers and crashing waves. And as we all know, water provides an endless source of wonder and excitement: from snorkeling and diving to skiing and ice-skating.

On a more essential level, we humans have always understood water's profound value. Without it, life would be impossible. Life began in, and emerged from, the ocean. Water is the foundation of all terrestrial and marine ecosystems. Our bodies are more than 65 percent water; it is the basic component of every cell. To stay alive we must drink two liters of fresh water every day (directly or indirectly). Water is essential to all our food: from crops and livestock to fish and shellfish. Throughout history, people have made their homes near water. Our great civilizations emerged where water was abundant.

Yet despite its immeasurable spiritual and practical importance, humans have a long history of water abuse. This is primarily because in addition to using water for inspiration, recreation, transportation, irrigation, and hydration, we have also made water our favored mode of sanitation. We've used water to clean up and wash away our messes. Our garbage, including our own bodily wastes, usually went directly into the nearest body of water. And once we entered the modern era, the vast toxic dregs from chemical and industrial production became a whole new source of water abuse. Slowly, after much sickness and death, we've begun to realize that what we do to water we do to ourselves.

In 1862, Abraham Lincoln's 12-year-old son, Willie, and his brother, Tad, both contracted typhoid fever from drinking the polluted water that entered the White House from faucets fed directly by the Potomac River.[1] Tad survived, but Willie, the son who held the most cherished place in Lincoln's heart, died after weeks of misery and suffering. Long after the burial, the President repeatedly shut himself in a room so that he could weep alone. Many who knew Abe well believed that he was never the

---

[1] Gary, Ralph. *Following Lincoln's Footsteps.* (NY: Carroll & Graf), 2001: 332–3.

same after Willie's death. Lincoln was not alone in his grief. Water pollution has been a major source of death and disease for thousands of years. Water contaminated by inadequate sewage treatment and disposal was the source of most of history's great typhoid epidemics.

Nearly a century after Willie's tragic death, water pollution – especially municipal sewage – finally gained the attention of federal lawmakers. In 1948, Congress passed the Water Pollution Control Act, which provided states with the first federal water pollution control funds and the first trickle of subsidies for local sewage disposal programs. Congress' commitment to subsidizing sewage treatment grew with the Federal Water Pollution Control Act (FWPCA) of 1956.[2] In the decade from FY 1961 to FY 1971, federal expenditures for state-based efforts to control water pollution rose from $50 million to $1.25 billion.[3] Unfortunately, this increased flow of federal dollars was not accompanied by strict, enforceable national water quality regulations and standards.

According to the Natural Resources Defense Council (NRDC): "No federal requirements were imposed on industrial polluters, and municipal dischargers benefited from federal dollars without any significant accompanying federal controls. Most notably, industries and cities did not need federal permits to discharge wastes into waterways."[4] Enforcement was infrequent and ineffectual (and remained focused on interstate pollution). The 1965 FWPCA was the strictest of these weak federal water pollution laws. Yet, even under the FWPCA, enforcers had to *prove* that a particular polluter caused violations of interstate quality standards. This was highly unlikely given the horde of polluters jamming the nation's major waterways and the primitive state of water quality science and monitoring.

During the industrial era, mining operators, paper mill owners and factory owners came to view nearby rivers, lakes and oceans as the cheap and easy way to dispose of their wastes. When challenged, they brazenly asserted their "right" to pollute and used their political connections to resist all efforts to stop them. Thus, by 1969, little had changed on the Potomac. A health conference in Washington, DC declared the river "a severe threat to anyone who comes in contact with it."[5] President Johnson condemned the condition of the Potomac as part of his pledge to clean up American waters by 1975. Unfortunately, the legal battle to confront water pollution was hampered by powerful polluters and antiquated and ineffectual legislation.

After two centuries of abuse and neglect, it became obvious that the nation's few feeble water pollution laws were incapable of restoring the health and ecological integrity of the nation's rivers, lakes, aquifers and coastal waters. In June 1969, the gravity of this crisis was dramatically confirmed in Cleveland where oil and industrial waste floating atop the Cuyahoga River burst into flame. *Time* magazine described

---

[2] The FWPCA was re-funded in 1961, 1965 and 1966.
[3] For a more thorough history of Washington's early efforts to address water pollution see: Kovalic, J. M. *The Clean Water Act of 1987*, 2nd ed. (Alexandria, VA: Water Environment Federation), 1987.
[4] Adler, Walter W., Jessica Landman & Diane Cameron. *The Clean Water Act 20 Years Later*. (Washington, DC: Island Press), 1993: 6.
[5] Adler, Walter W., Jessica Landman & Diane Cameron, 1993: 1.

the Cuyahoga as the river that "oozes rather than flows" and in which a person "does not drown but decays."[6] Soon thereafter, 250 million gallons of crude oil spewed from a Union Oil drilling blowout off the coast of Santa Barbara. Media coverage of the thick, gooey black ooze engulfing 30 miles of California's magnificent shoreline – killing helpless shorebirds, fish and marine mammals – stunned and infuriated the public.

In 1971, a Ralph Nader task force issued *Water Wasteland*, a disturbing 700-page report on the dire condition of U.S. waters. It caught national media attention.[7] According to Nader's report:

- Water pollution was costing the U.S. about $12.8 billion per year.[8]
- Thirty percent of all drinking water samples contained chemicals exceeding recommended health limits.[9]
- Eighty-seven percent of swordfish samples had mercury levels unfit for human consumption.[10]
- The Hudson River contained bacteria levels 170 times the safe limit.
- Record numbers of fish kills were reported in 1969. More than 41 million fish were poisoned by pollution – more than 1966, 1967 and 1968 combined.

Politicians from both parties scrambled to respond to the public demand for action by portraying themselves as defenders of clean water. Senator Edmond Muskie (D-Maine) and other legislators seeking the 1972 presidential nomination vied to be the country's environmental champion by proposing the toughest water pollution laws in history. Muskie introduced the Clean Water Act (CWA) to Congress by condemning the condition of the nation's waters, "Today, the rivers of this country serve as little more than sewers to the seas. Wastes from cities and towns, from farms and forests, from mining and manufacturing, foul the streams, poison the estuaries and threaten life in the ocean depths."[11]

---

[6] In fact, Cuyahoga River pollution caught fire nine times: in 1868, 1883, 1887, 1912, 1922, 1936, 1941, 1948 and – the most devastating of all – the 1952 blaze that resulted in nearly $1.5 millions in damage. Nor was the Cuyahoga River the only river to burn during that era. Pollutants fueled fires on a river into the Baltimore Harbor, the Buffalo River in upstate NY and the Rouge River in Michigan. Griffith, Susan. "Myths Surrounding the Cuyahoga River Fire 35 Years Ago" (Case Western University, June 17, 2004). Griffith, Susan. "Myths Surrounding the Cuyahoga River Fire 35 Years Ago," *Case Western University News Center* (October 29, 2004). http://www.case.edu/news/2004/10–04/cuyahoga_fire.htm.

[7] "Nader on Water," *TIME* (April 26, 1971). http://www.yachtingnet.com/time/magazine/article/0,9171,902895,00.html.

[8] Quoted in: "Nader on Water" (April 26, 1971). This estimation was made by Federal Water Quality Administration economist, Edwin Johnson.

[9] As reported by the Department of Health, Education & Welfare in July 1970 and quoted in: "Nader on Water" (April 26, 1971).

[10] According to a 1971 FDA study. Quoted in: "Nader on Water" (April 26, 1971).

[11] Quoted in: Kennedy, Robert F. "Congressional Testimony on the Clean Water Act" (October 8, 2002).

Not to be outdone in this effort to court concerned voters, President Nixon declared that "the 1970s absolutely must be the years when America pays its debt to the past by reclaiming the purity of its air, its water and our living environment. It is literally now or never."[12] Yet, when Congress delivered a tough CWA to his desk, Nixon demonstrated the depth of his commitment by vetoing it. To the relief of most Americans, Congress overrode the president's veto and signed the act into law. Compared to past clean water legislation, the CWA (formally known as the Federal Water Pollution Control Act of 1972), appeared to be a giant step forward.

CONGRESS TALKS THE TALK . . .

The bold print forthrightly affirmed Congress' determination to clean up and protect America's water resources once and for all. It declared, "The objective of this Act is to restore and maintain the chemical, physical and biological integrity of the Nation's waters."[13] The language Congress used to define the CWA's primary objective was clear and unambiguous. By calling for the *restoration and maintenance* of the chemical, physical and biological integrity of the nation's waters, Congress was going far past mere efforts to limit, reduce or even completely halt, water pollution.

The bedrock goal was to return the patient to *full health* – to completely rid the waters of all substances and practices that threaten human health or the integrity of the aquatic environment. Polluted waters must be restored to full health; unpolluted waters must be maintained and protected from future pollution.

Congress followed up on this admirable commitment by laying out three intermediate goals. "In order to achieve this objective, it is hereby declared that:

(1) It is the national goal that the discharge of pollutants into the navigable waters be eliminated **by 1985**;

(2) It is the national goal that wherever attainable, an interim goal of water quality which provides for the protection and propagation of fish, shellfish and wildlife and provides for recreation in and on the water to be achieved **by July 1, 1983**;

(3) It is the national policy that the discharge of toxic pollutants in toxic amounts be prohibited."[14]

The first goal became known as "zero discharge"; the second was dubbed "fishable & swimmable waters," and the third was called "no toxics in toxic amounts." To affirm Congressional commitment to these goals, Senator Muskie promised, "These are not merely the pious declarations Congress so often makes in passing its laws; on the contrary, this is literally a life or death proposition for the nation."[15]

---

[12] Adler, Walter W., Jessica Landman & Diane Cameron, 1993: 1–2.

[13] *The Clean Water Act,* § 101 (a).

[14] *The Clean Water Act,* § 101 (a) (1)–(3).

[15] Congressional Research Service. *History of the Water Pollution Control Act Amendments of 1972,* ser 1, 93rd Congress, 1st session (1972): 164.

BUT DOES IT WALK THE WALK?

Congress' commendable goals, no matter how vociferously professed, were only as good as the law designed to achieve them and the regulatory efforts of the agency in charge of enforcement. Looking back over the decades since the act was passed, it is patently obvious that the CWA's legal structure and enforcement have been woefully incapable of reaching the law's stated goals.

Even though the CWA removes more than a billion pounds of toxic pollutants and 900 million tons of untreated sewage from the nation's waters every year,[16] the act has not come close to restoring the chemical, physical and biological integrity of the nation's waters. The act's 1985 goal of eliminating pollutants from our waterways remains about as distant today as it did back in 1972. When it comes to the well-being of our waterways, instead of restoring the patient to full health, she remains in serious condition.

There is no doubt that some specific improvements have been made: the Cuyahoga River is no longer combustible, oil drilling is prohibited off the coast of California and Lake Erie is no longer considered dead. Surely, the nation's rivers, lakes and streams would be worse off without the CWA. Yet, after three decades, Congress appears to be as far from fulfilling its promise to restore the health of the country's waterways as ever.

Today, most Americans live within ten miles of a polluted lake, stream, river or coastal area.[17] The EPA's most recent report – which many consider falsely optimistic – contends that of the waters tested, 61 percent of the river and stream miles, 54 percent of the lake acres, 49 percent of the estuarine square miles and 22 percent of the Great Lakes shoreline miles meet the law's most basic "fishable and swimmable" quality standards.[18] It estimates that 20,000 bodies of water throughout the country are too polluted to meet basic water quality standards.[19]

Pollution-caused beach closings and advisories are breaking old records; by 2004, there were nearly 20,000 – the highest number in 15 years.[20] Worsening conditions are especially apparent for America's estuaries – 13 percent more of which are too polluted to support their uses than just four years ago.[21] Impairment of estuaries has profound ramifications for the environment and for the economy because they are nurseries for many commercial and recreational fish species and most shellfish populations, including shrimp, oysters, clams, crabs and scallops.

Instead of "zero discharge," the EPA's Toxics Release Inventory (TRI), reports that polluters dumped more than 221,800,000 pounds of toxic chemicals into our

---

[16]   Adler, Walter W., Jessica Landman & Diane Cameron, 1993: 139.
[17]   EPA Inspector General. *Water Enforcement: State Enforcement of Clean Water Act Dischargers Can Be More Effective* (August 2001).
[18]   Kubasek, Nancy & Gary Silverman. *Environmental Law*, 5th ed. (NY: Prentice Hall), 2005: 236.
[19]   EPA & GAO. *Water Quality: Inconsistent State Approaches Complicate Nation's Efforts to Identify Most Polluted Waters*. GAO-02-186 (January 2002).
[20]   NRDC. *Testing the Waters 2005: A Guide to Vacation Beaches* (August 2005).
[21]   Kennedy, Robert F (October 8, 2002).

waterways in 2003.[22] However, Congress' Office of Technology Assessment (OTA) considers this TRI data extremely misleading. The OTA estimates that the TRI database reflects *less than 1 percent* of the actual quantities of toxic pollutants released.[23] The primary reason for this gross underestimate is the fact that the TRI covers only manufacturing industries; it does not include massive releases of toxics from oil and gas wells, mining and agriculture.[24]

After years of steady improvement, the sewage problem has returned. Throughout the country, sewer systems are rapidly aging and are becoming overwhelmed by urban sprawl and industrial development. At least 853 billion gallons of raw sewage are being dumped into U.S. waterways every year.[25] According to the EPA, sewage contamination will reach unprecedented levels by 2025 unless significant investments are made in wastewater treatment technologies.[26]

Decades after the CWA's missed its 1985 "zero discharge" deadline, a deadly mixture of pollutants still poisons our waters. A total of 362 contaminants, including metals such as lead and mercury, a broad array of pesticides and organic industrial chemicals (such as PCBs and dioxin) are commonly found in American waters. In the most thoroughly studied large bodies of water – the Great Lakes – 11 of these substances have been classified as pollutants of "critical concern." Lake Superior receives nearly 500 pounds of PCBs per year; while Michigan, Huron, Erie and Ontario receive up to 5,000 pounds annually. Between 1,000 and 5,000 pounds of mercury are discharged to each of the Great Lakes. Every year, more than 1,000 pounds of lead are discharged to Lakes Superior and Huron, more than 8,000 pounds are discharged to Lake Ontario, more than 30,000 pounds are discharged to Lake Erie and more than 50,000 pounds are discharged to Lake Michigan.[27]

HOW DANGEROUS IS WATER POLLUTION?

How many Americans die of water pollution? Anyone who says they have an accurate answer to this question is lying. Researchers think that waterborne toxins sicken and kill thousands of people every year without ever being detected as the cause. Because most of today's water pollution is odorless and tasteless, dangerous chemicals are often consumed without realizing it. Even after people become sick, they are frequently unaware of the source of their symptoms and continue to consume polluted water despite the accumulating hazards. When doctors are consulted, they are often unfamiliar with water

[22] EPA. *2003 Toxics Relief Inventory* (2003). http://www.epa.gov/tri/tridata/trio3/index.htm.
[23] Adler, Walter W., Jessica Landman & Diane Cameron, 1993: 141.
[24] Adler, Walter W., Jessica Landman & Diane Cameron, 1993: 141–2.
[25] US-PIRG. *Troubled Waters: An Analysis of CWA Compliance (2003–4)*: 3.
[26] US-PIRG. *Troubled Waters: An Analysis of CWA Compliance (2003–4)*: 3.
[27] Adler, Robert W. "Cleaner Water, But Not Clean Enough," *Issues in Science & Technology* (December 22, 1993). HighBeam Research (November 11, 2009). http://www.highbeam.com/doc/1G1-15155692.html; Morreale, David J. *A Survey of Current Great Lakes Research* (University of Buffalo: July 2002). http://www.eng.buffalo.edu/glp/articles/review.htm.

pollution diagnostics and dangers. Misdiagnosis and under-diagnosis of waterborne poisonings and diseases by the medical community may result in significant morbidity and mortality, particularly in vulnerable populations at increased risk, as a result of exposure to waterborne pathogens and chemical contaminants.[28]

The complexity of this problem and our ignorance of the multiple and synergistic impacts of aquatic pollutants keeps us from a reliable understanding of the risks and dangers. Water contamination by either chemical poisons or infectious diseases may affect the health of millions of Americans. According to a 2008 study published in the journal *Reviews of Environmental Contamination and Toxicology*, an estimated 19.5 million Americans fall ill each year from drinking water contaminated with parasites, bacteria or viruses.[29] This figure does not include illnesses caused by industrial chemicals and toxins. Research shows that about one in ten Americans have been exposed to drinking water that contains dangerous chemicals or fails to meet federal health standards.[30] A 1995 report by the NRDC estimated that 1,000 deaths and more than 400,000 cases of waterborne illness may be caused by contaminated water. This statistic is compatible with the estimates of the Centers for Disease Control and Prevention.[31] However, some estimates run much higher – to seven million or more.[32]

Virtually all water pollutants are hazardous to humans. Sodium is implicated in cardiovascular disease; nitrates in blood disorders. Mercury and lead can cause nervous disorders. Nitrates, a pollutant derived from fertilizer runoff, can cause a potentially lethal form of anemia in infants called blue baby syndrome (or methemoglobinemia). Many contaminants are carcinogens. DDT is toxic to humans and can alter chromosomes. PCBs cause liver and nerve damage, skin eruptions, vomiting, fever, diarrhea and fetal abnormalities.

More than 14 million Americans drink water contaminated with pesticides, and the EPA estimates that 10 percent of wells contain pesticides.[33] Dysentery, hepatitis, salmonellosis and cryptosporidium are among the maladies transmitted by sewage in drinking and bathing water. Throughout the United States, rivers, lakes and beaches along every coast have been ruined for swimming and recreation by industrial wastes, municipal sewage and medical waste. What happens when these chemical pollutants interact? This is a serious problem that scientists know little about. They do know that sometimes they become less toxic and sometimes they become much more toxic.

Toxins of all kinds tend to concentrate as they move up the food chain. This bioaccumulation presents a serious problem because we humans tend to eat at the

---

[28] Millichamp, Gordon G. "Is Our Water Safe to Drink?" (Fall 1995). http://www.nutrition4health. org/nohanews/NNF95WaterSafeToDrink.htm.

[29] Duhigg, Charles. "Toxic Waters," *New York Times* (September 13, 2009). http://projects.nytimes. com/toxic-waters.

[30] Duhigg, Charles (September 13, 2009).

[31] Kraft, Michael. *Environmental Policy and Politics*, 3rd ed. (NY: Pearson/Longman), 2004: 40.

[32] Olson, Erik & Diane Cameron. *Dirty Little Secret About Our Drinking Water*. (Washington, DC: NRDC), February 1995.

[33] MSN Encarta. Water Pollution. http://encarta.msn.com/encyclopedia_761572857/Water_Pollution. html.

top of the chain. Along many rivers and shores, fish and shellfish can no longer be eaten because their bodies contain concentrated doses of DDT, sewage, pesticides and industrial wastes. In 2004, 31 states had statewide fish consumption advisories and alerts because of toxic pollution.[34] Cognitive and other mental deficits have been documented in children born of mothers who were exposed to PCBs through consumption of large quantities of contaminated fish.

Humans are not the only victims of water pollution. Water pollution kills wildlife and destroys habitat from coral reefs, wetlands and estuaries to trout streams and kelp forests. Sewage; toxic chemicals; pulp mill, mining, medical, military and manufacturing wastes; fertilizers, herbicides and insecticides; soaps and detergents; radioactive wastes; plastics; oil, gasoline and other automobile wastes befoul our oceans and freshwater ecosystems far in excess of what the planet's natural filtering and recycling systems can sustain. The result is widespread harm to all creatures that require uncontaminated water to survive.

WHAT PREVENTS THE CWA FROM MEETING ITS GOALS?

Most Americans are well aware that water pollution remains a serious problem that current laws are not solving. A comprehensive review of more than 500 public opinion surveys conducted between 1993 and 1974 confirmed that Americans continue to rank water quality high among environmental problems. The review showed that most believe that water-quality problems are getting worse and the percentage of people who hold this view has increased since the CWA was enacted.[35]

But why isn't the CWA meeting its stated goals? Is the law itself flawed? Is enforcement the problem? Are its goals simply unrealistic?

THE CLEAN WATER ACT'S MAJOR FLAWS

The CWA is structured around four basic guiding principles:

(1) No one has *the right* to pollute the nation's waters.
(2) Using public waterways for waste disposal is illegal without a permit limiting the amount of the discharge.
(3) Before discharge, pollutants must be treated with the best treatment technology economically achievable, regardless of the condition of the receiving water.
(4) Effluent limits must be based on the effectiveness of the treatment technologies, but more stringent limits *may* be imposed if technology-based limits do not prevent violations of water quality standards for the receiving water.[36]

---

[34] US EPA. *2004, National Listing of Fish & Wildlife Advisories.*
[35] Adler, Walter W., Jessica Landman & Diane Cameron, 1993: 10–11.
[36] US-PIRG. *Troubled Waters: An Analysis of CWA Compliance (2003–4):* 4.

When Congress confronted the question of how to clean up America's waters, it recognized that one source of pollution was much easier to regulate and restrict than the rest. This was the type that went from a particular facility, through a particular conveyance, and into a particular body of water. Congress called this *point source pollution*. Point source pollution is much easier to identify, monitor and control than *non–point source (NPS) pollution*, like urban and agricultural run-off, whose origins are far more diffuse and, therefore, much harder to pinpoint and prevent. Thus, the CWA's major legal mechanism, the permit system, is directed at cleaning up point source pollution.

PERMITTING POLLUTION

Though the act has been amended several times,[37] the permit system remains the CWA's legal centerpiece. It requires every industrial and municipal facility that directly discharges[38] pollutants into any waterway[39] to have a permit. So all factories, mills, plants and public wastewater treatment facilities that use ditches or trenches; ducts or drains; canals or culverts; gutters or pipes to discharge their wastes into a waterway must have a permit.[40] Known as an NPDES[41] permit, it contains *effluent limitations* on the quantity and concentration of pollutants a facility can release and the specific treatment technologies that must be used to stay within those limitations. The permit may also contain water quality guidelines if technology based limits are not enough to prevent the degradation of receiving waters.

Although Congress reckoned that point source would be the easiest type of water pollution to stop, it still remains a serious problem three decades after the CWA passed. Many severe loopholes drastically undermine the permit system's success:

> (1) Permits do not require polluters to eliminate pollution or meet health and safety standards for their receiving waters. Instead, they require polluters to use the best treatment technologies they can afford to meet technology-based contamination limits.

---

[37] In 1977, 1987 and 1990.

[38] A "direct discharge" means through any "discreet conveyance" – like a pipe.

[39] The permit program applies to all discharges into the "navigable waters" of the U.S. However, "navigable waters" are not defined by whether boats can actually float on them. Rather they are defined to include all waters over which Congress has constitutional authority to regulate under the Commerce Clause. Thus, even intermittent streams and wetlands that only occasionally have water are considered navigable waters. Territorial waters of the U.S. include waters three miles from shore. Additionally, facilities other than boats, like oil platforms, that discharge into these territorial waters are required to have an NPDES permit.

[40] For purposes of CWA, large feedlots and factory farms are regulated as point sources. These "concentrated animal feeding operations" are responsible for phosphorus, pathogens and animal waste nutrients seeping into surface and ground water. Enforcement on these sites has been quite lax.

[41] "National Pollutant Discharge Elimination System."

(2) State water agencies and the polluters themselves control permit issuance, monitoring, compliance and enforcement, with limited EPA oversight.

(3) The inferior quality of the states' monitoring, data collection, assessment and enforcement – and the EPA's lax oversight – make it impossible to measure polluters' compliance with the permit system and the condition of the nation's waters.

(4) Because enforcement is sporadic and penalties are low, polluters violate and ignore their permit limitations constantly and seriously.

(5) One of every four major polluting facilities operates without any permits.

(6) The EPA-sanctioned use of *mixing zones* undermines the permit system by allowing polluters to create vast toxic regions that make water unsafe to drink, unfit to play in and incapable of supporting aquatic life.

(7) Flaws in the permit system tolerate the disposal of industrial toxins down public sewers. This creates a toxic sludge the EPA deceptively markets as beneficial fertilizer – safe for use on America's farms and gardens.

The first major problem with the permit system is that pollution limits are not set to protect public health or maintain the ecological welfare of a given body of water. The degree of restriction imposed on a contaminant is not based on the dangers it poses. Instead, discharge limits are based on the cost of reducing a particular contaminant, given the types of treatment technologies available. Older facilities that discharge conventional pollutants require the least stringent standards of pollution treatment. Newly built facilities, and those discharging nonconventional or toxic pollutants, must use more stringent (and costly) pollution control technologies.

What happens when a body of water becomes seriously poisoned by the combined discharges of many legally permitted polluters? In theory, the CWA requires states to establish Water Quality Standards (WSQs) that define the maximum concentrations of pollutants allowable in a particular body of water. These standards are supposed to protect the health and safety of waterways, communities and ecosystems overburdened by too many legally permitted polluters. However, states have yet to establish WSQs for many bodies of water and, where they do exist, they have been found to be highly inaccurate and misleading. Further, EPA guidelines are not legally binding on how states determine or categorize water quality. This makes it nearly impossible to compare or assess water quality across the nation[42] or to make states adopt higher WSQs.

To make matters worse, when it comes to assessing water quality, the EPA must rely almost entirely upon information gathered from the states. However, states frequently manipulate their scientific methods and conclusions to fit their political

---

[42] PEER. *Murky Waters: An Inside Look at the EPA's Implementation of the Clean Water Act* (May 1999).

and budgetary situations. State water agencies commonly use one method of assessing water quality when emphasizing their progress or disguising their lax enforcement and others when emphasizing the need for more funding or looking for the truth. These conflicting motives have caused Michigan to claim that all its watersheds are in dire need of restoration to secure federal watershed restoration funds and then assert that only 8 percent of its waterways are impaired in its yearly progress report.[43]

When assessing whether its waters were impaired by pollution or healthy enough to support "fishing and swimming," Ohio found that the answer was "all in the test." Quantitative chemical assessments indicated that a high proportion of the state's waterways were not impaired. Yet when more careful, expensive, qualitative biological assessments were performed on the same waters, impairment jumped from 39 to 64 percent. In other words, even though chemical tests seemed to indicate that aquatic life *should* be able to thrive in the water, more careful biological studies of what actually lived in the water revealed a far grimmer picture.[44]

In addition to their inaccuracy and manipulation, WQSs carry little legal weight. As long as polluters are abiding by the particular technical requirements of their NPDES permit, they are completely shielded from all CWA-based lawsuits. A polluter cannot be sued or fined for any pollutant it discharges that is not specifically mentioned in its NPDES permit, and it cannot be sued for violating general WQSs that are not specifically incorporated into its permit.[45]

The second major problem with the permit system is that issuance, monitoring, compliance and enforcement of permits are generally handled by the states and the polluters themselves, with limited EPA oversight.[46] Under the CWA, all but four states run their own NPDES permit programs. The CWA requires the industry to self-monitor its discharges and self-report its violations with occasional, predetermined onsite inspections by notoriously underfunded and apathetic state inspection and enforcement programs. Though the number of regulated polluters has more than doubled since 1999, state enforcement budgets have remained virtually static.[47]

But this is just part of the problem. The most powerful polluters in Washington, DC and each state capitol wield their tremendous influence to encourage regulators to turn a blind eye to their crimes. In West Virginia, for example, big coal companies have used their political clout to intimidate state regulators and discourage clean water enforcement. Several state regulators interviewed by *The New York Times* described how their enforcement efforts were "undermined by bureaucratic disorganization, a departmental preference to let polluters escape punishment if they promise to try harder, and a revolving door of regulators who leave for higher-paying jobs at the companies they once policed."[48] Meanwhile, in Washington, DC, EPA officials told *The New York Times* that enforcement lapses were particularly bad under

---

[43] PEER (May 1999): 23.
[44] PEER (May 1999): 27–9.
[45] Piney Run Preservation Association v. County Commissioners of Carroll County, Md.
[46] The EPA retains oversight over this process, but once states receive authorization to implement their own NPDES programs, the EPA's role becomes distant and minimal.
[47] Duhigg, Charles (September 13, 2009).
[48] Duhigg, Charles (September 13, 2009).

the administration of President George W. Bush. "For the last eight years, my hands have been tied," one official lamented. "We were told to take our clean water and clean air cases, put them in a box and lock it shut. Everyone knew polluters were getting away with murder. But these polluters are some of the biggest campaign contributors in town, so no one really cared if they were dumping poisons into streams."[49]

The extremely negligent and uneven history of state-directed efforts to control water pollution and industry's sordid record of malfeasance, obstruction and resistance should have discouraged Congress from crafting a law that gives states primary responsibility for operating the permit system and allows polluters to monitor their own compliance. The outcome has been disturbingly predictable. A 2009 investigation by *The New York Times* revealed that between 2004 and 2009, chemical factories, manufacturing plants and other businesses violated water pollution laws more than 506,000 times.[50] However, this statistic grossly underestimates the extent of CWA violations because companies generally test their pollution discharges only once per quarter, so the actual number of days when they broke the law is often far higher. Also, some companies illegally avoid reporting their emissions, so infractions go unrecorded.

About 60 percent of these 506,000 recorded violations fall into the most serious range, such as dumping toxins at concentrations that may cause cancer, birth defects and other illnesses. Yet fewer than 3 percent of CWA violations have resulted in fines or other significant punishments.[51] In fact, the EPA generally declines to prosecute polluters or force states to strengthen their enforcement by threatening to withhold federal funds or take away powers the agency has delegated to state officials.[52]

The third problem with the permit system is that its effectiveness is impossible to evaluate. Efforts to measure the level of industry compliance with the CWA have been unsuccessful because of the miserable state of EPA record-keeping in this regard. According to a report issued by EPA and state agency insiders and members of Public Employees for Environmental Responsibility (PEER), neither polluting industries nor state agencies are motivated to deliver accurate or consistent water quality data and compliance reports to EPA.[53] *The New York Times* investigators found the EPA's information on CWA enforcement so inadequate that they were forced to obtain and compile hundreds of thousands of water pollution records through Freedom of Information Act requests to every state and the EPA. Their efforts produced a national database of water pollution violations far more comprehensive than those maintained by either the states or the EPA.[54] *The New York Times*

[49] Duhigg, Charles (September 13, 2009).

[50] Duhigg, Charles (September 13, 2009).

[51] Duhigg, Charles (September 13, 2009).

[52] Duhigg, Charles (September 13, 2009).

[53] PEER (May 1999). Gives an insider account of how EPA and its state partners, through a mix of politics, bureaucratic inertia and bad science, perpetuate the fiction that official water quality reports are valid by routinely presenting Congress and the public with conflicting, erroneous and manipulated data containing little accurate information on the actual condition of the nation's waterways.

[54] For an interactive version, which can show violations in any community, visit http://www.nytimes.com/toxicwaters. Duhigg, Charles (September 13, 2009).

investigators discovered that the number of facilities violating the CWA grew more than 16 percent during the final years of the Bush administration.

Even the *The New York Times'* best efforts were marred by serious flaws in the available data. Often, states will report one set of sanguine figures on water quality for national inventory purposes and more ominous statistics to obtain federal watershed restoration funds. According to PEER General Council, Todd Robins, "EPA has yet to reject a state water quality report no matter how incomplete or scientifically invalid. It even allows states to simply ignore reporting requirements altogether, without any financial, administrative or regulatory consequences."[55] Thus states are free to manipulate numbers and falsify data in order to portray continuing water quality progress when, in fact, what fragmentary reliable data that exist suggest the opposite.[56] Efforts by public interest groups such as the Natural Resources Defense Council (NRDC), the U.S. Public Interest Group (US-PIRG) and PEER to gather and assess EPA data, recognize that "available data on water quality in the U.S. at best paints an incomplete picture of the pollution entering our waterways; at worst, it is a gross underestimate."[57]

In addition to the falsified, incomplete and inaccurate data supplied by industry and the states, the EPA undermines water quality assessment because it requires states to enter data only for "major" polluting facilities. As a result, the EPA has no compliance data on hundreds of thousands of polluters. The EPA admits that for many states, even the data on these major facilities is "incomplete and unreliable."[58]

The fourth problem with NPDES permits is that polluters constantly and seriously violate and ignore them. Even the EPA's sanguine statistics – that omit thousands of the country's polluters and are derived from industry self-reporting to state agencies with dismal enforcement records – disclose the abysmal state of CWA compliance. For the period between July 2003 and December 2004, the EPA's own records revealed that:

- Nationally, 3,700 major facilities (62 percent) violated their CWA permits.
- Together they racked up 29,000 violations during that period.
- On average, they exceeded their pollution limits by almost four times the permitted amount; there were 2,500 violations when permit limits were exceeded six-fold.
- There were 436 facilities in violation of their permits more than half the time.
- Thirty-five were in violation the entire time.
- The states that allowed the most violations were Ohio, Texas, New York, Louisiana, Tennessee, Indiana, West Virginia, Massachusetts and Illinois.[59]

[55] PEER (May 1999). Executive Summary.
[56] PEER (May 1999). Introduction by PEER Executive Director, Jeffrey Ruch.
[57] US-PIRG. *Troubled Waters: An Analysis of CWA Compliance (2003–4)*: 6; PEER (May 1999).
[58] US-PIRG. *Troubled Waters: An Analysis of CWA Compliance (2003–4)*: 6.
[59] US-PIRG. *Troubled Waters: An Analysis of CWA Compliance (2003–4)*.

This dismal enforcement record prompted the EPA's own Inspector General to conclude that "small fines and lengthy time limits to achieve compliance promote a pay-to-pollute mentality."[60]

Unfortunately, permit violation is only the beginning. The fifth problem, and bigger outrage, is that about one of every four major facilities operates without any permit. In 2000, a national review of all 6,700 NPDES permits for major facilities showed that in 12 states, more than half of all water pollution permits for major polluters were expired. More than one-third of all permits were expired in 17 states; and in 44 states (and the District of Columbia), more than 10 percent were expired.[61]

Nationwide, about one quarter of all major water polluters – more than 1,690 facilities – were operating without current permits to jettison their wastes to the nation's waters. More than 770 major facility permits had been expired for two years, and 251 had been expired for five years. These facilities illegally disgorge huge amounts of highly toxic effluents into our waters. In nine states, well over 50 major polluters operated with expired permits, topped by Texas (135), Louisiana (116), Ohio (96), California (85) and Indiana (81).[62]

In response to the EWG/FoE report and another by the EPA's own Inspector General's Office (IGO), the agency announced a campaign to renew expired permits for major facilities. The EPA went so far as to post a website in which its progress could be monitored. Two years later, the EPA's own website revealed that there had been virtually no progress toward meeting its goals. Since then, the website has been removed.[63]

THE MIXING ZONE LOOPHOLE

A sixth major flaw in the way the CWA's permit system is interpreted and enforced is the EPA-sanctioned use of mixing zones in states. The CWA's technology-based effluent restrictions were supposed to require pollution-reduction technologies that would become increasingly more stringent and would progress from end-of-pipe treatments to changes in manufacturing processes until zero discharge was achieved.[64] Congress expected this progression to continue to reduce pollutants while also reducing the economic burden associated with installing increasingly costly treatment technologies at the point of discharge. However, instead of proactively adopting cleaner, less-polluting production methods, industry pressured state

---

[60] EWG/PIRG. *Moneyed Waters: Political Contributions & the Attack on the Clean Water Act* (1995).

[61] Environmental Working Group and Friends of the Earth. *Clean Water Report Card: Falling Grades* (March 2000).

[62] Environmental Working Group and Friends of the Earth (March 2000).

[63] This page has been removed from the EPA website: http://www.epa.gov/owmitnet/permits/back-log/backlog.htm.

[64] CWA §§ 301 (b) (2) (A), 304 (b) (3).

agencies and the EPA to weaken the law by allowing them to go back to the use of mixing zones.

In 1983, the EPA allowed states to return to the pre-CWA mixing–zone dilution process. Instead of enforcing water quality standards at the point of discharge, state and federal regulators created mixing zones in the receiving water. Pollutant concentrations are measured at the outer boundary of the mixing zone rather than at the end of the discharge pipe. These toxic zones can extend from a few feet in length to miles downstream from the point of discharge. They allow industries to increase their pollution allowances based on the volume of their receiving water.

The EPA justified removing water quality protections from waters inside mixing zones based on the reasoning that Congress did not intend the CWA to protect the whole water body, but rather the *water body as a whole*. This bizarre legal interpretation completely contradicted the law's guiding principle that "dilution was no longer to be the solution to pollution" and contradicted its stated goal of totally eliminating all pollution into the nation's waters.

This loophole allows the polluter's point of compliance with human health and aquatic life standards to move far downstream from the actual point of release. Mixing zones condone the creation of vast toxic regions that make water unsafe to drink, unfit to play in and incapable of supporting aquatic life, thereby violating the goals and prohibitions of the CWA.

Of course, this system saves the polluter money because it legally allows them to avoid the expense of treating chemical wastes that frequently contain many of the most toxic pollutants known. Because they are released legally, most people never know that organochlorines (such as dioxin) and many pesticides, herbicides and carcinogens (such as benzene and polyaromatic hydrocarbons) are being dumped into public waters, but studies show that they are turning up at biologically active levels in living organisms worldwide.

THE LOOPHOLE IN THE SEWER

During the early years of the CWA, the EPA required many towns to construct sewage treatment facilities and funded 90 percent of their capital costs. The law required communities to make sure that their Publicly Owned Treatment Works (POTWs) could remove at least 85 percent of the pollutants passing through them by 1977. By 1976, the federal government was spending $50 billion per year to help cities achieve this goal.[65] In recent decades, things have changed. Since the Reagan era, the federal government has withdrawn virtually all sewage treatment funding; yet across the country, aging POTWs are in serious need of maintenance and expansion, and urban sprawl is once again outpacing sewage treatment capacity.

Sewage treatment plants treat human biological waste in large quantities. Sludge is the end product of the sewage treatment process. Once treated, some sludge is

---

[65] Stauber, John & Sheldon Rampton. *Toxic Sludge is Good for You!* (Monroe, LA: Common Courage Press), 1995: 103.

released into local waterways, but most sludge is disposed of on land. Sludge can make decent fertilizer provided it is properly treated and not laced with a toxic brew of industrial chemicals, radioactive wastes and heavy metals.

Under the CWA, POTWs are considered direct dischargers of point source pollution and therefore require a NPDES permit.[66] Unfortunately, the large industrial facilities that dump their hazardous wastes into the public sewage system are labeled "indirect dischargers" and therefore are "minor facilities" that do not require a NPDES permit.[67] States are not even required to report the violations or the compliance status of these minor facilities to the EPA. Thus, many big industrial plants and other huge polluting facilities choose to avoid the legal problems and treatment costs of being a NPDES-permitted discharger by simply dumping their chemical toxins down the drain and letting the nearby sewage treatment plant handle the problem.

Sewage disposal provides industrial polluters with a double loophole. First, it allows them to avoid the CWA's permit system. Second, because the main federal law governing hazardous waste disposal excludes domestic sewage from regulation,[68] sewage disposal allows industry to side-step expensive hazardous waste disposal requirements as well.

Alas, municipal sewage treatment facilities do not treat toxic chemicals; they only treat biological waste. So, *in theory*, indirect dischargers are not allowed to dump toxic chemicals and other hazardous contaminants directly into the sewer without submitting them to some type of *pretreatment*. CWA requires industries to pretreat their hazardous chemicals before dumping them down the drain to prevent them from destroying, or seriously damaging, the bacterial treatment systems used to decontaminate human waste. However, the EPA compels only "major" POTWs to require their indirect dischargers to have pretreatment programs – only 10 percent of the nation's 15,000 POTWs are considered "major."[69]

By 1987, Congress' Office of Technology Assessment (OTA) estimated that more than 160,000 industrial facilities were discharging more than one trillion gallons of wastewater containing untreated hazardous waste into the sewers each year. Industrial wastes account for 25 percent of municipal sewage nationally and can be almost 100 percent in some areas.[70]

---

[66] The financial difficulties faced by many municipal sewage treatment facilities, and the political problem of raising taxes needed to overcome them, forced the EPA to subject POTWs to less stringent technology-based standards than industrial point source polluters. This standard is called secondary treatment.

[67] The rationale for exempting these "indirect dischargers" from the NPDES program was that it would be redundant to require controls on discharges that would be subject to treatment at POTWs.

[68] See: the Resource Conservation and Recovery Act (RCRA) §1004.

[69] Major POTWs must have a daily flow of over five million gallons or have "significant" industrial inputs. Percival, Miller & Leape Schroeder. *Environmental Regulation: Law, Science & Policy.* (Boston, MA: Little, Brown), 1992: 919.

[70] Percival, Miller & Leape Schroeder, 1992: 917–18.

Unfortunately, neither state agencies nor the EPA are required to police industry pretreatment compliance.[71] The law gives this crucial job to each local POTW, so responsibility for regulating and handling nearly half of the toxic substances discharged by industry annually is left to 1,500 financially strapped, politically weak, local POTWs.[72] Patrolling all the industrial tie-ins to the public sewers to make sure untreated toxic wastes are not dumped into them is a nearly impossible task for most municipal wastewater facilities. Taxpayer-financed sewage systems are not only underfunded but they also generally lack the political will necessary to investigate and punish politically connected violators. At the local level, the political pressures to undermine, bypass and violate this process are even greater than at the state and federal levels. Punishment is made even more unlikely by the fact that indirect dischargers can be penalized only for toxic dumping that can be proven to have caused a POTW to violate its NPDES permit.[73] For all these reasons, virtually every review of the CWA's pretreatment program has rated it an abject failure.[74]

At the end of this failed pretreatment process, POTWs are left with pools of wastewater and mountains of sludge contaminated by thousands of tons of miscellaneous poisons. The nation's rivers, bays and estuaries become the recipients of much of this toxic residue. No less than 37 percent of the toxics entering the nation's waters and estuaries pass from industries through POTWs.[75]

After the CWA became law, environmentalists continued to pressure Congress to stiffen restrictions on the level of contaminants that POTWs flushed into the nation's waterways. But even though improving treatment meant cleaner wastewater at the end of the pipe, it elevated the level of industrial toxins trapped in sewage sludge. By 2000, the nation's POTWs were turning out eight million dry tons of sludge annually.[76]

Toxic sludge contains an unpredictable mix of heavy metals, PCBs, dioxins, many synthetic chemicals and industrial solvents, radioactive waste, medicines, pesticides, asbestos, petroleum byproducts, bacteria, viruses and other hazardous residues. More than 60,000 toxic substances and chemical compounds can be found in sludge; at least twenty-one of these substances are known carcinogens.[77] Meanwhile, industry turns out about 1,000 new chemicals every year.[78]

Much of this sludge was dumped into the ocean until 1988, when public outrage and environmental lobbying finally pushed Congress to pass the Ocean Dumping Ban Act. This act outlawed the transport and dumping of sewage sludge into the ocean

---

[71] The only federal monitoring of these indirect dischargers is the requirement that certain major industries semi-annually report their discharges and supply notification of any additional loads that would interfere with its local POTW.

[72] As noted earlier only 10 percent (1,500 out of 15,000) of the nation's POTWs are required to have pretreatment programs.

[73] See: *Arkansas Poultry Federation v. EPA* (8th Circuit Court, 1988).

[74] Percival, Miller & Leape Schroeder, 1992: 920.

[75] Percival, Miller & Leape Schroeder, 1992: 918.

[76] Orlando, Laura. "Toxic Avengers," *In These Times* (February 1999): 12.

[77] Bleifuss, Joel. "Nightmare Soil," *In These Times* (October 16, 1995): 12.

[78] Stauber, John & Sheldon Rampton, 1995: 104.

by 1991. In response to this ban, the EPA rewrote section 503 of the CWA that governs the disposal of sewage sludge. With the stroke of a pen, EPA transformed sewage sludge from a hazardous waste into a beneficial fertilizer.[79] By 1993, the EPA hired a PR firm to create a national program to rename toxic sludge "biosolids" and market it as safe for unrestricted use on farms and gardens.[80] In less than a decade, between two and three million tons of sludge was being spread on farmland every year.[81]

This transformation occurred, not because the sludge was any cleaner,[82] but because the EPA simply raised the legal limits of acceptable exposure to many contaminants so that most of the nation's sludge could still be classified as "clean." The EPA's new lead regulations increased the amount that could be applied annually to an acre of land via sludge from 111 to 267 pounds; the arsenic level was raised from 12.5 to 36 pounds per acre. Safe mercury levels jumped from 13.4 to 50 pounds per acre; and safe levels of chromium shot from 472 to 2,672 pounds per acre.[83] None of these changes was based on new scientific information showing these toxic substances to be less dangerous. Under rule 503, this sludge reclassified as fertilizer can be so contaminated it cannot be legally landfilled, but it is exempt from classification as a hazardous waste because it is a "marketable product."[84] Back in 1983, only seven of 30 municipal sludges tested clean enough to be used as fertilizer;[85] but after section 503 raised the allowable exposures, the toxic sludge of many cities suddenly became marketable.

Who benefits from this sludge-to-fertilizer scam? A close, corrupt associate of the EPA – the waste management industry – is the main beneficiary.[86] Waste management refuse collectors are hired by POTWs to haul and spread sludge. Between 1992 and 2002, New York City alone spent about $2.5 billion on sludge management programs.[87] A large portion of this money went to giant waste management contractors such as WMX Technologies and Browning-Ferris (whose CEO from 1988 to 1995 was two-time EPA chief, William Ruckelshaus). These contractors haul hundreds of tons of toxic sludge from big cities like New York to small farming communities like Sierra Blanca, Texas every day. Farmers buy it because it is marketed as safe (EPA approved) and it comes very cheap – some farmers have even been paid to take it.[88] However, once this toxic fertilizer is spread on the land, all liability transfers to the landowner.[89]

---

[79] Hanes, Spencer G. Jr. "Is Toxic Sludge Good for You?" *Vermont Journal of Environmental Law* (October 30, 2003). http://www.vjel.org/editorials/ED10039.html.

[80] Stauber, John & Sheldon Rampton, 1995.

[81] Orlando, Laura (February 1999): 12.

[82] Though better treatment methods have helped contain some heavy metals concentrations.

[83] Bleifuss, Joel (October 16, 1995): 12.

[84] Instead, it would have to be disposed of as toxic waste under the SWDA & RCRA.

[85] Bleifuss, Joel (October 16, 1995): 12.

[86] Montague, Peter. "EPA's New Landfill Rules Protect Only the Largest Garbage Haulers," *Rachel's Hazardous Waste News #268* (January 15, 1992). http://www.ejnet.org/rachel/rhwn268.htm.

[87] Orlando, Laura (February 1999): 12.

[88] Treatment plants pay for transportation, application and monitoring.

[89] Orlando, Laura (February 1999): 12.

The waste management industry isn't the only biosolids beneficiary. The "biosolids lobby" is a tight alliance of those who have a stake in the sludge production and marketing business. It includes POTW managers and operators, state and federal employees, waste management corporations, engineering firms, construction companies and equipment manufacturers and suppliers. Together they formed the Water Environment Federation (WEF) to defend and promote the use of biosolids in close coordination with the EPA.

How dangerous is sludge? It's nearly impossible to tell. Officially, the EPA and the biosolids lobby insist that it's perfectly safe and beneficial. In fact, they put millions of dollars into an extensive PR campaign to convince Americans they have nothing to worry about. Those who have dared to be critical of biosolids or raise damaging evidence have been denigrated, discredited and denounced. Meanwhile, those in the EPA who have championed the use of biosolids have been praised and rewarded.

Case in point: Terry Logan is a professor of soil chemistry at Ohio State University. As cochair of the EPA's Peer Review Committee on biosolids, Dr. Logan was given the job of assembling the best scientific talent and data to help develop EPA's new regulations on sludge. While it was clear that the agency wanted to loosen the restrictions on the use of sludge as fertilizer, Dr. Logan's committee was supposed to present an objective assessment of the risks surrounding biosolids.[90]

However, Dr. Logan's situation made objectivity difficult. He was being paid $2,400 per month as consultant and board member of N-Viro International Corporation, a firm that had patented a process for converting sludge to fertilizer. Thus, it was no surprise when Logan's committee recommended that the CWA's section 503 be modified to allow toxic sludge to qualify as fertilizer. A negative assessment could have seriously harmed the value of the stock options professor Logan held in N-Viro.[91]

You would assume that such ethical conflicts of interest might become a problem for the EPA or harm Dr. Logan's reputation. On the contrary, in 1994 the EPA bestowed its "Man of the Year" award on Dr. Logan, and presented N-Viro and two other organizations with a $300,000 Congressional grant to promote biosolids.[92]

Then there is the case of David Lewis. In 1996 and 1999, Dr. Lewis published two articles on biosolids in the British science journal *Nature*. His articles criticized the agency's lax sludge rules and the poor science behind them, and warned of the potential dangers sludge poses. His views carried some weight because he was a highly esteemed microbiologist who had worked as a researcher for the EPA more than 30 years.

In retaliation, the EPA denied him a promotion, demanded that he resign by age 55 for criticizing the agency's policies and charged him with violating ethical rules requiring "reasonably prominent" disclaimers that he did not speak for the EPA

---

[90] Small Wright, Machaelle. "Sewage Sludge/Biosolids: A Health and Environmental Crisis and Scandal," *Perelandra Health Watch* (September 12, 2002). http://www.perelandra-ltd.com/Sewage_3A_W288.cfm.

[91] Small Wright, Machaelle (September 12, 2002).

[92] Small Wright, Machaelle (September 12, 2002).

in his articles. Evidently, the size print used by the journal for its disclaimer wasn't large enough to be "reasonably prominent."[93]

Because Lewis continued to research and speak out on the risks of sludge, he remained a target of harassment and scorn by EPA officials and the biosolids lobby.[94] But as well contaminations, crop failures, livestock die-offs, human sicknesses and even deaths cropped up around the country, David Lewis gained a reputation as the only EPA scientist who would listen to the growing number of people who feared that toxic sludge was the culprit.

Until David Lewis examined the case, Brenda Robertson got nothing but disrespect, denial and disinformation from the EPA and state officials about what caused the death of her son, Tony. Tony rode his dirt bike through sludge on a hillside near his home in Osceola Mills, Pennsylvania on October 12, 1994. When he got home, Brenda recalls, "I hosed off the bike, and I made him go to the basement to take off his clothes. The smell was like – just a terrible smell! Then, he took a bath."[95]

By Monday, Tony was vomiting and had a headache and a sore throat. When a boil formed on his left arm, Tony was taken to a doctor, who diagnosed the flu and prescribed antibiotics. By the next day, Tony developed breathing problems and was taken by medevac to a hospital in Pittsburgh. By Friday morning he was dead.

The doctors said Tony died of a bacterial infection and asked whether he had eaten something bad, been bitten by an animal or played in poisonous plants. This didn't seem right to Brenda, "We couldn't think of any dangerous activity like that … I sat around for months wondering what had happened. Did something happen that I should have spotted? Had I done something wrong? How could I have prevented it?"[96]

Over the next five-and-a-half years, the official explanation for Tony's death changed four times, but despite their confusion, officials vehemently denied any possibility that Tony's death could have resulted from exposure to toxic sludge. Then, in March 1999, the mystery surrounding his death was raised to a new level when Brenda read in a local newspaper that the Pennsylvania Department of Environmental Protection (DEP) had investigated the case and come up with a new cause of death. Once again, DEP officials concluded that her boy had not died from exposure to sludge, but had died of a bee sting. This new report even asserted that sludge had not been applied to the hillside at the time that Tony rode his bike there.

Totally unaware of any new investigation, Brenda Robertson was dumbfounded by the article. "I just about died," she said. "I was in shock. All they needed to do is come to Osceola, go to the only funeral director, go to the only school. They could have found out. They made up a story about a bee sting … It was a complete lie, and yet

[93] Small Wright, Machaelle (September 12, 2002).

[94] Bleifuss, Joel. "The Sludge Report," *In These Times* (April 22, 2002). http://www.inthesetimes. com/issue/26/12/views1.shtml.

[95] Gibb, Tom. "A Terrible Waste Gets a Long Look," *Post Gazette News* (June 11, 2000). http://www. post-gazette.com/healthscience/20000611sludge4.asp.

[96] Gibb, Tom (June 11, 2000).

people walked up to me and said, 'We didn't know Tony died of a bee sting. Why didn't you ever tell us?' ... It made me look like an idiot."[97]

Brenda challenged the DEP's report: "I am upset. It's frustrating, and all I'm trying to do is get some answers ... I think there are people who don't want to admit they made a mistake."[98] State Representative Camille George (D-Houtzdale) accused the DEP of "deception and incompetence."[99]

Under fire, the agency did another probe and confessed that its report was incorrect. It admitted that Brenda's son didn't die of a bee sting and that sludge had been applied to the field Tony biked through. However, the cause of Tony's death was now blamed on exposure to a pathogen called *Staphylococcus aureus*, which the DEP asserted, "is not known to be found in bio-solids."[100]

Upon talking with David Lewis and other experts, Brenda discovered that the EPA does list *Staphylococcus aureus* as a pathogen in sludge, along with 11 others, although the agency contends it is of "minor concern." After examining the case, Dr. Lewis told Brenda that the lime used to disinfect sludge could have opened a lesion on Tony's arm. Then the staph infection could have crept into his blood stream through the abrasion. If the strain of staph had been an especially tough one, such as those originating in hospital waste, for example, it could have been fatal.[101]

Lewis told the press that he believed sludge was probably Tony's killer, "I'm hearing from people across the country who are getting sick just like Tony did. The case of Tony Behun is as clear a connection as you'll see ... They call it biosolids, but all it is is human waste after they've filtered out the tampon applicators. You take what's flushed down the toilet at a hospital, what's flushed out of a metal-plating plant, mix it and sell it as fertilizer. That's a bad idea."[102]

While scientists continue to disagree over the relative dangers of toxic sludge,[103] there is now undisputed evidence that toxic substances from sludge can enter plant roots.[104] As predicted by some EPA officials as far back as 1975,[105] evidence of the dangerous results of applying toxic sludge to farmland is beginning to emerge all over the country.

Patty Martin, the mayor of Quincy, Washington, led an investigation to find out why many local wheat and corn crops were so poor and the cows so sickly. All the

---

[97] Tuohy, John. "2 Mothers, 2 Deaths Too Many Questions," Alliance for a Clean Environment (July 31, 2000); Gibb, Tom (June 11, 2000).

[98] Gibb, Tom (June 11, 2000).

[99] Gibb, Tom (June 11, 2000).

[100] Tuohy, John (July 31, 2000).

[101] Tuohy, John (July 31, 2000).

[102] Gibb, Tom (June 11, 2000).

[103] See: Harrison, E. Z., S. R. Oakes, M. Hysell, & A. Hay. "Review: Organic Chemicals in Sewage Sludges," *Science of the Total Environment #367* (2006): 481–97. Available online: http://cwmi.css. cornell.edu/Sludge.html. Also: Harrison, E. Z., M. B. Mcbride, & D. R. Bouldin. "Land Application of Sewage Sludges: An Appraisal of the US Regulations," *International Journal on Environment & Pollution*, v. 11, n. 1 (1999): 1–36. http://cwmi.css.cornell.edu/PDFS/LandApp.pdf.

[104] Wilson, Duff. "Wasteland," *Amicus Journal* (Spring 1998): 35.

[105] Sanjour, William (EPA Chief Technology Branch, AW 465) "Policy Implications of Sewage Sludge on Hazardous Waste Regulation" (October 17, 1975).

evidence pointed to the high content of industrial chemicals in the fertilizer.[106] After spreading sludge on his 99-acre farm, Vermont dairyman Robert Ruane's cows started getting arthritis, and milk production dropped from 18,000 pounds per year to 14,000 pounds per year. Over a two-year period, 66 cows died. "They told me how much money it was going to save me on fertilizer," Ruane lamented. Tests revealed high levels of cadmium, lead, arsenic, radionuclides and dioxins in the fertilizer. Tissue and blood samples from the dead cows pointed to severe liver damage.

In all these cases and many more, the EPA and the biosolids lobby have insisted that the evidence is entirely circumstantial, but courts are beginning to disagree. In June 2003, a jury awarded $550,000 to a farmer whose land was destroyed from sludge application. The Boyce family farm had been using sludge from the city of Augusta on its land from 1986 to 1998.[107]

Even as evidence of the dangers of biosolids continue to mount, many industries have decided to take advantage of this legal loophole by copying POTWs and disposing of their hazardous wastes by mixing them with fertilizer and selling them to farmers. According to the NRDC and *Seattle Times* reporter Duff Wilson, the same dangerous yet legal scam is happening all over the country. Industries are getting rid of tons of toxic waste by giving it to fertilizer manufacturers for free or paying them to take it. By law, any material that has "fertilizing qualities" can be labeled and used as fertilizer – even if it contains dangerous chemicals and heavy metals.[108]

In Gore, Oklahoma, low-level radioactive wastes were mixed with other substances, sold as liquid fertilizer and sprayed on thousands of acres of grazing land. In Tifton County, Georgia, more than a thousand acres of peanuts were destroyed by fertilizer that turned out to be a toxic brew of hazardous waste and limestone. In southwest Washington, highly corrosive lead-laced pulp mill wastes were spread on crops used for livestock consumption.[109]

Bay Zinc Company of Oregon has a federal permit to store toxic steel mill waste. It is poured from railcars into the top of a large silo. Then it is taken out of the bottom of the silo as the raw material for fertilizer. "When it goes into our silo, it's a hazardous waste," admits Bay Zinc president Dick Camp. "When it comes out of the silo, it's no longer regulated. The exact same material! Don't ask me why. That's the wisdom of the EPA."[110]

Even though the EPA has steadfastly refused to reconsider its policy on biosolids, there appear to be ways to put the brakes on the use of toxic sludge as fertilizer. Unfortunately, the political path through Congress appears treacherous and slow. Congress stands squarely on the side of the sludge industry, the WEF and the EPA. Since 1997, Congress has given EPA almost $24 million to promote sewage sludge as a safe and beneficial fertilizer. The funds are earmarked for the EPA to give to the biosolids lobby (the WEF and the Water Environment Research Federation

---

[106] Wilson, Duff (1998): 34–8.
[107] This was a small fraction of the $12.5 million they sought in damages. See: Hanes, Spencer G. Jr. (October 30, 2003).
[108] Wilson, Duff (1998): 34–9.
[109] Wilson, Duff (1998): 34–9.
[110] Wilson, Duff (1998): 34.

[WERF])[111] and are designated for fighting the "opponents" of the EPA's programs who spread "misinformation." This misinformation includes complaints from citizens sickened by sludge, the opinions of physicians who have treated them and the research of scientists – some even at the EPA – showing that land application of sewage sludge can cause public health and environmental problems.[112]

Nevertheless, it appears that boisolids may go the way of nuclear power and for many of the same reasons. Despite the PR efforts of the EPA and the biosolids industry, as more people become aware that the hazardous contaminants in sludge may poison well water; ruin land values; harm or kill crops, livestock and people; and may even present enormous future clean up costs and liabilities, the opposition to sludge grows. As knowledge about sludge grows and its reputation goes down the crapper, farmers are starting to think twice about using it for fertilizer – even if it's "free."

NON−POINT SOURCE POLLUTION: A DISMAL FAILURE

So far, we have examined the CWA's most successful efforts to clean up the nation's waterways by going after the easiest type of pollution to eliminate – point source pollution. But all of the other sources of water pollution – agricultural, feedlot, mining, timber, storm drain and urban runoff – are neither discharged from a pipe nor put down a sewer. Each time it rains, water runs off the land and picks up toxic pesticides and fertilizers from farms and lawns; heavy metals and oils from cars and trucks; manure from giant animal feedlots; poisonous chemicals and metals from mining sites; and sediment from construction sites, farms and timber operations. This polluted runoff carries the contaminants into our groundwater, lakes, streams, bays and oceans. The origins of this non point source (NPS) pollution are copious, small, scattered and exceptionally difficult to regulate or manage once released. The EPA estimates that more than 50 percent of today's water quality problems result from this NPS pollution.

Section 303 of the CWA requires the regulation of both point source and NPS water pollution. However, at the federal level, the EPA has done little to bring this type of pollution under control. The CWA requires states to have comprehensive plans for protecting their water quality from both sources of pollution. But these EPA-approved state programs appear to be largely ineffective in reducing NPS pollution – especially agricultural runoff.[113] So far, most states have chosen voluntary approaches using what is known as "best management practices" to deal with NPS pollution.

In 1998, the Clinton administration proposed (and Congress approved) a new Clean Water Action Plan that provided $1.7 billion over a five-year period to help state and local governments come up with more effective ways to control NPS pollution. By 1999, the EPA proposed a new rule that would have toughened the CWA's WQS provisions by making them more enforceable and binding upon

---

[111] WEF/WERF are: The Water Environment Federation and the Water Environment Research Foundation. The WEF is the political arm of the biosolids lobby; the WERF is its research wing.
[112] Small Wright, Machaelle (September 12, 2002).
[113] Kubasek, Nancy & Gary Silverman, 2005: 236–7.

dischargers. The new provisions would have established a discharge quota system and allowed a form of effluent trading among polluters to encourage more cooperation between states and local water districts. However, objections to the new rules grew in Congress and in late 2002 the Bush administration dropped the whole plan as unworkable.[114]

THE CWA: SINK OR SWIM?

In January 2003, the Bush administration quietly directed EPA officials (and the U.S. Army Corps of Engineers) to stop protecting millions of acres of wetlands, streams and other waters unless they first obtained permission from national headquarters in Washington, DC. The directive stated that no permission was required to ignore CWA protections for these waters and that no records would be kept of decisions not to invoke the CWA.[115]

The directive severely narrowed the types of waterways considered protected under the CWA to those that were navigable year-round by commercial vessels. This is a major departure from all previous administrations' policies and all previous court interpretations of Congress' intent when using the term *navigable waters*. This term is defined in CWA, section 507(2), to mean "the waters of the United States." Based on legislative history indicating that Congress sought to extend federal regulation as broadly as possible under its constitutional authority to regulate interstate commerce, courts have interpreted "waters of the United States" to include virtually any surface waters, whether navigable or not.[116]

Unfortunately, recent Supreme Court rulings seem to be backtracking on their original interpretation of navigable waters. On June 19, 2006, the Court ruled on two landmark cases, *Rapanos v. United States* and *United States v. Carabell*, which together challenged federal CWA protections over nonnavigable streams and rivers that are tributaries to larger lakes, rivers and coastal waters, as well as to the wetlands that are nearby these streams and smaller rivers. Instead of clearly upholding CWA protections over these waters that have been in place for the last 33 years, the Supreme Court issued a 4–1–4 split opinion that lacked any majority opinion and muddied the waters surrounding the question of the act's jurisdiction.

The court's vague ruling around the meaning of navigable waters jeopardizes CWA protections of more than twenty million acres of wetlands and half of all streams (roughly 53–60 percent of the nation's waterways) that do not harbor boat traffic. This includes some of the most vital wetlands, tributaries, headwaters and other small bodies of water. According to Melissa Samet, senior director of water resources for American Rivers, "These smaller waterways play critical roles for our

[114] Kraft, Michael, 2004: 130.
[115] NRDC (press release). "Bush Administration Policy Makes America's Waters Vulnerable to Development, Pollution, Says New Report" (August 12, 2004). http://www.nrdc.org/media/press-releases/040812.asp.
[116] See: Percival, Miller & Leape Schroeder, 1992: 885.

nation's water. They provide flood protection, clean drinking water, wildlife habitat and offset water treatment costs."[117]

The Bush EPA took full advantage of this weakening of the CWA's coverage to withdraw enforcement of clean water regulations in these disputed areas. In response, more than 250 members of Congress signed on to letters to President Bush asking him to rescind his negative policy directives and restore protections to all U.S. waters. On May 2006, the House went further, with a 222–198 vote, it successfully approved an amendment to the Interior-EPA appropriations bill to prohibit implementation of the administration's new policy.[118] Also, a bill introduced in both the House and Senate, The Clean Water Restoration Act (CWRA), sought to make it clear that all waters of the United States should fall under the protections of the CWA.[119]

But Congressional action proved ineffective; the CWRA sat mired in committee and never made it to an official vote. Meanwhile, an internal EPA memo dated March 2008 found that the agency failed to pursue 304 CWA violations since July 2006 because of "jurisdictional uncertainty" caused by the Supreme Court's decisions, and that a total of 500 CWA cases had been negatively affected by the rulings.[120]

Restoring these protections by passing the CWRA would be the first small step the Obama administration and the 111th Congress could take to begin to reverse the federal government's dismal record on clean water. But industry, developers and conservative think tanks are trying to make sure the new legislation dies. On the other side, a broad coalition of more than 300 organizations endorses the CWRA. This coalition includes environmental groups such as the NRDC, the Sierra Club, Earth Justice and the National Audubon Society; as well as prominent members of the "rod and gun" lobby such as Trout Unlimited, Ducks Unlimited and the Izaak Walton League. If the Obama administration and the Democratic Party prove incapable of taking this small step, despite their majorities in both houses of Congress, there is little hope that anything of importance will be done to protect the declining quality of American waters for quite some time.

---

[117] Bronski, Peter. "Muddy Waters: The Push for Better Clean Water Protection," E Magazine.com. http://www.emagazine.com/view/?4574.

[118] Earth Justice. "House Rejects Bush Administration's Misguided Water Policy." (August 11, 2006). http://www.earthjustice.org/our_work/policy/2004/bush_administration_launches_effort_to_dismantle_clean_water_act.html.

[119] *Clean Water Authority Restoration Act* HR 962 and S 473.

[120] Bronski, Peter.

4

Superfund and RCRA – Toxic Trash

In *Silent Spring*, the pathbreaking bestseller that launched the modern environmental movement, biologist Rachel Carson created an ominous little parable she called *Fable for Tomorrow*. In it, an idyllic American hamlet suffers mysterious maladies. First, plants turn brown and wither, pets and livestock die, fish disappear from streams and birds no longer adorn the woodlands and meadows with their songs. Next, baffling illnesses ravage the town, killing children and elders while survivors desperately search for answers. Was this the work of some kind of evil spell or secret weapon? No, Carson explained, "No witchcraft, no enemy action had silenced the rebirth of new life in this stricken world. The people had done it themselves." Their own "wonder chemicals" had turned against them.

By the time *Silent Spring* hit the bookstores in 1962, the chemical industry had already produced, and stashed *somewhere*, about 100 trillion pounds of hazardous wastes, enough to create a highway to the moon 100 feet wide and 10 feet deep.[1] In addition, we now know from the industry's own internal documents that American and European chemical companies were engaged in a multidecade conspiracy to prevent regulators, the press and the public from discovering the insidious toxicity of their products and wastes.[2]

Realizing that Rachel Carson's book would expose the dark side of their industry, two major chemical and pesticide producers – Monsanto and Velsicol – threatened to sue Houghton Mifflin unless *Silent Spring*'s publication was cancelled.[3] Failing that, the entire agrochemical industry leapt into crisis management mode, unleashing its flacks to attack Carson and her book. The National Agricultural Chemical Association doubled its PR budget, inundating the media with op-ed pieces and book reviews slamming *Silent Spring*. It accused Carson of being part of a communist

---

[1] Montague, Peter. "What Has Gone Wrong? Part 1: Congress Creates A Monster – The ATSDR," *Rachel's Hazardous Waste News* #292 (July 1, 1992). http://www.ejnet.org/rachel/rhwn292.htm.

[2] *Trade Secrets: A Moyers Report* (PBS: 2005). http://www.pbs.org/tradesecrets/; Montague, Peter. "What We Must Do – Part 7: Toxics in Your Drinking Water – When Did People Know it was Bad?" *Rachel's Hazardous Waste News* #97 (August 22, 1988). http://www.ejnet.org/rachel/rhwn097.htm.

[3] Harremoes, Gee, et al., eds. *The Precautionary Principle in the 20th Century: Late Lessons from Early Warnings.* (London: Earthscan Publications Ltd.), 2002: 140.

plot to cripple American agriculture.[4] As a "childless spinster," Carson was questioned about her concern for future generations,[5] and her *Fable for Tomorrow* was mocked as nothing more than far-fetched, alarmist hyperbole written by an "hysterical woman."[6]

The industry could not have been more wrong.[7] Rachel Carson's disturbing parable was already assuming real-life dimensions in the form of a toxic catastrophe brewing beneath the community of Love Canal – a suburb near Niagara Falls in upstate New York.[8] Love Canal's toxic calamity didn't make national headlines until 1978. However, the contamination started back in 1944 when the City of Niagara signed an agreement with Hooker Chemical & Plastics Corporation, permitting it to discard industrial wastes into the empty, unfinished, mile-long canal named after its builder, William Love. Hooker Chemical later bought the trench and continued to dump wastes there. Between 1947 and 1952, the company jettisoned more than 352 million pounds of hazardous chemicals – including DDT and lindane (two pesticides banned from use in the United States), PCBs, dioxin, multiple toxic solvents and heavy metals – on top of refuse already deposited by the City of Niagara and the Army.[9]

In 1953, this toxic waste pit was buried under several feet of earth and sold for one dollar to the Niagara City school district, which was eager to develop the land. Just how thoroughly school board members understood the perils lurking beneath Love Canal remains unclear to this day.[10] However, there is no doubt that Hooker Chemical knew exactly what it was selling because it tried to shield itself from future liability by warning the district of the potential hazards lurking below.

---

[4] Cronin, John & Robert F. Kennedy, Jr. *The Riverkeepers.* (NY: Simon & Schuster), 1999, ch. 9; GM Watch. "Monsanto's Campaign Against Rachel Carson" (May 27, 2007). http://www.gmwatch.org/latest-listing/1-news-items/4681-monsantos-campaign-against-rachel-carson-.

[5] Oxford University Press Blog. "Rachel Carson: Saint or Sinner?" (March 2007). http://blog.oup.com/2007/03/rachel_carson_s/.

[6] Stauber, John & Sheldon Rampton. *Toxic Sludge is Good for You!* (Monroe, LA: Common Courage Press), 1995: 124; Oxford University Press Blog.

[7] Carson's final dramatic vindication came in a report prepared by President Kennedy's Scientific Advisory Committee, which spent eight months investigating the facts in Silent Spring. The report condemned the USDA and chemical industry scientists and recommended that the government eliminate the use of persistent toxic pesticides. The report endorsed all the principal findings of Carson's book and closed with praise for its author.

[8] See: Gibbs, Lois Marie. *Love Canal: The Story Continues.* (Canada: New Society Publishers), 1998.

[9] The amount of toxic chemicals dumped by Hooker Chemical varies widely with the source. 352 million pounds is the figure used by Carl Pope of the Sierra Club in his book *Strategic Ignorance* (p. 198). Two official EPA web pages vary from 199,900 to 21,000 tons. See: "U.S. Sues Hooker Chemical at Niagara Falls, New York." http://www.epa.gov/history/topics/lovecanal/02.htm; "EPA Site Fact Sheet on Love Canal." http://www.epa.gov/Region2/superfund/npl/0201290c.htm.

[10] For an account that insists that the school board was well informed of the toxic dangers the site contained see the free market libertarian emag article: Zuesse, Eric. "Love Canal: The Truth Seeps Out," *ReasonOnline* (February 1981). http://www.reason.com/news/show/29319.html.

However, back in the 1950s, few people outside the chemical industry grasped the depth and severity of this problem. A cloud of oblivious optimism muffled public concern over industrial chemicals during those "happy days." Advertising such as DuPont's "Better Living Through Chemistry" intentionally nourished this nonchalant naïveté.[11] Like the culture around them, the school board probably discounted and dismissed the toxic threat in their eagerness to build new homes and schools.

Over the next twenty-five years, approximately 800 homes, 240 low-income apartments and one elementary school were constructed on the 36-square-block site. In time, the toxic brew lurking beneath slowly revealed itself. Chemicals percolated to the surface, seeped into basements and emerged in yards and construction sites. Some leaking acid barrels actually exploded. Neighborhood children suffered chemical burns after playing with a crumbly white substance they found in a vacant lot.

The situation grew more perilous in the 1960s with the construction of the LaSalle Expressway. An environmental engineer explained what happened in a 1995 article for the journal *Environment*:

> With the construction of the expressway, groundwater became trapped, its passageway [to the Niagara River] blocked. In what became known as the "bathtub effect," groundwater and rainwater built up and overflowed the clay basin in which the waste sat, thereby carrying contaminants through the upper silt layer and along recently constructed sewer lines into the basements of houses situated to the east, west and north.[12]

By the mid-1970s, acrid fumes emanated from the site. Lawns, shrubs and bushes turned brown in the yards of the closest residents. Thick oils appeared in their basement pumps and industrial odors filled their homes.

By 1978, when residents of Love Canal finally discovered they were living on a toxic waste pit, many were already poisoned. Cancers, miscarriages, birth defects, stillbirths and urinary tract diseases afflicted the neighborhood. The short- and long-term effects of exposure to Love Canal's toxins remain a subject of considerable controversy.[13] At

---

[11] The phrase "Better Living Through Chemistry" is a variant of the DuPont advertising slogan, "Better Things for Better Living ... Through Chemistry." DuPont adopted it in 1935 and it was their slogan until 1982 when the "Through Chemistry" bit was dropped; in 1999 it was replaced by "the miracles of science."

[12] Hoffman, A. J. "An Uneasy Rebirth at Love Canal," *Environment* (March 1995): 4–31.

[13] Of course, science is not capable of proving toxic cause and effect. Multiple studies were carried out by all parties involved. As expected, they came up with different results. In 1984, the state Department of Health (DOH) presented a report stating that 12.1 percent of infants born in an area where contaminated water drained from Love Canal suffered from low birth weight, compared to an average of 6.9 percent in upstate New York. This was followed by another DOH report that confirmed there was a "statistically significant excess of congenital malformations in ... the neighborhood, primarily from 1955 to 1964, just after the chemicals were dumped." In 1985, another study conducted by biologist, Beverly Paigen, revealed that 17.9 percent of the babies born in the Love Canal area were born below normal weight, and 12.1 percent had birth defects (about twice the control group's rate). She also reported that the children suffered 2.45 times as many seizures, 2.25 times as many skin rashes, and 2.95 times as much hyperactivity as in the control group.

the time, a health study conducted by volunteer scientists and community members revealed that 56 percent of the children born between 1974 and 1978 suffered birth defects, including some with three ears, double rows of teeth, faulty hearts and kidneys, bizarre tumors, extra fingers and toes and mental retardation. The miscarriage rate increased 300 percent among women who had moved to Love Canal; urinary-tract disease increased 300 percent, with a great number of children being affected.[14]

Lois Gibbs was one of the many mothers whose children suffered chronic illnesses after moving to Love Canal. First, her best friend's son died and her own son fell ill; then she nearly lost her baby girl to a strange disease resembling childhood leukemia. These tragedies compelled her to organize the Love Canal Homeowners Association (LCHA) and transformed Lois into one of the country's most dedicated and tenacious anti-toxics activists.

LCHA fought tirelessly for more information, immediate medical attention and swift government relief. It deliberately focused public pressure and the media spotlight on the governor and other elected representatives. Its goal was to make the Love Canal crisis a high-profile campaign issue. The LCHA relentlessly dogged candidates and protested at party conventions. Lois gave hundreds of interviews to the news media.

LCHA put every candidate on the spot. During an election year, TV, radio, newspapers and magazines covered Love Canal mothers with children in their arms and tears in their eyes crying out for help. No politician could avoid the question: "What are you going to do about Love Canal?" In a final act of courage and utter desperation, Lois and her fellow LCHA activists locked a couple of EPA officials in a Love Canal home and refused to release them until they were promised a government buy-out of their homes and permanent relocation. The Carter administration relented.

On October 1, 1980, the president visited Niagara Falls to sign a bill authorizing the funding to permanently relocate all families who wished to leave. Love Canal residents reported that many of the chronic illnesses that afflicted them slowly disappeared after they moved away.

Love Canal was neither the first nor the worst toxic waste calamity in America, but thanks to Lois Gibbs and LCHA, it was the first to gain extensive media coverage and high-level political attention. It dramatized the serious dangers of toxic waste and compelled policymakers to devise a response. However, the Love Canal disaster was only the beginning. Within a few years, *Silent Spring*'s frightening fable became a tragic reality in one community after another as lethal chemicals poisoned small

---

[14] Gibbs, Lois Marie. "Learning from Love Canal: A 20th Anniversary Retrospective." *Orion Afield* (Spring 1998). http://arts.envirolink.org/arts_and_activism/LoisGibbs.html; EPA. *Testimony by Lois Gibbs at the Proceedings of the Superfund Relocation Roundtable Meeting* (May 2–4, 1996/Pensacola, FL). http://www.epa.gov/oecaerth/resources/publications/ej/nejac/nejacmtg/roundtable-relocation-0596.pdf.

towns across America from Times Beach (MO), West Dallas (TX) and Anniston[15] (AL), to Glen Avon (CA), Morrisonville (LA) and Sauget (IL).[16]

Responding to public alarm, politicians passed a tough-sounding Superfund law[17] and put the EPA in charge of enforcing it. Coupled with the Resource Conservation and Recovery Act (RCRA), passed in 1976, these two laws were Congress' answer to the problem of hazardous waste. Superfund and RCRA were designed to reinforce each other. RCRA gave the EPA "cradle-to-grave" oversight over the ongoing generation, transport, treatment and disposal of hazardous waste; while Superfund cleaned up old abandoned toxic sites by imposing strict cleanup liability on those responsible for creating them.

Although both laws have been on the books since 1980, more than 1,200 Superfund sites across the country still await cleanup. One in four Americans lives within three miles of one. Approximately three to four million children, who face developmental risks from exposure to toxic contaminants, live within a mile.[18] In addition, EPA officials admit there are still at least 114 *uncontrolled* toxic sites scattered across the country from New Jersey to California. More than 100 schools are located within a mile of these pockets of poison and twenty-five million people live within ten miles of one.[19]

Nevertheless, some say public alarm over hazardous chemicals is unnecessary and overblown.[20] After all, humans have unwittingly poisoned themselves throughout

---

[15] For more detail on Monsanto's 40-year contamination of Anniston see: Love, Dennis. *My City was Gone.* (NY: William Morrow), 2006; Grunwald, Michael. "Confidential: Read & Destroy," *Washington Post.* http://www.mindfully.org/Industry/Monsanto-PCBs-Anniston.htm. Also: Crean, Ellen. "Toxic Secret: Alabama Town Was Never Warned of Contamination," *CBS: 60 Minutes* (August 31, 2003). http://www.cbsnews.com/stories/2002/11/07/60minutes/main528581. shtml.

[16] By 1996, the EPA had relocated 15 entire communities due to toxic contamination. *Proceedings: Superfund Relocation Roundtable Meeting* (May 2–4, 1996/Pensacola, FL). http://www.epa.gov/compliance/resources/publications/ej/nejac/nejacmtg/roundtable-relocation-0596.pdf.

[17] Superfund is the name commonly used for CERCLA (The Comprehensive Environmental Response, Compensation and Liability Act).

[18] Steinzon, Rena & Margaret Clune. *The Toll of Superfund Neglect.* (Center for American Progress), 2006; U.S. EPA, *Superfund's 25th Anniversary: Capturing the Past, Charting the Future.* http://www.epa.gov/superfund/25anniversary/. According to: Miller, Anthony B. et al. *Environmental Epidemiology, Volume 1: Public Health and Hazardous Wastes.* (Washington, DC: National Academy Press), 1991: 76; the EPA estimates there are 32,000 potential Superfund sites, but Congress's Office of Technology Assessment estimates there are 439,000.

[19] Sapien, Joaquin. "Human Exposure 'Uncontrolled' at 114 Superfund Sites EPA Secrecy About Sites' Toxic Dangers Extends Even to Senators' Inquiries," *Center for Public Integrity* (May 18, 2007). http://projects.publicintegrity.org/superfund/report.aspx?aid=870.

[20] This was the opinion of one of the top bureaucrats at the Center for Disease Control, a physician named Vernon L. Houk. He died of cancer recently, but during his tenure at the CDC he was known for his public statements downplaying the dangers of dioxin and toxic waste in general. See: Montague, Peter. "What Has Gone Wrong? Part 1: Congress Creates A Monster – The ATSDR" (August 22, 1998). The Video Project. *Times Beach, Missouri* (Oakland, CA: 1994); Lapp, David. "Defenders of Dioxin: The Corporate Campaign to Rehabilitate Dioxin," *Multinational Monitor* (October 1991). http://multinationalmonitor. org/hyper/issues/1991/10/lapp.html.

history. Ancient Greeks noticed that slaves who worked in asbestos quarries developed lung ailments and died young. Roman aristocrats were poisoned by lead linings in their wine jugs and piped water. Over the centuries, many jobs have exposed laborers such as miners, hatters, tanners and printers to noxious miasmas containing mercury, lead and coal dust. But while these toxic substances posed a serious danger to certain segments of society, they never caused significant harm to the general population – until the Industrial Revolution.

The Industrial Revolution belched noxious substances on an ominous scale. By the nineteenth century, everyone living in the choking gray hubs of industrial civilization was threatened by the deadly byproducts of burning fossil fuels, manufacturing chemicals and cement, and smelting metal. Massive quantities of sulphuric acid, alkali, sodium carbonate and lead were essential for industrialization, but they poisoned land, air, water and people in the process. In addition, untreated sewage contaminated water supplies, unleashing deadly cholera epidemics that filled the graveyards of London, Liverpool, Paris and New York.[21]

As one English writer said of London, " . . . her inhabitants breathe nothing but an impure and thick mist, accompanied by a fuliginous vapor, which renders them obnoxious to a thousand inconveniences, corrupting the lungs, and disordering the entire habit of their bodies . . . " He goes on to describe the city's industrial smokestacks:

> Whilst these are belching forth their sooty jaws, the city of London resembles the face rather of Mount Aetnea, the Court of Vulcan, Stromboli, or the Suburbs of Hell than the Assembly of rational creatures . . . for when, in all other places, the air is most serene and pure, it is here eclipsed with such a cloud of sulphur, as the sun itself, which gives day to all the world besides, is hardly able to penetrate and impart it here, and the weary traveler, at many miles distance, sooner smells than sees the city to which he repairs.[22]

In England, Europe and America the advance of technology took its toll as the ever-increasing tonnage of industrial toxins was flushed into the surrounding environment. Coal tar dyes from the textile industry, acids for stripping corrosive materials from iron and steel, battery lead, sulphuric acid used as an electrolyte and nitrates employed to make high-powered explosives – all became part of the vast industrial waste stream that now had to be disposed of. But this was just the beginning.

The chemical age didn't really explode until the second half of the twentieth century, when petroleum became the feedstock for a wide range of synthetic organic chemicals and the source of an insidious variety of noxious extrusions. As Samuel Epstein explains in *The Politics of Cancer*, "petrochemicals are the quintessence of a 'process industry,' in which a small number of primary constituents from crude oil are

---

[21] For a graphic, eye-opening account from the time, see: Engels, Freidrich. *The Condition of the Working Class in England: From Personal Observation and Authentic Sources.* (Moscow: Progress Publishers), 1973: ch. 2; "The Great Towns."

[22] From John Evelyn's Fumifugium in: Jennings, Humphrey. *Pandaemonium 1660–1886: The Coming of the Machine as Seen by Contemporary Observers.* (NY: The Free Press), 1985: 8–9.

converted into a large number of intermediate chemicals in a still larger number of large scale end products."[23] The beguiling bonanza of new commodities produced through "the wonder of chemistry" seemed endless. Synthetic fabrics, paints, plastics, pesticides, cosmetics and even miracle drugs were derived from petrochemicals.

Unfortunately, many petrochemical products and their associated wastes were not biodegradable. Unlike water, cotton, wood, wool, rubber and other substances not concocted in the lab, most of these synthetic substances did not readily decompose into their organic components to become recirculated and reused throughout the ecosystem. Instead, they hung about poisoning the planet and climbing the food chain – an ever-rising tide of indestructible toxic ooze that no one knew how to handle.

For years, nobody lost much sleep over these substances because the chemical industry worked overtime to conceal their dangers beneath a shiny cosmetic coat of progress and public relations. It took several decades before people began to realize that "better living through chemistry" was a mixed blessing at best.[24]

After World War II, American industries produced about one billion pounds of hazardous waste per year; by the late 1970s, the yearly figure was up to nearly 100 billion – well over 350 pounds for every person in the country.[25] During this period, the basic attitude toward disposal was "out of sight, out of mind." Hazardous industrial, household and military wastes were deposited willy-nilly into lagoons, bays, open pits, deserted quarries, ravines, swamps, unused farmland and city dumps. Many unsupervised sites were simply buried, abandoned and forgotten. Slowly, their poisonous plumes invaded the surrounding environment – a silent, lethal, creeping catastrophe of enormous proportions.

Despite the public's heightened environmental awareness during the late 1960s and early 1970s, this toxic menace avoided detection. In 1970, the president's annual environmental report made no reference to hazardous waste and it was never mentioned by the EPA in the early years of its life. Air and water pollution were the primary concerns of the time. However, the production of hazardous waste increased fivefold over the decade, while the Clean Water Act (CWA) and Clean Air Act (CAA) denied industrial polluters unfettered access to the oceans, rivers, lakes and skies. Under these pressures and restrictions, more industries used illicit methods and remote locations to dispose of their toxic trash.

By the late 1970s, decades of careless uncontrolled disposal came back to haunt America. Although the media paid scarce attention to the thousands of toxic hot spots festering across the country, some sites – such as Love Canal, Stringfellow and Valley

---

[23] Epstein, Samuel. *The Politics of Cancer.* (NY: East Ridge Press), 1998.

[24] Today, scientists suspect that an estrogen-like compound in plastic may be causing an array of serious reproductive disorders. Bisphenol A (BPA) is one of the highest-volume chemicals in the world and is found in the bodies of most people. Used to make hard plastic, BPA can seep from beverage containers and other materials. It is used in all polycarbonate plastic baby bottles, as well as other rigid plastic items, including large water cooler containers, sports bottles and microwave oven dishes, along with canned food liners and some dental sealants for children.

[25] This is an average of higher and lower estimates reviewed in Block, Alan & Frank Scarpitti. *Poisoning for Profit.* (NY: William Morrow & Co.), 1985: 46.

of the Drums – made national news.[26] They revealed the federal government's lack of legal authority to intervene in these crisis situations.

In June 1979, the Carter administration submitted a bill to Congress to address this problem. It called for the creation of a new law – The Comprehensive Environmental Response, Compensation and Liability Act. This bureaucratic mouthful became known as CERCLA, or Superfund. CERCLA made culpable contaminators liable for cleaning up their own toxic messes. If the culprits were no longer in business or could not be identified, Superfund would pay for a government cleanup.

Carter signed CERCLA in 1980. By the time it reached the president's desk, fierce chemical industry lobbying had convinced Congress to strike a provision compensating the victims of exposure to hazardous spills and dumps.[27] In the same year, EPA officials identified 30,000 toxic hot spots across the nation, and the number continued to rise with each passing day.

By taxing 43 dangerous chemicals produced by the country's largest chemical companies[28] and imposing a 9.6-cent-per-barrel charge on crude oil, CERCLA established a $1.6 billion "Superfund" the EPA could use to restore *orphaned* sites – where the culpable parties were either unknown or out of business.[29] This trust fund could also finance cleanup on sites requiring emergency action or when recalcitrant contaminators tried to avoid liability in court. In these cases, the EPA could initiate decontamination immediately and then sue the guilty parties to replenish the Superfund.[30] Under CERCLA, the EPA can bill recalcitrant polluters up to triple the cost of cleanup.[31]

Alternatively, the EPA may use the courts to compel liable parties to clean up their own messes. The trust fund has been used to pay for about 30 percent of the EPA's priority cleanups, while liable corporations themselves have financed the other

---

[26] For a listing of toxic sites in your state see: http://www.eco-usa.net/sites/index.shtml.

[27] Victims of toxic exposures at hazardous waste sites may seek compensation under state laws. However, studies show their chances of winning compensation are extremely low for three reasons: the statute of limitations barrier; the burden of proof barrier requires demonstrating causality between the defendant's action and the harm suffered; and the cost barrier of trying to satisfy this burden of proof is usually extraordinary.

[28] Two-thirds of these tax revenues came from about a dozen big companies, such as Dow, DuPont, Exxon and Shell.

[29] This was later raised to $4 billion.

[30] Before 2000, all money recovered from companies for cleanups performed by the EPA went back into the trust fund to be spent on cleaning up other sites. But in 2000, a little-noticed change in EPA policy allowed cleanup reimbursements to be tucked away in site-specific accounts to be used only for future work on those sites. There are hundreds of these accounts and the EPA doesn't need Congressional approval to spend the money in them, unlike CERCLA's trust fund. Between 2000 and 2007, EPA diverted $709 million collected from Superfund polluters into these special accounts, putting hundreds of millions of dollars out of reach of other Superfund sites waiting for cleanup. See: Mullins, Richard & Joaquin Sapien. "EPA Diverts Money from Shared Superfund Pool," *Center for Public Integrity* (May 10, 2007). http://www.publicintegrity. org/Superfund/report.aspx?aid=871.

[31] Wolk, Julie. *The Truth About Toxic Waste Cleanups.* U.S. PIRG & Sierra Club (February 2004). TruthaboutToxicWaste#1ABC70.pdf.

70 percent. To avoid the possibility of being charged triple cleanup costs, most companies prefer to finance their own restorations.

Unfortunately, the creation of this cleanup fund came at a stiff price. The oil industry only conceded to CERCLA's tax on crude oil in return for an "exclusion" of all their production wastes from CERCLA cleanup liability.[32] This provision excluded petroleum wastes, even though they are extremely dangerous and often infused with hazardous chemicals such as benzene, toluene, xylene and lead.[33] Known as the "petroleum exclusion," this loophole is particularly onerous because many Superfund sites contain petroleum wastes. Today America is littered with aging underground petroleum storage tanks, leaking wastes and contaminating land and water supplies. Yet this loophole leaves the victims with no legal remedy for their harms.[34] In addition to being free of cleanup liability, oil companies cannot be sued by those harmed by their pollution under CERCLA because the law excludes toxic oil wastes from its definition of "hazardous."[35]

This oil waste exclusion was built into both CERCLA and RCRA. In RCRA it provides the oil industry with an inexpensive way to rid itself of the enormous amounts of toxic muck that comes with petroleum extraction. While RCRA requires other businesses to carefully document, transport and deposit their toxic waste in permitted treatment facilities, oil companies can legally dump toxic sludge in open pits and landfills. This practice poisoned people in nearby communities, like the folks in Grand Bois, Louisiana. For years, this courageous little Cajun community fought to protect itself from Exxon's deadly dumping practices in the courts and state legislature with little success.[36] Finally, Hurricane Katrina engulfed these sludge pits, doing uncalculated damage to the surrounding environment and inhabitants.[37]

Despite this outrageous petroleum waste loophole, the basic legal ethics behind CERCLA are sound and commendable. Superfund employs the "polluter pays" principle, which rests on the well-established childhood adage that people are responsible for cleaning up their own messes. Another attractive characteristic of CERCLA is its simplicity. It inflicts no complex regulatory process on business. Instead, by imposing potentially costly cleanup liability, CERCLA enlists industry's commercial instincts for the bottom line to discourage the illicit disposal of hazardous waste.

[32] Kennedy, Robert F. Jr. *Crimes Against Nature.* (NY: Harper Collins), 2004: 112.
[33] Courts interpreting the exclusion have generally held that the petroleum exclusion covers crude oil, crude oil fractions and hazardous substances that are indigenous to crude oil or are typically added to crude oil during the refining process, such as benzene, toluene, xylene, ethyl benzene and lead.
[34] Basile, Jason M. "Still No Remedy After All These Years: Plugging the Hole in the Law of Leaking Underground Storage Tanks," *Indiana Law Journal* (Spring 1998). http://www.law.indiana.edu/ilj/volumes/v73/no2/basile.html.
[35] US-EPA. *Scope of the CERCLA Petroleum Exclusion Under Sections 101l(14) and 104(a)(2)* (July 3, 1987). http://www.epa.gov/superfund/programs/er/triggers/haztrigs/whatsub3.htm.
[36] Roberts, J. Timmons & Melissa M. Toffolon-Weiss. *Chronicles from the Environmental Justice Frontline.* (NY: Cambridge University Press), 2001: 137–64.
[37] Allen, Barbara. "Environmental Justice and Expert Knowledge in the Wake of a Disaster," *Social Studies of Science* (Winter 2007): 103–10

The need for CERCLA's potentially severe liability costs became patently obvious after RCRA's enactment in 1976. RCRA required the many dangerous and substandard waste disposal facilities to comply with RCRA's rigorous treatment and disposal requirements or go out of business. This left scores of insolvent disposal sites unattended and thousands of corroding barrels and tank loads of toxic residue leaching into the surrounding environment. When CERCLA passed in 1980, it became responsible for cleaning many of these sites.

Worse yet, as the scarcity of licensed facilities drove up the cost of legal disposal, industry began sidestepping RCRA's labeling, transport and disposal regulations by resorting to illicit dumping more frequently. Since there are many clandestine ways to dispose of hazardous waste, violations of RCRA are easy to commit and difficult to discover. Thus, without the looming threat of CERCLA's punitive cleanup liability to discourage it, widespread midnight dumping and the abandonment of insolvent waste sites would have doomed RCRA's efforts to regulate hazardous waste disposal.[38]

CERCLA's *strict, joint and several* liability format is potentially quite stern and broad in scope. It makes anyone caught contributing to a toxic blight, whether negligent or not, responsible for the entire cost of rehabilitation, unless they can find other culprits and legally compel them to assume their share of the cleanup burden. This allows the EPA (and taxpayers) to avoid an expensive, time-consuming investigation to identify all the contributors to a toxic site. Instead, it can finger one or two *potentially responsible parties (PRPs)* and they will be forced to bear all the restoration costs unless they can locate other culpable contaminators. In addition, Superfund liability is *retroactive* – PRPs are responsible for cleaning up their toxic hazards even if they made them before CERCLA became law.[39]

CERCLA imposes cleanup liability on three categories of PRPs: the waste generators who produced the hazardous substances; the transporters who hauled them to their disposal destination[40]; and the owners and operators of the site where they were discarded, including anyone who purchased the site afterward. This broad definition of potentially responsible parties was consciously intended to draw lenders, insurers and corporate risk managers into the legal fold.

The dramatic decline in "midnight dumping" since CERCLA became law reveals how effective this liability threat can be. Yet despite CERCLA's apparently stern approach to illicit disposal, America remains pockmarked and poisoned by thousands of toxic tumors. Superfund's failures stem from flaws and loopholes in the law itself, stiff industry opposition and the EPA's pathetic record of enforcement.

---

[38] The Resource Conservation and Recovery Act of 1976.

[39] CERCLA's retroactivity is controversial. In a decision with potentially far-reaching implications, the United States District Court for the Southern District of Alabama ruled in United States of America v. Olin Corporation, that CERCLA cannot be applied retroactively to conduct that occurred prior to its enactment on December 11, 1980. This decision was overturned on appeal. But this issue won't go away until Congress clarifies its intent upon CERCLA's reauthorization and amendment.

[40] Including anyone who arranged for this transportation.

The agency has repeatedly used its considerable legal discretion to reduce the cleanup burden on polluters at the expense of their victims.[41] Nevertheless, CERCLA remains a costly thorn in industry's side. So, despite the EPA's deferential discretion, industry relentlessly endeavors to malign, disarm and dismantle Superfund. Overall, they have succeeded.

In 1994, proposed legislation to overhaul Superfund died in committee prior to the November elections. After the elections, intense lobbying by the oil and chemical industries prompted a series of Republican-controlled Congresses to let the petro-chemical taxes that subsidize the fund expire, despite yearly requests by the Clinton administration to renew them.[42] Without these taxes to keep the fund solvent, Superfund restorations slowed to a crawl. Lacking a substantial trust fund, the EPA's capability to initiate its own cleanups, or leverage corporate cleanups with the threat of triple charges, dropped dramatically. During the Bush administration, this situation went from bad to worse. Unlike every president since Carter, Bush did not include CERCLA's "polluters pay" tax in his budget proposals. Consequently, the burden of paying for toxic cleanups shifted dramatically from polluters to their victims by forcing taxpayers to pick up the tab to cleanse contaminated communities.

In 1996, when CERCLA still had a $3.8 billion cleanup fund accumulated from prior chemical tax revenues, only 18 percent of the program's cost was passed on to the public. According to Bush's 2003 budget plan, the public was supposed to assume 79 percent of the cleanup costs. But by October, the fund was empty and taxpayers were footing the entire bill.[43] Of course, the largest beneficiaries of these "reforms" were the president's cronies in the petrochemical industry, whose record profits and obscene CEO compensation packages were already legendary.[44]

In the absence of political will and resources, the number of completed Superfund restorations fell 50 percent below previous annual totals. Bush's EPA claimed that the numbers were misleading because the recent sites chosen for rehabilitation are more complex and expensive than those in previous years. But Congressional representatives who asked the EPA for documentation to substantiate this claim were snubbed.[45]

While the Superfund's bankruptcy may be the knockout blow that renders CERCLA catatonic, this law has been on the ropes since it was born. CERCLA came into the world with powerful enemies. Oil and chemical corporations hated paying taxes to finance the fund; culpable polluters (and their insurers) railed against cleanup standards and fees they considered burdensome and unreasonable as well as the stiff legal costs of trying to dodge them.

---

[41] See Chapter 1 for several examples.

[42] Industry opposition persists even though this feedstock tax has probably been passed forward as higher prices and backward to the IRS as a corporate tax profit deduction. Thus consumers and taxpayers have undoubtedly made a major indirect contribution to this "polluter pays" tax.

[43] Kennedy, Robert F. Jr., 2004: 113; Wolk, Julie (February 2004); "The Superfund," *Mother Jones* (September 3, 2003). http://www.motherjones.com/news/featurex/2003/09/superfund.html.

[44] *ABC News*. "Oil: Exxon Chairman's $400 Million Parachute" (April 14, 2006). http://www.abcnews.go.com/GMA/story?id=1841989.

[45] "The Superfund" (September 3, 2003).

Even though CERCLA's retroactive liability is not criminal, but only cleanup in nature, it has always been a particular source of corporate enmity. Over decades, General Electric dumped 1.3 million pounds of deadly PCBs into the Hudson River.[46] Their chronic discharges contaminated a 200-mile stretch of the Hudson, making it the largest Superfund site in America. Yet because this callous lethal act was committed before CERCLA became law, GE insists it should not pay for cleanup.[47] Most folks would agree that if you dent someone's car or break the window while doing something legal, you should fix it, but corporate America spurns such ethics. Instead, they argue that the public should bear the cost of cleaning their toxic messes. Evidently, it's the extra price we should pay for all the wonderful things they sell us. After all, doesn't GE "bring good things to life"?

CERCLA's early years were spent under the Reagan administration's first EPA chief, Anne Gorsuch. In Gorsuch, the president found a kindred spirit, someone who considered environmental regulation as onerous and unnecessary he did. Gorsuch was recruited by Reagan's transition team, led by the ultraconservative beer tycoon, Joseph Coors, one of Reagan's most generous campaign donors. As one of Colorado's worst polluters, Coors detested the EPA and the very notion of environmental regulation. He was impressed by Gorsuch's record in the Colorado legislature, in which she fought bills to control toxic waste and reduce auto emissions.[48] Coors reportedly chose Gorsuch after she satisfactorily answered the question: "Are you willing to bring the EPA to its knees?"[49]

As EPA chief, Gorsuch selected like-minded appointees by picking lobbyists from paper, asbestos, chemical, automobile and oil companies to run the EPA's principal departments. During her time in office, she slashed the agency's budget 60 percent, crippling its capability to write regulations or enforce the law.[50] By June of 1981, she had abolished the EPA's Office of Enforcement, demoting and disorganizing its functions by farming them out to disparate parts of the agency. Gorsuch then replaced the office with a chief enforcement counselor, recruited from Exxon, who reported directly to her.[51]

---

[46] The federal government classifies PCBs as probable human carcinogens. They are also associated with reproductive problems, low birth weight, reduced ability to fight infections and learning problems. Humans are exposed to PCBs primarily through eating contaminated fish. The body does not excrete these chemicals, so they accumulate in fatty tissue. Because of PCB contamination, New York State shut down the Hudson River fishery in 1977. Today, the New York State Department of Health recommends severe restrictions on eating Hudson River fish.

[47] "Hudson River PCBs," *Riverkeepers.* http://www.riverkeeper.org/campaigns/stop-polluters/contaminated-sites/pcbs/.

[48] Both Gorsuch and her future husband, Robert Burford, were appointed to executive offices for their anti-regulatory, anti-environmental zeal. As a rancher with a history of violating his BLM grazing permits, "Chuck" Burford had publicly called for the abolition of the Bureau of Land Management. Coors had Reagan appoint him to run the Bureau where he worked overtime to fulfill his promise. See: Durant, Robert F. *The Administrative Presidency Revisited.* (Herndon, VA: State University of New York Press), 1992.

[49] Lazarus, Richard. *The Making of Environmental Law.* (Chicago, IL: University of Chicago Press), 2004: 101.

[50] Cronin, John & Robert F. Kennedy, Jr., 1999.

[51] Block, Alan & Frank Scarpitti, 1985: 320; Kennedy, Robert F. Jr., 2004: 26.

Gorsuch's tenure as EPA chief proved especially debilitating for hazardous waste laws such as RCRA and Superfund. Fifty-five million dollars was immediately cut from the agency's hazardous waste program. After Love Canal, Carter's EPA listed 14,000 sites for priority cleanup and "fast-tracked" 114 for immediate action. But Gorsuch's reaction time to this emergency was glacial. In 1981, she used only $8 million of the $78 million available for decontaminating toxic sites. In 1982, only $71 million was spent on cleanup out of the $170 million appropriated.[52] Yet somehow, based on this amazing record of neglect, Gorsuch testified that the program was doing so well that, "I don't see the need to continue the Superfund beyond 1985."[53]

In 1982, the chemical eradication of the small Missouri town of Times Beach exemplified the EPA's gross disregard for the toxic contamination of American communities. During the 1970s, the roads, corrals and horse stables in and around the small riverside hamlets of Times Beach and Imperial were sprayed with waste oil laced with dioxin and PCBs. When Russell Bliss, the man responsible, applied the waste oil to control dust and weeds, he was completely unaware of the dioxin contamination. NEPACCO,[54] the chemical company that paid Bliss to dispose of its toxic refuse, never bothered to alert him to the toxicity of his cargo, although NEPACCO was well aware of it.

Dioxins are one of industry's most lethal byproducts. They are a family of 219 highly toxic chemicals created by the manufacture of some herbicides, wood preservatives and germicides as well as the incineration of solid waste. Dioxins are also generated by the production of paper and the infamous defoliating weapon, Agent Orange.[55] Industry documents, unearthed during discovery proceedings in a class-action lawsuit brought by Vietnam veterans exposed to Agent Orange, revealed that several major chemical companies conspired to hide the dangers of dioxin from the public as early as 1965.[56]

On TV, Dow chemical's president insisted, "There is absolutely no evidence of dioxin doing any damage to humans, except something called chloracne. It's a rash." Yet, behind the scenes, Dow was meeting with other chemical producers in a furtive effort to keep the news of dioxin's perils from exploding into a scandal and an outcry for governmental regulation. A participant in these meetings from Hercules Powder wrote: "They [Dow] are particularly fearful of a congressional investigation and excessive restrictive legislation on the manufacture of pesticides."[57]

Today, the EPA considers a "safe" level of dioxin exposure to be about 1/10,000th the size of a grain of table salt.[58] Dioxin causes cancer and birth defects in lab animals

---

[52] Block, Alan & Frank Scarpitti, 1985: 319–20.
[53] Williams, Gerald S. "Toxic Dumps: EPA's Hit List." *Newsweek* (January 3, 1983): 12.
[54] The Northeastern Pharmaceutical and Chemical Company (NEPACCO) of Verona, Missouri.
[55] Dioxins are also produced by the combustion of wood in the presence of chlorine, by fires involving PCBs and by the exhaust of automobiles burning leaded fuel.
[56] "Dioxin Puts Dow on the Spot," *Time/CNN OnLine* (May 2, 1983). http://www.time.com/time/magazine/article/0,9171,953860-1,00.html.
[57] "Dioxin Puts Dow on the Spot" (May 2, 1983).
[58] Montague, Peter. "Dioxin Part 2: Gauging the Toxicity," *Rachel's Environmental & Health Weekly* #173 (March 21, 1990). http://www.ejnet.org/rachel/rhwn173.htm.

in doses as low as five parts per trillion. Exposure can cause liver damage and can make the skin erupt in pus-filled blisters that spread across the face, neck and shoulders and then down the rest of the body. Severe cases leave scars and can result in permanent disfigurement.[59] The waste oil sprayed on Times Beach had dioxin levels two million times higher than the EPA's safe exposure level and 2,000 times higher than the dioxin level in Agent Orange. Guinea pigs fed dirt from the streets of Times Beach died almost immediately.[60]

Chemical industry flacks and free market ideologues such as ABC's John Stossel are fond of assuring the public that dioxin isn't really dangerous and Times Beach was just a ridiculous overreaction. As evidence, they point to a factory explosion that released a cloud of dioxin over Seveso, Italy in 1976. Stossel contends that this accident left the people of Seveso no less healthy than their fellow Italians.[61] However, follow-up research on the people of Seveso by Dr. Alberto Bertazzi has documented serious health problems resulting from the accident, including alarming increases in rare blood and liver cancers, a three-fold increase in rectal cancer and a six-fold increase in Hodgkin's disease and myeloma in women.[62]

Claims that some dioxin exposures have not increased cancer rates overlook the facts that cancer can take many decades to develop and that there are several kinds of dioxin, some more deadly than others. According to the EPA and the World Health Organization, the peer-reviewed science clearly shows that the most toxic form of dioxin, called TCDD, is a known human carcinogen.[63] The rest of the dioxin family fits into a lower category of "likely" human carcinogens. In 2004, Peter deFur, cochair of the EPA's three-year, peer-reviewed dioxin analysis, concluded that there is "clear and compelling evidence" of dioxin's multiple health effects including reproductive problems, diabetes, birth defects, liver ailments and increased cancer rates in humans.[64]

In the early 1970s, the EPA became aware that Times Beach could be contaminated, but did nothing to confirm it and told no one about it. Immediately after Russell Bliss sprayed the Shenandoah Stables in early 1971, 50 horses and many other animals on the property died. According to the stable owner, Judy Piatt, hours

---

[59] Montague, Peter. "Dioxin Part 2: Gauging the Toxicity" (March 21, 1990).
[60] "The Times Beach Story," by Marilyn Leistner (the last Mayor of Times Beach, Missouri). http://www.greens.org/s-r/078/07-09.html.
[61] Stossel, John. *Give Me a Break.* (NY: Harper Collins), 2005: 108–9.
[62] This study only covers the period 1976 through 1986 – 10 years after the Seveso accident. Since most cancers take longer than ten years to develop, the cancers reported in this study may represent only the earliest signs of more trouble to come. Bertazzi, Pier Alberto et al. "Cancer Incidence in a Population Accidentally Exposed to 2,3,7,8-Tetrachlorodibenzo-PARA-dioxin," *Epidemiology* (September 1993): 398–406.
[63] The International Agency for Research on Cancer (IARC), a division of the World Health Organization, has labeled the most potent dioxin, called TCDD, a known human carcinogen. See: McGregor, Douglas B. et al. "An IARC Evaluation of Polychlorinated Dibenzo-P-dioxins and Polychlorinated Dibenzofurans as Risk Factors in Human Carcinogenesis," *Environmental Health Perspectives* (April 1998): 755–60.
[64] "EPA Affirms Health Dangers from Dioxin," *New York Times* (September 13, 1994). http://query.nytimes.com/gst/fullpage.html?sec=health&res=9C00E6DA143BF930A2575AC0A962958260.

were spent raking up the dead birds that fell from rafters and trees. A veterinarian with the Missouri Division of Health confirmed that there were "bushel baskets full of dead wild birds."[65] Soon the whole Piatt family became sick and both children were hospitalized; one lost half her body weight after suffering a severe kidney disorder. When similar poisonings devastated nearby stables sprayed by Russell Bliss, their owners suspected his waste oil was the cause and asked the Centers for Disease Control (CDC) to investigate.[66]

CDC officials visited the stables, examined sick animals and sampled the soil. It took two years for them to issue their test results. Meanwhile, no one did anything to stop Russell Bliss from spraying toxic oil on the roads of Times Beach, Imperial and several other locations throughout eastern Missouri. In 1973, the CDC finally verified that the soil samples they collected contained dangerous levels of PCBs and dioxin. They shared their findings with the EPA and Missouri environmental officials; traced the contamination to Bliss's waste oil and discovered that he had sprayed it on dozens of sites around eastern Missouri.[67] Two more years passed before the CDC warned the EPA that the small community of Imperial was so seriously contaminated that it should be evacuated.[68] When it finally did, the EPA ignored the warning.[69]

Another four years passed. In 1979, a former employee of NEPACCO told local EPA officials that the chemical company had hired Russell Bliss to get rid of tank loads of dioxin-laced oil. Still, the EPA did nothing. For three more years the people of Times Beach were kept in the dark. In fact, the mayor wasn't alerted to the problem until November 1982, when a newspaper reporter asked her about the town's contamination. Taken by surprise, the mayor was stunned when a telephone call with EPA officials verified the accuracy of the reporter's facts.[70]

The news sent shock waves through the community. Residents remembered how roads turned purple and gave off foul odors after being sprayed; and how birds, squirrels and pets died in the weeks that followed. Everyone began comparing notes and wondering whether the health problems in their families were caused by dioxin. City officials were horrified when they recalled that after ordering Bliss to stop spraying, he'd drained the remainder of his tank load on vacant land that later became the town's ballpark.[71]

---

[65] "Death of Animals Laid to Chemical," *New York Times* (August 28, 1974): 36; "Why is EPA Ignoring Monsanto," *Rachel's Environment & Health News* #563 (September 10, 1997). http://www.rachel.org/bulletin/pdf/Rachels_fnvironment_Health_News_560.pdf.

[66] "Death of Animals Laid to Chemical" (August 28, 1974): 36.

[67] Eventually the identified contaminated sites numbered over 100. See: "Why is EPA Ignoring Monsanto" (September 10, 1997). http://www.rachel.org/bulletin/pdf/Rachels_fnvironment_Health_News_560.pdf.

[68] CDC testing in 2007 revealed that 112 of the 130 Imperial residents tested showed abnormalities in blood, liver or kidney functions. "Dioxin Puts Dow on the Spot" (May 2, 1983).

[69] Reinhold, Robert. "Missouri Now Fears 100 Sites Could Be Tainted by Dioxin," *New York Times* (January 18, 1983): A1, A23.

[70] "The Times Beach Story," by Marilyn Leistner (the last Mayor of Times Beach, Missouri). http://www.greens.org/s-r/078/07-09.html.

[71] "The Times Beach Story," by Marilyn Leistner (the last Mayor of Times Beach, Missouri). http://www.greens.org/s-r/078/07-09.html.

In response to the panic and bad press, EPA officials promised to investigate, but then did nothing for nine months, leaving the frightened folks of Times Beach to stew in their anxiety and dread. Their mood swung between disbelief, outrage and terror. People demanded answers and action from Reagan's EPA, but chief Burford did nothing. Finally, after townsfolk took up a collection to finance their own tests, EPA chemists suddenly appeared, sealed in protective haz-mat "moon suits," and began sampling soil in the streets, yards and playgrounds of Times Beach.

The panic was palpable. Was the whole town toxic? What should they do? Were their schools and homes safe? Terrified residents demanding answers confronted EPA officials at a press conference, but the only advice they offered was to avoid eating the dirt.[72]

Within weeks, things got much worse. Just as the EPA completed its first round of sampling, the Meramec River overflowed, leaving Times Beach under twenty-five feet of toxic water and muck. As the floodwaters subsided, evacuated residents desperately sought answers to their most pressing concerns: Was it safe to return and clean up their homes? What precautions should they take? Their frantic questions met with official silence until the day before Christmas Eve. When the community gathered at City Hall for the town's annual Christmas party, state and federal officials announced, "If you are living in town it is advisable for you to leave and if you are out of town do not come back."[73]

In the weeks before floodwaters engulfed Times Beach, a political storm was also brewing in the nation's capital. EPA chief Burford and her coterie of loyal appointees were under media scrutiny and Congressional investigation for suspicious shenanigans surrounding Superfund cleanups. Eventually, the investigation revealed that Burford's cabal of Reagan loyalists had favored well-connected polluters with lax enforcement and lucrative sweetheart deals gilded with million dollar discounts on Superfund cleanup fees. In addition, they manipulated cleanup timetables to create helpful publicity for Republican candidates in key congressional races.[74]

But this was merely the tip of an enormous malevolent iceberg. The EPA and its hazardous waste laws were in shambles. Deep budget cuts and forced layoffs had crippled the agency's capability to do research, make rules, or enforce the law. Gorsuch and her polluter-friendly appointees had gone out of their way to demoralize the agency and drive off anyone dedicated to environmental protection. They created hit lists of employees considered too green. Targeted officials were demoted

---

[72] The Video Project, 1994.

[73] "The Times Beach Story," by Marilyn Leistner (the last Mayor of Times Beach, Missouri). http://www.greens.org/s-r/078/07-09.html.

[74] Szasz, Andrew. "The Process and Significance of Political Scandals: A Comparison of Watergate and the 'Sewergate' Episode at the Environmental Protection Agency," *Social Problems* (February 1986): 202–17. This illicit act is called "election tracking" – the practice of timing key events, such as the announcement of cleanup funding, to assist the election campaigns of "friendly" politicians. The specific cleanups involved four Superfund sites: Stringfellow (in California), Berlin and Farrow (in Michigan) and Tar Creek (in Oklahoma). In the Stringfellow case, Reagan's EPA delayed cleanup because it did not want Governor Jerry Brown (a Democrat), then running for the Senate, to get the credit.

or "encouraged" to resign. In fiscal year 1981, more than 4,100 employees (about one-third of the entire staff) left the EPA.[75]

When Congress began investigating EPA malfeasance regarding Times Beach, Reagan ordered Burford to assert executive privilege and withhold subpoenaed documents. This touched off a constitutional confrontation with Congress and heightened speculation about a major cover-up.

As Congress and the press condemned Gorsuch's refusal to turn over documents relevant to the "Sewergate" scandal, the floodwaters receded from Times Beach. The nightly news broadcast the residents' desperate pleas for a government buyout of their contaminated homes. Seizing the opportunity to boost her image, Anne Gorsuch decided to come to the rescue. In February of 1983, she flew to Missouri to announce a $33 million buyout of the entire town.

Back at EPA headquarters, Gorsuch tried to point the finger of guilt at her top hazardous waste official: Rita Lavelle. She accused Lavelle of making secret agreements with Superfund polluters and demanded her resignation. Lavelle fought back. When asked to account for her mismanagement of Times Beach, she blamed Burford's poor leadership and the pervasive in-fighting and chaos in the EPA. The week before the EPA was supposed to turn over its internal records regarding Times Beach and other mishandled Superfund cleanups, two paper shredders were delivered to EPA headquarters. Critics cried "cover-up!" Their accusations were probably justified because many crucial documents, including those pertaining to the EPA's eight-year mishandling of the Times Beach fiasco were declared "lost."

Under oath, Lavelle lied to Congress about her influence over cleanup negotiations at the Stringfellow Superfund site – a toxic mess in California partially caused by her previous employer, Aerojet-General.[76] In the end, she was sentenced to six months in prison and fined $10,000 for perjury and obstruction of justice.[77] Anne Burford, under investigation by six congressional committees and the Justice Department, resigned in March 1983 along with nine other Reagan appointees.

Times Beach is but one of the many communities that have suffered at the hands of callous, corrupt corporations and negligent EPA officials. Unfortunately, the removal of Gorsuch, Lavelle and their confederates was only a minor victory that had a positive but limited impact on the agency's dismal long-range performance. Several presidents have come and gone since Times Beach and Sewergate were nightly news.

Through both Republican and Democratic administrations, EPA honchos have continued to work closely with industry to downplay and diminish the mounting evidence that dioxins are not just found in isolated pockets of contamination such as

---

[75] Waterman, Richard W. *Presidential Influence and the Administrative State*. (Knoxville, TN: University of Tennessee Press), 1989: 121.

[76] Dowd, Maureen. "Lonely at the EPA Top," *CNN/Time OnLine* (March 14, 1883). http://www.time.com/time/magazine/article/0,9171,951954,00.html.

[77] Lavelle served only three of the six months sentence. In 2004, a jury in Los Angeles federal court found Lavelle guilty of one count of wire fraud and two counts of making false statements to the Federal Bureau of Investigation (FBI) in an unrelated charge. For this she was sentenced to another 15 months in federal prison.

Love Canal and Times Beach. With each new study, scientists have warned that dioxin, PCBs, furans and other industrial toxins are far more pervasive, and considerably more toxic, than industry and the EPA care to admit.

Today, dioxin has been found in the bodies of every American tested. Most dioxin comes from incinerating garbage and hazardous waste, bleaching paper and manufacturing chlorinated plastics and pesticides. Although dioxin can directly enter our lungs, most of the dioxin in our bodies comes from dioxin emissions contaminating pastures, feed, soil and water consumed by poultry and livestock. Dioxin concentrates in their bodies as it moves up the food chain.[78] Finally, it enters our bodies when we eat meat, dairy, eggs and other products from contaminated animals.

In 1987, leaked EPA documents and internal industry reports revealed that senior EPA officials were collaborating with major polluters to limit public knowledge and concern about the ubiquitous hazards of dioxin and other dangerous chemicals. According to U.S. District Judge Owen M. Panner, the documents revealed an agreement, "between the EPA and the industry to suppress, modify or delay the results of the joint EPA/industry [dioxin] study or the manner in which they are publicly presented."[79]

The American Paper Institute (API), the main lobbying arm of the paper industry, realized that the public might stop buying many of its products – from disposable diapers[80] and coffee filters to paper towels and milk cartons – if they became concerned about the unsafe levels of dioxin consistently found in them.[81] To avoid new regulations and falling profits, the API mounted a full-scale campaign to fend off bad publicity and stiffer regulations. The "public affairs strategy" of their "dioxin response team" sought to suppress or counter all allegations of health risks in the media and collaborate with sympathetic EPA administrators to limit regulation and public concern.[82] An internal document revealed that API lobbyists felt they'd made major headway in convincing EPA chief Lee Thomas that dioxin was only a public perception issue, not a public health problem.

In this 1987 internal report, the API proudly claimed that, "Thomas indicated a willingness to cooperate with the industry to ensure that the public would not be unduly alarmed about this [dioxin] issue."[83] The same report explained that to turn the EPA's attention away from dioxin contamination of paper products, the API should "improve intelligence gathering within EPA," including identification of "allies" and "adversaries" within the agency.[84]

[78] USEPA (Office of Research and Development). *Exposure and Health Reassessment of 2,3,7,8-Tetrachlorodibenzo-p-Dioxin (TCDD) and Related Compounds, Part III Integrated Risk Summary and Risk Characterization for 2,3,7,8-Tetrachlorodibenzo-p-Dioxin (TCDD) and Related Compounds,* External Review Draft. (Washington, DC: June, 2000type="author").

[79] Stackelberg, Peter von. "White Wash: The Dioxin Cover-Up," *Greenpeace* (March/April 1989). http://www.planetwaves.net/contents/white_wash_dioxin_cover_up.html.

[80] "The Dioxin Connection in Disposable Diapers," *Mothering* (Fall 1989). http://findarticles.com/p/articles/mi_m0838/is_n53/ai_8011827.

[81] Stackelberg, Peter von (March/April 1989).

[82] Stackelberg, Peter von (March/April 1989).

[83] Stackelberg, Peter von (March/April 1989).

[84] Stackelberg, Peter von (March/April 1989).

Many companies fear the potential liabilities associated with dioxin in their products and wastes. To prevent what happened to the tobacco industry, a broad coalition led by Monsanto, BASF and Dow Chemical; and managed by their lobbying groups, the American Chemistry Council (ACC)[85] and the Chlorine Chemistry Council (CCC), have pressured Congress, the White House and the EPA to overlook the vast body of credible evidence (including the EPA's own studies) of dioxin's dangers.[86] During the Clinton administration, the EPA created faulty dioxin risk assessments and refused to release more accurate and damaging studies to the public.[87] This collusion and cover-up – persisting from Carter to Bush – prompted one disillusioned environmental activist, Teri Swearingen, to comment, "money can make dioxin safe on cornflakes."[88]

It is this same tight relationship between the polluter police and the polluters that has made it so difficult to keep Superfund alive and effective. Research by the Center for Public Integrity reveals that 100 companies linked to more than 600 of the nation's worst Superfund sites spent more than $1 billion lobbying the White House, Congress and the EPA from 1998 through 2005. Seventy-one of these companies spent more than $123 million in campaign contributions during the same period.[89]

On Capitol Hill, these large corporations find it easy to outspend and outlobby environmental organizations. For instance, between 1998 and 2005, Exxon Mobil, a giant polluter linked to 111 Superfund sites, spent more than $66 million on lobbying. This sum is about eight times what three environmental groups – Environmental Defense, the Sierra Club and the National Environmental Trust – collectively spent on lobbying during the same time.[90] In addition, some polluters have formed industry front groups such as the Superfund Action Alliance and the Superfund Settlements Project to weaken CERCLA's liability and cleanup provisions.

---

[85] Formerly the Chemical Manufacturer's Association, this industry trade association represents hundreds of chemical producers.

[86] Center for Health, Environment and Justice. *Behind Closed Doors* (April, 2001). http://www.besafe-net.com/BCDreport.htm; Casten, Liane C. "EPA Collusion with Industry," *Synthesis/Regeneration* (Summer 1995). http://www.mindfully.org/Air/Dioxin-EPA-Industry-Collusion.htm; *Dioxin: The Orange Resource Book* (Summer, 1995). http://www.greens.org/s-r/07-8toc.html; "Pandora's Poison," Eric Coppolino *Synthesis/Regeneration* (Summer 1995).

[87] Montague, Peter. "A Sea of Troubles Engulfs Incineration," *Rachel's Democracy and Health News #325* (February 17, 1993). http://www.rachel.org/bulletin/index.cfm?issue_ID=804.

[88] Shabecoff, Philip. *Earth Rising*. (Washington, DC: Island Press), 2000: 116; Pianin, Eric. "Dioxin Report by EPA on Hold Industries Oppose Finding of Cancer Link, Urge Delay," *Washington Post* (April 12, 2001). http://www.mindfully.org/Pesticide/Dioxin-Industries-Oppose.htm; Lester, Stephen U. "Industry's 'True Lies': The Politics Behind the Scientific Debate on Dioxin," *Consumer Law Page*. http://consumerlawpage.com/article/truelies.shtml; Appel, Adrianne. "Tiny Town Demands Justice in Dioxin Poisoning," *Inter Press Service* (July 15, 2007). http://www.ipsnews.net/news.asp?idnews=38667.

[89] This figure includes their PACs and employees. Narayanswamy, Anupama. "Lobbying the EPA Takes Money – and Connections," *Center for Public Integrity* (April 22, 2007). http://www.publicintegrity.org/superfund/report.aspx?aid=852.

[90] Narayanswamy, Anupama (April 22, 2007). http://www.publicintegrity.org/superfund/report.aspx?aid=852

Polluter lobbying and influence peddling makes it difficult, but not impossible, for Superfund to work. Experience shows that when citizens organize, protest, hold officials' feet to the fire and refuse to take no for an answer, Superfund can provide valuable resources to clean up and restore contaminated communities or relocate their residents. In fact, CERCLA has functioned as a safety net in hundreds of cases when hazardous substances threatened communities after nature and industry collided. For example:

- In the late 1980s and early 1990s, the West Dallas Coalition for Environmental Justice fought for a Superfund cleanup to remove the lead contaminating their neighborhood. The cleanup finally commenced when they won their environmental racism suit against the EPA, Dallas and the state of Texas after years of struggle in the courts and the streets.[91]
- When Arkansas' 15 Mile Bayou flooded in 1980, water surged into the Gurley Pit Superfund site, inundating residences and farmland with 500,000 gallons of hazardous waste. Superfund cleaned up the site and ensured that future flooding would no longer threaten local residents.
- In 1997, Idaho's Milo Creek flooded, leaving 50 homes awash in toxic mining waste. CERCLA funds were used to decontaminate homes and stabilize the creek's channel to protect the neighborhood from future floods.[92]
- In 1999, Hurricane Floyd dumped seven inches of rain over a twenty-four-hour period in southeastern Pennsylvania. The resulting floodwaters washed toxic contaminants from an industrial area into a nearby suburb. Using Superfund, the EPA identified the abandoned landfills leaching this toxic brew and began planning a long-term cleanup to protect the neighborhood by 2001.

Yet even these notable success stories have their formidable downside. In 1996, at a rare conference involving EPA officials and community leaders from contaminated neighborhoods, citizens voiced bitter criticisms of the EPA's cleanup, relocation and buy-out efforts. One after another, neighborhood leaders condemned the EPA for a long list of failures and abuses. Among the most prominent were:

- Ignoring or downplaying health problems and making a haphazard effort to compile and evaluate relevant health information.
- Discriminating against minority communities in nearly every aspect of the Superfund process, including longer response times to contaminations of minority neighborhoods and inequitable resources devoted to cleanups, health monitoring, buy-outs and relocations.

---

[91] Countryman, Carol. "Getting the Lead Out – West Dallas, TX, Lead Contamination," *The Progressive* (November 1993).

[92] Fidis, Alex. *Empty Pockets: Facing Hurricane Katrina with a Bankrupt Superfund* (U.S. PIRG) (December 2005).

- Studying a problem to death without doing anything.
- Favoring polluters with cheaper, less effective cleanup standards.
- Meeting secretly with polluters.
- Hiding vital information from the community.
- Ignoring and avoiding community input into the cleanup process.
- Leaving families stranded for long periods in substandard, temporary housing before offering a buy-out.
- Buying out homes at well below the purchase price of equivalent homes.
- Treating people as case numbers and demonstrating complete bureaucratic insensitivity to their stress, suffering and pain.
- Ignoring the critical needs of "fenceline communities" (along the borders of a Superfund site or a buy-out zone) even though homeowners from these neighborhoods suffer great losses in property value and are often unable to get insurance, sell their homes or get mortgages. People move out, but no one moves in. The community slowly dies.[93]

By 2006, CERCLA had permanently restored 294 (or 21 percent) of the 1,375 sites on the EPA's list of the worst toxic sites in the nation. Only sites that make the list qualify for the funds necessary for a thorough, *remedial* cleanup, so contaminated communities must fight hard just to make the National Priorities List. Sites that don't qualify for remedial cleanup may qualify for a "removal" cleanup, designed to temporarily contain or control the toxic threat. CERCLA has performed more than 7,000 of these removal cleanups since 1980. In addition, the Government Accountability Office estimates that there are between 150,000 and 500,000 toxic sites that remain completely unaddressed by CERCLA.[94]

Even as CERCLA's cleanup funds run dry, Superfund has evolved beyond conducting cleanups at traditional hazardous sites. It has been used to respond to acts of toxic terrorism and natural disasters such as the World Trade Center collapse and the devastating Midwest floods of 1993. Environmentalists believe Superfund could provide essential revenues for cleaning up Hurricane Katrina's toxic aftermath if its trust fund was restored, but the Bush administration seemed determined to prevent this.[95]

An empty cleanup fund has multiple negative consequences. If the EPA cannot initiate cleanups, it is unable to respond to emergencies or leverage polluter cleanups with the threat of triple charges. Also, without the threat of costly cleanup liability, toxic waste generators may try to side-step RCRA's expensive disposal and treatment procedures by returning to their old habit of midnight dumping.

---

[93] *Proceedings: Superfund Relocation Roundtable Meeting.* Pensacola Civic Center (May 2–4, 1996). http://www.epa.gov/compliance/resources/publications/ej/nejac/nejacmtg/roundtable-relocation-0596.pd.
[94] Fidis, Alex (December 2005).
[95] US-PIRG. *Superfund 25th Anniversary Report Finds America's Safety Net is Weakest When Needed Most Groups Call on EPA Superfund to Lead Hurricane Katrina and Rita Pollution Cleanup with Special Appropriation.* http://www.besafenet.com/NarrativeSuperfundReport.pdf.

Before RCRA became law, industry often cast its untreated hazardous wastes into the same garbage dumps used by everyone. There it mixed, mingled with and eventually transformed more benign forms of rubbish into toxic trash. Hazardous chemicals were routinely stored in unlabeled containers, transported by haulers who had no idea what they were carrying and discarded anywhere polluters could discreetly get rid of them. These careless practices left the country pockmarked with thousands of toxic ravines, fetid beaches, noxious bays and poisonous rivers.

In creating RCRA, Congress' central concern was to protect the public and the environment from these dangerous wastes. To this end, much of RCRA is devoted to creating strict procedures for the containment, transport, treatment and disposal of hazardous and "non-hazardous" solid wastes. However, RCRA lawmakers admitted that simply promoting safer methods of storage and disposal was ultimately a costly, losing battle and that the best solution to the hazardous wastes problem was "source reduction" – to avoid producing them. As part of RCRA, Congress advocated a policy of source reduction that closely resembles a somewhat broader approach that goes by at least three names: *Clean Production, Zero Waste and Industrial Ecology.*[96]

Industrial Ecology is an integrated, holistic system that endeavors to meet the goal of generating Zero Waste by employing Clean Production technologies and practices in every aspect of the economic process. Industrial Ecology aims to fundamentally change the way materials flow through society. Philosophically, it rests on the realization that the wastefulness of our industrial society is compromising the ability of nature to sustain our needs and the needs of future generations. In practice, Clean Production focuses on establishing a broad social commitment to source reduction, waste prevention and recycling.

Industrial Ecology looks at "waste" not as a problem to be buried or burned but as an opportunity to recover valuable resources, create jobs, save money and reduce pollution. Clean Production strikes at the heart of the waste problem by tackling the way products are designed and changing the way waste is handled so that products last longer, materials are recycled, or, in the case of organics, composted.

Industrial Ecology is enthusiastically endorsed by environmentalists and is being pioneered by leading corporations, municipalities and progressive governments around the world.[97] By calling for source reduction, Congress and RCRA are paying lip service to the importance of this approach as the ultimate remedy to the hazardous waste dilemma. Yet, in practice, source reduction has been either marginalized or simply ignored. There are several reasons why source reduction has been shunned. They speak volumes about the fundamental inability of our political and economic system to sacrifice short-range profit and power to protect the long-range health of the public and the environment.

---

[96] Chalfan, Larry. "Industrial Ecology: The Path to Sustainability," *Zero Waste Alliance* (October 16, 1999). http://www.zerowaste.org/publications/ie_pres/index.html; *Extended Producer Responsibility: A Prescription for Clean Production, Pollution Prevention and Zero Waste* (July 2003). http://www.grm.org/epr/epr_principles.html.

[97] *The Case for Zero Waste.* http://www.zerowaste.org/case.htm; *Clean Production Action* (July 2003). http://www.cleanproduction.org/Steps.Closed.Zero.php.

Of course, Congress could move toward a Zero Waste policy by simply ordering industries to begin phasing out all toxic substances from their production processes and waste streams. This type of technology-forcing legislation has worked successfully with lead in gasoline and CFCs in all their applications. When sources of toxic waste cannot be completely eliminated, often they can be transformed into useful products such as compost. Some success has been made in the breeding of bacteria that convert toxic organic waste into less dangerous forms. There are also treatments for some toxic wastes that can reduce their hazardous characteristics and make them safer for landfill or reuse.

However, in the eyes of most CEOs and politicians, Zero Waste has one giant drawback: Clean Production policies would require companies to be accountable to the public for their decisions. Inevitably, this would limit the freedom companies now have to make the products they wish with the materials and methods they like, with little regard for the consequences to the environment or public health. The sanctity of this corporate prerogative is enshrined in RCRA's specific commitment to avoid interference in the production process.[98] This commitment frustrates any movement toward source reduction. In practice, the EPA's desire to avoid meddling in production decisions has subordinated the need for public and environmental protection to the profit-driven prerogative of the private corporation.

Another reason why the EPA remains unenthusiastic about source reduction is its illicit relationship with the powerful waste management industry. Waste management has become one of the largest businesses in America and, in many respects, the industry owes its existence and continued success to the EPA. Conversely, many high-ranking EPA officials owe their post-EPA careers to the waste management industry.[99]

The EPA has formed a tacit alliance with the corporate giants of the waste management industry such as Chemical Waste Management, Integrated Environmental Services Inc. (IESI), Browning-Ferris (BFI), Waste Management Inc. (WMI), Allied Waste and Rollins Environmental Services.[100] These multinational, mega-waste

---

[98] As the committee report accompanying the House version of the 1976 Act explained in the provisions applicable to generators of hazardous wastes, "rather than place restrictions on the generation of hazardous waste, which in many instances would amount to interference with the production process itself, the committee has limited the responsibility of the generator of hazardous waste to one of providing information." See: Percival, Robert V., Alan S. Miller, Christopher H. Schroeder & James P. Leape. *Environmental Regulation: Law, Science and Policy.* (Boston, MA: Little, Brown & Co.), 1992: 217.

[99] Scores of federal and state employees have gone on to careers in the hazardous-waste industry, including three out of the five EPA administrators. (Of the other two, one left the agency in disgrace and one was a millionaire already.)

[100] It may appear that there are many local waste management firms, but these are usually subsidiaries of the few giant firms. Setting up hundreds of subsidiaries is a key part of the industry's grand strategy for profiting from the nation's waste crisis. Creating many subsidiaries has major advantages. It reduces the company's tax burden and, more importantly, each subsidiary has only limited assets, so if they get sued for harming people or the environment, they quickly become an empty pocket. The parent company is shielded from liability. See: Montague, Peter. "What We Must Do – Part 5: Winning Corporate Strategies," *Rachel's Hazardous Waste News #93* (September 5, 1988). http://www.ejnet.org/rachel/rhwn093.htm.

corporations own most of the landfills and all the incinerators in this country and have branched out into other countries as well. Many of the corporate officers running these firms – such as William Ruckelshaus, Douglas Costle, Walter Barber, Lee Thomas and Joan Bernstein – were the same EPA officials who wrote and "enforced" the regulations that created the modern waste management industry.[101]

This incestuous relationship runs deep. Various deputy, acting, assistant and regional EPA administrators, as well as several enforcement attorneys, have moved into high-level positions with these firms. Currently, many top EPA officials – the ones who make policy – can look forward to lucrative jobs in this industry when they retire from government service. In fact, a 1993 study found that 80 percent of the top EPA officials who worked in the area of hazardous waste after 1980 joined firms involved in Superfund cleanups and RCRA hazardous waste disposal.[102] In addition, these corporations have a long history of making generous campaign contributions to politicians from the president down to the local level. Therefore, it is hardly surprising that government has decided it has an obligation to provide the waste management business with the things it needs to keep their profit margins climbing.

The EPA works closely with waste management to portray the industry as green and environmentally sound. But commercial waste management is a private business, not a community service. As such, it aims to maximize income and minimize costs. Taking in wastes through the gate produces income; costs are incurred by treating the waste so that it won't poison people and the environment.

Therefore, one of the keys to profitability in this industry is a steady abundant flow of waste to dispose of. In fact, until 1994, most waste incinerators insisted on "put-or-pay" contracts with local governments, stipulating that they must deliver a guaranteed tonnage of waste or pay a stiff penalty. This definitely put a crimp in any community's campaign to "reduce, reuse and recycle." Fortunately, this illicit "flow control" practice was ruled unconstitutional by the Supreme Court.[103]

Besides increased tonnage, profit is generated by finding the cheapest ways to dispose of the waste taken in. Obviously, waste management's bottom-line interests sharply conflict with the needs of the public and the environment, which require the safest, most effective treatment and disposal of a steadily shrinking waste stream. Yet, when disputes arise, the EPA has generally sided with industry.

In fact, the EPA's own rules have forced local municipalities, state environmental agencies and the EPA itself to become heavily dependent on a few noncompetitive waste management companies to haul and dispose of the nation's growing volume of waste. In 1991, the EPA enacted RCRA regulations that required the country's 6,500 municipal garbage dumps to install liners and leachate collection systems

---

[101] Griscom, Amanda. "The EPA's Revolving Door," Salon.com (April 30, 2004). http://dir.salon. com/story/opinion/feature/2004/04/30/muck_epa/print.html.

[102] Hackett, Steven C. *Environmental and Natural Resources Economics: Theory, Policy, and the Sustainable Society*, 2nd ed. (Armonk, NY: M. E. Sharpe), 2001: 167–8.

[103] On May 16, 1994, the U.S. Supreme Court struck down an ordinance of Clarkstown, New York that required all nonhazardous solid waste generated within the town to be deposited at a town-sponsored transfer station constructed and operated by a private contractor (Carbone v. Clarkstown, 1994 W. L. 183594).

within two years or shut down. These regulations were touted as an essential part of the effort to control the migration of hazardous chemicals from dumpsites.

However, by the agency's own admission, the new RCRA mandated liners and leachate collection systems were not environmentally sound and were sure to leak as their liners broke down.[104] According to the EPA's official handbook on the subject, "eventually liners will either degrade, tear or crack and will allow liquids to migrate out of the unit."[105] In fact, so many of these high-tech disposal sites have already failed that 20 percent of today's Superfund sites were formerly RCRA-regulated disposal sites.[106]

Since these new containment technologies were unaffordable for most communities, they had to close their local dumps and contract with major regional or statewide corporate disposal facilities to handle their wastes.[107] Thus, instead of 6,500 local dumps, the nation was left with about 1,000 large regional dumps, owned and operated huge waste companies such as Browning-Ferris Industries (BFI), WMI, Safety-Kleen, Allied Waste and Chambers Development. Under these conditions, competition was strangled and waste management firms were free to charge ever-higher prices for their services because they could simply deny other haulers access to their dumpsites and incinerators.

In some large cities such as New York, competition in the waste hauling business was already extinct. Waste hauling and disposal had been dominated by organized crime for decades and crime bosses made sure the industry was anything but competitive. Consequently, many cheered when Browning-Ferris worked with law enforcement to break the mob's grip on the waste industry in New York and New Jersey.[108] Yet, as soon as their grip was broken, the major waste firms moved in and began jacking-up their prices and copying many of the mob's practices, only on a broader scale.[109] According to one small waste hauler squeezed out of business by the

---

[104] The EPA contends that the protective parts of landfills – the liners and leachate collections systems – will last about 30–100 years. The manufacturers of liners only guarantee their products for twenty years. EPA's own regulations only require landfill operators to try to protect the environment for 30 years after a dump is filled and closed. If they meet their design potential, modern landfills will protect the environment only until our grandchildren start paying taxes. If they don't meet their design potential – and experience tells us many won't – they will pollute the land and water of our children.

[105] U.S. Environmental Protection Agency, *Lining of Waste Impoundments and Disposal Facilities [Sw-870]* (Springfield, VA: National Technical Information Service), March 1983.

[106] Clifford, Mary. *Environmental Crime*. (MD: Aspen Publishers), 1998: 393.

[107] These new facilities cost upwards of $10 million. Many of the old dumps became Superfund sites.

[108] Some scholars have produced convincing evidence that organized crime was never really ousted from its hegemonic position over the solid and hazardous waste disposal business in these areas. Instead, they assert, the mafia quietly "merged" with legitimate industry and colluded with corrupt government officials to maintain their lucrative position in this business. See: Block, Alan & Frank Scarpitti, 1985.

[109] As of 1984, BFI was under investigation in seven states for suspected monopolistic practices such as price-fixing, charges that it denied but often settled out of court for amounts totaling $15 million by 1989. The problem was intensified in 1985, when a BFI toxic dump in Williamsburg, Ohio, was repeatedly closed by both state and federal environmental authorities. A grand jury also brought criminal charges against BFI for contaminating a nearby stream.

majors, "the only difference between the majors and 'the boys' [the mob] is that the majors don't actually kill you."[110] Thus, instead of providing any lasting environmental benefits, the EPA's landfill rules cost the public about $33 million only to force local garbage facilities out of business and put the nation's waste-disposal needs at the mercy of a few powerful uncompetitive corporations.[111]

As a consequence, government became so dependent on the services provided by a few multinational waste disposal firms that it couldn't afford to crack down on them, even though they were some of the country's worst criminal polluters. Most waste management companies have extensive criminal rap sheets. For example, both WMI and BFI have long sordid criminal histories involving price fixing, bid rigging, insider trading and fraud, as well as scores of environmental offenses.[112]

Yet the EPA balks at canceling their business licenses or barring them from taking government contracts. "If we blacklist hazardous waste haulers in an area where they are the only haulers, we put ourselves in a bad situation. We need someone to move that waste," admitted Bob Meunier, compliance chief for an EPA grants division. The director of the agency's enforcement branch, Elaine Stanley, agreed, "They have facilities located in areas where we need to use them. We don't have too much of a choice in some cases."[113]

It appears that the EPA even avoids imposing substantial penalties for fear of harming their associates in the waste industry. Fines are often bargained away. After stalling and haggling for 2 years over a $2.2 fine for illegally dumping toxic hospital waste, WMI convinced the EPA to fine them only $423. According to Laurel Price, New Jersey's assistant attorney general, "criminal fines amount to little more than a license to pollute. The deterrent is not great."[114]

By the mid-1980s, a growing number of communities were refusing to put up with the expense and danger of hazardous and solid waste landfills. As the perils became obvious, Congress enacted amendments to RCRA that severely restricted the land disposal of hazardous waste. The EPA's revised RCRA rules required states to come up with another plan for disposing of their hazardous wastes by 1989 or lose Superfund cleanup monies. But instead of moving toward source reduction and zero waste, the large waste disposal firms enlisted the EPA and the Department of Energy into their campaign to promote incineration as the ideal way to deal with toxic waste. This had the effect of pitting communities who feared they would lose their Superfund cleanup monies against those who refused to allow hazardous waste incinerators into their neighborhoods.

Suspicions about the safety of incineration surfaced almost immediately. They only deepened when state and local government officials – from Taylor County,

---

[110] Royte, Elizabeth. *Garbage Land*. (NY: Little, Brown & Co.), 2003: 73.
[111] Montague, Peter. "EPA's New Landfill Rules Protect Only the Largest Garbage Haulers," *Rachel's Hazardous Waste News* #268 (January 15, 1992). http://www.ejnet.org/rachel/rhwn268.htm.
[112] Royte, Elizabeth, 2003: 71.
[113] Montague, Peter. "What We Must Do – Part 4: A License to Pollute," *Rachel's Hazardous Waste News* #91 (August 22, 1988). http://www.ejnet.org/rachel/rhwn091.htm.
[114] Montague, Peter. (August 22, 1988).

Georgia to Kern County, California – were caught making secret deals with waste management firms to locate hazardous waste incinerators in poor, rural and minority communities behind the backs of their citizens.[115]

When secrecy failed, big waste firms tried to buy community acquiescence to hazardous waste incinerators by promising jobs, paying waste taxes to local governments and making donations to educational programs and community projects. At the national level, industry CEOs tried to head off opposition and establish their green bona fides by contributing large sums to major environmental organizations and getting themselves appointed to their managing boards.[116]

EPA and industry hype made incineration sound wonderful. Incineration firms gave themselves green names such as U.S .Ecology and American Ecology Corporation and portrayed themselves as environmentally sound recyclers – turning toxic trash into energy. Their trade association – the Environmental Technology Council – assured the public that modern incinerators were not the old inefficient waste incinerators of yesteryear.[117]

To get the point across, they renamed their incinerators Waste-To-Energy plants (WTEs). They claimed that by using the latest scrubbers, electrostatic precipitators, flue-gas cleaners and combustion controls, WTEs could convert a single day's trash into enough electricity to power 50,000 homes, all while meeting state and federal air quality regulations.[118] In fact, they boasted, "If all air emission sources were as well designed, controlled, operated and regulated as hazardous waste incinerators, we would not have an air pollution problem in this country today."[119]

Of course, their strategy was to make incineration sound beneficial while either buying off or discrediting environmentalist and neighborhood opposition. The industry hoped their tactics would isolate any local protest movements that arose in remote rural areas or poor minority communities from the sympathy and support of national environmental organizations and put them at odds with coopted municipal governments and county officials in their area. If their cause gained any media coverage at all, incinerator protestors would be portrayed as hysterical, irrational, selfish NIMBY know-nothings. Some major environmental groups were successfully silenced with industry money. They chose to ignore or minimize the dangers of hazardous waste incineration and refused to support grassroots community opposition. But others, such as Greenpeace, refused to take the bait.

Despite industry's best efforts, resistance to incineration became intense and relentless. Greenpeace allied itself with numerous community groups fighting

[115] Office of Planning & Research for Governor Gray Davis. *Environmental Justice in California State Government* (October 2003). http://www.opr.ca.gov/planning/publications/ OPR_ EJ_Report_Oct2003.pdf; Greenpeace Video. *Rush to Burn* (1988).

[116] For example, WMI's founder, Dean Buntrock and its chief executive, Phil Rooney. See: Montague, Peter. "WMI: A Culture of Fraud and Dishonesty," *Rachel's Democracy & Health News #556* (July 24, 1997). http://www.rachel.org/bulletin/bulletin.cfm?Issue_ID=567.

[117] The ETC website is: http://www.etc.org/whoistheetc/.

[118] Royte, Elizabeth, 2003: 77.

[119] "Hazardous Waste Incineration: Advanced Technology to Protect the Environment," *The Environmental Technology Council.* http://www.etc.org/technologicalandenvironmentalissues/treatmenttechnologies/incineration/.

incinerators. By the early 1990s, hazardous waste incinerators, and the web of regulations intended to make them operate safely, were under scathing criticism from government scientists, private researchers and even the *Wall Street Journal*.[120]

After Greenpeace obtained and publicized several suppressed EPA studies on incineration that refuted their rosy hype, agency officials and private research scientists were forced to admit that hazardous waste incinerators emit hundreds of times more dioxins and other toxic air pollutants than EPA regulations allow.[121] Jeff Bailey's *Wall Street Journal* article exposed a record of malfunctions, including explosions and major releases of toxins that incinerator operators had covered up and EPA officials seemed powerless to curtail.[122]

Clearly, the whole truth behind incineration was far more complicated and considerably less rosy than officialdom wanted to admit. Although state-of-the-art incinerators can reduce or filter out some of the dangerous effluents pouring from their smokestacks – such as sulfur dioxide, carbon monoxide and nitrogen oxides – many other noxious WTE emissions still poison our lungs.

WTE smokestacks release radioactive materials and toxic heavy metals (arsenic, lead, chromium, cadmium, beryllium and mercury) that cannot be destroyed by incineration. In addition, incinerators release products of incomplete combustion (PICs). PICs include some of the most deadly chemicals known to science, such as furans and dioxins. Chemical analyses of the PICs in smokestack emissions have revealed the presence of 192 volatile organic compounds.[123]

A major blow to the waste industry's sanguine picture of incineration came in Arkansas. A week before he became president, Governor Bill Clinton ordered the EPA to burn twenty two million pounds of dioxin-laced toxic waste abandoned by the VERTAC corporation of Jacksonville. A majority of Jacksonville's citizens had expressed their opposition to incineration through referendums and public meetings, but Governor Clinton and EPA officials ignored their protests and insisted the VERTAC incinerator would emit zero dioxin into the surrounding community.[124]

This lie was exposed when Pat Costner of Greenpeace caught government scientists falsifying the results of dioxin blood level tests.[125] By the time the VERTAC incineration was halted by a federal judge, the dioxin blood levels of nearby residents had risen 22 percent. The incineration itself was a drastic failure; it transformed the

[120] Bailey, Jeff. "Concerns Mount Over Operating Methods of Plants That Incinerate Toxic Waste," *Wall Street Journal* (March 20, 1992): B1, B5.

[121] Costner, Pat. *The Incineration of Dioxin in Jacksonville, Arkansas: A Review of Trial Burns and Related Air Monitoring at VERTAC Site Contractors Incinerator, Jacksonville, AR.* (Washington, DC: Greenpeace Toxics Campaign), January 29, 1992.

[122] Bailey, Jeff (March 20, 1992): B1, B5.

[123] Montague, Peter. "Incinerator News," *Rachel's Democracy and Health News #592* (April 2, 1998). http://www.rachel.org/BULLETIN/index.cfm?St=4.

[124] Montague, Peter. "Corruption Out of Control in Arkansas," *Rachel's Democracy and Health News #345* (July 8, 1993) & *#311* (November 12, 1992). http://www.ejnet.org/rachel/rhwn345.htm; http://www.ejnet.org/rachel/rhwn311.htm.

[125] Stelzer, C. D. "Weak in Math," *Riverfront Times* (July 12, 1995). http://lists.essential.org/1996/dioxin-l/msg00784.html.

9,600 drums of organochlorine waste into 13,730 drums of dioxin-laced residue for a net gain of 43 percent![126]

Real-world incinerators operate at considerably lower levels of efficiency and safety than the claims made for them by WTE operators and their friends in government. In the VERTAC case mentioned previously, Judge Reasoner asked the EPA's attorney if he could produce the data to prove VERTAC's incinerator actually destroyed hazardous wastes at the level of efficiency the agency claimed it could. The EPA lawyer's response: "No sir, we could not."[127]

By law, incinerators must destroy 99.99 percent of the hazardous materials they burn. This means that an incinerator burning 10,000 tons of hazardous waste per day can lawfully spew one ton of toxic chemicals into the air every twenty-four hours.[128] After this legal level of efficiency is achieved in a controlled test burn, the incinerator's actual daily smokestack emissions are rarely monitored by anyone except the incinerator operators.[129]

However, trial burns are poor indicators of burn efficiency on a daily basis. During trial burns, when licensing is at stake and EPA officials are watching, operators make sure that all systems are operating at peak efficiency: waste feed, temperature, oxygen flow and pollution control devices are carefully maintained to optimize performance. However, on a day-to-day basis, smokestack emissions may be considerably more toxic. Internal EPA records revealed that, among the eight major hazardous waste incinerators studied, none could achieve 99.99 percent destruction rate required by law.[130] Consequently, the EPA simply didn't bother to enforce its own standards. When violators were identified it was almost always the work of vigilant citizens or whistleblower employees, not EPA inspectors.[131]

And then there is incinerator ash. The toxics filtered out by the scrubbers and screens designed to improve the safety of a WTE's smokestack emissions must go somewhere. So the chromium, copper, manganese, lead, arsenic, dioxin and vanadium removed from the plume now collects in the filters or falls through the grates on the boiler's floor to become incinerator ash. But RCRA contained a loophole that exempted this ash from being *legally* defined as hazardous even though it was highly toxic. Consequently, WTEs could sidestep the expense of handling their toxic ash

---

[126] Montague, Peter. "A Sea of Troubles Engulfs Incineration," *Rachel's Democracy and Health News #325* (February 17, 1993). http://www.rachel.org/bulletin/index.cfm?issue_ID=804.

[127] Montague, Peter. (February 17, 1993).

[128] If the rate of efficiency were to fall by just 0.99 percent, 100 tons of toxic chemicals would be dumped into the atmosphere.

[129] Montague, Peter. "All Hazardous Waste Incinerators Fail to Meet EPA Regulations, EPA Says," *Rachel's Hazardous Waste News #280* (April 7, 1992). http://www.ejnet.org/rachel/rhwn280.htm; Montague, Peter. "Hazardous Waste Incinerators: A Technology Out of Control?" *Rachel's Hazardous Waste News #281* (April 15, 1992). http://www.ejnet.org/rachel/rhwn281.htm; Montague, Peter. "A Sea of Troubles Engulfs Incineration," *Rachel's Democracy and Health News #325* (February 17, 1993). http://www.rachel.org/bulletin/index.cfm?issue_ID=804.

[130] Trenholm, A. et al. *Performance Evaluation of Full-Scale Hazardous Waste Incinerators. vol. I, Executive Summary.* [EPA/600/2- 84/181A]. (Washington, DC: U.S. Environmental Protection Agency), 1984.

[131] Bailey, Jeff (March 20, 1992): B1, B5.

like hazardous waste. Instead, they deposited it in sanitary landfills as if it were household rubbish.[132]

In 1994, this exemption was eliminated when the Supreme Court ruled that RCRA does not allow toxic ash to be disposed of as nonhazardous waste.[133] So the EPA came up with a new trick. It allowed incinerator operators to transform their mountains of toxic ash into cash by "recycling" them into cement. Both WTEs and many unlicensed boilers and kilns (operating on the grounds of industrial plants) were legally allowed to burn toxic waste, mix their toxic ash with other materials, and sell it. According to industry and the EPA, this mixture called "aggregate" can be safely folded into cement and used for road building and construction. Industry scientists and PR flacks contend that once the ash is mixed into these construction materials it is "locked away" and therefore no longer hazardous.[134]

This safety claim is a treacherous combination of denial and wishful thinking. Waste management studies provide some evidence that ash wastes, mixed with lime or cement, may remain "locked away" for a time. But they have no data on the long-term durability of this material because it hasn't been around long enough. Critics list a number of known factors that make it impossible for cement-ash mixtures to remain intact for long.[135] In the words of respected incinerator critic, Peter Montague:

> The fundamental problem is the unlimited duration of the hazard. Lead, cadmium, arsenic and other toxic metals simply do not degrade as time passes. They remain toxic, waiting to poison the next generation, or the generation after that, as soon as the waste "containment" system breaks down. The hazard is of infinite duration, but human "containment" systems are all subject to the ravages of time. Humans have never constructed anything that lasts "forever," yet the natural hazards of heavy metals DO last forever. That is the fundamental problem facing the producers of incinerator ash; it is the very same problem faced by those who create radioactive wastes.[136]

WTE operators are really not concerned about the long run. Instead, they're betting that they'll be long gone by the time serious problems arise. This is just another version of the all-too-familiar "out of sight out of mind" attitude that gave us Love Canal, Times Beach and every other Superfund site.

[132]   Montague, Peter. "Incinerator Ash – Part 2: All Wastes Must Go Somewhere Forever," *Rachel's Democracy and Health News* (July 18, 1990). http://www.rachel.org/bulletin/bulletin.cfm?Issue_ID=1547.

[133]   The Supreme Court's decision was the result of extensive efforts by the Environmental Defense Fund (EDF) to force regulation of incinerator ash as RCRA hazardous waste. Environmental Defense Fund v. Wheelabrator Technologies, Inc.

[134]   Forrester, Keith E. & Richard W. Goodwin, "Engineering Management of MSW Ashes: Field Empirical Observations of Concrete-like Characteristics." in Theodore G. Brna & Raymond Klicius, eds., Vol. I of *Proceedings International Conference on Municipal Waste Combustion* (April 11–14, 1989/Hollywood, FL): 5b–16.

[135]   Montague, Peter. "Incinerator Ash – Part 4: Dump Now, Let the Children Pay Later," *Rachel's Democracy and Health Weekly #192* (August 1, 1990). http://www.rachel.org/bulletin/bulletin.cfm?Issue_ID=943.

[136]   Montague, Peter. (August 1, 1990).

The "burn it up" option requires only incinerators and an EPA willing to ignore their perils. In sharp contrast, the zero waste approach requires thought, planning, investment in new technologies, and a commitment to the health of our children and grandchildren and to social values that reach beyond the next quarter's profit margins.

Widespread grassroots opposition made it impossible for the waste industry to build the 200–250 new incinerators they hoped would be burning 75 percent of the nation's waste by 1992. In the face of stiff opposition, no new WTE's were built after 1996; by 2005, there were only 90 licensed WTEs operating in the country.[137]

Citizens took on the incineration industry in many ways. A frontal assault was launched to halt incineration at the local level. In addition, communities developed waste reduction, recycling and composting programs that starved incinerators by diverting trash. Eighty percent of solid waste can be recycled and composted. However, communities that build incinerators must feed them, thus they foreclose their recycling and composting options for the lifetime of the furnace.

In the 15-year period between 1980 and 1995, a broad-based, loosely organized movement against incineration blocked the construction of 300 incinerators across the country. But while incinerators, especially *hazardous* waste incinerators, met a wall of grassroots resistance, more hazardous waste was being burned than ever before. The EPA quietly decided to bypass the licensing and community approval procedures that stymied the construction of hazardous waste incinerators. The agency's "solution" to this dilemma was to allow industrial boilers and cement kilns to burn toxic waste as "recycled fuel"; this renaming gimmick exempted them from RCRA's toxic waste disposal licensing and permitting requirements.

Back in 1980, Congress exempted "recycled" chemical wastes from control under RCRA. Based on this exemption, the EPA ruled that toxic waste burned as fuel in boilers and industrial furnaces (BIFs)[138] was being recycled and, therefore, was exempt from RCRA regulation.[139] Enormous quantities of hazardous waste escaped RCRA's disposal regulations through this loophole. Instead of paying to get rid of their toxic trash at expensive state-of-the-art incinerators, businesses found they could save money by magically renaming their hazardous waste "recycled fuel" for combustion

---

[137] See: Montague, Peter. "The Recent History of Solid Waste: Good Alternatives Are Now Available," *Rachel's Hazardous Waste News #28* (June 10, 1992). http://www.ejnet.org/rachel/rhwn289.htm; Royte, Elizabeth, 2003: 81.

[138] Boilers and Industrial Furnaces (BIFs) that burn toxic waste are sometimes referred to as HWCs – Hazardous Waste Combustors.

[139] The trend toward sending hazardous waste to cement kilns was also encouraged by EPA's decision to exclude hazardous waste sent to BIFs for "recycling" as fuel from the reporting requirements of the Emergency Planning and Community Right to Know Act of 1986. Prior to 1988, hazardous waste generators were required to report wastes shipped off-site for "reuse as fuel/fuel blending" on EPA's Toxics Release Inventory (TRI) forms. In that year, however, EPA decided that wastes that were "recycled" (including wastes used as fuel) would no longer have to be reported in the TRI forms. Generators could thus ship wastes to BIFs or to fuel blending operations and claim credit for reducing the amount of waste "released" to the environment. This provided a strong incentive to send wastes to BIFs for "recycling."

in cement kilns and industrial furnaces.[140] In the words of Clinton's EPA chief, Carol Browner, "We have one set of standards for hazardous waste incinerators. We have another, weaker set of standards for cement kilns."[141]

Under Clinton, the BIF regulations appeared to become stricter. However, of the 925 boilers burning toxic waste in operation when the new BIF rule was finalized, 600 of them were virtually exempt because they qualified as "small quantity burners."[142] By 1995, 90 percent of all liquid hazardous waste was being burned in these less efficient, minimally regulated BIFs instead of RCRA-licensed incinerators.[143] Fifty billion pounds of toxic waste were being torched in these industrial boilers, furnaces and kilns, while only five billion pounds were incinerated in officially regulated WTEs.[144]

Hugh Kaufman, an engineer in the EPA's Office of Solid Waste, charged that BIF regulations were specifically tailored to benefit the cement kiln industry. According to Kaufman, the EPA:

> . . . appears to be engaged in a pattern and practice of accommodating the regulated cement kiln hazardous waste incineration industry with nonexistent, or at best loose, regulation . . . As a direct result of the lack of the RCRA regulations, many sectors of the cement kiln industry have been transformed into major commercial hazardous waste disposal companies. The public and the environment have not been protected from the adverse consequence of these incineration activities.[145]

[140] Richardson, J. D., & Mark A. *Recycling or Disposal? Hazardous Waste Combustion in Cement Kilns: An Introduction to Policy and Legal Issues Associated with Burning Hazardous Waste in Cement Kilns* (A Briefing Paper of the American Lung Association Hazardous Waste Incineration Project, April 1995); Montague, Peter. "Hazardous Waste Incineration in Cement Kilns: 'Recycler's' Paradise," & "Citizens Slow Growth of Incineration," *Rachel's Democracy & Health News #174* (March 1990), & *206* (November 1990). http://www.rachel.org/bulletin/index. cfm?St=4.

[141] Browner, Carol. EPA Administrator (July 28, 1995). Quoted in: *Myths and Facts About Protecting Human Health and the Environment: The Real Story About Burning Hazardous Waste in Cement Kilns.* http://www.downwindersatrisk.org/ DARNCCKC Myths And Facts About Burning Hazardous WasteIn CementKilns.htm.

[142] Kopel, David B. "Burning Mad: The Controversy Over Treatment of Hazardous Waste in Incinerators, Boilers, and Industrial Furnaces," *Environmental Law Reporter* (April 1993): 10216–27. http://davekopel.org/env/ipincine.htm.

[143] Federal law imposes some requirements on hazardous waste-burning kilns located within municipalities with populations of at least 500,000, but all kilns currently burning hazardous waste are located in or near smaller communities.

[144] These figures come from: Montague, Peter. "Hazardous Waste Incineration in Cement Kilns: 'Recycler's' Paradise," *Rachel's Democracy & Health News #174 & 206* (March 28, 1990). http://www. ejnet.org/rachel/rhwn174.htm; similar, but somewhat different figures are given by: Richardson, J.vD. & A. Mark. *Recycling or Disposal? Hazardous Waste Combustion in Cement Kilns: An Introduction to Policy and Legal Issues Associated with Burning Hazardous Waste in Cement Kilns* (A Briefing Paper of the American Lung Association Hazardous Waste Incineration Project, April 1995). http://www.mindfully.org/Air/Cement-Kilns-Burning-WasteIntro.htm.

[145] Letter from Hugh Kaufman, an engineer with EPA's Office of Solid Waste, to William Reilly, Administrator, EPA (December 7, 1990). Quoted in: Kopel, David B. "Burning Mad: The Controversy Over Treatment of Hazardous Waste in Incinerators, Boilers, and Industrial

The EPA has issued some regulations and guidelines that may limit the emissions of certain toxic chemicals from the smokestacks of all hazardous waste combustion units, but these rules are being challenged in court and the jury is still out on their effectiveness.[146]

The cement industry brazenly claims to be doing society a big favor by burning toxic waste in its kilns. According to industry literature, "Using these wastes is a key service that cement companies can provide to society. As well as reducing the amount of fossil fuel needed to produce cement, it prevents large volumes of material from going to landfills or being burned in incinerators."[147] However, cement kilns are designed to make cement, not dispose of hazardous waste. A study by the U.S. Center for the Biology of Natural Systems, found that emissions of dioxins are eight times higher from cement kilns that burn hazardous waste than those that do not burn it.[148]

For some of the more shameless companies – such as Marine Shale Processors of Louisiana – producing cement "aggregate" became a false front for making money by illicitly hauling and incinerating hazardous waste.[149] According to the EPA, companies that claim to be burning hazardous waste for fuel in the production of another product (such as aggregate) are considered recyclers, not hazardous waste disposal facilities. There is virtually no EPA review process to check the claims of these "small quantity burners" or their operations. Thus, a fraudulent company, bent on making money through unregulated toxic waste disposal, has an easy time exploiting this RCRA loophole.[150]

One final alarming aspect of the toxic waste problem is the virtually unregulated disposal of toxic military wastes. The defense establishment has a long and sordid record of resisting congressional and grassroots attempts to identify and clean up vast stretches of public land poisoned by enormous quantities of hazardous waste. One of the few reliable accounts of this scandal is Seth Shulman's groundbreaking investigation, *The Threat at Home*.[151]

Furnaces," *Environmental Law Reporter* (April 1993): 10216–27. http://davekopel.org/env/ipincine.htm.

[146] According to the National Research Council, the EPA rules require incinerators to reduce emissions to a standard known as "maximum achievable control technology," or MACT. The NRC report says compliance with MACT regulations will diminish the exposure of local populations to emissions, but it is unclear what effect compliance will have on a metropolitan or regional scale, since little is known about the risks posed by collective emissions from several incinerators. See: NRC. *Waste Incineration and Public Health* (2000). http://books.nap.edu/catalog.php?record_id=5803.

[147] Baue, William. "Hazardous Waste as Fuel: Conservation or Corporate Irresponsibility?" *Social Funds Newsroom* (September 11, 2002). http://www.socialfunds.com/news/article.cgi/924.html.

[148] Greenpeace. *Types of Incineration.* http://www.greenpeace.org/international/campaigns/toxics/incineration/types-of-incineration.

[149] U.S. Department of Justice [Press Release]. "U.S., Louisiana Secure $35 Million Settlement with Two Companies to Clean Up Hazardous Waste and Reopen Incinerator," (September 12, 1997). http://www.usdoj.gov/opa/pr/1997/September97/379enr.html.

[150] Marine Shale Processors in Amelia, Louisiana, was finally closed down by EPA after national TV threw a spotlight on the corporation's malfeasance. It is hard to estimate how many others are doing the same and remain unidentified.

[151] Shulman, Seth. *The Threat at Home.* (NY: Beacon Press), 1992.

Shulman chronicles a ghastly toxic legacy of malfeasance, secrecy and cover-up perpetrated under the presumption of national security and tolerated under the specious legal doctrine known as "the unitary theory of the executive." The Reagan administration advanced this legal theory to justify Executive Order 12580, which forced the EPA to gain Justice Department approval before enforcing environmental laws against military installations and other federal facilities. Reagan wanted the defense establishment to vigorously pursue his arms race against the USSR without worrying about toxic collateral damage or the troublesome environmental laws they would violate.

The unitary theory of the executive asserted that the EPA could not bring legal action against the Department of Defense to enforce environmental compliance because one body of the executive branch cannot sue another. To prevent states from filing suit against military polluters within their borders, the administration advanced the doctrine of "sovereign immunity," which spared military facilities from paying any punitive fines issued by state environmental agencies.

After years of dodging environmental laws through these dubious legal exclusions, the Pentagon has become the nation's premier polluter. For decades it has flagrantly ignored all the EPA's final cleanup orders. The DOD discharges more than 750,000 tons of hazardous waste every year – more than the top three chemical corporations combined. In 2001, the EPA estimated that the cleanup costs of toxic military sites would exceed $350 billion – five times the Superfund liability of private industry.[152] Of the 1,255 sites on CERCLA's Superfund list, the Pentagon owns 129; the most of any entity. In addition, the DOD has about 25,000 other contaminated properties in all 50 states.[153]

Scores of military facilities across the country threaten nearby communities with highly toxic dumpsites, from Indiana's Jefferson Proving Ground and Nebraska's Cornhusker Ammunition Plant to the installation known as "Earth's most toxic square mile" – Colorado's Rocky Mountain Arsenal. Yet, no matter who sits in the Oval Office, the White House and the Justice Department have stymied every effort by community groups, state governments and the EPA to make the Pentagon obey environmental laws. Any reversal of this long-standing policy by the Obama administration would be a pleasant and extremely improbable surprise.

[152] Joshua, Frank. "The Pentagon is America's Biggest Polluter," *AlterNet* (May 12, 2008). http://www.alternet.org/healthwellness/85186/.

[153] Layton, Lyndsey. "Pentagon Fights EPA on Pollution Cleanup," *Washington Post* (June 30, 2008). http://www.truthout.org/article/pentagon-fights-epa-pollution-cleanup.

5

TSCA – The Toothless Tiger

The Toxic Substances Control Act (TSCA) bestows sweeping authority upon government officials. It empowers the EPA to completely ban or sharply restrict any potentially dangerous chemical. With such massive regulatory clout over chemical production, one would hardly expect TSCA to be popular with Monsanto, GE, Dow or DuPont – but it is. In fact, a phalanx of industry cheerleaders and bodyguards zealously defend TSCA from all critics and would-be reformers. The managing director of the American Chemistry Council raves, "TSCA not only protects health and the environment, it also fuels innovation."[1]

Industry's bewildering enthusiasm for TSCA is further confounded by its universal disrepute among environmentalists. No one in the Sierra Club, Friends of the Earth, Environmental Defense or Greenpeace has a good word to say about it. Ken Cook, of the Environmental Working Group, dismisses TSCA as a "largely toothless statute."[2] But how could anyone call a law toothless that thoroughly screens chemicals and keeps dangerous ones off the market? If this law is powerful enough to prevent further contamination of our country, eliminate toxins from our food, remove hazardous substances from the products we consume and reduce the tonnage of toxic waste, why aren't environmentalists singing its praises?

But maybe industry likes TSCA precisely because it isn't really the regulatory powerhouse it appears to be. Perhaps TSCA is a toothless tiger whose fierce regulatory countenance conceals its utter inability to prevent industry from concocting and selling any noxious substance (or should I say miracle product?) it can tempt us to buy. This would account for TSCA's shabby reputation among environmentalists as well as its popularity with industry. But do the facts bear out this explanation?

TSCA was not always the darling of the chemical industry. In fact, when it was introduced in 1972, the Chemical Manufacturers Association (CMA) launched a well-coordinated assault that nearly killed the act in Congress. The CMA vehemently

---

[1] Hogue, Cheryl. "The Future of U.S. Chemical Regulation: Two Views on Whether Current Law Overseeing Commercial Chemicals in the U.S. is Tough Enough," *Chemical & Engineering News* (January 8, 2007). 34–8. http://pubs.acs.org/cen/government/85/8502regulation.html.

[2] Brown, Mary Ashby. "Litigation Update. Key Teflon Chemical: Center of Lawsuits and Debates," *Sustainable Development Law & Policy* (May 2006). http://vlex.com/vid/335529.

resisted further government supervision of chemical safety. Company flacks claimed existing regulations were adequate, and TSCA would stifle innovation and ruin the industry. Today, these same industry mouthpieces extol TSCA for encouraging innovation and protecting public health.

Passing TSCA took four years, two high-profile environmental calamities and widespread public alarm to overcome industry intransigence and congressional inaction. The first environmental scandal to counteract legislative lethargy was the discovery that General Electric had been poisoning the Hudson River for 28 years by discreetly draining massive amounts of PCB-laden wastes into its waters.

The second trigger involved Kepone, a highly toxic and carcinogenic pesticide produced by the Life Sciences Chemical Plant of Hopewell, Virginia. The plant's negligent safety and disposal procedures resulted in the poisoning of its workers and the James River. These two tragedies unleashed a flurry of public concern about the rising tide of man-made chemical concoctions flooding the environment. *Time* magazine warned readers that "chemists are introducing new compounds at the rate of more than 1,000 a year" and encouraged Congress to enact a law that would "carefully spot and screen potentially hazardous substances before they get into the environment."[3] This is exactly what TSCA was supposed to do.

It was intended to be the mother of all toxic control laws. Unlike other statutes, TSCA possessed a proactive preventive mandate of sweeping breadth and scope. It could restrict or ban dangerous chemicals *before* they were marketed in specific products, used in particular settings or transformed into pollution. Because of its broad precautionary nature, ecology activists expected great things from TSCA, but they were sorely disappointed.

TSCA's regulatory fangs were knocked out in congressional back rooms where the embryonic act was assaulted by lobbyists from the pharmaceutical, nuclear power, cosmetic, pesticide, food and tobacco industries. Publicly, TSCA was heralded as a screening process for "all chemicals and mixtures," but behind closed doors, industry flacks insisted their products should get a free pass because they were already covered in some way by other statutes. So pesticides, tobacco, nuclear material, drugs, cosmetics and certain food additives were all excluded from TSCA's controls.

Section 6 of TSCA sounds quite strict. It gives EPA the authority to control any chemical that presents an *"unreasonable* risk of injury to health or the environment." However, *unreasonable* is a very slippery "wiggle-word" that chemical company lawyers have used time and time again to successfully challenge chemical regulation in court. In fact, the lead author of the GAO's 2004–2005 report on reforming TSCA contends that it could be significantly improved with a few simple word changes:

> Many of the changes recommended by GAO are simple word changes, such as requiring that the EPA show a chemical poses a "significant" rather than

---

[3] "Tragedy in Hopewell," *Time* (February 2, 1976).

"unreasonable" risk, or that it "may" rather than "will" present health risks. It sounds small, but in practice, it makes a huge difference.[4]

Since TSCA exempts chemical producers from demonstrating the safety of their products and forces the EPA to prove a chemical dangerous before imposing any controls, unbiased thorough chemical testing is essential. However, serious flaws in TSCA make careful, systematic, impartial testing impossible.

THE TESTING LOOPHOLE

From the beginning, industry was dead set against the government testing the safety of its chemicals, and Congress was well aware that no federal bureaucracy had the capacity to assess all the new substances deluging the market. National scientific institutions have a very limited capacity to conduct chemical safety research. For example, the National Toxicology Program (NTP), a consortium of eight federal agencies, manages to study the carcinogenic effects of 12 to 24 new substances each year.[5] Effects on the nervous, reproductive, immune and endocrine systems, and on major organs such as the kidneys, liver, heart and brain are simply not considered.

While the NTP busies itself studying the cancer effects of a few dozen chemicals, about 1,000 new compounds flood commercial markets. Fully evaluating the dangers of 1,000 new chemicals every year, especially in combination with the 70,000 already in use, is far beyond the budget of the EPA or any other governmental body. This lack of capacity, combined with industry's stiff opposition to government-controlled testing, convinced Congress to turn most chemical assessments over to the very companies seeking to market these new chemicals – hardly an objective source of information! Consequently, to make their case for regulating a chemical, the EPA is usually forced to rely on the incomplete, biased testing data provided by the company that wants to profit by marketing it.

TSCA's chemical testing system is tailor-made for deception and fraud. Procedures are obscure, results are subjective and regulators are outflanked and overwhelmed by an evaluation process easily manipulated by chemical manufacturers. The traditional definition of science as the pursuit of knowledge and understanding just doesn't apply in the rapacious world of chemical regulation. On this high-stakes battleground, industry wields science like a weapon. Ponderous reports, inscrutable studies and archaic language are strategically deployed to baffle, deceive, outmaneuver and disarm the EPA and the public.

In the same year TSCA gave industry responsibility for testing its own chemicals, lawmakers were confronted with alarming evidence that science had been conscripted and corrupted to serve the interests of the chemical producers. In April 1976,

---

[4] Quoted in: Monforton, Celeste. "Public Health Calls for TSCA Reform," *The Pump Handle* (November 13, 2007). http://thepumphandle.wordpress.com/2007/11/13/public-health-calls-for-tsca-reform/.
[5] See the NTP's website: http://ntp.niehs.nih.gov/.

Industrial Bio-Test Laboratories (IBT), the nation's premiere toxicology laboratory, was exposed as a fraud. At the time, IBT conducted 35–40 percent of all toxicology testing in the United States, including industry-financed tests submitted to the EPA and the FDA to verify the safety of thousands of products, from cosmetics and drugs to pesticides. After suspicions were raised by chemical studies that seemed too good to be true, regulators discovered that dozens of these studies were total fakes. Eventually, investigators determined that of the 10,000-plus studies used to gain safety approval over the years, the vast majority were "invalid." Yet many of these substances remain on the market.[6]

One FDA investigator concluded that IBT "was hell bent on providing their clients with favorable reports. They didn't care about good science. It was about money. They really had what was almost an assembly line for acceptable studies."[7] But IBT was only part of the problem. Soon evidence turned up that Monsanto executives knew their studies were phony but sent them to the EPA and the FDA anyway.[8] Some years later, Craven Laboratories was caught pulling the same scam.

Amazingly, none of these scandals moved the EPA to crack down on corrupt labs and fraudulent testing practices. The agency's oversight program is just shy of non-existent. An EPA Inspector General's report in 1991 found that the agency had never inspected 600 of the 800 labs conducting chemical safety studies and had audited only 1 percent of their 220,000 studies. In fact, the EPA had never issued a single civil or criminal penalty for laboratory malpractice.[9]

While blatant fraud on the level of IBT or Craven Labs may be rare – or just rarely uncovered – the sophisticated, subtle slanting of scientific studies is a constant and continuous practice among chemical companies determined to get their products to market. According to Nicolas Ashford, MIT professor of technology and policy, "It's possible to co-opt the system without telling a lie." Using animals that are resistant to cancer, keeping doses low, shortening the duration of an experiment and many other clever gimmicks can be employed to produce results that make chemicals seem less dangerous than they are.

Industry often gripes about the cost of testing their chemicals, but they are deeply opposed to handing this process over to government. Their goals are to maintain control over the chemical testing process and keep their requirements as limited and voluntary as possible. Limited testing saves money and maintains a veil of blissful ignorance around their "miracle" products; control over the testing process makes industry the sole source of "expert knowledge" surrounding their wares. Independent studies and government research pose a threat because they may contradict the rosy reputation industry likes to bestow upon their "wonder chemicals."

---

[6] Schneider, Kenneth. "Faking it: The Case Against IBT Laboratories," *Amicus Journal* (Spring 1983). http://planetwaves.net/contents/faking_it.html.

[7] Fagin, Dan & Marianne Lavelle. *Toxic Deception* (Monroe, LA: Common Courage), 1999: 34.

[8] Fagin, Dan & Marianne Lavelle, 1999: 34.

[9] Knoz, Kenneth A. Asst. Inspector for Audit, Office of the Inspector General, EPA, *Memorandum to Linda J. Fischer, Asst. Administrator for Prevention, Pesticides and Toxic Substances, EPA.* (September 30, 1992).

INNOCENT UNTIL PROVEN DANGEROUS

For testing and regulatory purposes, TSCA divides chemicals into two categories: existing (or old) chemicals and new chemicals. Section 5 of TSCA covers new chemicals; section 4 covers old chemicals. Any chemical not included in the TSCA's inventory of existing chemicals is considered "new," while those listed in the inventory are considered "old". The TSCA Inventory is a list of all chemical substances in commerce prior to December 1979. By volume, about 99 percent of all chemicals on the market today are considered existing chemical substances. To assess the potential dangers posed by these existing chemicals requires careful testing.

However, the EPA has even less authority to require tests for old chemicals than for new ones and TSCA's testing rules make further testing almost impossible. Over the objection of environmentalists, the agency decided that thorough testing of all substances listed in TSCA's inventory was unnecessary. Instead, an Interagency Testing Committee was empowered to categorize existing chemicals as high priority or not. High priority chemicals could require further testing because they were suspected of causing cancer, mutation or birth defects.

Of course, no manufacturer wants their chemical classified as high priority because this means it may be subject to further investigation and testing. Yet most of the information used to make the initial high priority determinations came from the manufacturers.[10] This gave manufacturers a strong motivation to minimize and sanitize the information it provided the EPA about its existing chemicals.

Once the Interagency Testing Committee placed a chemical on the high priority list, the EPA had 12 months to assess its risk or issue testing rules if it had insufficient data to make an assessment. Each time the agency wanted to test a particular chemical for a specific effect such as cancer, it had to go through a nearly impassable rule-making process. To require further testing, the agency needed to demonstrate to the court that the chemical may present an "unreasonable risk," but without further testing this was often impossible. Thus TSCA's test rules confounded the testing process by putting the agency in the classic Catch-22 conundrum: to get permission for further testing, it had to provide evidence of harm that could only be derived from further testing!

Twenty-two years after TSCA became law, the EPA had tested a grand total of 263 high-priority chemicals for some specific effect, or only about 0.4 percent of the approximately 70,000 existing chemicals in commercial use.[11] To add insult to injury, instead of testing the safety of these high-priority chemicals, the EPA decided to trust the manufacturers to test about half of them. In 2005 and 2006, the GAO's TSCA report lamented that:

EPA officials say the act's legal standards for demonstrating unreasonable risk are so high that they have generally discouraged EPA from using its authorities to ban or

---

[10] This information is supposed to be updated every 4 years.

[11] EWG, *The Chemical Industry Archives* (2009). http://www.chemicalindustryarchives.org/factfiction/testing.asp.

restrict the manufacture or use of existing chemicals. Since Congress enacted TSCA in 1976, EPA has issued regulations to ban or limit the production of only five existing chemicals or groups of chemicals.[12]

Unfortunately, getting chemicals tested was just the first barrier to regulating dangerous substances already on the market. To restrict a chemical's use after testing, the agency not only had to prove that the chemical presented an "unreasonable risk" but it had to also demonstrate that: (1) it chose the least burdensome regulation to reduce risks to a reasonable level; and (2) the benefits of regulation outweighed the costs. The EPA must prove all three of these factors for every old chemical they wish to restrict.

The agency's effort to regulate asbestos clearly revealed the near impossibility of restricting chemicals already in commercial use. Ten thousand Americans die each year – a rate approaching 30 deaths per day – from diseases caused by asbestos, according to a detailed analysis of government mortality records and epidemiological studies by the Environmental Working Group.[13] Asbestos kills thousands more people than skin cancer each year, and nearly the number that are slain in assaults with firearms. The ailments linked to asbestos exposure overwhelmingly affect older men.

Industry became aware of asbestos' potential as a deadly killer back in the 1930s. As the decades passed, the evidence became overwhelming and irrefutable; asbestos was conclusively linked to an ever-growing number of lethal health risks. In 1949, Exxon admitted in a confidential internal document that asbestos causes lung cancer, silicosis, fibrosis and erythema.[14] In recent years, a small library of unearthed industry documents has revealed that many companies were involved in covering up the truth about asbestos for decades.[15]

The list of culpable conspirators reads like a "Who's Who" of corporate America. While hundreds of thousands of people died from asbestos exposure, Exxon, Dow (Union Carbide), DuPont, Bendix (now Honeywell), The Travelers, Metropolitan Life, Dresser Industries (now Halliburton), National Gypsum, Owens-Corning, General Electric, Ford and General Motors were actively concealing its perils from their workers and the public. Asbestos-related mortality continues today in the United States at a rate of at least 5,000 deaths per year.[16]

In 1989, after ten years of research, public meetings and regulatory impact analyses, the EPA issued a final rule under Section 6 of TSCA to prohibit the future manufacture, importation, processing and distribution of asbestos in almost all products. The asbestos industry challenged the EPA's ban and took its appeal to the Fifth Circuit Court of Appeals.

In a landmark case – *Corrosion Proof Fittings v. EPA* – the court all but eliminated the EPA's ability to use TSCA to restrict dangerous chemicals. The court held that the EPA had presented insufficient evidence (including risk information) to justify its

[12] Quoted in: Monforton, Celeste (November 13, 2007).
[13] EWG. "The Asbestos Epidemic in America." http://reports.ewg.org/reports/asbestos/facts/fact1.php.
[14] EWG. "Something in the Air: The Asbestos Document Story." http://reports.ewg.org/reports/asbestos/facts/fact3.php.
[15] EWG, "Something in the Air: The Asbestos Document Story."
[16] EWG, "The Asbestos Epidemic in America." http://reports.ewg.org/reports/asbestos/facts/fact1.php

asbestos ban. The court found that: (1) the agency had not used the least-burdensome regulation to achieve its goal of minimizing risk; (2) had not demonstrated a reasonable basis for the regulatory action; and (3) had not adequately balanced the benefits of the restriction against the costs to industry.

In its conclusions the court held that "the EPA's regulation cannot stand if there is any other regulation that would achieve an acceptable level of risk as mandated by TSCA" and that "EPA, in its zeal to ban any and all asbestos products, basically ignored the cost side of the TSCA equation."[17] Such a sharp rebuke from the court put the kibosh on EPA efforts to use TSCA to restrict dangerous chemicals already in production.

NEW CHEMICAL REGULATION

Under TSCA, the centerpiece of the EPA's regulation of new chemicals is the premanufacture notice (PMN), sometimes referred to as a "section 5 notice." Section 5 requires that EPA receive a section 5 notice from the manufacturer of any new chemical 90 days before it goes onto the market. This notice is supposed to contain a significant amount of information about the chemical, including test data on its potential impact on human health and the environment. However, such tests are not mandatory; therefore, if the company is fearful of certain side effects, it may simply not test for them. During the 90-day PMN process, EPA staff can ask for some limited data on the toxicity and physical characteristics of a chemical, although they rarely do.

The EPA is inundated and overwhelmed by the number of PMNs it must consider. The agency must assess between 2,000 and 2,500 new chemical PMNs a year, or between 40 and 50 new chemical applications every week. If the EPA does not require further testing of a new chemical, or act to restrict or ban its use within 45 days of notification, the substance is free to be marketed. Yet when it comes to requiring further tests on new chemicals, the agency faces the same Catch-22 dilemma it confronted with old ones. Before it can require further tests, EPA must show that the chemical may present an "unreasonable risk." However, because TSCA requires only "known" data to be reported and does not require the manufacturer to provide any toxicity data in the PMN,[18] more than half of all PMNs submitted contain no toxicity data whatsoever.[19] Consequently, the EPA usually has no scientific basis upon which to require additional tests. In addition, because the contents of a PMN are not binding, there is no incentive for a manufacturer to ensure that its original premanufacture notice is accurate or reliable.

[17]   Quoted in: Lowell Center for Sustainable Production. "The Promise and Limits of the United States Toxic Substances Control Act" (October 10, 2003). http://www.chemicalspolicy.org/downloads/ Chemicals_Policy_TSCA.doc.
[18]   Ji, Qingsong & Bo Yan. *EPA's New Chemicals Program Under TSCA: The Basics.* Chem Alliance. http://www.chemalliance.org/Articles/Regulatory/reg000921.asp.
[19]   EWG. "The Most Poorly Tested Chemicals in the World," *The Chemical Industry Archives* (March 27, 2009). http://www.chemicalindustryarchives.org/factfiction/testing.asp.

Once EPA has finished its 45-day review of a PMN, the manufacturer need not limit the uses or production levels of this chemical to those described in the PMN. Manufacturers are even allowed to revise PMNs while the EPA is reviewing them. After learning that EPA was considering controls on a chemical, manufacturers have gone back and revised the exposure estimates to avoid regulatory action. In addition, they have revised PMNs to show lower releases than previously estimated and they have added claims that the chemicals will be used in zero-discharge systems. Finally, if the EPA decides to regulate a chemical, it must select the "least burdensome control." If the EPA takes no action, the manufacturer is free to use the new chemical after the 90-day period has transpired.

Both environmentalists and industry are critical of the PMN process. Chemical manufacturers say the procedure is expensive, requiring unnecessary red tape. After all, they argue, they would not produce unsafe chemicals because if they did they could be liable in tort for negligence. Environmentalists point out that the EPA has issued stop or limit orders for only 0.5 percent of all new chemicals. Eighty percent of all new chemicals are approved within three weeks, with or without test data; and 90 percent of the 23,971 new chemicals approved by EPA between 1976 and 1994 were approved with no restrictions on their proposed use and production and with no requests for additional test data, regardless of the paucity of data contained in the PMN.[20]

Under TSCA, any chemical company that becomes aware of "any information that indicates that their chemicals present a substantial risk of injury to human health or the environment" must report this information immediately to the EPA. Absolute certainty is not necessary; any reasonable indication that a chemical is potentially dangerous must be reported.

According to *The TSCA Compliance Handbook*, this reporting requirement is critical. "The EPA views its information gathering under this section as an early warning mechanism for keeping the agency and citizens apprised of newly discovered chemical hazards."[21] Because Congress and the EPA realized that chemical producers are motivated to delay or avoid reporting the dangerous effects of their new chemicals, TSCA requires industry to submit such reports within 15 days of discovery or face a penalty of $6,000 for each day over the time limit. Yet because these fines were rarely imposed, many suspected that the chemical industry was ignoring their reporting obligation. Nevertheless, it took 14 years for the EPA to finally realize that TSCA's early warning system was essentially worthless.

One blatant example of this failure was the EPA's four-year legal battle with Monsanto over its Santogard PVI pesticide. In 1990, Monsanto finally agreed to pay a fine for failing to report scientific data acquired in 1981 showing that Santogard PVI causes cancer in lab rats. At $6,000 per day for failure to report, Monsanto should have paid a fine of $19.7 million. Instead, EPA settled for less than one percent of that sum. Monsanto's fine of $198,000 was chump change for a company with sales of $9 billion that year.[22]

---

[20] EWG. "The Most Poorly Tested Chemicals in the World." (March 27, 2009).
[21] Griffin, Ginger L. *The TSCA Compliance Handbook*, 3rd ed. (NY: Wiley), 1996.
[22] McHugh, Josh. "Chemicals," *Forbes* (January 13, 1991): 118.

But this demonstration of EPA feebleness was only a small indication of TSCA's inability to compel industry to hand over incriminating information on their new chemicals. In the wake of this dismal showing, the EPA decided to get some hard data on how seriously industry was taking its legal obligation to report potentially dangerous chemicals. The agency sent a letter to all chemical manufacturers urging them to submit any data they had failed to report in the past.

Six months later, the CMA met with EPA officials to hammer out an "amnesty" program. They struck a deal whereby companies that had violated TSCA's reporting requirements year after year would send the EPA all the data they had illegally withheld. In return, the EPA would limit fines to $15,000 for any human study and $6,000 for any animal study withheld. In addition, no corporation's total fines would exceed $1 million.[23]

This proved to be an astounding Get-Out-of-Jail card for the chemical industry. During the amnesty period, more than 120 companies sent the EPA 11,000 illegally withheld reports on the adverse health effects of their chemical products. DuPont alone submitted 1,380. Some of these adverse health studies had been around since 1960 and had not been submitted, as required, when TSCA was enacted in 1976. Under the law, any such study submitted in 1991 should have drawn a fine of $32.9 million.[24] Thus, the EPA's amnesty program saved these chemical corporations – and short changed taxpayers – hundreds of millions, if not billions, of dollars.

The EPA's amnesty program clearly demonstrated that DuPont, Monsanto, Dow and the other big chemical manufacturers had been shamelessly thumbing their noses at the agency and the law for years. No one can estimate how many people were poisoned because of their criminal negligence. Yet, after these corporate outlaws were caught red-handed, the EPA bent over backward to minimize any penalties for their crimes.

Believe it or not, the EPA pronounced its amnesty program a resounding success. Why? Because the agency grievously debased its definition of success. Instead of measuring success by compliance with the law or the number of dangerous chemicals kept out of circulation, the EPA set its sights considerably lower. Success meant getting industry to come clean about how many potentially dangerous chemicals it had slipped past regulators over the years by ducking the law and bamboozling the agency. And how was this great success achieved? By bribing these giant corporate outlaws with paltry penalties for their multimillion-dollar crimes.

According to the *National Law Journal*, "EPA views the program as an important success, and it has already attempted to duplicate it."[25] And so it did. To induce the natural gas industry to comply with another chemical reporting law, the agency waived the law's $25,000-per-day fines, agreed to limit a company's liability to $3,000 per chemical and to cap it at $90,000. Next, the EPA applied its amnesty principle to the nation's Right-to-Know Law. The agency sent amnesty letters to

[23] Montague, Peter. "On Regulation," *Rachel's Democracy & Health News* #538 (March 20, 1997).
[24] Montague, Peter. (March 20, 1997).
[25] Lavelle, Marianne. "EPA's Amnesty Has Become a Mixed Blessing," *The National Law Journal* (February 24, 1997): A1, A18.

thousands of food processors that had ignored this law for years. It offered to waive their $25,000-per-day fines and cap each corporation's liability at $2,000.[26] And the EPA called this successful enforcement.

Behind this laughable definition of successful enforcement lies a deeply disturbing admission of the agency's utter inability to enforce TSCA and other laws. Clearly, the EPA is powerless against giant chemical corporations armed with larger budgets and far more attorneys than the agency can ever hope to muster. *The National Law Journal* puts it this way: "EPA policy makers have themselves concluded that they cannot count on the traditional techniques of deterrence to prevent crime on this beat. Not with thousands of factories, hundreds of thousands of products and a complex set of laws – the meaning of which are subject to perpetual debate."[27]

In return for granting amnesty to corporate scofflaws, the EPA collected a tiny percentage of the fines it was entitled to levy. More importantly, the agency hoped to compile a more complete database on the nature of the chemicals being used around the country. However, the EPA was so overwhelmed by the deluge of studies and reports that its staff nicknamed the system for sorting and storing them "the triage database." At first, the staff tried to organize this flood of chemicals into "high," "medium" and "low" levels of concern. But it never completed the job. Thus, this mountain of studies remains part of the agency's vast unexplored backlog of unscreened chemicals in circulation.[28]

A year after amnesty ended, a report on TSCA released by the Environmental Defense Fund (EDF) concluded, "For most of the important chemicals in American commerce, the simplest safety facts still cannot be found. This report documents that, today, even the most basic toxicity testing results cannot be found in the public record for nearly 75 percent of the top-volume chemicals in commercial use."[29] This is a dismal finding, but did amnesty improve the situation? Hardly. In 1984, the National Research Council carried out a toxicity-testing survey. The NRC looked for toxicity data on 100 chemicals randomly chosen from a broader list representing the 3,000 new chemicals marketed in high volumes each year. They concluded that 78 percent of these chemicals lacked even "minimal toxicity information."[30] In 1997, after amnesty, the EDF carried out a similar procedure. They found that 71 percent of the chemicals surveyed lacked minimal toxicity information – a 7 percent improvement in 13 years.

Furthermore, the EDF report found that even the minimal screening information used to determine whether a chemical is likely to pose a hazard to human health was widely unavailable. For example, among the high-volume chemicals surveyed:

- Carcenogenity tests were missing for 63 percent;
- Reproductivity toxicity data were unavailable for 53 percent;
- Neurotoxicity tests were missing for 67 percent;

[26] Montague, Peter. (March 20, 1997).
[27] Lavelle, Marianne. (February 24, 1997): A1, A18.
[28] Fagin, Dan & Marianne Lavelle, 1999: 15.
[29] Roe, David et al. *Toxic Ignorance: The Continuing Absence of Basic Health Testing for Top-Selling Chemicals in the United States.* (NY: EDF), 1997.
[30] National Research Council, *Toxicity Testing.* (Washington, DC: National Academy Press), 1984.

- Immune system toxicity tests were unavailable for 86 percent;
- Studies evaluating the impact on children were not done on 90 percent of high-priority chemicals; and
- More than half (58 percent) had not been tested for any form of chronic toxicity.[31]

The chemical industry's expensive PR and advertising campaigns continually remind the public how vital chemicals are to our modern society. They frame the issue as a choice between rationality and irrational fanaticism. Either you are for chemicals and their beneficial contribution to society or you are some fanatic, opposed to all chemicals and plastics, and therefore can't be taken seriously. They insist that current laws such as the TSCA do an ample job of protecting society from dangerous chemical exposures. Therefore, rational people don't concern themselves with unsafe chemicals in kids' toys and baby formula, formaldehyde in building supplies, endocrine disrupters in our bodies or industrial solvents and fuel additives in our drinking water. But as the gaping loopholes in TSCA demonstrate, there is ample reason to worry about the potential risks posed by the tens of thousands of chemicals currently authorized for use and the thousands of new chemicals that enter the marketplace every year.

Outside of the chemical industry, few will argue that the current system is working well and doesn't need a major overhaul. In the 1990s, researchers discovered that some chemicals could interfere with the body's hormones at levels once thought to be inconsequential. Such disruption can cause serious health problems during critical life stages, particularly during fetal development. Also, the new technology of bio-monitoring has revealed that nearly all blood and urine contain trace levels of industrial chemicals. These findings challenge long-held assumptions that the general public has little or no exposure to many commercial substances. Europe fully recognized this new reality and has initiated a new EU-wide chemicals policy known as REACH, which stands for Registration, Evaluation, Authorization and Restriction of Chemical Substances. Among the most fundamental principles of REACH is that instead of assuming that chemicals are safe, until regulators with minimal authority and inadequate resources can prove otherwise, the burden of proof should be on chemical manufacturers to establish that the chemicals they sell are safe.[32]

Within the United States, the effort to reform TSCA has been unable to overcome chemical industry opposition, presidential disdain and congressional indifference. Thus, TSCA has remained ineffective and unaltered since it was signed into law by Gerald Ford. But recently, the call for reform has gained strength and the coalition demanding TSCA reform has grown well beyond a few national environmental organizations. Unions representing chemical plant workers are chiming in, along

[31] Roe, David et al. 1997.
[32] Some environmental groups, like Greenpeace and Friends of the Earth, have been critical of the limited list of candidate chemicals covered by REACH thus far. See: Greenpeace, "First REACH Hazardous Chemicals List is a Drop in the Ocean," *Greenpeace European Unit* (October 28, 2008). http://www.greenpeace.org/eu-unit/press-centre/press-releases2/First-REACH-hazardous-chemicals-list-is-a-drop-in-the-ocean.

with animal welfare groups who want to move chemical safety testing away from reliance on laboratory animals and toward the use of genomics and cell-based technologies.[33] Even some businesses have joined the call for reform because they want the law to require health and safety information on the chemicals contained in the products they purchase.

Across the Atlantic, REACH has gotten the attention of U.S. lawmakers and chemical producers. The impact of Europe's new precautionary policy cuts American chemical producers out of European markets unless they change their ways. Meanwhile, the pressure for reform is mounting in many states as well. Some have stiffened chemical laws on their own. For example, California has adopted legislation to phase out toxic compounds from consumer products and encourage the development of eco-friendly chemicals, while other states and localities have banned hazardous substances such as brominated flame retardants. This inconsistent patchwork of state and local laws causes headaches for bulk chemical manufacturers and suppliers of finished products.

There are indications that Obama's EPA chief, Lisa Jackson, may favor rewriting TSCA. In a memo sent to EPA employees just after she was sworn in, Jackson declared, "It is now time to revise and strengthen EPA's chemicals management and risk assessment programs."[34] Only time will tell if this growing movement to reform TSCA will generate meaningful improvements or suffer the Washington equivalent of death by a thousand cuts.

---

[33] Hogue, Cheryl. "Change is Coming: Converging Forces Spur Modernization of U.S. Chemical Control Law," *Chemical & Engineering News* (March 16, 2009). http://pubs.acs.org/cen/government/87/8711gov3.html.

[34] Hogue, Cheryl (March 16, 2009).

6

The Endangered Species Act – Noah's Ark or Titanic?

Without biodiversity, humans would perish. Biodiversity, or biological diversity, is succinctly defined as *the entire, interdependent web life on Earth*. The Rutgers University Biodiversity Initiative defines it more thoroughly as:

> ...the sum total of all the plants, animals (including humans), fungi and micro-organisms, along with their individual variations and the interactions between them. It is the set of living organisms and their genetic basis that make up the fabric of the planet earth and allow it to function as it does, by capturing energy from the sun and using it to drive all of life's processes.[1]

This complex web of life is humanity's life support system. It provides us with food, clothing, medicine, shelter and even the air we breathe; it regulates our climate and purifies our water; it recycles our wastes, keeps our soil fertile and our crops pollinated. In addition, biodiversity is the storehouse for the genetic heritage of millions of years of evolution.[2]

Today this web of life is being shredded. Many of the creatures that make up this network are going extinct. Should humans be concerned? The renowned ecologist, Paul Ehrlich, used the following metaphor: If you noticed someone popping rivets out of an airplane you were about to board, would you be alarmed? What if the person assured you that a few rivets would not make any difference? You might be persuaded, but at what point would you insist that the rivet popper stop? How many rivets can a plane lose without falling apart in the sky? Ehrlich's metaphor is valuable because it warns us that losing biodiversity on "spaceship Earth" is very similar to losing airplane rivets. Many species may disappear with little *apparent* impact on the web of life; but when do we reach the critical point where the web can no longer support human life? Ecologists cannot answer this question because they have identified only a fraction of

---

[1] Rutger's Biodiversity Center Homepage. *What is Biodiversity?* http://aesop.rutgers.edu/~biodiversity/whatis2.htm#DEFINE.

[2] According to the UN's 1995 Global Biodiversity Assessment, humans share the planet with an estimated 13 million other species. A generation ago, that estimate was 1.3 million, but more species are discovered every year. About 90 percent of the world's species, mostly insects and fungi, have not yet been studied or even given scientific names.

Earth's species and are far from understanding the intricate, interwoven lifelines of the biosphere's elaborate tapestry.

No creature exists in a vacuum. All living things survive within ecosystems – communities of plants and animals adapted to particular types of physical environments. Some creatures are part of coral reef ecosystems, others live within desert ecosystems, some thrive in wetlands, while others are adapted to tropical rainforests. Working together, Earth's interconnected ecosystems create a delicately balanced, tightly woven planetary network called the biosphere.

The removal of a single species from an ecosystem can set off a chain reaction affecting many other creatures and even other ecosystems. It has been estimated, for example, that a disappearing plant can take with it up to 30 other species, including insects, higher animals and even other plants.[3] This makes the impact of each new extinction even harder to predict than Ehrlich's rivet metaphor would indicate. The full significance of any extinction is not readily apparent; and the long-term consequences are nearly impossible to assess.

However, we do know that some ecosystems are more fragile than others. Ecosystems with greater diversity are better able to withstand disruption. This may be because these ecosystems have *redundancy* – that is, more than one way of doing the same thing. If one species disappears, others fill in, taking over its function in the ecosystem. Or if environmental conditions change, a more diverse ecosystem will possess a greater genetic capacity for adapting.

Fossil studies reveal that the diversity of life on our planet has gone up and down over the past half-billion years. There have been five major "extinction crises" during which life was so imperiled that a significant portion of its diversity was lost. The most famous of these was the one that wiped out the dinosaurs 65 million years ago. However, there have been other, even more drastic, crises that may have reduced diversity by upward of 90 percent. After each of these extinction episodes, diversity eventually returned, but the organisms were different, and recovery took millions and millions of years.

Today, most biologists believe we have entered a sixth major extinction episode.[4] According to the renowned paleoanthropologist, Dr. Richard Leakey, this sixth extinction crisis:

> ... means the annihilation of vast numbers of species. It is happening now, and we, the human race, are its cause ... Every year, between 17,000 and 100,000 species vanish from our planet. For the sake of argument, let's assume the number is 50,000 a year. Whatever way you look at it, we're destroying the Earth at a rate comparable with the impact of a giant asteroid slamming into the planet, or even a shower of vast heavenly bodies.[5]

---

[3] Alaska Department of Fish & Game. *Why Save Endangered Species?* http://www.adfg.state.ak.us/specialesa/why_save.php.

[4] Seventy percent according to: The American Museum of Natural History. Press Release. *National Survey Reveals Biodiversity Crisis – Scientific Experts Believe We Are in Midst of Fastest Mass Extinction in Earth's History* (April 20, 1998). http://www.amnh.org/museum/press/feature/biofact.html.

[5] Leaky, Richard & Roger Lewin. *The Sixth Extinction* (Doubleday: 1995). http://www.well.com/user/davidu/sixthextinction.html.

The implications of the statistics Leaky assembles are staggering. Humans use almost half of the photosynthetic energy available to sustain life on Earth, and this figure will only grow as our population leaps from 5.7 to 10 billion inside the next half-century.[6] At this pace, Leaky predicts that half of the Earth's species will vanish within 100 years. Such a dramatic and overwhelming mass extinction threatens the entire biosphere, including the species responsible for it – Homo sapiens.

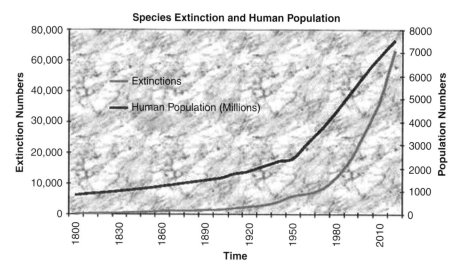

This rapidly accelerating rate of extinction is astonishing and almost entirely the product of human activity. During the 300 years between 1600 and 1900, human activity led to the extinction of about 75 species of birds and mammals – about one species every four years. This rate increased slightly during the first half of the twentieth century. Biologists estimate that by the mid-1970s, human-caused extinction rose to about 100 species per year. Harvard biologist, Edward O. Wilson, perhaps the world's leading expert on biodiversity, believes that by the mid-1980s, the rapidly accelerating extinction rate had reached at least 400 times the natural rate (but possibly as high as 10,000 times the rate prior to the arrival of human beings). By 1987, the Office of Technology Assessment (OTA) warned Congress that the loss of biodiversity had reached "crisis proportions." Today, Wilson believes between 27,000 and 50,000 species vanish every year – or three to six species per hour – mostly from the destruction of forests, coral reefs, mangrove swamps and other key habitats in the tropics.[7]

---

[6] Leaky, Richard & Roger Lewin (1995).

[7] Forests are home to much of the known terrestrial biodiversity, but about 45 percent of the Earth's original forests are gone, cleared mostly during the past century. Despite some regrowth, the world's total forests are still shrinking rapidly, particularly in the tropics. Up to 10 percent of coral reefs – among the richest ecosystems – have been destroyed, and one-third of the remainder face collapse over the next 10–20 years. Coastal mangroves, a vital nursery habitat for countless species, are also vulnerable, with half already gone. Kraft, Michael E. *Environmental Policy & Politics*, 3rd ed. (NY: Pearson/Longman), 2007: 53.

In 1995, the United Nations Environment Programme (UNEP) published its *Global Biodiversity Assessment*. This report – the work of 1,500 scientists from around the world – warns that the current mass extinction crisis may wipe out 24 percent of the world's mammals within 30 years (including tigers, rhinos, Asian elephants, cheetahs and mountain gorillas); 12 percent of birds and more than 5,000 plants.[8] Like the loss of a single rivet, the disappearance of some obscure, seemingly insignificant creature may appear trivial or go completely unnoticed. But the sheer volume and pace of these "minor losses" moves us quickly toward the precipice of a planetary collapse of the ecosystems that sustain us.

How are humans shredding Earth's priceless web of life? Threats to biodiversity include road and dam building; the expansion of agriculture, mining and oil drilling; urban sprawl and other activities that destroy and fragment habitat; harvesting of wild species for food, lumber and other products; introduction of nonnative animals and plants; pollution of the air, water and soil with toxic chemicals and wastes; and increased ultraviolet radiation and climate disruption resulting from a broad range of human activities. These are the immediate causes of biodiversity loss. Underlying these processes, however, are forces even less amenable to regulation:

(1) A competitive global economy requiring ceaseless, rapid growth and dependent upon the combustion of fossil fuels;

(2) The constant expansion of human population; and

(3) Failure to recognize the true value and vital importance of biodiversity.

THE ENDANGERED SPECIES ACT: A LEGAL NOAH'S ARK?

The foremost American law directed at preserving biodiversity is the Endangered Species Act (ESA). It is famous for its protection of certain well-known animals such as the bald eagle, the spotted owl and the grey wolf. The media commonly portrays the law as an altruistic effort on the part of society to prevent the extinction of some creatures considered worthy of protection and preservation. Environmentalists have fostered this image by using the charisma of certain cute, cuddly animals such as sea otters, harp seals and pandas; or magnificent creatures such as bald eagles, grizzly bears, whales, elephants, gorillas and tigers to rally the public behind the ESA.

Although this approach has produced widespread citizen approval for the act, public support remains somewhat superficial and susceptible to attack. After all, what happens when the cost of preservation rises and the species threatened has an image problem? Should we spend precious tax dollars, sacrifice economic growth and jobs just to save a slug, a beetle, a weed or a fungus?

In these cases, the response of most environmental organizations has been to bolster the public's sagging enthusiasm by reminding them of the many medicines and other benefits we receive from even the lowliest of life forms. A treatment for cancer was found in the bark of the Pacific Yew – a scrawny, shrub-like tree that was

---

[8] UNEP (V. H. Heywood & R. T. Watson). *Global Biodiversity Assessment: Summary for Policy-Makers*. (NY: Cambridge University Press), 1995.

once discarded as worthless during logging operations.[9] Another obscure plant, the rosy periwinkle, produces treatments for childhood leukemia, testicular cancer, Hodgkin's disease and high blood pressure. Lifesavers such as penicillin and tetracycline come from fungi and bacteria. Of America's top 150 selling prescription drugs, 79 percent originate in nature, while in the developing world, 80 percent of all people rely on traditional medicines (derived from the healing properties of plants) as their primary source of health care.[10]

In addition to medicines, microscopic creatures such as bacteria have been used throughout history to help us make wine, beer, cheese and bread. Today, some bacteria are used to clean up oil spills and researchers have identified other methane-munching microbes that can help to clean up hazardous waste dumps and landfills by breaking down more than 250 nasty pollutants into harmless molecules.[11] They are assisted in this process by certain obscure weeds in the mustard family that possess the power to clean the environment of toxins, asbestos and heavy metals.[12]

Since every species is a potential source of medicine or other benefit (yet less than 2 percent of all *known* plant species have been adequately screened), the medicinal argument is a far more convincing and inclusive rationale for making major sacrifices to preserve biodiversity than the "cute and charismatic" justification. Nevertheless, the medicinal argument is still partial, short-sighted and myopic compared with the fundamental reason humans must do whatever it takes to halt this extinction crisis – our survival depends on it!

Besides medicines, we depend on plant life – from towering trees to tiny phyto-plankton – for the air we breathe, the food we eat, the clothes we wear, the homes we live in and the ozone layer that protects us from the sun's radiation. While *living* forests purify our water, regulate rainfall, moderate climate, prevent floods and erosion, provide habitat for valuable creatures and enrich our spiritual and recreational lives, their harvested timber gives us shelter, furniture and paper.

In addition, the genetic diversity of plant life keeps our crops healthy and resistant to blight and disease. Just three species – corn, wheat and rice – provide half the world's food. This small group of plants upon which human survival depends is susceptible to devastating insect infestations and blights. Perhaps the best way to protect domestic crops from such disasters is to cross-breed them with wild varieties. In the 1970s, a corn blight in the United States was controlled by cross-breeding domesticated corn with a wild Mexican variety. In 1992, scientists protected domestic wheat from a harmful leaf rust by cross-breeding it with a wild variety from Brazil. Protecting plant species such as the endangered Texas wild rice could hold the key to controlling future threats to domesticated rice crops and combat threats to human survival.

---

[9] The Sierra Club. *Species at Risk: The Pacific Yew.* http://www.sierraclub.org/lewisandclark/species/pacificyew.asp.

[10] Lewis, Barry. "Biodiversity: Why Should We Care? What Does it Mean?" *Academy of Natural Sciences* (January 1997). http://www.acnatsci.org/education/kye/nr/biodiv1.html.

[11] "Stalking the Mysterious Microbe," *Capital Times* (June 9, 2005).

[12] Marcus, Adam. "Scientists Modify Plants to Remove Environmental Toxins," *Genome News Network* (October 18, 2002). http://www.genomenewsnetwork.org/articles/10_02/plant_arsenic.php.

Animal life is essential to human survival as well. Insects pollinate our crops, create our topsoil and recycle our wastes. Many animals provide us with food and labor on our behalf. Even the tiniest microbes are absolutely essential for detoxifying our environment and decomposing our wastes.

Thus the most irresistible, overpowering motivation for protecting biodiversity is that without it, humans will go the way of the dinosaurs. This is the lesson people must grasp in order to steadfastly and ardently endorse all measures necessary to maintain biodiversity.

THE ENDANGERED SPECIES ACT — LOOPHOLES IN THE ARK

In 1973, Congress passed the Endangered Species Act (ESA) with an enthusiastic bipartisan vote of 355 to 4.[13] When he signed the Act into law, President Nixon said, "Nothing is more priceless and more worthy of preservation than the rich array of animal life with which our country has been blessed."[14] Although the ESA was primarily directed at saving American wildlife, Congress explicitly linked it to the global effort to protect ecosystems and contain the rate of extinction through the various international agreements designed to protect biodiversity worldwide. ESA protections are administered by the Secretary of the Department of the Interior (DoI) through its subordinate agency, the Fish and Wildlife Service (FWS). However, marine species, including some marine mammals, are the responsibility of the Secretary of Commerce, acting through the National Marine Fisheries Service (NMFS).

These secretaries and the government services beneath them have been enforcing the ESA for more than 30 years. Have their efforts had a positive impact on the rate of extinction? Back in 1973, when the ESA became law, scientists figured the global rate of extinction to be about 100 species per year. Currently, they estimate that between 17,000 and 100,000 species vanish from our planet annually. Thus, in the 30 plus years that the ESA and its associated treaties have been in force, the global rate of extinction has gone up between 170 and 1,000 percent. But perhaps this is unfair. After all, the ESA is a U.S. law; it should be judged primarily on its performance within the borders of the United States.

The fundamental goal of the ESA is clear and unambiguous – the *recovery* of all species threatened with extinction. The act defines recovery as "the process by which the decline of a threatened or endangered species is arrested or reversed, and threats to its survival are neutralized, so that its long-term survival in nature can be ensured."[15]

[13] The ESA (16 U.S.C. 1531–1543) was passed in 1973, but was preceded by weaker acts in 1966 and 1969. It has been amended on numerous occasions since then: 1976, 1977, 1978, 1979, 1980, 1982 and 1988. It has been reauthorized three times, each time by large bipartisan majorities in Congress.

[14] Committee on Scientific Issues & the Endangered Species Act, National Research Council. *Science and the Endangered Species Act*. (Washington, DC: National Academy Press), 1995. http://www.nap.edu/readingroom/books/esa/executive.html.

[15] Committee on Scientific Issues & the Endangered Species Act, National Research Council. *Science and the Endangered Species Act*. (Washington, DC: National Academy Press), 1995. http://www.nap.edu/readingroom/books/esa/executive.html.

Since the ESA's primary goal is the recovery of species to levels where protection is no longer necessary, a key measure of the law's effectiveness is its recovery rate. What portion of all the species listed for ESA protection has improved enough to be considered recovered? Of the 1,311 species protected by the act since 1973,[16] the ESA is credited with recovering 12 – a dismal 0.09 percent rate of recovery.[17]

Only 10 percent of all protected species are improving; 30 percent are stable; the remaining 60 percent continue slipping toward extinction.[18] Because these statistics focus only on the rate of recovery for species officially listed for protection under the act, they are far too rosy. Unfortunately, weaknesses and loopholes in the law – magnified and exploited by the agencies responsible for enforcement – effectively exclude most imperiled species from ever qualifying for ESA protection.

By the Numbers: Endangered Species Recovered

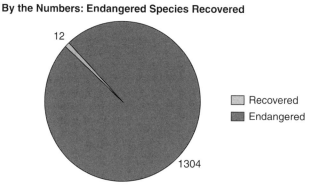

LOOPHOLE # 1: MAKING "THE LIST"

No creature – no matter how close to extinction – may qualify for ESA protections unless and until it becomes officially *listed* by the Interior Secretary as *threatened* or *endangered*.[19] Unfortunately, the listing process is so flawed that most imperiled species never make the list.

---

[16] In addition to the 1,311 species listed as of May 2007, an additional 14 species were listed and de-listed for reasons other than recovery over the last 30 years and 12 have recovered for a grand total of 1,337 species under ESA's protection over the Act's 34-year history.

[17] Pombo, Richard W. (R-CA), Chairman. *Committee on Resources Report – The ESA at 30: A Mandate for Modernization* (April 2004). http://resourcescommittee.house.gov/issues/more/esa/whitepaper.htm.

[18] Committee on Scientific Issues & the Endangered Species Act, National Research Council. *Science and the Endangered Species Act.* (Washington, DC: National Academy Press), 1995. http://www.nap.edu/readingroom/books/esa/executive.html.

[19] Endangered species is defined by the ESA as "any species which is in danger of extinction throughout all or a significant portion of its range". A threatened species is defined as "any species that is likely to become an endangered species within the foreseeable future throughout all or a significant portion of its range".

Population biologists estimate that 500,000 species (roughly 5 percent of the world's total) are native to the United States.[20] So far, only about 150,000 of these species have been identified, and considerably fewer have been carefully studied.[21] Since we know virtually nothing about the approximately 350,000 remaining unnamed species, none of them qualifies for listing, no matter how desperate its condition.

Some biologists reckon that one-third of all species native to the United States – approximately 165,000 – are threatened with extinction; others calculate the number of imperiled plant and animal species to be as low as 6,480.[22] These divergent estimations mean that the 1,311 plant and animal species officially listed under the Endangered Species Act are between 20 and 0.8 percent of all species in the United States at risk of extinction.

Thus, *at least* 80 percent of the nation's imperiled species receive no ESA protection. Why? Because the official listing process that all species must navigate to qualify for ESA safeguards is so strict, slow and constrained by scientific ignorance, political pressure, bureaucratic intransigence and budgetary shortfalls that many species disappear before becoming identified or studied enough to meet the law's rigorous listing qualifications.[23] Unable to qualify for ESA protections, hundreds of imperiled species are left to languish for years or go extinct while on the DoI's roster of "candidate species."[24]

While some presidents have been more openly opposed to the ESA than others, the listing problem has grown from one administration to the next. Under Clinton, the Inspector General's Office (IGO) of the DoI released its investigation into the listing problem:

---

[20] This estimation is made mainly on the basis of the U.S.'s proportional representation of relatively well-known groups of organisms.

[21] President's Committee of Advisers on Science and Technology (Panel on Biodiversity and Ecosystems). *Teaming with Life: Investing in Science to Understand and Use America's Living Capital* (March 1998). http://clinton4.nara.gov/WH/EOP/OSTP/Environment/html/teamingsec2. html.

[22] President's Committee of Advisers on Science and Technology (Panel on Biodiversity and Ecosystems) (March 1998); American Lands Discussion Paper. *Broken Promises of Recovery: The Clinton Administration's 10-Prong Attack on Endangered Species* (January 2000). http://www. defenders.org/esa-9.html.

[23] The ESA directs the Interior Secretary to determine whether a species is listed based upon five factors: (1) the present or threatened destruction, modification or curtailment of its habitat or range; (2) over-utilization for commercial, recreational, scientific or educational purposes; (3) disease or predation; (4) inadequacy of existing regulatory mechanisms; (5) other natural or man-made factors affecting its continued existence. The determination must be based on "the best scientific and commercial data available."

[24] Species recommended for listing because the available evidence appears to justify the need for protection are called candidate species. If there is enough evidence that the species needs to be listed, but there is inadequate funding to finish the process, the FWS usually declares the species' listing "warranted but precluded." This has been the situation with the Florida Black Bear since 1992.

We found that ... timely progress has not been made toward officially listing and protecting endangered and threatened plant and animal species. Approximately 600 domestic candidate species deemed ... to merit immediate protection under the Act have thus far not been officially listed ... an additional 3,000 species are suspected to be threatened or endangered, but action has not been taken to list and protect these plants and animals.

During the last 10 years, at least 34 animal and plant species have been determined to be extinct without ever having received full benefit of the Act's protection, and those species currently known to merit protection, as well as those candidate species eventually determined to need protection, are similarly in jeopardy of extinction ... It may take 38 to 48 years at current listing rates to list just those species now estimated to qualify for protection ... this length of time to list and protect endangered species is ... likely to result in additional extinction of certain plants and animals during the period.[25]

Evidently, the IGO's 1990 report had no impact. Under the Bush administration, opposition to listing became so blatant that in December 2000, the director of the FWS ordered his staff to stop work on all ESA listings unless a court ordered otherwise.[26] By 2004, a report released by the Center for Biological Diversity revealed that systematic delays, including lengthy waits on the candidate list, contributed to the extinction of 83 species between 1974 and 1994. Seventy-nine percent of the 225 species on the candidate list have been there for at least ten years, 38 percent have waited at least 20 years and 28 percent have been waiting since 1975. On average, candidate species wait 17 years to be listed.[27]

Unfortunately, the listing logjam went from bad to worse under the administration of George W. Bush. During his administration, nearly half of the FWS employees who work with endangered species reported that they had been directed by their superiors to ignore scientific evidence that would result in listing recommendations for imperiled species. "We are not allowed to be honest and forthright, we are expected to rubber stamp everything," wrote an FWS biologist as part of the survey. "I have 20 years of federal service in this, and this is the worst it has ever been."[28]

The ESA's listing process is a formidable loophole because it effectively ignores thousands of imperiled species and allows hundreds more to languish for years on the candidate roster. Unfortunately, the listing process is just one of the ESA's flaws. The

---

[25] Center for Biological Diversity. *Scientists, Congress, Government Auditors and the U.S. Fish & Wildlife Service's Own Biologists Repeatedly Confirm That Imperiled Species Are Not Being Added to the Endangered Species List Fast Enough.* http://www.sw-center.org/swcbd/activist/ESA/ critique.html.

[26] *Green Earth Journal.* "Endangered Species Act Endangered" (December 22, 2000). http://www. greenjournal.com/showarticle.asp?404;http://www.greenjournal.com/article216.asp.

[27] Clarke, Chris. "Groups Petition Bush to List 225 Species," *Faultline: California's Environmental Magazine* (May 5, 2004). http://www.faultline.org/archives/001331.html.

[28] These are the results of a 2005 survey of more than 1,400 service biologists, ecologists and botanists conducted by Public Employees for Environmental Responsibility, a nonprofit organization. See: Clarren, Rebecca. "Inside the Secretive Plan to Gut the Endangered Species Act," Salon.com (March 27, 2007). http://salon.com/news/feature/2007/03/27/endangered_species/.

others become apparent when we ask: *What becomes of the species lucky enough to qualify for ESA protection?*

THE "CRITICAL HABITAT" LOOPHOLE:

If the protection of endangered and threatened species depends in large measure on the preservation of the species' habitat, then the ultimate effectiveness of the Endangered Species Act will depend on the designation of critical habitat.
– United States Congress, 1976

Habitat loss is a major obstacle to the recovery of species battling extinction. Habitat encroachment due to logging, livestock grazing, dams and other water projects, mining, urban sprawl and other factors is the leading threat to 80 percent of species listed as threatened or endangered.[29] According to one study, it affects more than 95 percent of all listed species.[30] Thus, rehabilitating most species poised on the brink of extinction involves the protection, maintenance and expansion of their habitat.

To move endangered species toward recovery, the ESA requires the Interior Secretary to designate *critical habitat* and develop a *recovery plan* for every listed species. The legal definition of critical habitat is "the geographic area containing physical or biological features essential to the conservation of a listed species or an area that may require special management considerations or protection." The courts have ruled that critical habitat designation should promote the recovery, not just the survival, of the listed species.[31] Yet, in practice, the Interior Secretary and the FWS have narrowly defined critical habitat as the last refuge of species on the verge of extinction – the bare bones of their living quarters.

In addition, the ESA gives the DoI and the wildlife services under it the discretion to grant exceptions to the critical habitat requirement. The Interior Secretary can avoid assigning critical habitat if the service considers it "not prudent" because habitat designation would harm the species (e.g., by encouraging vandals, poachers or collectors). In addition, the secretary may postpone designation for up to one year if the information needed for designation is "not determinable." Finally, critical habitat designations do not affect private landowners' actions unless they are seeking official approval or funding from the federal government. While privately held land may be

[29] American Lands Discussion Paper (January 2000).
[30] For a deeper analysis of the important role critical habitat designation plays in the preservation and recovery of endangered species see: CRS Report to Congress [RS20263]. *The Role of Designation of Critical Habitat Under the Endangered Species Act* (July 16, 1999); St. Clair, Jeffrey. "Going Critical: Bush's War on Endangered Species," *Dissident Voice* (June 9, 2003). http://www.dissidentvoice.org/Articles5/St.Clair_ESA.htm; The Endangered Species Coalition. *In-depth Look: Endangered Species Act.* http://www.stopextinction.org/cgi-bin/giga.cgi?cmd=cause_dir_custom&page=indepth&cause_id=1704.
[31] Ivester, David. "Critical Habitat Should Promote Recovery, Not Just Survival, of Endangered Species, Says Court," *Stoles Rives* (March 1, 2002). http://www.stoel.com/resources/articles/environment/news-mar01-2.shtm.

designated as critical habitat, activities on that land are only affected if a federal action (e.g., some type of license, loan or permit) is involved.

These legal exclusions and exceptions appear reasonable on paper, but in reality they have been severely abused by the Interior Secretary, the FWS and the NMFS. The "not prudent" provision is supposed to be used only in the rare circumstance where designation of critical habitat would be detrimental to the species. However, these agencies declared that designating critical habitat was "not prudent" in 200 consecutive species listings between 1996 and 2003, prompting several successful legal challenges.

A frequent justification used in "not prudent" findings is that publishing precise location maps in the *Federal Register* would increase the threats of vandalism, poaching or collection of the endangered creature. However, the FWS has used this justification regardless of whether there has ever been a documented instance of vandalism or collection of the species or whether a species is confined to a few acres or ranges across hundreds of thousands of acres. Also, the "not prudent" determination is often issued even when locality information for the species is already well distributed in the public domain and neither vandalism nor collection has resulted.[32] Between 1973 and 2002, the DoI was so reluctant to grant critical habitats that it used its discretionary powers to block critical habitat designations for 88 percent of the ESA's listed species.[33]

Environmental groups such as the Center for Biological Diversity and Earth Justice have challenged many of these "not prudent" and "not determinable" findings. Frequent successful rulings resulted in court orders and court-approved settlement agreements requiring the FWS to issue new critical habitat determinations for many imperiled species.[34]

A sad example of the consequences of avoiding critical habitat designation is the dusky seaside sparrow. This sparrow was listed as endangered, but its critical habitat was not established for another ten years. The sparrow inhabited parts of coastal Florida used by NASA's space program and other parts valued for development and

---

[32] This was true for two endangered San Francisco Bay tidal marsh plant species. The Suisun thistle and the soft bird's beak were listed as endangered species in November 1997, but were never given a critical habitat designation until 2003 when the court supported a lawsuit by the Center for Biological Diversity requiring the Service to act.

[33] Several lawsuits have forced the FWS to designate critical habitat in recent years, thus the percentage of species with critical habitat designation had risen to 36 percent (445 species of the 1,244 listed) by July 2004. Department of the Interior/Fish & Wildlife Service. "Endangered and Threatened Wildlife and Plants; Final Designation of Critical Habitat for the Topeka Shiner," Final Rule (Part II), *Federal Register* Rules & Regulations, v. 69, n. 143 (July 27, 2004). http://mountain-prairie.fws.gov/species/fish/shiner/FRtshinerfinalCH.pdf; Scarpello, Robert J. *Statutory Redundancy: Why Congress Should Overhaul the Endangered Species Act to Exclude Critical Habitat Designation* (2003). http://www.bc.edu/schools/law/lawreviews/meta-elements/journals/bcealr/30_2/04_TXT.htm; St. Clair, Jeffrey (June 9, 2003); Endangered Species Coalition. "Critical Habitat" (2003). http://www.stopextinction.org/ESA/ESA.cfm?ID=86&c=21.

[34] Press Release. Center for Biological Diversity. "Lawsuit Filed to Protect Endangered Tidal Marsh Plants: Bush Administration Continues to Withhold Critical Habitat for Imperiled Species" (November 19, 2003). http://www.biologicaldiversity.org/swcbd/press/tidal11-19-03.html.

tourism. As its habitat shrunk the remainder was sprayed to eradicate mosquitoes. This combination proved deadly. The last of its species perished in 1987.[35] Hundreds of other species, including the Florida panther, Arizona's pygmy owl and the California red-legged frog, face a similar fate if they are denied critical habitat designation.

Critical habitat designations offer necessary protections, but often they are too incomplete and inadequate to foster recovery. Although the listing of any species is supposed to be based solely upon a scientific assessment of the species' condition, other considerations are permitted when agencies determine critical habitat. The law permits the FWS and the NMFS to balance the habitat needs of the imperiled species against the economic and social needs of society. Thus, portions of an endangered species' critical habitat can be sacrificed if the agency feels the economic benefits outweigh the costs.

Case in point: The National Association of Home Builders went to court to get rid of all critical habitat designations for the northwest salmon and steelhead. It claimed the designations established by the FWS and the NMFS were "excessive, unduly vague, not justified as essential to conserve the listed species and not based upon a required analysis of economic impacts."[36] In response, the Bush White House directed the services to settle the lawsuit by completely withdrawing all the habitat protections.

To the great pleasure of the home construction industry, which had donated almost $1.2 million to Republicans in the 1999–2000 election cycle, the administration withdrew critical habitat designations and protections for 19 species of salmon and steelhead in California, Washington, Oregon and Idaho.[37] The move covered fish in more than 150 different watersheds, rivers, bays and estuaries in four states, including Puget Sound and the Columbia and Snake rivers. It cleared the way for extensive timber sales, home construction and water diversions throughout this region. Next, the administration began redrawing the existing habitat maps to exclude areas highly prized by oil and timber companies. Between 2001 and 2003, the Bush administration reduced the land area contained within critical habitat by more than 50 percent with no credible scientific basis to support the shrinkage.[38]

Craig Manson, Bush's Assistant Interior Secretary for Fish, Wildlife and Parks, justifies the agency's failure to designate and defend critical habitat by arguing that it "provides little additional protection to most listed species, while preventing the Service from using scarce conservation resources for activities with greater conservation benefits." Manson contends that, "In almost all cases recovery of listed species

---

[35] Walters, Mark Jerome. *A Shadow and a Song: The Struggle to Save an Endangered Species.* (Post Mills, VT: Chelsea Green Publishing Co.), 1992.

[36] Hattam, Jennifer. "No Habitat, No Problem," *Sierra* (July/August 2002). http://www.sierraclub.org/sierra/200207/lol.asp.

[37] Hattam, Jennifer. (July/August 2002).

[38] Center for Biological Diversity. *Reagan Redux: A Review of the Bush Critical Habitat Record* (April 21, 2003). www.biologicaldiversity.org/ swcbd/activist/Bushrecord.pdf; St. Clair, Jeffrey. (June 9, 2003).

will come through voluntary cooperative partnerships, not regulatory measures such as critical habitat."[39]

However, according to two long-delayed reports quietly submitted to Congress by the FWS in June 2003, species with critical habitat designations are more than twice as likely to make progress toward recovery as species without them.[40] This figure would be considerably higher if critical habitats weren't constantly diminished and reduced by agencies, restricted by budget limitations and compromised by conflicts of interest and political pressure. These problems are magnified when the agencies in charge of protecting endangered species go to bat for the very interests bent on gutting or eliminating the ESA altogether. Bush appointees to the DoI and the FWS have ranged from covertly antagonistic to openly hostile toward the ESA and the need for critical habitat.

Case in point: Julie MacDonald, Bush's choice for Deputy Assistant Secretary of the Interior for Fish and Wildlife and Parks. Hundreds of pages of records, obtained by environmental groups through the Freedom of Information Act, chronicle a long-running battle between MacDonald and FWS scientists over whether to safeguard plants and animals from oil and gas drilling, power lines and real estate development. MacDonald was renowned for her cozy relationship with hired guns such as Steve Quarles – a powerful litigator for the logging, pesticides, meat and development industries – who helped create a lobby group to drum up support for Congressman Pombo's failed effort to eviscerate the ESA in 2005. To further the interests of Quarles, Pombo and their corporate cohorts, Deputy Secretary MacDonald used her position to prevent the placement of dozens of imperiled species on the endangered species list, block the protection of millions of acres of critical habitat and overrule agency scientists when they attempted to prevent or reduce the destruction of wildlife habitat.

In one instance reported by the *Seattle Times*, MacDonald complained in an email to the FWS biologists about their aggressive protection of the threatened delta smelt, indigenous to the Sacramento–San Joaquin estuary. According to the *Times*, "MacDonald then called and read her email to a California Farm Bureau Federation lawyer." The Farm Bureau promptly "filed a motion to reopen its case seeking to exempt the smelt from ESA protections and citing MacDonald's email as evidence that the government's science was flawed."[41]

In March 2007, a report to Congress by the DoI's Inspector General accused MacDonald of violating federal rules and called for her to face punishment for leaking information about endangered species to industry groups. However, MacDonald resigned the week before a House oversight committee was scheduled

[39] Shogren, Elizabeth. "Bush Weighs Endangered Species Delay," *Los Angeles Times* (April 19, 2003). http://www.commondreams.org/headlineso3/0419-06.htm; *Environmental News Service.* "Comment Welcome on Mexican Spotted Owl Habitat Reports" (March 29, 2004).

[40] *Center for Biological Diversity.* "U.S. Fish and Wildlife Service Reports Show That Critical Habitat Enhances Recovery of Endangered Species" (October 2003). http://www.biologicaldiversity.org/swcbd/Programs/policy/ch/sub1.html.

[41] Welch, Craig. "Bush Switches Nation's Tack on Protecting Species," *Seattle Times* (September 27, 2004). http://seattletimes.nwsource.com/html/nation-world/2002047271_bushesa27m.html.

to hear testimony about her violations of the ESA, censorship of scientific reports and mistreatment of FWS staff.[42]

THE "RECOVERY PLAN" LOOPHOLE: DEATH
BY A THOUSAND CUTS

Closely related to the designation of critical habitat, successive amendments to the ESA require the FWS and the NMFS to develop *recovery plans* for all listed species. Recovery plans include (1) a detailed description of the species' current situation; (2) a recovery threshold and benchmarks for indicating when this threshold has been achieved; (3) an implementation schedule of tasks and projects necessary to ensure recovery; and (4) a method for assessing the effectiveness of the recovery plan.

A host of problems undermine recovery plans. Perhaps the most serious is that about 500 of all listed species still languish without them.[43] There are two loopholes that permit the FWS and the NMFS to evade recovery plans. First, the ESA permits the agency to dodge the recovery plan requirement if it finds that a recovery plan would "not promote the conservation of a species." Second, the agency does not have to make or follow deadlines for the promulgation and implementation of recovery plans. So far, the responsible agencies have stretched and bent these legal exceptions to deny recovery plans to more than 40 percent of all listed species.[44]

Often, however, species *with* recovery plans fare little better than those without them. This seems perplexing at first glance. Recovery plans appear to possess the ideal characteristics of enforceable guidelines to make sure that agencies take the necessary measures to conserve and rehabilitate listed species. They are prepared by experts, they are supposed to direct FWS and NMFS monies toward identifying and pursuing the steps necessary to promote recovery and they should identify which agencies are responsible for carrying out specific conservation tasks. Unfortunately, at least three court cases have rendered recovery plans legally unenforceable.[45]

Although the FWS and the NMFS are required by law to develop recovery plans for all listed species, there is no explicit legal requirement for any government agency whose programs affect endangered species to implement recovery plans, nor are plans typically detailed enough to clearly establish whether they are being followed.[46] All too often, involved state and federal agencies ignore critical habitat designations and evade implementation of recovery plans. This forces concerned citizens and

---

[42] Cart, Julie. "Interior Department Official Resigns," *Los Angeles Times* (May 2, 2002). http://www.latimes.com/news/science/environment/la-na-macdonald2may02,1,7983114.story?track=rss&ctrack=1&cset=true.

[43] Bean, Michael J. "Endangered Species – Endangered Act?" *Environment* (January 1999). http://www.findarticles.com/p/articles/mi_m1076/is_1_41/ai_53709851.

[44] Helmy, Eric. "Teeth for a Paper Tiger: Redressing the Deficiencies of the Recovery Provisions of the Endangered Species Act," *Environmental Law* (September 22, 2000). http://www.accessmylibrary.com/article-1G1-70393144/teeth-paper-tiger-redressing.html.

[45] Cheever, Frederico. "The Road to Recovery: A New Way of Thinking About the Endangered Species Act," *Ecology Law Quarterly* (Winter 1996): 1–78.

[46] Cheever, Frederico (Winter 1996): 1–78.

environmental groups to file expensive lawsuits in order to defend listed species. Their record of success in court is uneven at best.

During the Clinton administration, the Mexican spotted owl was listed as threatened due to high logging rates on U.S. Forest Service lands. But even though 90 percent of all known Mexican spotted owls live in the national forests of Arizona and New Mexico, no acres within these forests were designated as critical habitat. To defend the Mexican spotted owl's habitat, the Center for Native Ecosystems, the Center for Biological Diversity and Diné Citizens Against Ruining the Environment took the FWS to court.

"The Fish and Wildlife Service is refusing to protect all of the owl's key habitat," said Jacob Smith of the Center for Native Ecosystems. "They didn't even include all the places we know the spotted owl lives. How can they protect this magnificent forest bird without even protecting the most important habitat? This is standard operating procedure for the Fish and Wildlife Service. They simply refuse to protect wildlife unless citizens sue them."[47] The suit was successful; the court required the FWS to expand the owl's habitat designation.

Based on the amended habitat designation, the FWS recovery plan proposed specific guidelines for protecting known spotted owl populations and their habitat. However, under Clinton and Bush, the Forest Service consistently ignored and violated Fish and Wildlife's guidelines for owl recovery by allowing the logging of protected habitat and nesting areas.[48] The court ruled that recovery plans are not legally binding and cannot be used to prohibit the Forest Service from further destruction of spotted owl habitat. To make matters worse, in August 2004, Bush's FWS director axed nearly five million acres from the Mexican spotted owl's critical habitat designation.

Recovery plans have other weaknesses: they are notoriously incomplete, outdated and too vague to guide the day-to-day decisions officials must make to improve the condition of an imperiled species or avoid putting its survival in greater jeopardy. Take the recovery plan for the black-capped vireo, an endangered bird found largely on privately owned land in Oklahoma and Texas. Obviously, influencing how private landowners handle the vireo and its critical habitat is vital to any successful recovery plan. Yet the FWS's recovery plan offers the following vapid recommendation: "Use various methods to protect vireos and their habitat on private lands. This should be a major part of recovery because little public land occurs in the vireo's range."[49] What those various methods might be and how to persuade private landowners to cooperate in their use are neither discussed nor defined in the plan.

---

[47] Press Release. *Center for Native Ecosystems.* "Colorado Groups to Join Mexican Spotted Owl Critical Habitat Suit" (March 28, 2001).

[48] Earth Justice. *Judge Orders Cattle off Mexican Spotted Owl Habitat* (December 12, 2002). http://www.earthjustice.org/accomplishments/display.html?ID=142; Center for Native Ecosystems. *Notice of Intent to Sue Over Spotted Owl* (March 28, 2001). http://www. nativeecosystems.org/mexicanspottedowl/010328_noi.htm.

[49] U.S. Fish and Wildlife Service, *Black-Capped Vireo Recovery Plan.* (Washington, DC: Government Printing Office), 1991: 45.

A National Academy of Science (NAS) study of the ESA concluded that requiring government officials to develop and implement recovery plans according to set deadlines, and with improved scientific standards, would greatly increase the rate of recovery and delisting. The NAS recommended that all recovery planning should include an element of "recovery plan guidance" that details how the ESA should be implemented to recover the species. According to the NAS, these changes would help ground recovery plans in the principles of conservation biology and make them more quantifiable, meaningful and effective in rehabilitating endangered species.[50]

Strong critical habitat designation and recovery plan provisions are essential to the ESA's capability to safeguard imperiled species and move them off the list and toward recovery. However, by abusing and stretching the law's limited exclusions, the FWS and NMFS have created loopholes that effectively deny critical habitat to 64 percent, and recovery plans to 40 percent, of all listed species. Furthermore, the critical habitat and recovery plan provisions have been so diluted and poorly implemented that even the species protected by them seldom recover.

SECTIONS 7 & 9: LIFE SUPPORT, NOT RECOVERY

The most well-known sections of the ESA are not intended to move listed species toward recovery. Their aim is more modest. Sections 7 and 9 were crafted to prevent further attrition of listed species' populations. Section 7 is directed at protecting listed species from the actions of government agencies, while section 9 is designed to protect listed species from the harmful actions of any citizen.

Known as the jeopardy prohibition, section 7 requires all federal agencies to ensure that their actions (including those regulating private actions) are "not likely to jeopardize the continued existence" of any endangered or threatened species, nor "adversely modify" its critical habitat. *Actions* are broadly defined: They include anything authorized, funded or carried out by the agency, including permits and licenses.

When any federal agency plans to fund, authorize or carry out an action, it must check with the appropriate service (FWS or NMFS) to determine whether their plans could harm protected species. If the agency is informed that their action "may affect" a species' survival, the agency must initiate consultation with the FWS or the NMFS. The service will then prepare a *biological opinion* indicating whether the proposed action will jeopardize the continued existence of the protected species.

If the FWS or the NMFS finds the action would jeopardize the species, it must suggest "reasonable and prudent alternatives" that would avoid such harm. The *reasonable and prudent alternatives* process has become the primary mechanism for resolving conflicts between federally authorized projects and the survival of protected species and the preservation of their habitats. This section has the potential to be a powerful tool for protecting listed species. However, because most species have no

[50] Kurpis, Lauren. (EndangeredSpecie.com.) *Facts About Endangered Species.* http://www. endangeredspecie.com/Interesting_Facts.htm.

designated critical habitat, the protections of section 7 are considerably weakened. Still, ESA opponents often accuse environmentalists of abusing section 7 powers to prohibit developments they primarily oppose for reasons other than protecting endangered species.

But the facts indicate that section 7 prohibitions have had an extremely minor impact on federal projects. Of the 1,869 consultations undertaken over one five-year period, only 181 resulted in a "jeopardy opinion" identifying conflicts. In 158 of the 181 cases, the agencies offered at least one reasonable and prudent alternative that allowed the project to go forward without violating section 7.[51] Thus, during the five-year period studied, the ESA's jeopardy prohibition prevented 0.03 percent of all proposed federal actions. A longer-term study showed that only about one in every 3,500 projects is prevented by section 7.[52] Even when section 7 prevents an action, proponents can apply for an exemption. While exemptions are not granted easily, they *must* be granted if the Secretary of Defense determines that an exemption is necessary for national security.[53]

Section 9 is known as the takings provision. Under its authority, all *takings* of listed species would be prohibited, whether on state, federal or private land. The term *takings* refers to all attempts by "any person" to "harass, harm, pursue, hunt, shoot, wound, kill, trap, capture or collect an endangered or threatened species." Restrictions are less stringent for plants than for animals. Violation of the prohibition against taking a threatened or endangered species can result in criminal sanctions. The degree to which section 9 protects critical habitat for species is still a subject of great dispute.

Congress created significant exemptions to section 9. The ESA authorizes the FWS and NMFS to issue *incidental take statements and permits. Take statements* allow federal projects to proceed, even if they will probably kill members of a species, as long as the killings are *incidental*, not intentional, and the deaths won't jeopardize the existence of the entire species. In addition, *incidental taking permits* may be issued to anyone whose actions might harm endangered species. To obtain this permit, applicants must submit a *Habitat Conservation Plan (HCP)* to the federal agency in charge of protecting that species. The plan must specify the harms likely to result from their activity, the steps that will be taken to minimize these harms and the other alternatives they've considered. The FWS or NMFS will then solicit and review public comment and issue an incidental take permit if it finds that the taking will be incidental, steps will be taken to minimize the impact on the species, the applicant

[51] Barry, D. L., L. Haroun, & C. Halvorson. "For Conserving Listed Species, Talk is Cheaper Than We Think: The Consultation Process Under the Endangered Species Act," *World Wide Fund For Nature*. (Washington, DC, 1992).

[52] Davidson, Bob & Jeff Curtis. "The Endangered Species Act: 30 Years on the Ark," *Open Spaces* (September 13, 2004). http://www.open-spaces.com/article-v5n3-davison.php.

[53] An Endangered Species Committee (composed of six specified federal officials and a representative of each affected state) must decide whether to allow a project to proceed despite future harm to a species; at least five votes are required to pass an exemption. The law includes extensive rules and deadlines to be followed in applying for such an exemption, and some stringent rules for the Committee in deciding whether to grant an exemption.

will fund the plan and the taking "will not appreciably reduce the likelihood of the survival and recovery of the species in the wild."

Private landowners, corporations or state and local governments who clear land, cut timber or alter habitats in some other way that might incidentally harm a listed species must get an incidental take permit by developing an HCP. As of December 2002, 414 HCPs had been approved, covering approximately 30 million acres of nonfederal lands and protecting 200 endangered or threatened species.

FROM BUSH TO OBAMA

In the final days of his administration, President Bush took a final shot at crippling the Endangered Species Act by issuing two regulations designed to:

(1) Eliminate the U.S. Fish and Wildlife Service's role as an independent, scientific watchdog over potentially species-threatening federal projects such as mines, dams and timber sales;

(2) Exempt coal-fired power plants, federal fuel efficiency standards and all other greenhouse gas-emitting activities from Endangered Species Act review.

The president's second regulation specifically banned federal agencies from protecting the imperiled polar bear from greenhouse gas emissions and oil and gas development.

These policies were intended to cripple the FWS's oversight and enforcement powers and prevent the ESA from confronting the greatest future threat to endangered species: global climate change. Bush's 11th-hour regulations drew lawsuits from major environmental groups and nine states. Soon after his election, President Obama and Congress took the first steps toward revoking both regulations, and the Center for Biodiversity delivered 94,000 petitions to Interior Secretary Ken Salazar, requesting that he take action to rescinded the rule blocking FWS oversight under the ESA.

The president signed into law an omnibus appropriations bill giving Secretary Salazar the power to rescind both rules. According to the Center for Biodiversity, Salazar was pressured to use his power to restore FWS authority and protect the polar bear from climate change by 49 members of Congress; 35 members of the California legislature; more than 13,000 scientists; scores of law professors; and more than 200,000 citizens represented by more than 130 conservation organizations.[54] But Salazar chose to retain the rule preventing the ESA from protecting the polar bear from climate change.

Although Secretary Salazar admitted that "the single greatest threat to the polar bear is the melting of Arctic sea ice due to climate change," he said the global risk from greenhouse gases, generated worldwide, requires comprehensive policies, not

---

[54] Center for Biological Diversity. "Cleaning Up the Bush Legacy." http://www.biologicaldiversity. org/campaigns/cleaning_up_the_bush_legacy/index.html.

the disjointed efforts of multiple statutes and government agencies to protect specific species.[55] This seems like a reasonable justification, but it contradicts the Obama administration's policy of pursuing greenhouse gas restrictions under the Clean Air Act, whose national air pollution standards are hardly the ideal legal vehicle for crafting a comprehensive policy on energy and global climate change.

Some environmental groups fear that the Obama administration's uneven enthusiasm for a "comprehensive approach" may be an excuse to block several legal efforts to compel government agencies to rein in greenhouse gases through a variety of statutes – including the ESA and the Clean Water Act (CWA). In May 2009, a CWA lawsuit filed by the Center for Biological Diversity finally prompted the EPA to begin assessing the risk of ocean acidification caused by atmospheric CO_2 absorbed in seawater. Scientists monitoring the coastal waters off Washington state report that ocean acidification is already affecting seawater pH and disturbing marine ecosystems. According to an NAS report released in 2008, the pH of Washington's coastal waters has declined more than 0.2 units since 2000, violating the state's water quality standard.[56] By law, once a body of water is listed as "impaired," the EPA (or the state) must limit the emission of the offending pollutant into the specified waterway to prevent further deterioration. In this case, the CWA would require limits on CO_2 emissions that contribute to ocean acidification.[57]

Ocean acidification decreases the capability of many marine organisms to build their shells and skeletal structure. It may soon endanger tens of thousands of marine species that build shells and skeletons from calcium carbonate. Increased ocean acidification is expected to cause massive corrosion of coral reefs and seriously damage marine ecosystems. These adverse conditions would have dire implications for the millions of people who depend on sea life for their survival. According to Martin Rees, President of the Royal Society, the U.K.'s national academy of science:

> Everybody knows that the increasing concentration of carbon dioxide in the atmosphere leads to climate change. But it has another environmental effect, ocean acidification, which hasn't received much political attention. Unless global CO_2 emissions can be cut by at least 50% by 2050, and more thereafter, we could confront an underwater catastrophe, with irreversible changes in the makeup of our marine biodiversity. The effects will be seen worldwide, threatening food security, reducing coastal protection and damaging the local economies that may be least able to tolerate it.[58]

[55] Revkin, Andrew C. "U.S. Curbs Use of Species Act in Protecting Polar Bear," *New York Times* (May 8, 2009). http://www.nytimes.com/2009/05/09/science/earth/09bear.html.

[56] Environment News Service. "First Ocean Acidification Lawsuit Filed Against EPA," (May 14, 2009). http://www.ens-newswire.com/ens/may2009/2009-05-14-091.asp.

[57] Environment News Service (May 14, 2009).

[58] Guardian.co.uk. "Carbon Emissions Threaten 'Underwater Catastrophe', Scientists Warn," (June 1, 2009). http://www.guardian.co.uk/environment/2009/jun/01/carbon-emissions-ocean-acidification.

Martin's statement underscores the extensive, synergetic global interaction between environmental threats such as climate change, water pollution and biodiversity. These problems have multiplied and outgrown the restricted efforts of national governments to address them through domestic policies unless they are part of a coordinated international response. Unfortunately, international measures to confront these potentially catastrophic global problems are so primitive and ineffectual they make America's environmental laws appear downright rigorous.

7

Planetary Problems – Cooperation or Collapse?

America's environmental laws are poorly enforced and riddled with loopholes. Yet they definitely rank a cut above global environmental accords. After all, if a wealthy superpower like the United States can't protect its environment, how can a fractious gallimaufry of nations hope to prevent planetary ecological crises like climate disruption and plummeting biodiversity? Negotiating agreements between scores of rivalrous nations is like herding cats. Ultimately, nations recognize no lawmaking authority greater than themselves and there is no global government capable of enforcing the few environmental treaties that achieve ratification. Therefore, many international relations scholars contend that establishing effective environmental agreements is a virtually futile endeavor.

PROSPECTS FOR ENVIRONMENTAL COOPERATION – FOUR THEORIES

Neorealism, which is arguably the most prominent theory of international relations, considers such ventures dubious and potentially hazardous. Neorealist theory asserts that all nations are entrenched in an *anarchic* international system lacking any global peacekeeping authority. Neorealists maintain that this situation compels states to prioritize security and elevate power above all other assets. Power is the nation's capability to defend its interests (especially its very existence) and get what it wants. And because power can be meaningfully measured and employed only in relation to potential threats, obstacles and adversaries – it is relative.

The dog-eat-dog nature of world politics envisioned by the neorealists discourages prolonged cooperation between nations. Temporary security alliances may prove advantageous for bolstering power and overcoming mutual rivals. However, protracted cooperation to protect the environment is another story because it requires considerable sacrifice, loss of maneuverability and limitations on national sovereignty. In addition, pollution taxes and regulations are not popular with economic elites.

Neorealists believe that nations cannot afford to comply with environmental treaties that impose prolonged sacrifices without enforceable guarantees that others will not cheat and free ride. Yet, in their estimation, such guarantees are precluded by the system's anarchic nature, which encourages nations to advance their interests by exploiting the weaknesses of others. Consequently, neorealists see environmental treaty making as an impractical folly with the potential to seriously jeopardize the power and security of those involved. For neorealists, the only situation that could possibly facilitate some level of lasting cooperation would be one that was fostered, induced, imposed and enforced by a sanctioning superpower – a hegemon like the United States.[1]

Another prevalent theory of global affairs, neoliberalism, is more sanguine about the prospects for protecting the planet through cooperation. Neoliberals disagree with the neorealists' depiction of the international system as an anarchic, beggar-thy-neighbor power struggle. Instead, they recognize a system in which nations are embedded in a network of *complex interdependence*, involving the pursuit of economic growth through world trade and the mutual exchange of information. Neoliberals believe this interdependence has become more pervasive, influential and essential to every nation's well-being over time.[2]

In their estimation, the survival and security of nations rests on their capability to benefit from this cooperative process of global exchange. Therefore, neoliberals believe the neorealists' preoccupation with security through military power is misplaced. Martial conflict disrupts economic exchange and destabilizes the international system. Thus, nations should pursue warfare only as a measure of last resort, not as a first line of defense.

Neoliberals consider cooperation far more pervasive and essential to the nature of the international system than neorealists realize. In their view, cooperation and controlled competition must trump conflict for the system to survive. Just as the conflict between two boxers is governed by a set of mutually accepted rules of engagement, so the conflicts and rivalries within international capitalism are bounded by generally acknowledged economic and political contracts, norms and standards.

Although neoliberals consider economic cooperation vital to national prosperity and the health of the international system, they are more tentative about *environmental* cooperation because it often conflicts with the very economic activities that countries and corporations find so profitable – from plundering marine ecosystems to burning rain forests and fossil fuels. This tension between economic and environmental cooperation gives neoliberals pause. Because they are wedded to the notion that world trade generates growth and reduces international conflict, they are hesitant to inhibit this process by imposing restrictions to protect the environment. Instead, they promote profitable solutions for protecting the planet. In some cases, these solutions have worked or at least postponed the day of reckoning. In others, they have failed miserably by either trading one type of pollution for another, exacerbating the problem or even creating new ones.

---

[1] Snidal, Duncan. "The Limits of Hegemonic Stability Theory," *International Organization*, v. 39 (Fall 1985): 579–614.

[2] Keohane, R. & J. Nye. *Power and Interdependence: World Politics in Transition*, 2nd ed (Boston, MA: Little-Brown), 1989.

Neoliberals remain undeterred. For them, economic growth supersedes environ-mental protection. This inclines them toward two potentially disastrous implicit assumptions. First, it is far more important that any purported environmental fix be profitable than truly effective. Second, if there is no *profitable* solution to an environ-mental problem, then perhaps there is no problem (or acceptable solution) at all. These two assumptions are part and parcel of the cherished neoliberal axiom that there is no fatal contradiction between capitalism's need to ceaselessly maximize growth and the ecological and resource limitations of our planet.[3]

Thus, unlike neorealists, neoliberals do not scoff at the futility of global environ-mental cooperation. Instead, they champion agreements that employ market mech-anisms and technological fixes in the hope that environmental protection can turn a profit.[4] Unfortunately, because their overriding concern is economic growth, neo-liberals often favor, advocate and defend these types of solutions whether they work or not.

World systems theory (WST) provides an alternative assessment of world affairs and the prospects for global environmental cooperation.[5] Where neorealists see nations preoccupied with *security* and vying for *power* in an anarchic international system and neoliberals see a community of nations benefiting from *interdependent economic growth*, world systems theorists see a system of global capitalism based on *dominance* and *exploitation, inequitably* divided between the rich core countries of the North and the poor peripheral countries of the South.

Inequity lies at the very heart of this hierarchical world system in which power protects wealth and wealth begets power. A handful of the world's wealthiest and most powerful nations and corporations stand at the apex, or the *core*, of this world system. The core's dominance facilitates the exploitation of the periphery's cheap resources and labor to produce an endless stream of products marketed to the higher-paid workers, professionals and businessmen in the core through the institutionalized glorification of mindless, wasteful consumption known as advertising.

World systems theorists believe dominance and exploitation incite recurrent resistance. During the twentieth century, this resistance launched national independ-ence movements in Asia, Africa and Latin America, forcing the core to abandon direct colonialism. But core elites soon turned this setback to their advantage by coopting independence leaders with a share of the wealth produced by the laboring classes beneath them. The few third world leaders who refused to take the bait were vilified, discredited, isolated, subverted, driven from power and even eliminated by the counterinsurgency strategies of the core.

Once emancipated from absolute colonial rule, even the most compliant Southern elites have tried to increase their share of the wealth derived from the people and resources of their country. To accomplish this and bolster their dwindling popularity,

[3] Simon, Julian L. *The Ultimate Resource 2.* (Princeton, NJ: Princeton University Press), 1996.
[4] Schmidheiny, Stephan. *Changing Course: A Global Business Perspective on Development and the Environment.* (Boston, MA: MIT Press), 1992.
[5] See: Wallerstein, Immanuel. *World-Systems Analysis: An Introduction.* (Durham, NC: Duke University Press), 2004; *After Liberalism.* (NY: New Press), 1995.

Southern elites champion the cause of "development" and insist on more equitable relations between North and South.[6]

For world system theorists, the inequitable, exploitive relationships at the heart of the global economy present formidable barriers to international environmental cooperation. Southern elites are justifiably mistrustful of calls for mutual sacrifice to protect the environment. They question why poor nations should restrain their development plans to help prevent ecological problems they had little part in creating.

Core elites, in turn, duck their own historic responsibility for global ecological crises while pointing the finger at rapidly developing nations such as China, Brazil and India for exacerbating them. Meanwhile, they advocate and finance solutions that reinforce their continued hegemony. Finally, outside the citadels of power, everyday people in both the core and periphery fear that elites will impose draconian and/or ineffective environmental policies that benefit the wealthy and impose further hardships on everyone else.

In sum, world systems theorists insist that global capitalism is driven to maximize growth and profit through inequitable relationships of exploitation and coercion. Therefore, they consider cooperation to protect the environment extremely unlikely in an aggressively expansionist world system divided between exploiters and exploited, oppressors and oppressed.

Recently, a fourth view of international relations and the prospects for environmental cooperation has emerged. Known as the *green* or *ecological* perspective, this outlook holds much in common with world systems theory. Green theory agrees with WST that all nations are embedded in a global capitalist economy whose insatiable drive for profit and growth necessitates rapacious exploitation of labor and resources coupled with obsessive, wasteful consumption.[7] But for Greens, the imperatives of profit and growth are not the only forces behind incessant expansion. Like neorealists, Greens contend that as long as humanity is divided into rival nation-states, governments will seek security, wealth and power through military might. This condition promotes arms races and amplifies the system's expansionist metabolism.

For Greens, the anarchic nature of the international system is just one of several forces behind escalating militarism. Military power is wielded by core nations to gain control of territory or resources, assert their dominance over the periphery and stake out spheres of influence between themselves. In addition, military coercion is employed to repress popular resistance and retain elites in power. And finally, some core nations amass enormous profits from weapons manufacture and trade.

The most meaningful way Greens diverge from all the other perspectives is their estimation that the high-energy global society we take for granted is utterly *unsustainable*.[8] For Greens, global industrial capitalism faces two imminent, insurmountable

---

[6] Wallerstein, Immanuel. *Historical Capitalism.* (London: Verso), 1995.
[7] Goldfrank, Walter L., David Goodman, & Andrew Szasz, eds. *Ecology and the World-System.* (Westport, CT: Greenwood Press), 1999.
[8] Daly, Herman. *Beyond Growth: The Economics of Sustainable Development.* (Boston, MA: Beacon Press), 1996.

limitations. First, it is rapidly depleting vital nonrenewable resources, especially its primary energy source – fossil fuels. Second, it is poisoning itself and the biosphere with its wastes.[9]

Unsustainable – the significance of this conclusion cannot be overstated. If Greens are right about the approaching demise of our wasteful, rapid growth, overconsumptive society, the immediate future looks challenging and potentially quite grim. The longer people remain either oblivious or in denial about the impending crisis, and the longer elites resist making essential changes because they are not profitable or politically expedient, the worse the situation will become. Conversely, the sooner and more thoroughly we change course and move toward a sustainable, nontoxic way of life, the better off all of us, and our planet, will be.

Greens are of two minds about the prospects for global environmental cooperation. Their determination that the modern world is overshooting its ecological limits elicits an uncomfortable dichotomy of pessimism and hope. Greens assert that widespread ecological and social calamities are unavoidable without unprecedented cooperative action. Yet because government and corporate elites profit from the status quo, Greens doubt their willingness to self-impose strict limitations upon their freedom to extract resources and pollute unless confronted with profound breakdowns of the current system. Even then – without widespread, bottom-up political pressure for cooperative solutions – there is no guarantee that nations won't spurn collaboration and engage in devastating clashes over the dwindling resources of a degraded planet.

To avert this ominous prospect, Greens place whatever hope they have for efficacious environmental cooperation upon the increasing organization and influence of civil society.[10] World opinion and public perceptions have been increasingly shaped and mobilized by grassroots social movements and global activist networks of nongovernmental organizations (NGOs). Without citizen-based pressure, Greens doubt that world leaders would have gathered to demonstrate their concern at the Earth Summit in Rio de Janeiro, or that nations would have engaged in deliberations around ozone depletion, climate change or biodiversity. However, it remains to be seen whether this groundswell of ecological populism will be enough to compel policymakers to come to the table and negotiate truly effective, binding cooperative agreements.

Greens generally believe that one key determinant of whether nations decide to cooperate is the conceptual framework used to understand environmental problems. If a problem is perceived as a looming, universal threat, cooperation is far more likely than if it is framed as a predicament of scarce, diminishing resources. Fighting over crumbs is a selfish and rivalrous free-for-all, but overcoming mutual threats calls for cooperation.

Although the nature of some problems is clear-cut, others can be seen from competing angles. For example, from one perspective the energy crisis can be framed as an ever-shrinking supply of fossil fuels. Depicting it in this manner encourages

---

[9] Sachs, Wolfgang, ed. *Global Ecology: A New Area of Political Conflict.* (London: Zed Books), 1993.
[10] Lipschutz, Ronnie D. & Judith H. Mayer. *Global Civil Society and Global Environmental Governance: The Politics of Nature from Place to Planet.* (Albany, NY: SUNY Press), 1996.

nations to engage in geopolitical rivalry over remaining petroleum reserves. Yet the energy crisis can also be viewed as an impending ecological disaster brought on by burning fuels that overload the atmosphere with greenhouse gases (GHGs). This interpretation of the problem elicits the need for collaboration to seek out clean, renewable energy sources and forestall climate disruption.

ROADMAPS AND ROADBLOCKS TO RATIFICATION

While framing problems to encourage cooperation is important, this is only a small part of the daunting quest to achieve successful environmental treaties. Unfortunately, none of the prominent approaches to international relations provides even the most rudimentary roadmap for undertaking this onerous journey. Practical pathways and prominent roadblocks in the path to cooperation are revealed only when successful and unsuccessful attempts to negotiate ecological agreements are thoughtfully analyzed and compared.

The global agreement to protect the Earth's ozone layer is arguably the most successful example of international environmental cooperation. Known as the Montreal Protocol, this agreement committed countries to a relatively rapid phase out of chlorofluorocarbons (CFCs) and other ozone depleting substances (ODSs). It took a mere decade to negotiate – only about half as long as the unfinished, faltering efforts to establish an effective climate change treaty. Despite some weaknesses in the ozone treaty's implementation and enforcement, there has been a dramatic drop in the production of ODSs since the Montreal Protocol's ratification and subsequent improvement.[11] Thus, compared with most environmental agreements, including the Kyoto Climate Treaty, the ozone agreement stands out as a rare example of effective international environmental cooperation.

What accounts for this exceptional level of international collaboration to halt ozone depletion compared with the tentative attempts to replicate this success around climate change? The answer to this question is not readily apparent because along many dimensions, ozone and climate change negotiations appear quite similar. For example:

(1) Both negotiations address atmospheric problems with close ecological and scientific relations to each other.
(2) Scientific uncertainty surrounds each issue, requiring policymakers to rely on an international community of scientists for their

---

[11] Parties to the Montreal Protocol have so far made five modifications, four of which strengthened the control provisions of the instrument. These modifications include the: London Amendment (1990); Copenhagen Amendment (1992); Vienna (1995) Montreal Amendment (1997); and the Beijing Amendment (1999). The London Amendment made substantive revisions regarding technology transfer and financing. In London, the Multilateral Fund was also created as the interim financial mechanism of the Protocol and, in 1992, became the permanent facility managed by the World Bank, UNEP, UNDP and UNIDO. The Copenhagen Amendment included the phase-out in the production and consumption of several halocarbon compounds by the end of 1995, and halons.

understanding of the sources, severity and social implications of both problems.

(3) Potentially disastrous consequences, public alarm and environmental activism have pushed policymakers into action on both issues.

(4) Both crises present nations with a *tragedy of the commons* dilemma[12] that pits their need for long-term environmental cooperation against the immediate advantages of cheating or free riding on the efforts of others.[13]

(5) Solutions to both problems impose short-range regulatory costs in order to realize more distant, future benefits.

(6) Preventive action around both problems has been obstructed by shortsighted yet powerful economic and political interests.

(7) Historically, developed nations were the major source of both problems, although some developing nations became substantial contributors.

(8) Developed nations are the only countries with the resources and technological capacity to address these problems.

(9) Long-term solutions to these two problems are impossible without the participation of the major developing nations.

This leads directly to one final obvious, but crucial, similarity:

(10) Neither problem can be solved by a few countries. Therefore, *to succeed, negotiations must engender extensive international consensus around a viable solution.*

THE STRUGGLE FOR CONSENSUS – ACTORS AND ISSUES

As negotiations commenced, both climate change and ozone deliberations generated three rival coalitions composed of like-minded parties who viewed their interests in a similar way. *Activist coalitions* formed around governments, IGOs and NGOs who supported the timely ratification of effective atmospheric agreements. Those who profited from these polluting activities joined *blocking (or veto) coalitions* to foil effective regulations by stalling and promoting cosmetic agreements to "study the problem" indefinitely. And finally, *equity coalitions* of developing nations threatened to reject agreements that did not satisfactorily address the inequities between rich and poor nations surrounding these two atmospheric problems. Although both ozone and climate change negotiations involved these three coalition types, the particular actors involved in each of them differed and shifted as negotiations unfolded.

---

[12] Hardin, Garrett. "The Tragedy of the Commons," *Science*, v. 162 (September 1968): 1243–8. The Ecologist. *Whose Common Future?* (Philadelphia, PA: New Society Publishers), 1993; Hardin, Garrett. "Political Requirements for Preserving Our Common Heritage," *Wildlife in America*, H. P. Bokaw, ed. (Washington, DC: Council on Environmental Quality), 1978.

[13] Buck, Susan J. *The Global Commons: An Introduction*. (Washington, DC: Island Press), 1998; The Ecologist. *Whose Common Future? Reclaiming the Commons*. (Philadelphia, PA: New Society Publishers; UK: Earthscan Publications), 1993.

From the outset, members of the blocking and equity coalitions resisted the prompt ratification of an effective treaty. Both would have preferred to free ride on the environmental efforts of others. But realistically, this "have-your-cake-and-eat-it-too" preference was moot because extensive free riding renders any potential pact so burdensome and ineffective that even activists abandon it. Consequently, the blocking coalition's first preference was no agreement – or some cosmetic agreement requiring no significant action at all. If this option proved indefensible, blockers favored a viable multilateral agreement over the option they considered most repugnant: self-imposed unilateral regulations. While the equity coalition agreed that unilateral action was the worst option of all, it favored an effective, *equitable* multilateral agreement over some hollow cosmetic treaty.

As negotiations unfolded, blocking and equity coalition resistance assumed the form of three roadblocks to ratification. These three roadblocks have no established order in which they must be overcome, but the same logical sequence emerged in the course of both negotiations.

The first barrier was scientific uncertainty. Countries resist involving themselves in the costly, time-consuming process of international negotiations unless they become convinced that a serious threat requiring their attention confronts them. Without some degree of scientific certainty that these atmospheric problems posed a grave peril, countries balked at engaging in negotiations, much less making binding costly commitments to halt them. Consequently, the first obstacle to building a viable treaty was the sharp disagreement over what level of scientific evidence was compelling enough to trigger international action.

Blockers claimed that ozone depletion and global warming were merely theoretical and that scientists were divided over whether these alleged problems posed any real, significant danger. They insisted upon absolute proof before costly regulatory measures were negotiated. Whereas activists considered absolute proof a potentially disastrous requirement for initiating precautionary action. They urged countries to combine extensive research with sensible protective measures that could be adjusted and upgraded to meet an evolving appreciation of the threat.

The cost-benefit roadblock moved center stage as soon as countries realized the gravity of the atmospheric threats they faced. Immediately they began assessing their own interests in relation to them. What are the costs and benefits of any particular response? What would be the impact of doing nothing? These concerns are inseparably linked to the issue of scientific uncertainty because nations are generally unwilling to bear any significant costs unless they are fairly certain they face a dire calamity.

Yet even when science conclusively demonstrates the existence of a serious menace, blocking coalitions continue to resist any agreement that appears more costly than business-as-usual. Cooperation is especially difficult if improved science indicates that some might benefit, while others will suffer, from atmospheric disruption. But even if it becomes clear that everyone will suffer, the cost-benefit calculus of those most imperiled by ozone depletion and climate change diverges dramatically from those who currently profit handsomely from the activities that cause them. These divergent interests lie at the heart of the contention between activist and blocking coalitions.

Cost-benefit calculations are further complicated by the difficulty of comparing a broad spectrum of policy alternatives and by the more immediate, focused burdens of regulation compared with the more long-term, diffuse benefits derived from averting atmospheric calamity. Yet unless all essential parties can agree upon policies to contain these threats that appear less costly than ignoring them, consensus is impossible. Ultimately, activists must deploy a compelling mix of persuasion, perks and pressures to alter blockers' interest calculations in favor of an agreement. This requires the activist coalition to employ strategies to convert, diffuse, outmaneuver, coopt and erode blocking coalition resistance.

Equity presents the next obstacle to ratifying an effective agreement. Questions of how to equitably share the regulatory hardships of any treaty become the focus of contention as soon as negotiators recognize the seriousness of the problem and the costs of confronting it. Consensus will fail unless rich and poor nations agree upon provisions that distribute the burdens of addressing these atmospheric crises in a manner deemed relatively fair by all. This is no simple task. Sharp disagreements exist over what constitutes fairness. Policymakers from affluent nations often insist that equity means that all nations must share the burden of confronting atmospheric crises *equally*.

Developing nations in the equity coalition disagree. For them, fairness means accountability – thus, the polluter should pay. Poor nations point out that rich nations created and profited from the activities that cause these ecological problems for many decades. Therefore, fairness requires affluent nations to assume most of the liability for atmospheric protection. This involves taking the lead to reduce their own harmful emissions and funding the technology transfers needed for poor nations to do the same.

Wealthy nations generally have the power to stonewall these equity claims unless their mounting desire for an effective agreement can be leveraged by the threat of an equity coalition boycott. To exercise this holdout strategy, poor nations must convince rich nations that they will exercise their collective power to withhold their signatures from any agreement they consider inequitable. This feat is much easier said than done. The particular nature of each atmospheric problem has a major impact on the viability of this strategy. Once again, it is the activist coalition that must mediate this impasse by crafting equity provisions acceptable to both sides.

Achieving consensus requires activist coalitions to devise atmospheric agreements that all parties consider:

- Necessary to avoid a real, imminent threat;
- Less costly than ignoring the problem;
- A fair distribution of the regulatory burden.

To clear these three hurdles, activist leadership must pursue strategies designed to either (1) win the other two coalitions over to their view of these issues; (2) impose enough political and economic pressure to secure their assent; or (3) satisfactorily address their concerns without sacrificing the final agreement's ability to arrest the impending crisis. Once these barriers are overcome, all three coalitions can merge into a single consensus coalition committed to ratifying a successful treaty.

FORMAL NEGOTIATIONS – THE TIP OF THE ICEBERG

Traditionally, international negotiations are pictured as rarefied, formal affairs in which high-level diplomats engage in stately decision making deliberations. According to this view, decisions follow rationally from a careful analysis of possible options for mitigating environmental problems. Such analyses employ conventional risk analysis, involving cost-benefit estimates for each course of action being considered, with appropriate allowances for uncertainties in the probabilities and magnitudes of each outcome. Government policymakers then assess each option based on their values and preferences and try to negotiate some acceptable compromise between them.

In the real world, environmental negotiations, and especially the wider process of consensus building that surrounds them, are more like rugby than rational analysis; and policy decisions are more likely to be the cumulative result of complex stakeholder rivalry and bargaining under conditions of extreme uncertainty. Unlike rational analysis, this convoluted, multilevel process emphasizes the role of domestic, transnational and international coalition politics – including scientific research, shaping public opinion, shifting alliances, lobbying, influence peddling, persuasion and learning – as the key to understanding how negotiators ultimately determine their interests and options.

Consequently, the valuation of environmental risks, the assessment of response costs and the equitability of various methods of distributing those costs all become important political battlefields in which contending coalitions attempt to advance their interests by winning over key policymakers to their positions. Thus, the outcome of international negotiations is highly dependent upon who national policymakers decide to listen to; what information they trust; and what values they use to weigh the costs, benefits and risks involved in each course of action. Of course, all these factors are heavily influenced by the correlation of political interests and pressures brought to bear upon them.

Formal atmospheric deliberations involving a handful of high-level negotiators are only the tip of the consensus-building iceberg. For both ozone and climate change, diplomats adopted a negotiating format known as the framework-protocol approach. This incremental process commits parties to an ongoing series of formal negotiating sessions spread out over several years. At the first official session, negotiators attempt to craft a framework convention. Usually this is little more than a statement of concern over the problem that affirms their desire to study it further and meet again to determine whether further action is necessary. At subsequent sessions, known as *protocols*, diplomats reexamine the problem and attempt to negotiate more effective responses if needed.

The framework-protocol approach has proven more successful and effective than a big, "all-or-nothing," one-shot treaty negotiation. It permits an ongoing process of learning, persuasion and bargaining to foster consensus and improve the effectiveness of the treaty over time. Even though this approach can be maddeningly and dangerously slow, it allows activists more time to research the problem, get organized, educate the public and pressure government policymakers to adopt more effective commitments with each successive protocol.

These formal negotiations are embedded in a complex milieu of informal public discussion, debate, interest peddling and advocacy involving a much broader array of participants. This consensus-building activity does not stop between negotiating sessions. It is an ongoing process carried out by an extensive ad hoc network of activist-minded citizens, educators and knowledgeable authorities; prominent public figures; local, national and transnational environmental NGOs; research institutions and scientific panels; government agencies, policymakers and diplomats; intergovernmental organizations; alternative technology inventors, investors and entrepreneurs; and even insurance, banking and business executives.

Besides negotiation and diplomacy, consensus building involves education and persuasion, political organization and pressure, scientific research and computer modeling, technological innovation, economic analysis and policy planning. It takes place through conversation and the printed word; over cyberspace, radio and TV; in homes, offices, courtrooms, boardrooms and classrooms as well as laboratories, field experiments and workshops; through marches, petitions and demonstrations; and during Congressional hearings and election debates. Consensus building goes on everywhere and anywhere some folks are trying to convince others that these human-induced atmospheric threats pose grave dangers requiring immediate cooperative action.

Consensus building predated, laid the groundwork for, and eventually included formal negotiations. Well before ozone depletion or climate change gained international salience, incipient activist and blocking coalitions were locked in struggle over how to handle them. Between these two rival blocs were the vast multitudes of the uninformed, undecided and uncommitted, as well as an emerging coalition of developing nations willing to participate as long as their disadvantages, aspirations and equity concerns were adequately addressed.[14]

Each of these coalitions pursues a general strategy of advancing its interests, expanding its size and influence, winning over the uncommitted and undermining its rivals. Both environmental and business NGOs try to win over national policymakers by participating as much as possible in the actual negotiating sessions. At both the domestic and international levels, they attempt to affect national policy by (1) directly lobbying, petitioning and electing government officials; and (2) indirectly influencing their perceptions through the media, the scientific (expert) community and public pressure. Thus, the press, the scientific community and the public are seen as potential assets in the campaign to sway policymakers to their side and undermine the credibility of their opposition.

Activist NGOs recognize that (1) the potential ally with the most legitimacy (to policymakers, the media and the public) is the scientific community; (2) the potential venue with the greatest capacity to shape public opinion and elicit popular concern is the media; and (3) their most politically powerful potential ally is a mobilized citizenry. Thus, the degree to which the activist coalition's position is validated and supported by the scientific community, gains media exposure and wins

---

[14] In both negotiations, the equity coalition formed well after the other two.

public support is closely related to the political weight it will carry with national policymakers.[15]

The international community's willingness to initiate negotiations demonstrated the blocking coalitions' politically untenable position in the preliminary phase of both atmospheric negotiations. Blockers could not credibly claim that deliberations were unnecessary because the risks were *surely* insignificant. Instead, blockers had to accept the reality of scientific uncertainty and concede the possibility that the risks posed by ozone depletion and global warming *might* be significant (or even devastating). Therefore – at a bare minimum – they had to grant the need for the international community to support further scientific study and deliberation around these problems.

Further research could potentially enhance the blockers' position if it demonstrated an insignificant threat, remained inconclusive or revealed that the environmental hazards would not be universal (especially if they fell primarily upon less consequential nations).[16] However, more often than not, new research justified the activists' call for immediate action by providing further evidence that the environmental risks were severe and spread relatively evenly.[17]

Yet in due course, both the blocking and equity coalitions held a formidable strategic advantage: veto power. Ultimately, an effective agreement must include enough stakeholders from the blocking and equity coalitions to make the agreement work. This puts the activist coalition at a distinct disadvantage. Since activists must win over *all* stakeholders essential to a viable treaty, a few, or even one, party considered vital to an effective agreement can thwart their efforts. This strategic advantage allows blocking interests to concentrate their resources and lobbying efforts on a few key governments rather than attempting to win broad acceptance for their position.

By holding out and threatening to free ride, a small but decisive minority can scuttle an agreement despite its apparently overwhelming support. Of course, depending on the resources at their command, the activist majority can exact steep costs for noncooperation. If they can increase public pressure and impose trade sanctions or other penalties, they can make free riding quite uncomfortable. But if

---

[15] Lerner, Steve. *Earth Summit: Conversations with Architects of an Ecologically Sustainable Future.* (Bolinas, CA: Common Knowledge Press), 1992: 214.

[16] An unevenly spread risk may be conducive to an agreement as long as the wealthiest most influential countries are most threatened by atmospheric disruption. Since, in both cases, it was known that the industrial activities of the North were the main cause of these problems, and that these same countries were in the best position to respond to the problem, it quickly came down to a question of how desperately these same countries were to negotiate a response that encouraged and incorporated Southern participation. If they perceive the dangers as serious and the South's participation as essential to an effective agreement, an unevenly spread risk may actually facilitate the crafting of a of side payment package acceptable to all.

[17] Because new research often reveals serious environmental dangers, blocking interests have lobbied behind the scenes to reduce the budgets of the principal scientific organizations studying ozone depletion and climate change. See: Montague, Peter. "Killing Science," *Rachel's Environment & Health Weekly* #462 (October 5, 1995). http://www.ejnet.org/rachel/rehw462.htm.

and when a crucial holdout finally concedes, it may extract concessions that severely undermine the treaty's effectiveness.

In sum, successful atmospheric agreements require three distinct negotiating blocs to reconcile their differences around three major issues. So far, only ozone negotiations have succeeded. Meanwhile, climate change deliberations have limped along for years, mired in contention. Explaining why requires careful comparative analysis of the negotiation process: the coalitions involved, the magnitude of the roadblocks confronting them and the activist coalitions' ability to surmount them.

ROADBLOCK #1 – BREAKING THE UNCERTAINTY BARRIER

For both ozone and climate deliberations, the activist coalitions' first major challenge was to convince others that the science revealed an atmospheric threat menacing and credible enough to warrant a response. While many types of uncertainty surround the negotiation of each atmospheric agreement, scientific uncertainty pertains to questions like these: What level of consensus exists among scientists over the causes and potential effects of this problem? Are human activities responsible? What types of controls are necessary to abate it? What will happen if we do not respond? How bad will things get? How fast? Is the problem reversible? Will the effects harm some and benefit others, or impose relatively universal hardships? To address these kinds of questions, both atmospheric negotiations were preceded by numerous scientific studies of increasing complexity and scope and several international conferences designed to improve the scientific community's understanding of the problem, pool their information and focus attention on questions requiring further research.

But this is not simply a straightforward process of gathering and objectively analyzing scientific data. Science informs, but does not determine, judgments about whether, when and how to respond. Establishing a threshold of scientific certainty necessary to justify and motivate cooperative action is a contentious, politically charged ordeal. Comparison of both atmospheric negotiations clearly reveals that this threshold is not predetermined, fixed or objective.

Policymakers' and public perceptions of the seriousness of these two atmospheric problems constituted a strategic battleground between those who sought to advance or obstruct the negotiation process. Comparative analysis reveals that negotiators were willing to take action based on considerably lower levels of certainty, if they perceived the atmospheric threat as real, fairly immediate, universally devastating and virtually irreversible.

REAL MENACES OR IMAGINARY SCARES?

The debate over whether or not ozone depletion and global warming were genuinely dangerous enough to deserve policymakers' attention began long before the initiation of formal negotiations. Initially, a relatively small group of scientists and environmental activists endeavored to persuade policymakers that these problems were serious and salient enough to become part of the domestic and international agenda.[18]

American scientists were the first to recognize the seriousness of both problems because of the relatively advanced nature of atmospheric science and climate modeling in the United States. Their concerns were quickly grasped and popularized by environmental NGOs. The ozone issue eventually generated enough media coverage and public apprehension to grab policymakers' attention in the United States and several Scandinavian countries with light-skinned populations prone to skin cancer (and no CFC industry). For climate change, the small island nations and low-lying countries most threatened by sea level rise, coral bleaching and increased tropical storms pushed hardest to get the issue onto the international agenda.

Once these issues gained an international platform, this forum was used to improve the research on these issues, educate the public and convince the uncommitted and all essential members of the other two coalitions[19] that these problems were real and perilous enough to warrant a proactive response. For both ozone and climate change, this struggle was led by international panels of atmospheric scientists from many nations organized and coordinated by UNEP and WMO. Environmental NGOs and policymakers from activist nations popularized their findings. In each case, these respected scientific panels eroded the blocking coalition's skepticism with a growing body of evidence that a grave threat existed. At the same time, NGO activists educated and alerted the public and pressured policymakers "from below" for an effective agreement.

Compared with climate change, it took far less time and evidence to convince ozone diplomats to act on these scientific assessments. Efforts to reduce the levels of scientific uncertainty surrounding ozone depletion and global warming began during the 1970s. Investigating the impact of CFCs on the ozone shield began in 1974, shortly after F. Sherwood Rowland and Mario Molina published their theory that CFCs could migrate into the upper atmosphere and devour ozone.[20] After presenting their research to the American Chemical Society, Rowland told reporters that significant damage to the ozone layer may already be inescapable and could take many decades to repair. He warned that skin cancers could be expected to rise drastically from increased human exposure to solar ultraviolet radiation and suggested that the atmosphere was not an inexhaustible sink into which human waste could be dumped and forgotten. Rowland and Molina maintained that even though their evidence was not conclusive, their theory was strong enough and the dangers persistent and severe enough, that CFC production – an $8 billion industry in the United States alone – should be phased out.

It took 14 years to verify their theory; but fortunately, countries were willing to act on a far lower level of certainty than definitive proof. Years before the theory was

---

[18] In this initial phase, both the scientific and environmental activists and the policymakers they sought to win over were generally from Europe and the United States.

[19] Generally the equity coalition remained fairly aloof from this struggle. However, the activist coalition's efforts to educate representatives from the equity coalition about the seriousness of the problem and the necessity of a cooperative response had an impact on later struggles over the nature of an equitable agreement.

[20] Molina, Mario & F. Sherwood Rowland. "Stratospheric Sink for Chlorofluoromethanes: Chlorine Atom – Catalyzed Destruction of Ozone," *Nature*, v. 249 (June 1974): 810–12.

verified, the United States and a few other countries removed CFCs from "nonessentials" such as aerosols. By 1987, when ozone negotiators met in Montreal, even the most die-hard blockers acceded to substantial CFC cuts months *before* NASA-led missions over Antarctica confirmed that they were destroying the ozone shield.[21]

By contrast, despite 30 years of extensive research and a high level of scientific consensus that climate change poses a clear and present danger, diplomats have yet to negotiate GHG reductions comparable to the CFC cuts made in Montreal. There are several interrelated reasons why ozone negotiators were willing to act on considerably less evidence than their climate change counterparts.

THE OZONE HOLE – THE DREAD FACTOR LOWERS THE BAR

The discovery of a "hole"[22] in the ozone shield over Antarctica had a profound impact on the willingness of policy-makers to take preventive action well before conclusive evidence established that CFCs were the cause. There were three main steps to verifying the CFC-ozone hypothesis:

(1) Evidence that CFCs were arriving in the stratosphere unaltered;
(2) Evidence that these CFCs were being broken up by UV radiation and releasing chlorine atoms (called free radicals); and
(3) Evidence that these chlorine free radicals initiated a catalytic reaction that destroyed enormous amounts of ozone.

During the 1970s, the U.S. scientific community mounted a major research campaign involving the National Academy of Sciences (NAS) and a growing number of prominent chemists, meteorologists, physicists and space scientists from NASA, the National Oceanic and Atmospheric Administration (NOAA) and leading universities.[23] Throughout 1975, they used an arsenal of high-flying aircraft and balloon-borne instruments to detect CFCs 15 miles or more above the Earth's surface. By July, NOAA and NCAR researchers established for the first time that CFCs did indeed reach the stratosphere. Further studies revealed that CFCs were being zapped by the sun's ultraviolet rays and releasing ozone-destroying chlorine.[24] Thus, by 1976, two of the three steps necessary to verify the theory were complete.

---

[21] Watson, R. T. et al. *Present State of Knowledge of the Upper Atmosphere 1988: An Assessment Report.* National Aeronautics & Space Administration (August 1988).

[22] Because the depletion was never total, the term "ozone hole" is technically inaccurate. Many members of the blocking coalition objected to it because of its crisis bearing psychological connotations. They preferred to speak of "temporary ozone loses." According to some, names that include repeated sounds, like the three "O's" in ozone hole have "an advantage in the marketplace of ideas." Editorial. "Mysterious Seriousness," *Los Angeles Times* (November 1986): 28. I choose to use the term since it has gained widespread acceptance even in the scientific journals.

[23] Benedick, Richard Elliot. "Lessons from 'the Ozone Hole'," *Greenhouse Warming: Negotiating a Global Regime.* World Resources Institute, ed. (Washington, DC: WRI), 1991: 9–12; Benedick, Richard E. *Ozone Diplomacy.* (Cambridge, MA: Harvard University Press), 1991.

[24] Machta, Lester. "Ozone and its Enemies," *NOAA Magazine* (January 1976): 5.

The industry-led blocking coalition clung tenaciously to the notion that CFCs were benign because of the continuing absence of step three: solid proof that chlorine free radicals in the stratosphere actually devoured vast amounts of ozone. However, their steadfast demand for proof crumbled well before conclusive evidence of this third step finally surfaced in 1987.[25] In fact, the blocking coalition's intransigence began to dissolve in 1985, after British scientists discovered an ominous cavity in the ozone shield over Antarctica.

More than a decade before the ozone hole was discovered, Rowland and Molina's hypothesis began generating headlines and apprehension that CFCs might deplete the planet's ozone shield. By 1975, a battle ensued over how much evidence was needed to justify action against CFCs. A growing activist coalition of atmospheric scientists, climate modelers and environmentalists promoted a "better-safe-than-sorry" approach. They realized that if Rowland and Molina were right, but the United States and other governments waited years for irrefutable proof, the world could face a severe and prolonged degradation of the Earth's ozone layer that shields life from the sun's deadly UV rays. Environmental groups advocated precautionary action in addition to further study. The Natural Resources Defense Council (NRDC) and Friends of the Earth petitioned the Consumer Products Safety Commission for a ban on all nonessential aerosol sprays containing CFCs.

A smaller group of scientists and chemical industry flacks opposed taking any action against CFCs based on the uncertainties surrounding the Rowland-Molina hypothesis. They became the nucleus of an incipient blocking coalition committed to using the persistent uncertainties surrounding the CFC-ozone hypothesis to play down the alleged dangers and deny the need for any regulatory response. Their basic position was "no proof, no regulation."

For the chemical industry, considerable profits were at stake. The production of CFCs increased steadily after their development as a refrigerant in 1928.[26] Marketed by DuPont under the name Freon, CFCs became coolants for refrigerators and air conditioners, propellants in aerosol sprays and insulators in the manufacture of a wide range of rigid and flexible plastic foams. In addition, their stable, nonflammable, nonreactive properties made them seemingly perfect solvents for cleaning microchips and sensitive telecommunications equipment. Thus, from 1960 to 1974, U.S. Freon

---

[25] In 1987 and 88, NASA, NOAA and the National Science Foundation spearheaded two expeditions. Over 100 scientists from ten countries employed specially designed equipment – placed in satellites, balloons, a DC-8 flying laboratory and a high altitude U-2 aircraft – to detect telltale signs of a CFC-ozone reaction in the Antarctic stratosphere. Their results vindicated the Rowland-Molina hypothesis and concluded that the evidence "strongly indicates that man-made chlorine species are primarily responsible for the observed decrease in ozone." In addition, the UN's scientific panel announced that losses of ozone in the Northern Hemisphere were twice those predicted and that the Earth had already lost more ozone than the EPA had estimated would occur under the Montreal Protocol by 2075. The panel's conclusions made headlines all over the world. Watson, R. T. et al. (August 1988); Roan, Sharon. *Ozone Crisis.* (NY: Wiley Science Editions), 1989: 231.

[26] Although they were developed as refrigerants in 1928, the chemistry for producing chlorofluorocarbons (CFCs) was invented by the Belgian chemist, Swarts, in the 1890s.

production rose 533 percent, from 150,000 to 800,000 metric tons per year.[27] U.S. production accounted for nearly half of the global fluorocarbon production; the remainder being concentrated mainly in Europe, with limited amounts in Japan, the USSR, Canada, China, India and Latin America.[28]

In the summer of 1975, Richard Scorer, a respected British scientist and former editor of the *International Journal on Air Pollution*, toured the United States criticizing Rowland and Molina's theory as "doomsaying" and dismissing the need for CFC regulation. The world's largest public relations company, Hill & Knowlton, organized his tour. It was hired by the chemical industry to devise an extensive PR strategy to counter the negative publicity CFCs were receiving.[29] The basic theme of the campaign was captured by one full-page ad that proclaimed, "We believe in what US law holds clearly and we cherish dearly: you are innocent until proven guilty."[30]

Consumers did not seem to agree that chemicals had the same rights as humans. The public was alarmed by the increased potential for skin cancers caused by ozone depletion. A series of polls revealed that people were apprehensive about the potential dangers of CFCs; they were using fewer aerosol products and responding to environmentalists' calls for political action.[31] The CFC-ozone theory generated more letters to the federal government than any issue since the Vietnam War and polls were indicating that about half of all consumers had stopped buying aerosol products because of it.[32] The activists' cautious approach seemed to resonate with the public.

Throughout the Carter administration, the activists' demand for precautionary action gained momentum. In 1976, the NAS released its study of the CFC-ozone issue. It indicated that although the jury was still out, all the relevant studies validated the basic accuracy of the Rowland-Molina hypothesis and concluded that ozone depletion could be expected to cause many more skin cancers.[33] In response, the Carter White House launched a task force to assess the CFC-ozone issue that included representatives from every relevant federal agency. The Chairman of the President's Council on Environmental Quality, the Commissioner of the Consumer Product Safety Commission (CPSC) and the EPA's Assistant Administrator for R&D all came out in favor of precautionary CFC regulations. A few weeks later, the FDA proposed a phase out of all nonessential uses of CFCs in the products under its regulatory purview. The EPA followed suit by announcing it would seek a ban on all nonessential CFC uses. By May 1977, the EPA, FDA and CPSC jointly announced a timetable for CFC phase out. Production of CFCs for nonessential use would cease by October 1978.

Two important bills that eventually became part of the 1977 Clean Air Act (CAA) Amendments clearly established Congress' willingness to regulate CFCs at a

---

[27] Chemical Manufacturers Association. *Production, Sales, and Calculated Release of CFC-11, and CFC-12 Through 1987.* (Washington, DC: CMA), 1988.

[28] Benedick, Richard E, 1991: 25–6.

[29] Roan, Sharon, 1989: 61.

[30] Roan, Sharon, 1989: 62.

[31] Roan, Sharon, 1989: 63.

[32] Roan, Sharon, 1989: 58.

[33] National Academy of Sciences. *Halocarbons: Effects on Stratospheric Ozone.* (Washington, DC: NAS), 1976.

threshold of certainty well below irrefutable proof.[34] The 1977 CAA Amendments Congress explicitly required the director of the EPA to:

> ... control any substance, practice, process or activity (or any combination thereof) which in his judgment *may reasonably be anticipated to affect* the stratosphere, especially the ozone in the stratosphere, if such effect in the stratosphere *may be reasonably anticipated to endanger* public health or welfare.[35]

This *reasonable anticipation* standard mandated the EPA to regulate CFCs at a considerably lower threshold of certainty than waiting for conclusive proof.

In 1979, a second NAS report, using refined modeling procedures, concluded that expected ozone loss by the late twenty-first century would be more than twice what was predicted by its 1976 report. NAS warned that a "wait-and-see" approach to the problem was not practical and that the United States should take the lead in pursuing international cooperation to control CFCs.[36]

Canada, Norway, Sweden and Denmark promptly joined the activist coalition by emulating the U.S. ban on nonessential uses of CFCs. These governments quickly decided the evidence and the dangers were strong enough to warrant immediate action. Since Canada was a very small CFC producer, while Sweden, Norway and Denmark produced none, these governments determined that the health risks of inaction for their light-skinned, cancer-prone populations far outweighed any regulatory burden.

At a major meeting in Oslo, representatives from the United States, Canada, Sweden, Norway, Denmark and the Netherlands urged all nations to immediately begin reducing CFCs from all sources and asked UNEP to convene an International Conference on the Ozone Layer. The conference produced a *World Plan of Action on the Ozone Layer* that called for a treaty to protect the Earth from a potentially disintegrating ozone shield.

Six years after Rowland and Molina's theory went public, the activist coalition had grown remarkably in scientific credibility, political influence and geographic scope. Led by the Carter administration, this multinational activist coalition appeared well on its way to laying the groundwork for a strong global accord to phase out CFCs based on substantial, if not irrefutable, evidence that these chemicals posed a dire threat to the ozone shield and, therefore, merited precautionary regulation. Then suddenly, everything changed. By the end of the 1970s, the growing international effort to regulate CFCs ran into three formidable obstacles: the chemical lobby, the Reagan administration and the European Community (EC).

---

[34] HR 3118, "Stratospheric Research & Protection Act of 1975," in the House and similar bill in the Senate, S 3219.

[35] see: Benedick, Richard E., 1991: 23; Parker, Larry. "Stratospheric Ozone Depletion: Implementation Issues," *CRS Issue Brief for Congress* (December 7, 2000). http://www.ncseonline.org/nle/crsreports/stratospheric/strat-5.cfm.

[36] National Research Council. *Stratospheric Ozone Depletion by Halocarbons: Chemistry & Transport.* (Washington, DC: National Academy Press), 1979.

While the Scandinavian governments considered the CFC-ozone theory strong enough to require international action, this was not the case throughout the rest of Europe. The EC was the world's second largest producer of CFCs. Led by the U.K., it formed the core of the blocking coalition. EC policymakers concluded that the ozone-depletion hypothesis was dubious because of the absence of clear-cut proof that CFCs were harming the ozone layer and the unreliability of computer models to predict what actually occurs in the atmosphere.

Even though European atmospheric science lagged well behind the United States, European policymakers were suspicious of American science.[37] They considered it a political overreaction to exaggerated environmentalist fears. Some European officials saw Washington's call for international CFC controls as a ploy to undermine the competitive advantage European chemical producers had gained as a result of the U.S.'s domestic ban on CFCs in aerosols.[38] Also, they feared the ban had encouraged American chemical producers to develop CFC substitutes they could swiftly deploy to dominate the world market should CFCs be outlawed by international accord.[39]

In addition, public pressure in Europe to address ozone depletion was relatively weak. Unlike Europe, American media had actively covered the CFC story. Consequently, American consumer groups, environmental organizations and the public at large were far more active around this issue than their European counterparts who were more troubled by other pressing problems such as acid rain, chemical spills, nuclear weapons and nuclear power. Thus, at the inception of ozone negotiations, the domestic activist coalitions inside most European countries were embryonic at best.[40]

Back in the United States, CFC regulation ran into stiff resistance from a resurgent blocking coalition. American scientists close to the chemical industry insisted that this rush to regulation was based on flimsy evidence. Echoing European skeptics, they argued that science's evolving understanding of ozone depletion was based mainly upon unreliable and inaccurate computer models. They attacked the models' validity because they generated significant discrepancies and fluctuations in the predicted effects of CFCs upon the ozone layer. For instance, they failed to generate relatively constant projections for future ozone depletion. In 1974, various projections of ozone loss 50 to 100 years into the future hovered around 15 percent; they fell to around 8 percent in 1976; climbed up to 19 percent in 1979; and then dropped to around 3 percent by 1983. Thus, even though laboratory and modeling studies confirmed the validity of the chlorine-ozone linkage, skeptics insisted the models were flawed and there was no proof that lab experiments accurately replicated what actually transpired in the stratosphere.

[37] There was no equivalent in Europe to the NASA-NOAA research and satellite monitoring initiatives on the ozone layer, nor the series of National Academy of Sciences studies. Benedick, Richard E, 1991: 29.

[38] Maxwell, James H. & Sanford L. Weiner. "Green Consciousness or Dollar Diplomacy? The British Response to the Threat of Ozone Depletion," *International Environmental Affairs*, v. 5, n. 1 (1993): 19–41; Benedick, Richard E, 1991: 24.

[39] Dotto, Lydia & Harold Schiff. *The Ozone War*. (NY: Doubleday), 1978.

[40] Benedick, Richard E, 1991: 27–8.

The chemical industry worked overtime to turn these discrepancies to its advantage. In 1979, DuPont officials stated, "No ozone depletion has ever been detected despite the most sophisticated analysis ... All ozone-depletion figures to date are computer projections based on a series of uncertain assumptions."[41] This position became the rallying point for powerful interests on both sides of the Atlantic. DuPont officials used their influence to raise the certainty threshold much higher, insisting that any further movement toward regulation must be based upon undeniable proof that CFCs were seriously damaging the ozone layer.

During the 1970s, a wealthy industry alliance – led by DuPont[42] and the industry's influential lobbying organization, the Chemical Manufacturers Association (CMA) –resisted the CFC ban in aerosols.[43] By 1980, after failing to prevent the ban, these fluorocarbon users and producers had redoubled their efforts to prevent further regulation by organizing a broader lobbying coalition they called the Alliance for a Responsible CFC Policy.[44]

Through intense lobbying and substantial campaign contributions, this powerful alliance of more than 400 of the country's major CFC producers and users set out "to convince government – Congress the White House and anyone else – that EPA's proposal to restrict CFCs is ill-advised."[45] When the EPA asked for public comment on proposed CFC regulations, the Alliance organized a letter-writing campaign that generated more than 2,000 letters. CFC producers and users argued that there was, as yet, no conclusive evidence that CFCs harmed the ozone layer and that the latest model estimates of ozone loss were now converging on very low numbers. Thus, there was ample time for further study and research before embarking on any heavy-handed regulation.

The chemical industry considered Ronald Reagan's election a great victory – they now had a friend in the Oval Office. CFC regulation did not sit well with the antienvironmentalist, antiregulatory bent of the Reagan White House and the Alliance for a Responsible CFC Policy lobbied hard to keep it that way.[46] The new administration backtracked from Carter's precautionary approach to CFCs and

[41] Roan, Sharon, 1989: 96.
[42] With its headquarters in the U.S. and with subsidiaries and joint ventures in six other countries, DuPont was the world leader in CFC production. It held 50 percent of the U.S. market and was responsible for about 25 percent of global production; it was also the only company that produced CFCs for all major markets: North America, Europe and Japan. To its credit, DuPont had been the first to investigate what became of CFCs once they were released into the atmosphere. In 1972, DuPont issued an invitation to other CFC manufacturers to attend a seminar on "The Ecology of Fluorocarbons" and employed scientists to study the problem. But the DuPont scientists only studied the lower atmosphere, not the stratosphere. See: Haas, Peter M. "Banning Chlorofluorocarbons: Epistemic Community Efforts to Protect Stratospheric Ozone," *International Organization*, v. 46, n. 1 (1992): 187–224.
[43] CMA was the 19-member industry trade and lobbying association. They also financed their own CFC research.
[44] Haas, Peter M (1992): 187–224.
[45] An Alliance representative quoted by *The New Yorker* cited in: Roan, Sharon, 1989: 102. Information on campaign contributions is given by Roan on page 109.
[46] Roan, Sharon, 1989: 104–9.

withdrew from the activist coalition. This defection seriously hobbled the activist coalition's ability to garner further international support for an ozone treaty. Reagan's new EPA chief, Anne Burford, pleased industry by expressing skepticism that the science justified any CFC controls whatsoever, even in aerosols.[47]

Citing inconclusive science and regulatory hardships, the Reagan administration stalled the implementation of domestic CFC regulations and remained aloof from international efforts to draft an ozone agreement. Despite this policy reversal, Washington continued to insist that the EC should replicate America's ban on CFCs in aerosol products to remove Europe's competitive advantage in this market.

Enthusiasm for ozone negotiations waned as the chemical industry's trans-Atlantic blocking coalition pressured their governments to wait for proof before imposing CFC regulations. At the intergovernmental level, UNEP strove to keep the process alive by pooling and synthesizing the growing body of scientific knowledge on the issue and encouraging governments to commit themselves to a series of open-ended deliberations. Between 1981 and 1985, UNEP's respected director, Mostafa Tolba, used his influence to make sure the first session of formal ozone negotiations in Vienna was as productive as possible.

To advance scientific understanding, UNEP established the Coordinating Committee on the Ozone Layer (CCOL), composed of representatives from inter-governmental and nongovernmental organizations with active ozone layer research programs. This group reported its findings over the next decade in the *Ozone Layer Bulletin*. In 1981, UNEP's Governing Council approved a Swedish motion to estab-lish an ad hoc working group of legal and technical experts to formulate the legal framework for an international treaty to protect the ozone layer.[48] But despite UNEP's efforts, enthusiasm for ozone negotiations hit rock bottom by 1983. It appeared that neither Europe nor the United States was willing to move forward as long as the threat posed by CFCs remained unproven.

However, beneath the surface, things were changing. In March, Anne Burford resigned her post as EPA chief beneath a cloud of scandal and corruption. Under media scrutiny and Democratic pressure, Reagan appointed two successive replace-ments – William Ruckelshaus and Lee Thomas – who both appeared genuinely concerned about ozone depletion.

With public and bipartisan congressional support for an ozone treaty and the White House leery of further negative press, Ruckelshaus and Thomas enjoyed considerable latitude in developing the U.S. negotiating position on ozone. This allowed activist factions within government who favored domestic and international CFC controls to reassert themselves. EPA and State Department activists argued that, whether or not the Reagan White House genuinely favored controlling CFCs, it had everything to gain and nothing to lose by continuing to call for an international ozone

---

[47] In her book, Reagan's head of EPA, Anne M. Burford, refers to ozone depletion as a scare issue that she was savvy enough to dismiss as unimportant. Burford, Anne M. *Are You Tough Enough?* (NY: McGraw-Hill), 1986.

[48] Morrisette, Peter M. "The Evolution of Policy Responses to Stratospheric Ozone," *Natural Resources Journal*, v. 29 (Summer 1989): 794–820.

accord. Confident that the EC would oppose any stringent agreement, U.S. support for an international accord allowed the United States to maintain the moral high ground while pressuring Europe to match America's aerosol ban, thus depriving European producers of the competitive advantage they had gained since the United States outlawed CFCs in aerosol sprays.

Soon after Burford's resignation, environmentalists initiated legal action to compel the EPA to implement the increased CFC reductions required by the 1977 CAA Amendments.[49] Fear of court imposed, unilateral CFC cuts gave the EPA's new leadership further impetus to promote an international agreement. The agency agreed to sponsor a series of international ozone workshops before and after the first session of negotiations in Vienna in return for postponing immediate unilateral reductions.

However, no CFCs reductions were adopted in Vienna. European opposition and U.S. ambivalence produced a framework agreement to keep researching and discussing the issue. Negotiators put off deciding whether or not to regulate CFCs until 1987 when they agreed to meet again in Montreal. Over the two-year span between Vienna and Montreal, NASA, WMO and UNEP undertook an ambitious effort "to provide governments around the world with the best information currently available on whether human activities represent a substantial threat to the ozone layer."[50] Nevertheless, by the time negotiators reconvened in Montreal there was still no conclusive evidence that CFCs were (or were not) damaging the ozone shield.

This uncertain condition persisted until *after* the Montreal Protocol was drafted in 1987. In fact, on the eve of the final negotiating session, the NOAA concluded that the "scientific community currently is divided as to whether existing data on ozone trends provide sufficient evidence that chlorine-induced ozone destruction is occurring now."[51] Nevertheless, negotiators agreed to a 50 percent CFC reduction in Montreal *before* any scientific consensus confirmed a causal relationship between CFCs and ozone depletion.

So why were Montreal negotiators, especially European members of the blocking coalition, willing to agree to such a stiff regulatory regime before the scientific community was totally convinced that CFCs had an impact on stratospheric ozone? This dramatic change of heart was largely prompted by an ominous discovery that came just a few months after negotiators left Vienna.

In May 1985, British scientist Joseph Farman and his colleagues from the British Antarctic Survey warned the world about the extremely low levels of ozone they had measured over Antarctica. According to Farman, ozone concentrations recorded during the Antarctic spring had fallen about 50 percent below their 1960 levels. This ozone cavity had spread by 1985 to cover an area greater than the United

---

[49] The Natural Resources Defense Council argued that, under the 1977 Clean Air Act Amendments, the EPA was required to regulate CFCs if they were deemed harmful to the environment. In 1980, the EPA had proposed CFC regulations but they had not been implemented during the first four years of the Reagan administration.

[50] WMO. *Atmospheric Ozone 1985: Assessment of Our Understanding of the Processes Controlling the Present Distribution and Change* (Geneva: 1986): 4.

[51] Albritton, Daniel L. et al. *Stratospheric Ozone: The State of the Science and NOAA's Current and Future Research.* (Washington, DC: National Oceanic & Atmospheric Administration), 1987: 22.

States. Farman did not seek to explain the gap, he simply stated that "chemical causes must be considered" and presented a graph showing a definite correlation between atmospheric concentrations of CFCs and ozone depletion.[52]

NASA confirmed this menacing and completely unexpected revelation after reexamining its own satellite data. U.S. satellites had not previously recognized this problem because their computers were programmed to automatically reject ozone losses of this magnitude as anomalies far beyond the error range of existing predictive models.[53] The corrected results showed no dramatic ozone loss until the late 1970s. Then an abrupt decline was apparently triggered by some unknown atmospheric development. Scientists were stunned and mystified. These drastic ozone losses had not been predicted by any of their atmospheric models. UNEP/WMO announced that, "these data indicate that some mechanism is at work in the cold southern polar night or polar twilight that is not generally included in models. This clearly warrants further investigation."[54]

It is important to note that Farman's discovery did not clarify or improve scientific understanding of how CFCs affect stratospheric ozone. Quite the opposite; it showed atmospheric modelers just how little they really knew. In fact, the ozone hole discovery confirmed the chemical industry's view that ozone science was uncertain and computer models of the atmosphere were still crude. However, foreboding satellite images of a giant cavity in the ozone shield over Antarctica brought home the realization that uncertainty is a double-edged sword. Instead of being less dangerous than the models predicted, the problem could be much worse.

Farman's disturbing find thrust the ozone crisis back into the headlines. Sherry Rowland told the *New York Times* that Farman's discovery was evidence of a problem, "that was harder to label just a computer hypothesis." He added, "Industry always said we'd have plenty of advanced warning of any ozone problems, but now we've got a hole in our atmosphere that you can see from Mars."[55]

The EPA began exhibiting a willingness to act on a much lower level of scientific certainty soon after the hole's discovery, even though the science was muddier than ever. By March 1986, EPA chief Lee Thomas had adopted an activist position on scientific uncertainty that put him at odds with Reagan's White House:

> In the face of all this scientific uncertainty, one might ask why has the EPA embarked on programs to assess the risk and to decide whether additional CFC regulations are necessary? Why not simply adopt a 'wait-and-see' attitude and hold off a decision until depletion is actually confirmed? Let me address this question squarely, EPA does not accept, as a precondition for decision, empirical verification that ozone depletion is occurring. ... [We] may need to act in the near term to avoid letting today's 'risk' become tomorrow's 'crisis'.[56]

---

[52] Farman, Joseph, B. G. Gardiner, & J. D. Shanklin. "Large Loses of Total Ozone in Antarctica Reveal Seasonal ClOx/NOx Interaction," *Nature*, v. 315, n. 6/85 (1985): 207–10.

[53] Collins, Craig. *Interview: Sherwood F. Rowland, University of California Irvine* (May 1991); Benedick, Richard E, 1991: 19.

[54] WMO (1986): 791.

[55] Quoted in: Roan, Sharon, 1989: 144.

[56] Quoted in: Brodeur, Paul. "Annals of Chemistry: In the Face of Doubt," *New Yorker* (June 1986): 86.

Although Thomas's position was not widely accepted within the Reagan administration, it had significant institutional support at NASA and in the State Department's Bureau of Oceans and International Environmental and Scientific Affairs.[57] This activist nucleus within the administration became largely responsible for trying to nudge the United States back into the activist coalition.[58]

Policymakers in the EPA and the State Department – in close alliance with NASA and NOAA scientists – actively pursued a policy of moving the international community toward consensus around a precautionary approach toward scientific uncertainty. Official U.S. policy openly supported the American and international scientific community's efforts to coordinate research and assess the problem through UNEP, WMO and the NASA-led Ozone Trends Panel. In addition, the State Department organized a series of bilateral and multilateral scientific meetings to parallel the ongoing negotiations and offered to undertake joint ozone research with the USSR and Japan. This strategy produced a more uniform understanding of the problem and moved these two countries toward the activist coalition's precautionary position. Finally, the U.S. Information Agency's telecommunications system allowed NASA's Robert Watson (head of the Ozone Trends Panel) and the U.S. chief ozone diplomat, Richard Benedick, to appear in a year-long series of live, televised question-and-answer sessions involving policymakers and scientists in more than 20 capitals in Europe, Latin America and Asia. This series attracted considerable foreign media attention and helped increase global concern over ozone depletion.[59]

Following Farman's discovery, the sense of urgency and danger leading up to the Montreal negotiations was further enhanced by a week-long international conference on the health and environmental risks of ozone loss. The June 1986 conference, sponsored by UNEP and EPA, produced a compendium of scientific papers followed by a multivolume EPA risk assessment. Taken together, these two documents presented the most thorough, up-to-date study of the dangers of ozone depletion.[60]

These assessments acknowledged that, although the link between UVB radiation and skin cancer was well established, any decreases in ozone would have been too recent to account for the rising trend in skin cancer since the 1970s. Nevertheless, future ozone depletion would have serious consequences. EPA estimated that there would be more than 150 million new cases of skin cancer in the United States alone among people currently alive or born by 2075, resulting in approximately three million deaths. On the basis of the same parameters, EPA projected 18 million additional eye cataract cases in the United States, many resulting in blindness. Research also indicated the strong possibility that increased levels of UVB radiation could suppress the human immune system as it had done in laboratory experiments on animals. However, it was not possible to determine the extent of increased human susceptibility to infectious diseases.[61]

[57] Haas, Peter M (1992): 187–224.
[58] Benedick, Richard E, 1991: 42; Roan, Sharon, 1989: 114–15.
[59] Benedick, Richard E, 1991: 56.
[60] EPA. *An Assessment of the Risks of Stratospheric Modification (revised draft)*. (Washington, DC: EPA), 1987; Titus, James G., ed. *Effects of Changes in Stratospheric Ozone and Global Climate*. (Washington, DC: EPA), 1986.
[61] EPA, 1987; Titus, James G., ed., 1986.

Major damage to agriculture was expected as well. In the lab, two-thirds of the 200 plant species tested were sensitive to UVB radiation. Long-term field studies of soybeans indicated substantial yield loss. Also extremely worrisome, but as yet unquantified, was the potential impact on the productivity of the world's fisheries via possible disruption of the aquatic food chain caused by radiation damage to phytoplankton and other organisms living or reproducing near the ocean's surface.[62] While both of these assessments increased the level of general concern about the consequences and costs of ozone depletion, the growing evidence of its impact on agriculture and fishing was of particular concern to policymakers from developing nations.

Even though scientists were more confused than ever about how CFCs affect the ozone shield, the discovery of the hole and the increased awareness of the dangers from rising UVB exposure had a powerful impact on negotiators' willingness to, consciously or subconsciously, lower the certainty bar necessary to implement a strong regulatory regime in Montreal. Some highly credible sources disagree with this assertion. They point out that when negotiators gathered in Montreal, they explicitly decided to ignore the Antarctic aperture because its causes had yet to be determined. For this reason, some ozone diplomats, including the chief U.S. negotiator Richard Benedick, officially deny that the hole had any significant impact on the decision to make deep CFC cuts in Montreal.[63]

> The hole over Antarctica did attract additional public attention to the ozone issue … It may also have influenced some of the participants in the negotiations as evidence of the fragility of Earth's atmosphere. Significantly, however, Antarctica was never discussed at the negotiations, which were based solely on the global models.[64]

Benedick and his fellow diplomats had sound strategic reasons for downplaying the hole's psychological impact upon the negotiations.[65] By explicitly ignoring the hole and refusing to discuss it during deliberations, negotiators sought to protect the treaty from efforts to dismantle or undermine it should the Antarctic aperture prove unconnected to CFCs. At one point in his account of the negotiations, Benedick admits that American diplomats and scientists "worried that linking the US position with the ozone hole would risk its being undermined if that phenomenon turned out to be unrelated to chlorine."[66]

---

[62] UNEP. *Synthesis Report.* UNEP/OzL.Prog.WGII(1)/4 (November 13, 1989); EPA, 1987; Titus, James G., ed., 1986.

[63] Benedick, Richard E, 1991: 18–20.

[64] Benedick, Richard E, 1991: 20.

[65] While Benedick at the State Department, Thomas at EPA and Watson of NASA all took this position, not everyone involved in the issue was as hesitant to recognize the galvanizing impact of the hole on the negotiations. Sherry Rowland told the LA Times, "The hole changed everything. It got the governments to believe there is a problem." For other examples, see: Sand, Peter. "Protecting the Ozone Layer," *Environment,* v. 27 (June 1985): 18–20, 40–3; Crawford, Mark. "United States Floats Proposal to Prevent Global Ozone Depletion," *Science,* v. 46 (November 1986): 927.

[66] Benedick, Richard E, 1991: 56.

Thus, negotiators wanted to make it clear to those that might seek to reverse or weaken the treaty in the future that the scientific evidence warranted such precautions *even if the hole was found to have no link to CFCs*. However, if negotiators really felt this was true, then the CFC cuts they adopted in Montreal should have been made back in Vienna when the science behind them was, if anything, more confident than it was after the breach was discovered.

Clearly, other factors were urging policymakers to act despite the monkey wrench of uncertainty and confusion caused by Farman's finding. One of those factors was dread. Risk perception analysts have identified a set of characteristics that help explain how peoples' perceptions of different hazards affect their willingness to tolerate them. The public expects policymakers to respond when hazards possess particular characteristics that elicit "dread." High-dread hazards are those that people consider to be globally catastrophic, increasing, threatening to future generations, hard to prevent, not easily reduced, involuntary and personally threatening.[67] Besides dread, risk analysis has identified two other factors that impact how people react to potential threats: familiarity and exposure. People find unfamiliar, high-exposure risks more threatening and less tolerable.

The ozone depletion possessed all these "dreadful" characteristics in spades. The increased risk of skin cancer is a universal problem that is increasing, threatening to future generations, hard to prevent and not easily reduced. Furthermore, UV exposure is personally threatening and essentially involuntary, unless you spend your life indoors. In addition to its potentially high exposure factor, ozone depletion is disturbingly unfamiliar because increased levels of UV radiation are unobservable, while their affects are delayed and poorly understood by scientists and those exposed.[68]

The growing gap in the ozone shield exaggerated the overall sense of dread, unfamiliarity and exposure by confounding the experts and shocking the world with tangible confirmation of an ecological disaster in the making. In doing so, it fundamentally altered the course of negotiations by transforming the political context in which they occurred. The hole galvanized world opinion and provided dramatic justification for precautionary action that negotiators could hardly ignore, despite their official decision to do so. Once it was discovered, scientific uncertainty lost all validity as an argument for protecting industry from onerous CFC reductions. The hole provided concrete evidence that it was no longer industry, but the ozone layer, that required protection.[69]

Even though public alarm generally works in the activist coalition's favor, attempts to manipulate it to suit their political ends can backfire. Despite industry's fondness for labeling environmentalists "doomsayers" and "alarmists," the loss of credibility and trust resulting from raising false alarms prevents most activists from overstating

---

[67] Slovic, Fischhoff & Lichtenstein. "Facts and Fears: Understanding Perceived Risk," *Social Risk Assessment: How Much is Enough?*, v. 181 (Summer 1980): 168–94.

[68] Morrisette, Peter M (Summer 1989).

[69] Morrisette, Peter M (Summer 1989); Litfin, Karen. *Ozone Discourses: Science and Politics in Global Environmental Cooperation.* CIAO Books (2006).

the dangers and exaggerating the crisis. Those who make a habit of overembellishing environmental hazards run the risk of ending up like the boy who cried wolf – discredited and mistrusted. Thus, although public alarm lowers the certainty threshold and moves policymakers toward a proactive response, overplaying the crisis is a precarious strategy that can backfire, causing more harm than good. To work in the activists' favor, public alarm and policymaker concern must be grounded in solid theories and sound facts, not alarmist hyperbole.

CLIMATE CHANGE – KEEPING THE CERTAINTY BAR HIGH

No eye-opening shocker like the growing breach in the ozone shield has galvanized global attention and lowered the certainty threshold for climate change negotiators. Instead, the unsettling symptoms of this creeping crisis have revealed themselves in waves, like a swelling tide. Although the cumulative impact of climate disruption may be catastrophic, so far its effects have not been extremely startling or unique. Instead, they have been ominous but incremental magnifications of phenomenon that are familiar aspects of an ever-changing climate. Weather patterns shift, producing more floods, droughts and forest fires; sea levels rise, gradually eroding coastlines; tropical storms become more frequent and severe; coral reefs bleach and slowly die; permafrost thaws, snow pack shrinks and glaciers retreat; while pests and disease vectors migrate steadily toward the poles. These disquieting symptoms have yet to trigger the alarm and dread unleashed by the discovery of the ozone hole.

This important difference has played into the hands of the climate change blocking coalition. Lacking the sudden appearance of any startling new menace, blockers have argued that all the alleged symptoms of human-induced climate change are simply normal variations in the Earth's climate system. After all, glaciers come and go, the number of tropical storms rises and falls, droughts and floods have always been with us, so all these climatic events can be explained without blaming human interference.

In 1988, the UN General Assembly chose UNEP as the venue for organizing the scientific community's rapidly evolving understanding of climate change. To this end, UNEP created the Intergovernmental Panel on Climate Change (IPCC).[70] Eventually, the IPCC involved about 2,000 of the world's preeminent climatologists selected by their governments to assemble and assess the latest peer-reviewed research and determine what was known and unknown about this problem.[71] Their goals were to ascertain whether human activities were altering global climate patterns, and if so, how drastic these disruptions would be.

To establish broadly accepted scientific legitimacy, UNEP designed scientific assessment panels respected by all negotiating parties regardless of their current level of knowledge of the problem, skepticism about the science or misgivings about the equity of the negotiating process. Like the Ozone Trends Panel, the

---

[70] UN General Assembly Resolution 43/53 (1988).
[71] IPCC/WMO/UNEP. *Report of the First Session of the IPCC* (Geneva: 1988).

IPCC included scientists with a broad range of attitudes toward climate change from most participating nations, even those with no established atmospheric research programs. A primary purpose for the scope and structure of the IPCC was political. UNEP sought to mitigate junk science, entrenched skepticism and nationalistic biases by increasing the global legitimacy of peer-reviewed science and creating commonly accepted international scientific assessments of the problem.

The debate over how to respond to climate change was heating up well before the IPCC released its first assessment report in 1990. As with ozone depletion, basic philosophical disagreements emerged over how to approach policymaking under conditions of significant scientific uncertainty. Once again, the skeptics put proof ahead of precaution, stressing the unreliability of climate models; while activists favored prevention, highlighting the disastrous possibilities of waiting to respond until the evidence was irrefutable.

The IPCC's first report was moderately activist in tone.[72] It concluded that within fewer than 50 years (if we carry on business as usual), the Earth will experience temperatures never before felt while humans have inhabited the planet. IPCC scientists acknowledged that many uncertainties remained, but they cautioned policymakers that their assessment was more likely to be an underestimation than an exaggeration of the problem.[73] The panel recommended that a global climate treaty be negotiated as soon as possible.

Environmentalists were encouraged by the IPCC's analysis, although they felt it understated the dangers and the urgent need for action. Greenpeace stressed that IPCC scientists openly admitted their assessments were "likely to be an underestimate" and that "the aspects of the climate system omitted from the computerized climate-simulations on which their predictions are based are such that the warming is most likely to be amplified by natural processes."[74]

Prominent scientific activists, such as Jeremy Leggett of Greenpeace and Michael Oppenheimer and Robert Boyle of the Environmental Defense Fund (EDF), pointed out that climate change, like ozone depletion, has two menacing features that require a farsighted, preemptive response: (1) irreversibility; and (2) the lag time between emissions and effects.[75] These characteristics distinguish global warming and ozone depletion from many other environmental issues, and they each have the

---

[72] More than 170 scientists from over 25 countries contributed directly to the report and another 200 were involved in the peer review of the draft.

[73] They felt their conclusion were probably conservative because the aspects of the climate system omitted from their computer models were such that the actual warming is most likely to be amplified by the unconsidered natural processes. IPCC: Working Group I. *Scientific Assessment of Climate Change* (June 1990).

[74] Leggett, Jeremy, ed. *Global Warming: The Greenpeace Report.* (NY: Oxford University Press), 1990; Greenpeace Staff. "Juggling the Greenhouse Numbers," *Greenpeace Magazine* (May/June 1991): 4; IPCC. *Intergovernmental Panel on Climate Change: First Assessment Report (Overview)* (August 31, 1990); IPCC, Working Group II. *Potential Impacts of Climate Change* (June 1990).

[75] Oppenheimer, Michael & Robert Boyle. *Dead Heat: The Race Against the Greenhouse Effect.* (NY: New Republic), 1991: 77.

pernicious consequence of increasing the need for an urgent response while at the same time making it politically difficult to achieve.

According to these activists, as long as GHGs are emitted in quantities close to current amounts, the Earth will become warmer and warmer for an indefinite period lasting at least hundreds of years. If emissions increase continuously, as they have in the past, warming will accelerate. If emissions are reduced, GHG levels will still remain elevated for centuries, making their consequences irreversible in any human time frame.

In their testimony before Congress, activist scientists explained that GHGs in the atmosphere resemble water in a sink with a nearly closed drain and a wide-open faucet. Far more GHGs are released into the atmosphere by human activities than the Earth's natural "drains" can accommodate. Thus, the level of GHGs in the atmosphere keeps rising. In the case of the most prominent GHG – CO_2 – the drains are oceans and forests, which can presently absorb only about half of each year's CO_2 emissions. The process of removing the remainder from the atmosphere is so gradual that if all human CO_2 sources were eliminated today, the extra gas already accumulated would remain airborne for more than 300 years.[76] Compared to the GHG "faucet," the "drain" is nearly shut tight, so the GHG buildup is effectively irreversible.

Lag time means that the climatic impact of today's GHG emissions is not fully realized until about 40 years after their release. Without the ocean, the atmosphere would heat quickly; but because heating the great mass of water on the Earth takes a long time, global warming is a slower process. This may seem like a good thing, but for the same reason, any efforts made to reduce atmospheric GHGs will not affect global temperatures for several decades after they are made. Thus, if policymakers wait for proof of serious climatic disruptions, climate change will continue to worsen for many decades thereafter, with unpredictable consequences no matter what control measures are adopted.

As with ozone depletion, environmentalists have been especially critical of the panel's refusal to spell out a worst-case scenario arising from its conclusions. When Ozone Trends Panel scientists avoided discussing their deep concern about the probable link between CFCs and the newly discovered hole over Antarctica, Friends of the Earth, the NRDC and Greenpeace criticized their silence and alerted the public to these *possible* links and *potential* threats well ahead of the panel.

The same has been true of their willingness to warn the public of potential for unleashing a *runaway greenhouse effect*.[77] This term is used to describe the potential for global warming to spiral out of control. Many scientists worry that melting Arctic permafrost could release vast quantities of GHGs[78] or that the white, heat-reflecting

[76] U.S. Senate. *Testimony of James Hansen Before the Senate Committee on Energy and Natural Resources: The Greenhouse Effect and Global Climate Change.* 100th Congress, 2nd Session 40 (June 1988); Oppenheimer, Michael & Robert Boyle, 1991.

[77] Greenpeace. *The Climate Time Bomb.* (Amsterdam, The Netherlands: Stichting Greenpeace Council), 1994; Leggett, Jeremy. "Global Warming: The Worst Case," *Bulletin of the Atomic Scientists*, v. 85 (1992): 28–32.

[78] The frozen soil (permafrost) beneath the Arctic tundra contains enormous stores of methane hydrate – a potent greenhouse gas.

layer of polar ice and snow could melt, exposing the dark, heat-absorbing surfaces of the ocean and land to the sun's rays. These are just two of the possible scenarios that could trigger a self-reinforcing feedback loop that would be unstoppable once it passed a critical tipping point. Huge natural forces would take over, drastically disrupting the climate and decimating ecosystems all over the planet.

For activist NGOs, this disturbing possibility plus the dual problems of lag time and irreversibility are compelling reasons for discarding the "prove-it" approach to uncertainty. However, they recognize that these dual dilemmas also put policymakers in an awkward position. Without action, climate disruption will increase indefinitely and irreversibly; yet even with dramatic emission reductions, the climate will continue to warm for quite some time, the public will see no immediate benefit and the situation will get worse for some time before it gets better. The short time horizons of economic and political elites – whose main concerns (whether next quarter's profit margins or reelection) rarely exceed ten years – tend to conflict with the extended time frame necessary to address climate change. To counteract this myopic inertia and head off the possibility of a runaway greenhouse effect, activists argued that policymakers must provide public education and strong, patient, visionary activist leadership.[79]

In the weeks leading up to the IPCC's first climate conference, half of the Nobel Prize winners living in the United States and half of the members of the NAS published a full-page plea in the *Washington Post*, urging George H. W. Bush to honor his campaign pledge to combat the greenhouse effect with "the White House effect." According to its signatories:

> There is broad agreement within the scientific community that amplification of the Earth's natural greenhouse effect by the buildup of various gases introduced by human activity has the potential to produce dramatic changes in climate .... Only by taking action now can we insure that future generations will not be put at risk.[80]

But the White House refused to heed their call to action. Instead, Bush's conference speech stressed the high level of uncertainty surrounding global warming and the lack of consensus in the scientific community.[81] He insisted that "what we need are facts, the stuff science is made of"[82] and cited a recent television interview in which scientists disagreed on the extent of global temperature change: "Two scientists, two diametrically opposed points of view. Now where does that leave us? Without enough information to justify policy responses ... Politics and opinion have outpaced the science."[83] When questioned about the IPCC's view that the science was

[79] Oppenheimer, Michael & Robert Boyle, 1991.
[80] Weisskopf, Michael. "Bush Says More Data on Warming Needed," *Washington Post* (April 18): A1.
[81] Weisskopf, Michael (April 18, 1990): A1.
[82] The White House, Office of the Press Secretary. *Remarks by the President in the Opening Address to the White House Conference on Science and Economics Research Related to Global Change* (April 17, 1990).
[83] Weisskopf, Michael (April 18, 1990): A1.

certain enough to justify action, Bush replied, "My scientists are telling me something very different."[84]

But was the scientific community really split over how to approach climate change? Who were these scientists the president found more credible than the vast assembly of climate experts working with the IPCC? At the time of Bush's speech, a small media-savvy cabal of climate skeptics was gaining an inordinate amount of publicity and influence in the White House through the President's chief of staff, John Sununu.[85] They insisted that no climate treaty was necessary because global warming was merely an unproven theory that would probably prove beneficial if it ever materialized. Like the small group of scientists who once fronted for the CFC industry, these climate skeptics accentuated the uncertainties and downplayed the dangers of climate change. But the meager efforts of the ozone "denialists" were completely outclassed by the highly polished operation of their climate change counterparts. Financed by the giants of the fossil fuel industry, their campaign of obfuscation and denial raised junk science to a whole new level of devious legerdemain.

The skeptics directed their message at two strategic audiences: beltway policy-makers and the American public. As long as the president and Congress considered GHG cuts unnecessary, and the American people tolerated their inaction, the United States would remain in the blocking coalition. Since the United States contributed 25 percent of humanity's CO_2 emissions and was the world's number one source of GHGs, it could effectively scuttle any cooperative effort to control climate change.

Throughout the 1990s, the evidence of climate change became more undeniable and menacing with each successive IPCC assessment. In response, the number of scientists critical of the IPCC's activist position steadily dwindled, and the worldwide demand for action gained momentum. However, in the United States, the media's preferential treatment of the publicity-prone coterie of climate skeptics generated the illusion that the scientific community remained deeply divided over the issue. This false impression persisted for many years, long after numerous investigations revealed that nearly all the remaining skeptics had strong financial and/or ideological motivations for their denial.[86]

Although the research of this dwindling handful of skeptics was usually sponsored by the fossil fuel industry and was seldom peer-reviewed, these facts didn't seem to raise any red flags in the press about the detached impartial character of their conclusions.[87] Instead, the media continued to endow this shrinking cabal with the same level of coverage and credibility as the broad international body of scientists appointed to study the problem.[88]

---

[84] Quoted in: Rowlands, Ian H. *The Politics of Global Atmospheric Change.* (Manchester: Manchester University Press), 1995: 80.

[85] Beardsly, Tim. "Profile: Political Engineer," *Scientific American* (April 1991): 26.

[86] Gelbspan, Ross. *Boiling Point: How Politicians, Big Oil and Coal, Journalist and Activists Have Fueled the Climate Crisis – and What We Can Do to Avert Disaster.* (NY: Basic Books), 2004.

[87] Gelbspan, Ross, 2004.

[88] Even respected sources like PBS's NOVA and Frontline used the skeptics to give "balance" to their coverage of climate change without critically analyzing their funding sources or their lack of peer-reviewed research.

With their research and traveling expenses covered by various oil and coal interests, the skeptics sought every opportunity to gain media attention. When negotiators met to draft a climate treaty before the 1992 Earth Summit in Rio, the skeptics turned out in force. At all six preliminary deliberations leading up to the summit, they held press conferences and actively lobbied delegates. In February 1991, they published a letter, signed by 50 scientists, which was highly critical of the precautionary orientation of the United Nations' effort to craft a climate change treaty:

> As independent scientists, researching atmospheric and climate problems, we are concerned by the agenda for the United Nations Conference on Environment and Development (to be held in June 1992 at Rio de Janeiro) being developed by environmental activist groups and certain political leaders ...
>
> [The] policy initiatives derive from highly uncertain scientific theories. They are based on the unsupported assumption that catastrophic global warming follows from the burning of fossil fuel and requires immediate action. We do not agree ...
>
> We are disturbed that activists, anxious to stop energy and economic growth, are pushing ahead with drastic policies without taking note of recent changes in the underlying science. We fear that the rush to impose global regulations will have catastrophic impacts on the world economy, standard of living and health care, with the most severe consequences falling upon developing countries and the poor.[89]

The core of politically libertarian/conservative scientific skeptics that produced this letter came from two overlapping groups that became known as the Phoenix Group and the Virginia Conspiracy. The Phoenix Group centered around Robert Balling, Jr. from Arizona State University and Sherwood Idso, a USDA physicist from Phoenix. The Virginia Conspiracy revolved around Patrick Michaels and S. Fred Singer, both associated with the University of Virginia. Also prominent among the skeptics was Richard Lindzen, a noted meteorologist from MIT.

The Phoenix Group originally consisted of 24 scientists who met in Phoenix in 1990 to draft a research program designed to promote the hypothesis that the climate apocalypse is not at hand. The results of that meeting were detailed in *Global Climatic Change: A New Vision for the 1990s*, a report distributed by Robert Balling. According to the report:

> The consensus of the scientists in this research prospectus is that there is considerable evidence that the impact of future climatic change may be neutral or even beneficial. The lines of evidence include:
>
> • *The Magnitude of Observed Warming.* The historical record of observed temperature change suggests that global warming for a doubling of carbon dioxide will be far below the 4.2° that fuels the Popular Vision.
> • *The Timing of Observed and Projected Warming.* More refined climate models tend to project most of their warming to occur in high latitude

[89] Quoted in: Michaels, Patrick J. *Sound and Fury: The Science and Politics of Global Warming.* (Washington, DC: CATO Institute), 1992: 183.

winter, which partitions most warming into the night. This prevents most of the deleterious effects and in fact lengthens growing seasons. The warmth of 1990 was consistent with this projection as were the world-averaged average crop yields.

- *The Growth Enhancement Caused by Carbon Dioxide.* Carbon dioxide is currently a limiting nutrient for plants, and a voluminous scientific literature demonstrates enhanced growth and water use efficiency as its concentration increases. In fact, except for the height of the ice ages, both global temperature and CO_2 concentration are currently near their lowest values for the last 100 million years.[90]

Patrick Michaels, one of the conference participants from the University of Virginia, declared in his book, *Sound and Fury*, that attendance at the Phoenix conference revealed that, "there is clearly a strong professional motivation to explore the emerging view of neutral or possibly beneficial climatic change."[91] What he declined to mention was the financial motivation behind adopting such a position.

At a hearing on the environmental costs of coal burning before the Minnesota Public Utilities Commission, Balling, Michaels and Lindzen were all hired to testify as expert witnesses by the Western Fuels Association (WFA) – the coal industry's major lobbying group.[92] In his testimony, Dr. Balling admitted receiving extensive funding from fossil-fuel interests since 1989. Sources of funding for Dr. Balling's work included the government of Kuwait, foreign coal and mining corporations and Cyprus Mining Company (a U.S. coal mining company and sponsor of the anti-environmentalist group *People for the West!*). In 1995, Dr. Balling admitted to receiving approximately $700,000 from American coal and oil interests between 1989 and 1995; and more than $200,000 from coal and oil interests in the U.K., Germany and several OPEC nations.[93]

USDA physicist, Sherwood Idso, another prominent member of the Phoenix Group, produced one of the major contributions to the climate debate – a video entitled *The Greening of Planet Earth*, which premiered in 1991 and was shown frequently in the Bush White House. This half-hour video – funded by the coal lobby – argued that CO_2 would enhance plant growth, resulting in "a better world, a more productive world." The WFA distributed 16,000 copies of its video, which reportedly cost $250,000 dollars to produce, to people and organizations in the United States and roughly 30 other countries.[94]

[90] Balling, Robert Jr. *Global Climactic Change: A New Vision for the 1990s* (1990). Actually this was not a consensus position. Three of the 24 members of this conference expressed substantial disagreement with these conclusions. See: Michaels, Patrick J, 1992: 185.
[91] Michaels, Patrick J, 1992: 184.
[92] Gelbspan, Ross. "The Heat is on," *Harpers* (December 1995): 31.
[93] "The Ties that Blind," *The Arizona Republic* (November 24, 1995): A2; Gelbspan, Ross (December 1995): 31.
[94] Guerro, Peter. "House Subcommittee to Hear Debate Over Climate Models," *Global Change* (electronic edition, November 1995): 8.

The WFA was also quite instrumental in promoting Patrick Michaels's rise to prominence as a global warming skeptic. In 1991, Michaels was given a position on the Science Advisory Panel of the Information Council on the Environment (ICE) – a PR group organized by the WFA and composed of 24 coal companies, mining associations and public utility corporations. The political goal of ICE's PR campaign was to target public opinion in key congressional districts in the United States with the message that global warming is an environmentalist hoax. Over the next four years, Michaels received more than $115,000 from coal and energy interests.[95]

In 1992, the WFA financed and distributed the *World Climate Review*, a quarterly magazine edited by Michaels that sought to counter "the current popular vision of climate gloom and doom."[96] By late 1994, roughly 15,000 copies of each issue were printed and distributed in the United States and elsewhere. In 1995, the WFA abandoned the *World Climate Review* and replaced it with an Internet publication, *The World Climate Report*,[97] also edited by Michaels. According to Fredrick D. Palmer, the General Manager and Chief Executive Officer of the WFA, the report is, "an antidote to the vision of apocalypse promoted by the professional environmental community and by the United Nations."[98]

Michaels also received funding for travel and research from Edison Electric Institute, the German Coal Mining Association and – along with Idso and Balling – the Cyprus Minerals Company.[99] Behind the battle over climate science, Michaels saw an effort on the part of the activist-oriented nations of Europe to impose global regulations that would undermine the competitive edge of countries such as the United States and Australia who have access to cheap fossil fuels. In his statement to the Coal Producer's Conference in Australia in May 1996 Michaels said:

> Any attempt to force emissions reductions will impose further stringencies on economic machines that are already well-oiled. There is clearly advantage to some, decadally stagnant economies [referring to European countries] if they can, by force of the UN or other international law, reduce the productivity of the competition [referring to the USA and Australia].[100]

Scientifically, the credibility of Michaels's research hardly passed muster with his peers. His work on pattern detection of climate change was seriously flawed, according to peer reviews by the IPCC. IPCC scientists concluded that "There are a number of serious problems with this [Michaels'] analysis," and presented a detailed discussion of the matter in the IPCC's Second Assessment Report (SAR). According to Dr. Tom Wigley, a lead author of the report, "Michaels' arguments are irrelevant,

[95] Gelbspan, Ross (December 1995): 31.
[96] Michaels, Patrick J. *The Political Science of Global Warming*. CATO Institute Conference on Global Environmental Crises: Science or Politics? (June 5–6, 1991).
[97] *World Climate Report*. http://www.worldclimatereport.com/.
[98] Hurley, Brad. "Skeptics on Climate Change," *Energy and Climate Information Exchange Digest* 2.6 (1992): 3.
[99] CAN. "Patrick Michaels: A Correction," *ECO: Climate Talks NGO Newsletter* (July 16, 1996): 3.
[100] CAN (July 16, 1996): 3.

and merely expose his ignorance or deliberate misrepresentation" of the science.[101] Even Michaels's book (*Sound and Fury*, published by the CATO Institute, a conservative-libertarian think tank),[102] which attempts to discredit the "popular vision" of global warming, is flawed by the omission of any effort to cite sources for an abundance of questionable facts and assertions.[103]

Like Patrick Michaels, Fred Singer is another overlapping member of the Phoenix Group and the Virginia Conspiracy. Singer was the deputy assistant minister of the EPA under Nixon and the chief science advisor to the U.S. Department of Transportation from 1987 to 1989.[104] In addition to his association with the University of Virginia, Singer heads the Science and Environmental Policy Project (SEPP) – a small but highly active[105] affiliate of the Washington Institute for Values in Public Policy. This think tank is sponsored by the infamous Unification Church – the reverend Sung Myung Moon's ultraconservative cult, better known as "the Moonies."[106] Singer's relationship with the Moonies raises questions about his credibility because of its rabidly antienvironmental religious doctrine and political activities.[107]

Singer sat on the advisory board of the Unification Church's magazine, *The World and I*; appeared at many church-funded, antienvironmental conferences; had three of his books published by the church; and his organization, SEPP, received a year of rent-free office space in a church-owned building.[108] After adverse media exposure prompted Singer to sever SEPP's financial ties with the Moonies, SEPP became an affiliate of the Institute for Contemporary Studies (ICS) whose major funders include British Petroleum, Chevron, Ford, Texaco, Mobil, Monsanto and the Forbes Foundation. Singer became a consultant on atmospheric science for Exxon, Shell, ARCO, UNOCAL and Sun Petroleum.[109]

Since he places the blame for many of the world's social crises squarely on the environmental movement, Singer's views have made him a popular panelist at antienvironmental conferences. He believes that global warming is most likely a natural occurrence; burning fossil fuels increases the world's food supply; and a global climate treaty will have catastrophic impacts on the world economy, on jobs, standards of living and health care. Singer published a compilation of critiques of the IPCC report and he did a survey of IPCC scientists in 1991. He claimed that

---

[101] CAN (July 16, 1996): 3.
[102] Among CATO's major backers are the American Petroleum Institute, ARCO Foundation, Association of International Automobile Manufacturers, Exxon, Ford Motor Co., NBC and Toyota. Deal, Carl. *The Greenpeace Guide to Anti-Environmental Organizations.* (Berkeley, CA: Odonian Press), 1993.
[103] Michaels, Patrick J, 1992.
[104] Nightline. "Is Environmental Science for Sale?" ABC (February 23, 1994).
[105] SEPP has published articles, letters to the editor, and an avalanche of press releases in its effort to influence the media's spin on climate change. SEPP's literature boasts of being mentioned in "the major media more than 250 times."
[106] Deal, Carl, 1993: 89.
[107] Nightline (February 23, 1994).
[108] Nightline (February 23, 1994).
[109] Nightline (February 23, 1994); Atmosphere Alliance. *Life Support: A Citizen's Guide to Solving the Atmospheric Crisis.* (Olympia, WA: Earth Island Institute), 1995.

Policymaker Summaries of the IPCC's Scientific Assessments were written by small steering groups that did not represent the consensus of contributing scientists. According to Singer, 40 percent of the IPCC reviewers and authors believed that the summary conveyed a misleading impression of the nature of upcoming climate change.[110]

Of all the skeptics, Richard Lindzen, noted meteorologist at MIT, is perhaps the most respected. Lindzen's theory maintains that greenhouse warming is self-limiting: he says that the earth cools by convection, not by radiation; as greater levels of GHGs warm the earth, water vapor will increase in the atmosphere and enhance convection, providing a strong cooling effect.[111] Although the preponderance of the early evidence indicated that Lindzen's theories were probably wrong, they were not conclusively disproved until 1993.[112]

Nevertheless, Lindzen has not changed his opinion about global warming or the IPCC's consensus:

> Five years ago, IPCC wasn't sure about human effects on climate; now they've changed their minds and think they can see an effect ... Their statement now is that all the changes are not due to natural variability, that some part ... might be due to man. But that's saying nothing. The predictions of global warming are based entirely on computer modeling results, and a lot of what you're seeing is defending models. It's become pretty clear that models are incapable of handling all the positive and negative feedbacks you'd need to make accurate forecasts.[113]

Lindzen contends that the amount of plus-or-minus error built into the computer models is actually greater than the global warming deviation the scientists are looking for. According to the Pulitzer Prize–winning science journalist Ross Gelbspan, Lindzen charges oil and coal interests $2,500 per day for his consulting services. His 1991 trip to testify before a Senate committee was paid for by the coal industry, and his speaking tour, *Global Warming: the Origin and Nature of Alleged Scientific Consensus*, was underwritten by OPEC.[114]

---

[110] Quoted in Michaels, Patrick J, 1992: 181–2.
[111] Lindzen, Richard S. *Reasons for Questioning Global Warming Predictions.* CATO Institute Conference on Global Environmental Crises: Science or Politics? (June 5–6, 1991).
[112] Hurley, Brad (1992): 3; Rind, D. et al. "Positive Water Vapour Feedback in Climate Models Confirmed by Satellite Data," *Nature*, v. 349 (February 1993): 500–3. A team of NASA and NOAA scientists now writes in Nature: "we use some new satellite-generated water vapor data to investigate this question. From a comparison of summer and winter moisture values in regions of the middle and upper troposphere that have previously been difficult to observe with confidence, we find that, as the hemispheres warm, increased convection leads to increased water vapor above 500 mbar in approximate quantitative agreement with the results from the current climate models. The same conclusion is reached by comparing the tropical western and eastern Pacific regions. Thus, we conclude that the water vapor feedback is not overestimated in models and should amplify the climate response to increased trace-gas concentrations." The instrument used is the SAGE II (Stratospheric Aerosol and Gas Experiment) aboard the Earth Radiation Budget Experiment satellite.
[113] Lindzen, Richard S (June 5–6, 1991): 12.
[114] Gelbspan, Ross (December 1995): 31.

Even though the underlying interests motivating this vocal group of skeptics raise deep concerns about the objectivity of their research and conclusions, from a purely scientific standpoint they have every right to challenge mainstream theories and point out their weaknesses. To advance climate science, critiques should be welcomed and not automatically dismissed as wrong. The general consensus on global warming does not establish the existence of absolute proof. And, of course, you can find many examples in history where the consensus view turned out to be wrong and the skeptics were right.

Consensus does not prove who is right, but proof may require several more years of research. And that could be a huge problem if it turns out that climate change is a grim reality. Waiting until absolute proof is in will only make the problem worse and the response more costly and less effective. Acting on consensus gives policymakers a head start. This head start many be vital if the scientific uncertainties cause scientists to underestimate rather than overstate the potential threats, as in the case of ozone.

For this reason, scientific consensus is important to policymakers because it indicates the probable existence of serious risk. In the face of uncertainty, policymakers have to weigh the risks of responding one way or another (including not responding at all). Thus, as the number of scientists who see climate change as a legitimate, high-risk problem grows, it becomes harder for policymakers to justify inaction, regardless of the remaining uncertainties.

Consequently, the policymaking process can be manipulated and impeded if powerful economic and ideological interests, with sizable stakes in the outcome, can exaggerate the level of disagreement and manipulate the scientific debate by funding the research of a small group of skeptics and blitzing the media with their views to make it appear to policymakers and the public that the scientific community remains deeply divided. By keeping the debate focused on whether there is a problem in the first place, the skeptics can effectively silence the debate over what to do about it. In his investigation into the oil industry's effort to distort the scientific debate, Ross Gelbspan characterizes these industry-hired skeptics as "interchangeable ornaments on the hood of a high-powered engine of disinformation. Their dissenting opinions are amplified beyond all proportion through the media while the concerns of the dominant majority of the world's scientific establishment are marginalized."[115]

Despite some internal dissention, the skeptics' "prove-it" position dominated the climate change policy of George H. W. Bush. At the Earth Summit, the United States conceded that "lack of full scientific certainty should not be used as a reason for postponement" and agreed to a Framework Convention on Climate Change (FCCC) similar to the preliminary ozone convention adopted in Vienna. However, the United States refused to agree that the science justified specific, mutually-agreed-upon targets and timetables for actual GHG reductions. While most developed nations saw climate change as a clear and present danger, U.S. skepticism had a corrosive impact on the activist policies they were prepared to

[115] Gelbspan, Ross (December 1995): 31.

adopt. Following the summit, the EU downgraded its carbon tax proposal in part because of U.S. inaction.[116]

Unfortunately, the differences between the Clinton/Gore administration and its predecessor were more rhetorical than real. While professing confidence in mainstream climate science and a willingness to adopt an activist policy, Clinton quickly buckled under Congressional opposition to his BTU tax and thereafter avoided any mandatory GHG reductions. By the second half of his first term, the Clinton White House was fighting a defensive battle against a Republican Congress dedicated to killing any climate treaty on the grounds that global warming was – in the words of Dana Rohrabacher (R.-CA) – "unproven at best, liberal claptrap at worst."[117]

Conservative congressional leaders such as Rohrabacher, DeLay and Doolittle were fervent ideological opponents of the IPCC's activist consensus and openly hostile to international efforts to control both ozone depletion and global warming. They promoted legislation to lift a ban on key ozone-depleting compounds, disputed the science underlying the ban on CFCs and questioned the connection between health and ozone depletion.[118] Also, Republicans sought a 40 percent reduction in the funds being spent by the Clinton administration to promote voluntary (and far from adequate) GHG reductions.[119]

In September 1995, the WMO announced that stratospheric ozone concentrations over the Antarctic had reached record lows. Although larger than predicted, further losses were expected because the CFCs released in the decades preceding the Montreal Protocol had not yet reached the stratosphere where they would continue destroying ozone for many decades.[120]

The news prompted policymakers in many countries to consider additional restrictions on ozone-depleting compounds. It had the opposite effect on Congress. Less than two weeks after the WMO announcement, the U.S. House Committee on Science, Subcommittee on Energy and Environment launched a series of hearings on *Scientific Integrity and Public Trust: The Science Behind Federal Policies and Mandates*. The Republican majority initiated these hearings because they maintained that an unholy alliance of environmental alarmists and scientists seeking greater federal research funding had exaggerated these atmospheric problems. They claimed that this unholy alliance had systematically suppressed scientific views that could undermine their activist agenda.

The first two hearings, "Stratospheric Ozone: Myths and Realities" and "Climate Models and Projections of Potential Impacts of Global Climate Change," were

---

[116] Paarlberg, Robert L. "A Domestic Dispute: Clinton, Congress and International Environmental Policy," *Environment* (October 1996): 16.

[117] Wright, Robert. "Some Like it Hot," *The New Republic* (October 5, 1995): 6.

[118] Climate News. "Congressional Ozone & Climate Hearings," *EcoNet* (December 25, 1995).

[119] Cushman, J. H. "Spending Bill Would Reverse Nation's Environmental Policy," *New York Times* (September 22, 1995): 1.

[120] CFC molecules take an average of 15 years to go from the ground level up to the upper atmosphere, and it can stay there for about a century, destroying up to 100,000 ozone molecules during that time. See: http://en.wikipedia.org/wiki/Ozone_depletion.

chaired by Rep. Rohrabacher.[121] The hearings gave prominence to the testimony of the scientific skeptics who Rohrabacher characterized as "people who do not profess conventional wisdom." He suggested that such people have been "shut out of the process," raising doubts about whether the United States is "getting objective science from our regulatory agencies."[122]

Fearing that further studies would turn up even more evidence of the need to control ozone depletion and climate change, the very Republican blockers so insistent on proof now demanded funding cuts in atmospheric research. The Republican majority justified these cuts by arguing that the NASA/EPA research program was merely politicized science, the product of the "Vice President of the United States' zeal for this particular issue," a zeal equivalent to "environmental fanaticism."[123]

Over the course of the hearings, witnesses and subcommittee members made a number of serious allegations. They accused NASA and EPA scientists of deliberately overstating the risks of stratospheric ozone depletion, understating the inherent uncertainties in climate models and distorting research results to secure continued federal funding.[124] The EPA was accused of conspiring to distort the risk of CFCs and that grant applications for climate research had been inappropriately denied on a political basis. Republican representatives claimed that skeptics had been systematically excluded from international scientific assessments of ozone depletion and global warming, even to the extent of denying data to one particular scientist critical of global warming.[125]

In the end, the hearings produced no credible substantiation of any scientific misconduct. Instead, it became evident that the scientific inquiry around these issues was being conducted by the IPCC in an objective and relatively apolitical manner. No actual cases of scientific fraud, unacceptable conduct or breakdowns in the scientific process were documented. In case after case, the record showed that the research had been carried out without preconceived political or scientific agendas and revealed extensive efforts to convey the complexity, uncertainties and limitations of their work. According to Rep. George E. Brown, Jr., "rather than ignoring contrary data or suppressing dissenting views, researchers demonstrated a remarkable commitment to the open and transparent process of scientific peer review."[126]

Even as climate science came under attack on Capitol Hill, new research was clarifying the connections between GHGs and climate disruption and improving the projections of atmospheric models. By factoring in the impact of sulfate aerosols, the backward projections of new models closely resembled actual patterns of climate change over the past century. According to Benjamin Santer, a climate modeler at

[121] Wright, Robert (October 5, 1995): 6.
[122] U.S. House of Representatives. *Hearing Series: Scientific Integrity & the Public Trust: The Science Behind Federal Policies & Mandates, Hearing #1: Stratospheric Ozone: Myths & Realities.* Committee on Science, Subcommittee on Energy & Environment (September 20, 1995).
[123] CSPAN Congressional Chronicle (Text from Congressional Record). *Comments of Rep. Dana Rohrabacher on the Omnibus Civilian Science Authorization Act of 1995.* http://www.c-spanarchives.org/congress/?q=node/77531&id=6957511.
[124] Brown, Rep. George E. Jr. "Environmental Science Under Siege," *Environment* (March 1997): 12.
[125] Brown, Rep. George E. Jr. (March 1997): 12.
[126] Brown, Rep. George E. Jr. (March 1997): 12.

Lawrence Livermore, "It's a very complex pattern and it's sort of difficult to see how other factors, such as natural variability or volcanoes, could have given you such a specific pattern of change."[127] These new results from fingerprint research by climatologists at Lawrence Livermore, the NOAA and climate research centers around the world, provided powerful new evidence to indicate that human-induced global warming had already begun.

Based on these improvements, the IPCC's SAR articulated a broader, more confident consolidation of the consensus opinion. Written and peer-reviewed by some 200 leading scientists and technical experts from approximately 130 countries, this assessment represented the most comprehensive and authoritative source of information on global climate change. The SAR concluded that:

- The balance of evidence suggests that there is discernible human influence on global climate.[128]
- These changes will have significant, often adverse, impacts on many ecological systems and socioeconomic sectors, including food supply, water resources and human health.[129]

---

[127] Vogel, Shawna. "Has Global Warming Begun?" *Earth*, v. 4, n. 6 (December 1995): 25.

[128] To paraphrase SAR: Humanity's emissions of greenhouse gases are likely to cause a rapid climate change. Carbon dioxide is produced by fossil fuels and deforestation. Methane and nitrous oxide are released from agriculture, changes in land use and other sources. CFCs and other gases also play a role. By thickening the atmospheric "blanket" of greenhouse gases, mankind's emissions are upsetting the energy flows that drive the climate system.

   Climate models predict that the global temperature will rise by about 1–3.5°C by the year 2100. This projection is based on current emissions trends and contains many uncertainties, particularly at the regional level. Because the climate does not respond immediately to greenhouse gas emissions, it will continue to change for hundreds of years after atmospheric concentrations have stabilized. Meanwhile, rapid and unexpected climate transitions cannot be ruled out. There is evidence that climate change may have already begun.

[129] To paraphrase SAR: Climate change will have powerful affects on the global environment. In general, the faster the climate changes, the greater will be the risk of damage. The mean sea level is expected to rise 15–95 cm by the year 2100, causing flooding and other damage. Climate zones (and thus ecosystems and agricultural zones) could shift towards the poles by 150–550 km in the mid-latitude regions. Forests, deserts, rangelands and other unmanaged ecosystems could become wetter, drier, hotter or colder. As a result, many may decline or fragment and individual species will become extinct.

   Human society will face new risks and pressures. Global food security is unlikely to be threatened, but some regions may experience food shortages and hunger. Water resources will be affected as precipitation and evaporation patterns change around the world. Physical infrastructure will be damaged, particularly by sea-level rise and by extreme events, which may increase in frequency and intensity in some regions. Economic activities, human settlements and human health will experience many direct and indirect effects. The poor are the most vulnerable to the negative affects of climate change.

   People and ecosystems will need to adapt to the future climate regime. Past and current emissions have already committed the earth to some degree of climate change in the twenty-first century. Adapting to these effects will require a good understanding of socio-economic and natural systems, their sensitivity to climate change and their inherent ability to adapt. Many strategies are available for promoting adaptation.

- Significant reductions in net GHG emissions are technically possible and economically feasible, and significant no regrets opportunities are also available in most countries to reduce net GHG emissions.[130]

The IPCC's conclusions appeared to deal a fatal blow to the uncertainty roadblock. But without any shocking discovery such as the ozone hole to raise the level of dread and the public's demand for action, the blocking coalition decided that it was still possible to defend the uncertainty roadblock by attacking the messenger. To this end, it assailed the integrity of the IPCC and disputed the credibility of the SAR conclusions.

As soon as the report was released, it was assaulted by industry lobbyists, OPEC nations, conservative policy institutes and their die-hard scientific skeptics. In the United States, the Global Climate Coalition, the Marshall Institute, the CATO Institute, the Committee for a Constructive Tomorrow and their affiliated skeptics led the campaign to discredit the IPCC's conclusions in the press.

At the forefront of this smear campaign was Dr. Fredrick Seitz, the man *Business Week* dubbed "the granddaddy of global warming skeptics." As a physicist, not a climate scientist, Dr. Seitz's credibility rested on his former position as president of the NAS during the 1960s. However, from the late 1970s to the late 1980s, Seitz had been a consultant to R. J. Reynolds, at which he oversaw the distribution of $45 million for research the tobacco giant used to promote its products.

According to *Business Week*, in 1972 Dr. Seitz became "a paid director and shareholder of Ogden Corp., an operator of coal-burning power plants." In the 1990s, when Ogden faced financial losses if the Kyoto Protocol became law, Seitz began publishing opinion pieces and circulating letters and petitions dismissing the dangers of global warming.[131] In 1998, Seitz circulated a report opposing the Kyoto Protocol and claiming carbon dioxide poses no threat to climate stability. The report was deceptively formatted to resemble a prestigious, peer-reviewed NAS journal article. The NAS promptly issued a statement disassociating itself from Seitz's devious gambit.[132]

---

[130] However, stabilizing atmospheric concentrations of greenhouse gases will require a major effort. Based on current trends, the total climatic impact of rising greenhouse gas levels will be equal to that caused by a doubling of pre-industrial CO_2 concentrations by 2030, and a trebling or more by 2100. Freezing global emissions at their current levels would postpone CO_2-doubling to 2100. Emissions would eventually have to fall to less than 30 percent of their current levels for concentrations to stabilize at doubled-CO_2 levels sometime in the future. Such cuts would have to made despite growing populations and an expanding world economy. WMO. "Key Points from the IPCC Second Assessment Report," *World Climate News* (January 1997): 5; Sawyer, Kathy. "Experts Agree Humans Have 'Discernible' Effect on Climate," *Washington Post* (December 1, 1995): A1.

[131] Woellert, Lorraine. "A Global-Warming Critic's Hot Stock," *Business Week* (June 5, 2000). http://www.businessweek.com/archives/2000/b3684066.arc.htm.

[132] Stevens, William K. "Science Academy Disputes Attack on Global Warming," *New York Times* (April 22, 1998). http://query.nytimes.com/gst/fullpage.html?res=9A02EED71F3CF931A15757C0 A96E958260.

As president of Marshall Institute[133] and science advisor to the Committee for a Constructive Tomorrow,[134] Dr. Seitz became part of a carefully orchestrated campaign to discredit and disparage the scientific consensus without revealing their financial ties to the petroleum industry. However, both of these conservative, free market think tanks were recipients of large contributions from big oil. A Greenpeace investigation into the financial reports of these conservative think tanks revealed that the Marshall Institute received $630,000 from Exxon Mobil between 1998 and 2005 and Committee for a Constructive Tomorrow received $472,000 from Exxon and $60,500 from Chevron between 1994 and 1998.[135]

Dr. Seitz charged the IPCC report's lead authors with deliberately deceiving the public and policymakers by deleting passages that expressed uncertainty about the human impact on climate change. His charges were printed in the *Wall Street Journal* and *The New York Times*.[136] Seitz directly accused one of SAR's lead authors, Dr. Benjamin Santer, with corrupting the peer-review process.

Dr. Santer replied that the charges "demonstrate his ignorance of the topic and the IPCC process" and added: "The irony of this situation is that I fought hard to keep the extended discussion of uncertainties. Now I am being accused by Dr. Seitz and others of suppressing them."[137] Forty prominent members of the IPCC replied to the charges leveled against Santer by signing a letter in support of SAR and the IPCC's peer-review process printed in the *Wall Street Journal*. Bert Bolin (IPCC chairman) and John Houghton and Luiz Gylvan Meira-Filho (the science group's cochairmen) expressed complete satisfaction with the final edition of the report. Echoing the Marshall Institute, the Global Climate Coalition sent letters with similar charges against the IPCC/SAR process to key members of Congress, the Clinton administration and other governments engaged in climate negotiations.

Despite their efforts, the Clinton administration's confidence in the integrity of the IPCC process was unshaken. In his testimony to the House of Representatives, State Department spokesman, Rafe Pomerance, declared that the energy industry's claims

---

[133] The Marshall Institute consists of several eminent scientists (Robert Jastrow, William Nierenberg and Frederick Seitz) who have published several critical reports on climate change theories and data. Jastrow is convinced that changes in the Sun's brightness may be responsible for any global warming that has occurred so far this century, and he warns that if the Sun enters a quiet phase in the next century (which appears likely based on long-term solar cycles), it could offset much or all the warming projected by models. Critics of the Marshall Institute dismiss its work as politically motivated, simplistic and naive "noisy junk science" (Jerry Mahlman of NOAA's Geophysical Fluid Dynamics Laboratory).

[134] The Committee For A Constructive Tomorrow (CFACT) was founded in 1985. It does policy and lobbying work on the environment from a libertarian perspective. http://www.source-watch.org/index.php?title=Committee_for_a_Constructive_Tomorrow.

[135] Greenpeace. *Exxon is Pumping Out Lies* (May 18, 2007). http://www.greenpeace.org/usa/news/exxonsecrets-2007; SourceWatch. http://www.sourcewatch.org/index.php?title=Committee_for_a_Constructive_Tomorrow.

[136] Seitz, Fredrick. "Renowned Scientist Finds 'Disturbing' Fault with IPCC Climate Change Report," *Wall Street Journal* (June 12, 1996): 2.

[137] Santer, Benjamin D. "A Chilling Reaction to Warnings of Global Warming," *San Francisco Examiner, Sunday Magazine* (July 3, 1996): 2.

were "absurd." State Department spokeswoman, Eileen Claussen, told the *London Guardian*, "There is very strong group of people who muddy the science. We call them the naysayers." *The Financial Times* cited U.K. Environment Minister John Gummer as dismissing those who "refused to believe the evidence before them," and the Canadian Council of Environment Ministers fully endorsed the IPCC's report at its May meeting. Finally, the European Union Council announced that it "recognizes that the IPCC SAR represents the most comprehensive and authoritative assessment in the science of climate change."[138] Ultimately, the SAR received the backing of 157 countries. Only 11 countries, mostly oil producers, opposed it: Iran, Kuwait, Saudi Arabia, Syria, China, Nigeria, Jordan, Lebanon, Oman, Qatar and the United Arab Emirates.

Buoyed by the ineffectiveness of all efforts to discredit the IPCC and SAR, members of the activist coalition were hopeful that the IPCC report would have a positive impact on the Second Conference of the Parties to the UN Climate Treaty to be held in Geneva in July 1996. A month before negotiations began, a transnational activist alliance of 365 environmental NGOs affiliated under the Climate Action Network (CAN) announced that it:

> strongly urges the Ministers to adopt a declaration in Geneva that would recognize that the impacts identified in the IPCC SAR for an equivalent doubling of CO_2 levels are clearly dangerous ... and that in order to achieve a stabilization of GHG concentrations ... 'at a level that would prevent dangerous anthropogenic interference with the climate system' it is essential to stabilize GHG concentrations well below the equivalent of doubling CO_2 from pre industrial levels.[139]

CAN called for negotiators to adopt a protocol that commits industrialized countries to binding targets and timetables for the reduction of CO_2 and other GHGs.

They were not disappointed. For the first time, the U.S. delegation forcefully backed a consensus declaration that stronger action must be taken – specifically, the adoption of legally binding targets and timetables for reducing GHGs by the end of 1997. Timothy Wirth, U.S. Undersecretary for Global Affairs, forcefully clarified the United States' new activist position on climate change science and policy:

> Since Berlin, our deliberations have benefited from the careful, comprehensive and uncompromised work of the Intergovernmental Panel on Climate Change. Their efforts serve as the foundation for international concern and their clear warnings about current trends are the basis for the sense of urgency within my government. We are not swayed by, and strongly object to, the recent allegations about the integrity of the IPCC's conclusions. The allegations were raised by ... naysayers and special interests bent on belittling, attacking and obfuscating climate change

---

[138] All quotes taken from: Lashof, Daniel A. "IPCC Second Assessment Report," *US Climate Action Network Hotline* (January 1996): 1–2.

[139] CAN. "Will the World's Ministers of the Environment Respond to the Science?" *US-CAN Hotline* (June 1996): 6.

science. We want to take this false issue off the table and reinforce our belief that the IPCC's findings meet the highest standards of scientific integrity ...

Let me make clear the US view: The science calls upon us to take urgent action ... This problem cannot be wished away. The science cannot be ignored and is increasingly compelling ... the United States recommends that future negotiations focus on an agreement that sets a realistic, verifiable and binding medium-term emissions target ...

... Continued use of non-binding targets that are not met makes a mockery of the treaty process. It leaves the impression that rhetoric is what counts rather than real emission reductions – an outcome that is both unacceptable and counterproductive.[140]

This bold and largely unexpected shift in U.S. policy at Geneva helped galvanize support among developed countries for seriously strengthening the climate treaty. With the White House agreeing for the first time to binding emission-reduction targets and timetables, only Australia, New Zealand, the OPEC countries and Russia dissented from the Geneva Declaration.

Signed by more than 150 countries, the Geneva Declaration advanced the negotiation process in three important respects. First, it strongly endorsed the conclusions of the IPCC's SAR. The Geneva Declaration made it clear that government ministers felt SAR provided "a scientific basis for urgently strengthening action ... to limit and reduce emissions of greenhouse gases." Second, the Declaration accepted the IPCC's warning that the continued rise in atmospheric concentrations of GHGs "will lead to dangerous interference with the climate system." This is significant because the Framework Convention signed in Rio committed countries to the objective of avoiding "dangerous" climate change. And finally, the Declaration called for "legally binding" objectives and "significant" reductions in future GHG emissions.[141]

The Geneva Declaration marked the demise of scientific uncertainty as a credible justification for obstructing the path to negotiating a viable global warming agreement. This does not mean that no uncertainty remained or that future evidence could not possibly undermine the consensus favoring action. It meant that, on the whole, international policymakers now agreed that existing uncertainties were no longer valid justifications for blocking the negotiation of some kind of binding agreement to reduce GHGs. This consensus laid the groundwork for the adoption of the Kyoto Protocol in 1997.

After Geneva, blockers could not credibly assert that the uncertainties justified inaction, therefore, the focus of contention shifted to the relative costs and benefits and the fairness of any proposed agreement. Even though the Clinton administration's adoption of the Kyoto Protocol was never ratified by Congress and his successor

---

[140] Wirth's speech is extensively quoted by Union of Concerned Scientists' staff scientist, Darren Goetze in "Geneva Breakthrough: World Leaders Endorse Stronger Climate Treaty," *No Sweat News* (Fall 1996). 1.

[141] Goetze, Darren (1996): 1.

withdrew from the process, the official justifications for these policy reversals were not based on scientific uncertainty. Instead, the Republican Congress and President Bush claimed Kyoto's requirements unfairly favored the developing nations and would harm the U.S. economy.

This does not mean scientific uncertainty was completely useless as an argument to justify inaction. Even though the evidence behind human-induced climate change was extremely difficult to deny, and the scientific consensus firmly supported the activist position, the American public was still confused, uninformed and apathetic. While most Europeans considered climate change real and dangerous, Americans remained relatively ignorant and unconcerned about the problem. This condition acted as an anchor, retarding U.S. policy by allowing the Bush administration to maintain its obstructionist position.

Following Kyoto, the coal industry, the American Petroleum Institute and especially Exxon Mobil redoubled their efforts to distort and discredit the accepted science and stall action on global warming. In 1998, a multimillion dollar disinformation campaign to foster public confusion and apathy was cooked up by PR experts from big oil companies, fossil fuel trade associations and conservative think tanks.[142] The scheme was outlined in an Exxon internal memo that claimed, "Victory will be achieved when uncertainties in climate science become part of the conventional wisdom" for "average citizens" and "the media." The memo said Exxon would recruit and train new scientists who lack a "history of visibility in the climate debate" and develop materials depicting climate activists as "out of touch with reality."[143] The planners decided to measure their progress by counting, among other things, the percentage of news articles that raised questions about climate science and the number of radio talk show appearances by their skeptics questioning the consensus view.[144]

To fund their plans, Exxon gave $16 million to 43 influential lobbying and advocacy groups between 1998 and 2005.[145] The Union of Concerned Scientists accused Exxon of imitating tobacco industry tactics by spreading uncertainty, misrepresenting peer-reviewed studies and emphasizing only selected facts.[146] Exxon deployed a similar strategy in the U.K. only to be publicly rebuked by the Royal Society who demanded that it withdraw all support for dozens of groups that have "misrepresented the science of climate change by outright denial of the evidence."[147]

---

[142] "Industrial Group Plans to Battle Climate Treaty," *The New York Times* (April 26, 1998). http://www.nytimes.com/1998/04/26/us/industrial-group-plans-to-battle-climate-treaty.html.

[143] "Industrial Group Plans to Battle Climate Treaty" (April 26, 1998). See memo at: http://www.euronet.nl/users/e_wesker/ew@shell/API-prop.html.

[144] "Industrial Group Plans to Battle Climate Treaty" (April 26, 1998).

[145] UCS. *Smoke, Mirrors & Hot Air: How Exxon-Mobil Uses Big Tobacco's Tactics to Manufacture Uncertainty on Climate Science* (2007). http://www.ucsusa.org/assets/documents/global_warming/exxon_report.pdf.

[146] AP. "ExxonMobil Paid to Mislead Public," *USA Today* (May 5, 2007). http://www.usatoday.com/money/industries/energy/2007-01-03-global-warming_x.htm.

[147] Adam, David. "Royal Society Tells Exxon: Stop Funding Climate Change Denial," *The Guardian UK* (September 20, 2006). http://www.guardian.co.uk/environment/2006/sep/20/oilandpetrol.business.

However, in the United States, it took Hurricane Katrina in 2005 – followed by Al Gore's award-winning film, *An Inconvenient Truth*, in 2006 – to significantly awaken the public to the dangers of climate disruption and Exxon's underhanded campaign to conceal them. Facing a public relations crisis and a shareholders' revolt for its nefarious activities, the oil giant claimed it was turning over a new leaf and would no longer fund and promote the pseudoscience of these conservative think tanks. In its 2007 Corporate Citizenship Report, released in time for its shareholder meeting, Exxon announced:

> In 2008 we will discontinue contributions to several public policy interest groups whose position on climate change could divert attention from the important discussion on how the world will secure the energy required for economic growth in an environmentally responsible manner.[148]

Thereafter, Exxon severed its ties with a few denialist groups like the Competitive Enterprise Institute. Its public pronouncements officially abandoned the defunct and discredited blocking position on scientific uncertainty. The company's vice chairman of public affairs, Kenneth Cohen, announced that "we know enough now – or, society knows enough now – that the risk is serious and action should be taken."[149] Yet, behind the scenes, Exxon continued to fund the pseudoscience and blocking policies of several naysayer think tanks.[150]

ALTERING INTEREST PERCEPTIONS – DISMANTLING THE COST-BENEFIT BARRIER

When atmospheric negotiators finally agreed that ozone depletion and climate change were clear and present dangers, the interest assessment roadblock moved center stage. The interest assessment roadblock refers to the conflicting perceptions that rival coalitions, and the national policymakers within them, have concerning the relative costs and benefits of responding (or not responding) to the problem. Interest assessment revolves around this question: What are the costs and benefits of doing nothing compared with other possible responses? There is virtually no chance that countries will impose binding atmospheric protections on themselves unless they become relatively certain that ignoring the problem will be more costly and hazardous.

Because the "no response" option is the baseline for assessing all the others, cost-benefit disagreements are closely linked to previous conflicts over scientific

---

[148] Adam, David (September 20, 2006).

[149] "Exxon Mobil Takes First Steps to Accept Climate Change Science and Cut Funding of the Denial Machine," *Climate Science Watch* (January 27, 2007). http://www.climatesciencewatch. org/index.php/csw/details/exxon-mobil-first-steps1/.

[150] Murray, James. "Exxon Shareholder Revolt Highlights Investor Climate Risks," *Business Green* (May 19, 2008). http://www.businessgreen.com/business-green/news/2216960/exxon-shareholder-revolt; "Exxon Still Funding Climate Change Deniers," *Greenpeace* (May 18, 2007). http://www. greenpeace.org/usa/news/exxonsecrets-2007.

uncertainty. This is why the discovery of the ozone hole helped accelerate the negotiation process in Montreal. Once countries believed that inaction would result in disastrous environmental, economic and political consequences, they began to consider which response options would mitigate the problem in a manner most conducive to their perceived interests.

Because interest perceptions differ, negotiators may agree in principle upon the need for some kind of action, but disagree on what that action should be. Rival coalitions, and the national policymakers within them, remain deeply divided over the relative costs and benefits of any given response. Blocking forces gravitate toward the position that the costs of regulation will be extreme, immediate and unlikely to outweigh any uncertain future benefits they might produce. To overcome their resistance, leaders of the activist coalition must craft an agreement that all essential parties believe will be more beneficial to their interests than doing nothing. This is a long, convoluted and uphill battle.

Once the no-response option becomes too discredited and politically hazardous to openly endorse, blockers can still obstruct progress by vetoing every proposed response on the grounds that it's too costly. Activists must publicly discredit these cost-based objections, thereby rendering them as politically unacceptable as the pretext of scientific uncertainty. In addition to public education and grassroots pressure, this effort requires policy and technology innovation, creative problem solving, exploration of mutual interests, hard bargaining and astute negotiation until all essential parties agree that there are policy options available that will minimize the burdens of regulation while effectively abating a serious atmospheric menace.

Policymakers' interest perceptions are based on a complex interaction of objective and subjective cost-benefit calculations. For both ozone and climate deliberations, national policymakers had to consider three important objective factors:

- The projected health, environmental and economic impacts of these atmospheric threats, if left unaddressed, upon the constituencies they represent;
- The projected cost-benefit calculus of any policy option upon the national economy as a whole and influential economic and political actors in particular;
- The relative advantages and disadvantages (vis-à-vis other nations) of any particular response – including no response.

New atmospheric research, alternative technology breakthroughs, promising policy innovations and shifting political pressures constantly modify how policymakers perceive these factors.

In addition, stakeholders perceive these factors through a subjective set of values, assumptions and beliefs shaped by their individual political allegiances and ideological-philosophical proclivities. For instance, activist policymakers with strong environmental ethics place a much higher value on the long-range health and ecological costs of atmospheric disruption than free market conservatives; while the situation is reversed when valuing the costs of regulation. Those with a large stake in manufacturing CFCs or producing fossil fuels (or politicians who consider them a valuable political constituency) will tend to downplay health and environmental consequences while concerning themselves mainly with the immediate economic costs of any particular policy response.

Public opinion is a major wild card in this debate. For better or worse, it can have a profound impact on policymakers' interest calculations. Environmentally concerned, aware and politically active consumers, voters, investors and citizens can fortify the political leverage of activist groups; alter the political allegiances of politicians; and modify the economic calculations of corporate officials. An unaware, apathetic (or even hostile) public can move policymakers in the opposite direction. Thus, a vital element in both activist and blocker strategy involves swaying the public behind their view of the issue.

Gathering empirical data on the pros and cons of various policy options is an indispensable component of assessing interests and evaluating alternatives. However, because of the unusually high level of uncertainty surrounding the cost-benefit calculus of any particular option, national policymakers are forced to base their policy choices largely upon rudimentary assessments of national interest.[151] Often these rough evaluations are based as much or more upon the strength of public opinion, the demands of the most politically influential stakeholders and the policymaker's own basic orientation toward the problem as they are upon detailed empirical comparisons of their relative merits.[152]

The activist coalition, and especially its environmentalist core, works to sway policymakers toward the precautionary approach – its guiding assumption being "an ounce of prevention is worth a pound of cure." Activists assume, unless proven otherwise, that even expensive climate protection policies are probably cheaper than the potentially disastrous consequences of inaction. They also tend to assume that the longer effective responses are delayed, the costlier they will become. The nations most threatened by atmospheric disruption gravitated quickly toward the activist position: Scandinavians for ozone depletion, and small island and low-lying states for climate change.

At the opposite end of the spectrum lies the blocking coalition's approach: "If it's not broken, why fix it?" This orientation assumes that there is only the faintest probability of disastrous consequences from alleged anthropogenic climate disruption. Because they assume that "nothing is broken," without overwhelming evidence and substantial political pressure it is hard to convince them that doing nothing wouldn't be cheaper than any conceivable response. Besides the die-hard ideological opponents of environmentalism and government regulation,[153] the first parties to

---

[151] CAN-US & Europe. *Independent NGO Evaluations of National Plans for Climate Change Mitigation.* (Washington, DC: CAN), 1995.

[152] CAN-US & Europe, 1995; Lashof, Daniel (NRDC). "Country Report: USA." *Independent NGO Evaluations of National Plans for Climate Change Mitigation (OECD Countries).* CAN-US & Europe, ed. (Washington DC: Climate Action Network), 1995.

[153] For example, see: Lehr, Jay H., ed. *Rational Readings on Environmental Concerns.* (NY: Van Nostrand Reinhold), 1992.

gravitate toward and promote this "do nothing" orientation were the economic and political interests that profit from these polluting practices.

Those parties who were less able to foresee how the issue would affect them and/or less committed to a particular perspective were less willing to commit themselves to a specific response without more extensive investigation into the stakes and the options. For this reason, think tanks of both activist and blocking persuasions worked hard to win over these uncommitted parties by churning out convincing cost-benefit analyses of various policy responses to atmospheric disruption. Of course, blockers' studies found the dangers to be minimal and the response costs exorbitant,[154] while activist studies concluded the opposite.[155]

[154] Using climate change as an example: Nordhaus, W. D. "Greenhouse Economics: Count Before You Leap," *The Economist* (July 7, 1990): 21; Shanahan, John. *A Guide to Global Warming Theory (Backgrounder #896)*. The Heritage Foundation (May 21, 1992); Balling, Robert Jr. (1990); Congressional Budget Office. *Carbon Charges as a Response to Global Warming: The Effects of Taxing Fossil Fuels*. U.S. Congress (August 1990); Deputy Undersecretary for Policy Planning & Analysis. *Limiting Net Greenhouse Gases in the United States*. U.S. Department of Energy, Office of Environmental Analysis (September 1, 1991); Dornbusch, Rudiger & James M. Poterba, eds. *Global Warming: Economic Policy Responses* (Cambridge, MA: MIT Press), 1991; Global Climate Coalition. *Comments of the Global Climate Coalition on the National Energy Strategy*. (Washington, DC: GCC), 1990; Global Climate Coalition. *Greenhouse Gas Emissions: Trends and Policy Options*. (Washington, DC: GCC), 1991; Global Climate Coalition. *A Reasoned Approach to Global Climate Change*. (Washington, DC: GCC), 1991; Norman, Colin. "Greenhouse Policy: A Bargain?" *Science* (April 12, 1991): 204. There were also studies that took a middle ground. For example: National Academy of Sciences. *Policy Implications of Greenhouse Warming*. (Washington, DC: National Academy Press), 1991.

[155] Using climate change as an example: Abrahamson, Dean Edwin. ed. "Global Warming: The Issue, Impacts, Responses," *The Challenge of Global Warming*. (Washington, DC: Island Press), 1989: 3–34; Chandler, William U., ed. *Carbon Emissions Control Strategies*. (Washington, DC: World Wildlife Fund & Conservation Foundation), 1990; Cline, William R. *Global Warming: Estimating the Economic Benefits of Abatement*. (Paris: OECD), 1992; Cline, William R. *Global Warming: The Economic Stakes*. (Washington, DC: Institute for International Economics), 1992; Darmstadter, Joel. *The Economic Cost of CO2 Mitigation: A Review of Estimates for Selected World Regions*. (Washington, DC: Resources for the Future, Discussion Paper ENR91–06), 1991; Dornbusch, Rudiger & James M. Poterba, eds. 1991; Dudek, Daniel J. & Alice LeBlanc. "Offsetting New CO2 Emissions: A Rational First Greenhouse Policy Step," *Contemporary Policy Issues* (July 1990); Manne, Alan S. & Richard G. Richels. *Buying Greenhouse Insurance: The Economic Costs of Carbon Dioxide Emission Limits*. (Cambridge, MA: MIT Press), 1992; OECD. *Convention on Climate Change: Economic Aspects of Negotiations* (Paris: OECD), 1992; Research/Strategy/Management Inc. *Global Warming and Energy Priorities: A National Perspective*. A Study for the Union of Concerned Scientists (November, 1989); Rosenberg, Norman J. et al. eds. *Greenhouse Warming: Abatement and Adaptation*. (Washington, DC: Resources for the Future), 1989; Rothenberg, Jerome. "Economic Perspective on Time Comparisons: Evaluation of Time Discounting." *Global Accord: Environmental Challenges and International Responses*. Nazli Choucri, ed. (Cambridge, MA: MIT Press), 1993: 307–32; Union of Concerned Scientists. *Fighting Global Warming: A Profitable Solution*. (Washington, DC: UCS), 1992; Union of Concerned Scientists. "Special Issue: The National Energy Strategy," *Nucleus* (Spring 1991): 3; Bryner, Gary C., ed. "Policy Options for Responding to the Threat of Global Warming," *Global Warming and the Challenge of International Cooperation*. (Provo, UT: David M. Kennedy for International Studies/Brigham Young University), 1992: 101–32;

COMPARING COSTS: THE OZONE HILL AND THE CLIMATE
MOUNTAIN

One of the primary reasons why ozone negotiations succeeded while climate negotiations floundered was the enormous difference in the estimated costs of confronting
these two threats. This is true for the particular economic sectors facing regulation as
well as the overall economies of the nations involved. Blockers' cost objections to
reducing GHGs appear far more credible than similar objections to phasing out
CFCs. Unlike CFCs, the buildup of GHGs results from a vast, complex, deeply
entrenched array of behaviors and processes at the very core of modern society.

Global economic growth, worldwide chains of production and international trade
and transport are all powered by the combustion of fossil fuels. Expectations for a
higher standard of living among the growing populations in the developing world are
premised upon abundant supplies of relatively cheap energy, while the entire economic life of some nations is utterly dependent on the extraction and sale of their
petroleum reserves. Consequently, the 60–80 percent reduction of GHGs necessary
to abate climate disruption will entail far-reaching, basic changes in the way people,
industries and governments go about their daily business.

Fossil fuels are central to the profitable operation of coal, oil and natural gas companies
and they are absolutely essential to the economic metabolism of most nations.[156] By
contrast, CFCs were never more than a small fraction of the chemical industry's overall
production and they played a relatively minor and easily replaceable role in the economic
life of most countries. Nearly all comparative studies estimate the costs of confronting
climate change to be far higher than reversing ozone depletion.[157] One prominent early
blocking study – the 1990 *Economic Report of the President* – estimated the cost of
compliance with the Montreal Protocol at $2.7 billion for the United States. The same
report projected the costs of reducing U.S. carbon dioxide emissions by 20 percent at
between $800 billion and $3.6 trillion.[158] This is between 300 and 1,333 times more

Chandler, William U., ed., 1990; GECR. "NGO Study Finds US Could Save Trillions by
Cutting CO2," *Global Environmental Change Report 3.21* (1991): 4.

[156] There are a few exceptions: like Iceland whose economy is powered by geothermal energy.

[157] Economists of the blocking persuasion argue that investments in technologies that slow climate
change will be very costly – from several hundred billion dollars to as much as $3.6 trillion in the
U.S. alone. These conclusions have met with sharp disagreements from activist economists who
argue that relatively easy and cost effective measures could be adopted to cut energy use
20 percent. Nevertheless, a 20 percent cut is only one third of the distance industrial nations
must go, according to IPCC scientists, to achieve the 60 percent cut in global carbon dioxide
emissions needed to stabilize atmospheric carbon. Past this point, most activists agree with
blockers that the cost will rise. However, mavericks like Amory Lovins argue that all the necessary
cuts and changes could be made in a very efficient and economic manner that would actually
save money in the long run. See: Brookes, W. T. "The Global Warming Panic," *Forbes*, v. 25
(December 1989): 96–102; Flavin, Christopher & Nicholas Lenssen. "Saving the Climate Saves
Money," *World Watch*, v. 3 (November/December 1990): 26; Lovins, Amory. "The Role of
Energy Efficiency," in Leggett, Jeremy, ed., 1990: 193–223.

[158] The President's report figures were based on: Manne, Anne S. & R. G. Richels. *Global CO2
Emissions Reductions – Impacts of Rising Energy Costs*. (Menlo Park, CA: Electric Power
Research Institute), 1990.

expensive. If these figures are remotely accurate,[159] they suggest that those opposed to significant GHG reductions may have a much stronger motivation for resisting regulation.

There are notable exceptions to these dismal cost calculations. World-renowned energy economists, Amory and Hunter Lovins, present a convincing argument that America's electric bill could be halved through energy efficiency measures and renewables that would mostly pay for themselves within a year. They explain in copious detail how the United States could benefit economically and politically over the coming decades by cutting oil imports to zero by 2040 and eliminating oil use entirely by 2050.[160]

Over the past few years, several respected studies have concluded that the costs of ignoring climate change will far outweigh the costs of confronting it. In 2006, a British study released by the respected economist Lord Stern concluded that avoiding the worst effects of climate change would cost 1 percent of global GDP per annum, while failure to make these investments could lower GDP as much as 20 percent. Less than two years later, Stern revised his assessment warning that it would be nearly twice as expensive to avoid serious climate disruption than originally expected and the cost of inaction would be far more catastrophic. "We badly underestimated the degree of damages and the risks of climate change … All the links in the chain are on average worse than we thought a couple of years ago." He warned that the release of methane from thawing permafrost, the acidification of oceans and the saturation of carbon sinks were causing GHG emissions to grow at a much faster pace than previously expected.[161] An IPCC report issued in 2007 argued that decarbonizing the global economy to a point where climate change should be manageable could cost 0.1 percent of global GDP. The authors concluded that, in some sectors, boosting energy efficiency would actually make money for businesses and homeowners.[162]

---

[159] For a critique of Manne-Richels estimates see: Williams, R. H. *Low Cost Strategies for Coping with Carbon Dioxide Emissions Limits.* (Princeton, NJ: Center for Energy and Environmental Studies), 1989. For conflicting assessments see: EPA. *Regulatory Impact Analysis: Protection of Stratospheric Ozone.* 3 vols. Washington, DC: unpublished report, 1988. For the cost-benefit assessments of several other nations see; EPA, Division of Global Change, Office of Air & Radiation. *Proceedings of the U.S. Environmental Protection Agency Workshop on Integrating Case Studies Carried Out Under the Montreal Protocol.* (Washington, DC: U.S. Government), 1990.

[160] Lovins, Amory B., et al. *Winning the Oil End Game: Innovation for Profits, Jobs, and Security* (Rocky Mountain Institute, Colorado/Earthscan, London). http://www.oilendgame.org. Another plan developed by Ken Zweibel, James Mason and Vasilis Fthenakis for *Scientific American* holds that the U.S. could make a massive switch from coal, oil, natural gas and nuclear power to solar power that could supply 69 percent of the U.S.'s electricity and 35 percent of its total energy by 2050. However, their plan would require a moderate $420 billion in subsidies from 2011 to 2050 to fund the infrastructure and make it cost-competitive. See: "A Solar Grand Plan," *Scientific American* (December 2007). http://www.sciam.com/article.cfm?id=a-solar-grand-plan.

[161] Fortson, Danny. "Stern Warns that Climate Change is Far Worse than 2006 Estimate," *The Independent* (April 17, 2008). http://www.independent.co.uk/news/business/news/stern-warns-that-climate-change-is-far-worse-than-2006-estimate-810488.html.

[162] Steiner, Achim. "The UN Role in Climate Change Action: Taking the Lead Towards a Global Response," *UN Chronicle* (February 2007). http://www.un.org/Pubs/chronicle/2007/issue2/0207p24.htm.

However, the cost-benefit calculus surrounding climate change remains even more controversial than the science. And, because it is the *perception* of high response costs that engenders focused opposition and general public reticence, these estimates need not be accurate – just believable and well-publicized – to dampen enthusiasm for GHG regulation and mobilize opposition from a broad range of industries fearful of bearing the costs. Further, while the major chemical producers could profit from international CFC restrictions by developing and marketing alternatives, generally this is not the case for the fossil fuel industry, especially the coal sector and the oil-producing nations.[163]

During ozone negotiations, activist efforts to alter the interest perceptions of CFC producers – through public pressure, consumer boycotts and aerosol bans – created defections from the blocking coalition and encouraged a search for alternatives. DuPont claimed that it abandoned its blocking position once it was convinced that CFCs probably caused ozone depletion. But there is strong evidence that two other factors played an important role as well: (1) its corporate image was seriously suffering; and (2) its head start in developing CFC alternatives positioned it to dominate the global alternatives market once CFCs were phased out.

DuPont spent an average of $2.5 million per year between 1974 and 1980 researching CFC alternatives. Although the link between CFCs and ozone depletion was never disproved, both American and European chemical producers decided to suspend their research programs in the early 1980s when it appeared that no further CFC regulation would be forthcoming.[164] However, by the time research was suspended, DuPont had identified several substances that possessed the necessary properties to replace several ozone depleting chemicals.[165]

Unlike its European competitors, DuPont resumed research into CFC alternatives after the ozone hole was discovered. Between 1986 and 1988, the company's $45 million effort[166] produced two classes of closely related substitutes: hydrochlorofluorocarbons (HCFCs) and hydrofluorocarbons (HFCs).[167] Although they caused minimal ozone depletion, these alternatives were harder to produce and two to five times more expensive than CFCs.[168] Consequently, DuPont officials reasoned that only global

---

[163] Cline estimated that oil-exporting nations stood to lose nearly 20 percent of their GDP by 2030 if national consumption taxes were applied to reduce global carbon emissions by 50 percent from the baseline they would otherwise follow. Cline, William R. *The Economics of Global Warming.* (Washington, DC: Institute for International Economics), 1992: 342.

[164] Makhijani, Arjun & Kevin R. Gurney. *Mending the Ozone Hole.* (Cambridge, MA: MIT Press), 1995: 267–73.

[165] Most notable among these was an alternative called HFC-134a, which has come into widespread use in the 1990s. Makhijani, Arjun & Kevin R. Gurney, 1995: 267–8.

[166] Reinhardt, Forest. *DuPont and Freon Products* (National Wildlife Federation: 1989): 12.

[167] Hydrochlorofluorocarbons and hydrofluorocarbons: in addition to these two basic classes of chemicals, DuPont also developed FC-134a, a chlorine-free refrigerant, to replace CFC-112. Its early development was also due to the head start DuPont achieved from its 1970s research program. Oppenheimer, Michael & Robert Boyle, 1991: 159, 160.

[168] Like CFCs, these substitutes are potent greenhouse gases. World Meteorological Organization, Global Ozone Research & Monitoring Project. *Scientific Assessment of Stratospheric Ozone: 1989* (vol. 1) (WMO: 1989).

CFC regulation would make them marketable. According to Dr. Joseph Steed, Environmental Manager of DuPont's Freon Division:

> Only regulation would force people to pay three times as much. By mid-1986, I saw that future regulation was definite. I concluded that there should be a real push for alternatives and that an international agreement was the only way to go.[169]

In addition to the market advantages it hoped to secure by developing alternatives, DuPont was concerned about the harm CFC production was doing to its corporate image. While CFCs were just a small part of its total business (2–3 percent of total sales), the media's coverage of Freon's possible link to the ozone hole undermined its slogan "better living through chemistry" and cast an unfavorable shadow over all its operations. Soon after the ozone hole was discovered, DuPont responded by taking the CFC issue out of the Freon Division's hands and turning it over to senior corporate management where, according to Sharon Roan, "the issue would be looked at in a broader manner."[170]

When the EPA's 1986 study estimated that skin cancers would increase markedly if CFC emissions went unabated, DuPont management began to consider the legal implications of resisting regulation. Lawsuits against cigarette manufacturers were holding them responsible for lung cancer. Chemical company executives worried that they could face similar legal problems in the near future.[171] And finally, American CFC producers feared that growing public pressures and the NRDC's lawsuit would compel the EPA to impose unilateral regulations. For all these reasons, the cost-benefit calculus of DuPont and other American CFC producers changed rapidly in favor of a strong ozone treaty before negotiators met in Montreal.

Industry's "change of heart" helped move the Reagan administration behind the goals of the activist coalition. In the months leading up to Montreal, the administration's most avid blockers were either converted or discredited and sidelined. Many were won over by a cost-benefit study from the President's Council of Economic Advisors, which concluded that the monetary benefits of preventing future skin cancer deaths far outweighed the costs of reducing CFCs. The Council's study vindicated the official activist policy and won over most of the remaining skeptics.

In desperation, an enduring handful of ideologically zealous blockers mounted a last-ditch effort to gain the upper hand. Influential remnants of the ozone-blocking coalition inside and outside the Reagan administration went public in an effort to oust the leadership of the U.S. negotiating team. Within the administration, Interior Secretary Donald Hodel used *The New York Times* to accuse chief negotiator, Richard Benedick, of a conflict of interest based on his acceptance of a position with an environmental NGO following the completion of ozone

---

[169] Quoted in: Litfin, Karen. *Power & Knowledge in International Environmental Relations: The Case of Stratospheric Ozone Depletion* (PhD thesis: University of California, Los Angeles), 1991: 28.

[170] Roan, Sharon, 1989: 193.

[171] Parson, Edward A. "Protecting the Ozone Layer," *Institutions for the Earth.* Peter M. Haas, Robert O. Keohane & Marc A. Levy, eds. (Cambridge, MA: MIT Press), 1993: 113; Roan, Sharon, 1989: 193.

negotiations.[172] Outside the administration, a prominent conservative-libertarian journal, *Human Events*, charged that "officials at the State Department, led by chief negotiator Richard Benedick and the EPA, have ... push[ed] their own radical negotiating program for international controls on CFCs, and they have done so largely out of sight of the Administration."[173]

Ironically, the entire libertarian position collapsed under the weight of its own absurdity after the press reported that Interior Secretary Hodel had proposed a program of "personal protection" – advocating the use of broad-brimmed hats, sunscreen and sunglasses instead of government regulation. Editorials and political cartoons lampooned his "program." Environmentalists parodied his idea by showing up at his press conference wearing cowboy hats and sunglasses, their faces smeared white with zinc oxide. They sarcastically asked how people should go about putting sunscreen and visors on cows and corn because animals and crops would also be affected.[174] Activists humorously ridiculed the cost-benefit assumptions behind Hodel's personal protection program. The NRDC's chief economist, David Donniger, pointed out that if each American had to buy two bottles of sunscreen per year, a hat and a pair of sunglasses, the bill would come to $40 per person, per year – an $8 billion national expenditure. He gibed, "It would be a lot less expensive to control pollution. Besides you couldn't get fish to wear sunglasses."[175]

In the face of mounting ridicule, Hodel backtracked, claiming he had been misquoted.[176] But the damage was already done; the ideologically motivated opponents of the emerging ozone treaty inside and outside the Reagan administration were dealt a politically embarrassing blow from which they never recovered. Hodel's remarks became symbolic of the stubborn, dangerous and irresponsible position on environmental protection held by so many in the Reagan administration. Also, his comments succeeded in focusing new attention on the need for a serious solution to a serious problem. A growing host of activist Senators and Congressmen labeled his idea "bizarre," "absurd," "laughable" and "a band-aid approach."[177] Within weeks, a resolution passed the Senate calling for CFC reductions of at least 50 percent, with a program for additional phase outs attached. The dispute was finally resolved in a

---

[172] Shabecoff, Philip. "A Wrangle Over Ozone Policy," *New York Times* (June 23, 1987): A1.

[173] Editorial. "The President Must Decide – State Department Pushes Radical Ozone Treaty," *Human Events* (June 20, 1987). See also: Benedick, Richard E, 1991: 62.

[174] Roan, Sharon, 1989: 200–3.

[175] Doniger, David D. "The Politics of the Ozone Layer," *Issues in Science & Technology*, v. 4 (Spring 1988): 89; Roan, Sharon, 1989: 202.

[176] This issue remains foggy. Both press accounts and Richard Benedick cite Hodel's own aides as the source of the leaked quote. Apparently the aides believed his "common sense" alternative would generate a backlash against overeager regulation. Sharon Roan credits the NRDC's David Donniger with alerting the press to Hodel's personal protection plan which was confirmed by State Department and other administration officials. Roan seems to accept Hodel's claim that he never meant or said his plan advocated sunglasses and hats. Benedick, Richard E, 1991: 60, 61; Roan, Sharon, 1989: 200–3.

[177] Green, Bill. "Congress: Policies on Global Warming and Ozone Depletion," *Environment*, v. 29 (April 1987): 5; Benedick, Richard E, 1991: 60, 61.

cabinet meeting where President Reagan affirmed his commitment to activist negotiating position.

As the most influential member of the activist coalition, the United States worked
closely with other activist nations and NGOs to bring European blockers and
uncommitted nations around to its side. According to the U.S. chief negotiator:

> US negotiators coordinated their diplomatic initiatives closely with like-minded
> governments, particularly Canada, Finland, New Zealand, Norway, Sweden and
> Switzerland. In addition, US negotiators and embassies developed close relation-
> ships with countries in the EC that seemed sympathetic to the concept of stricter
> controls on CFCs, in particular the Federal Republic of Germany because of its
> volume of production. The US also focused diplomatic attention on Japan, the
> USSR and key uncommitted developing-country governments.[178]

The United States made extensive use of its embassies in more than 60 countries,
providing them with detailed analyses of the issues and the rationale for American
positions.[179] State Department and EPA representatives met with the environmental
ministers, ambassadors and trade officials of key blocking nations while American
scientists from EPA, NASA and NOAA consulted their counterparts in Europe, Japan
and the USSR. The State Department even invited EC Commission officials to
Washington for bilateral consultations in an attempt to narrow the gaps between
them.[180]

To lend force to the U.S. negotiating position, Congressional activists Chafee
(R-Rhode Island) and Baucus (D-Montana) introduced bills designed to fortify the
U.S. negotiating position by imposing trade restrictions on countries that did not
follow the activist coalition's lead.[181] U.S. negotiators made effective use of these
Congressional initiatives, warning blocking governments that there might be a stiff
price to pay for not joining in meaningful efforts to protect the ozone layer.[182]

The world media played a critical role in activist strategy. According to Benedick,
"The US undertook major efforts to reach out to foreign public opinion, especially in
Europe and Japan, to counteract the previously unopposed influence of commercial
interests."[183] In addition to numerous speeches, TV and radio interviews and press
conferences given by U.S. officials in foreign capitals, Richard Benedick and Robert
Watson (from NASA) conducted live video discussions via satellite with experts,
policymakers and journalists from Europe, Asia and Latin America in order to
"amplify [their] persuasive voice."[184]

[178] Benedick, Richard E, 1991: 55.
[179] Benedick, Richard E. "Perspectives of a Negotiation Practitioner," *International Environmental
       Negotiation*, Gunnar Sjöstedt, ed. (London: Sage), 1993: 233.
[180] The invitation was declined. Benedick, Richard E, 1991: 73.
[181] Shimberg, Steven. "Stratospheric Ozone and Climate Protection: Domestic Legislation and the
       International Process," *Environmental Law* (1992 forthcoming); Parson, Edward A, 1993: 43.
[182] Benedick, Richard E, 1991: 29.
[183] Benedick, Richard E, 1991: 56.
[184] Negroponte, John D. *Protecting the Ozone Layer: Testimony Before the Senate Subcommittee on
       Toxic Substances & Environmental Oversight.* Department of State Bulletin (January 23, 6/87): 59.

At the nonstate level, American NGOs such as the World Resources Institute hosted meetings with European and Japanese environmentalists, urging them to become more active on this issue. The State Department openly encouraged American environmental groups to convince their counterparts in Europe and Japan to press for CFC controls more energetically.[185] During the intersession deliberations leading up to Montreal, representatives from several U.S.-based NGOs traveled to Europe to urge local environmental groups to demand a strong ozone treaty. In the U.K., Friends of the Earth ran a highly visible and effective campaign culminating in a boycott threat against 20 specific CFC-aerosol products.[186] In Germany an increasingly influential Green Party called for the government to break with the EC if necessary and sign a strong ozone agreement. After a few artful compromises in Montreal, Europe's blocking coalition collapsed under the external threat of U.S. trade sanctions against products containing CFCs and the internal strain of growing public support for an effective ozone agreement.

This contrasts sharply with climate change negotiations, where U.S. political leaders, the fossil fuel industry and the oil producing nations have stubbornly resisted all efforts to erode their blocking position. The politically powerful, heavily subsidized,[187] enormously profitable, vertically integrated, capital intensive nature of the overlapping petroleum, coal and electric utility industries make them highly resistant to the development of small-scale, carbon free, renewable energy alternatives.[188] Despite the many advantages of solar energy, these industries continue to shun every carbon-free alternative except nuclear power – a dangerous, nonrenewable, capital-intensive, subsidy dependent technology with deep financial ties to big oil.[189]

These underlying differences have produced a climate change blocking coalition that is far more influential, cohesive and intransigent than its ozone counterpart, and have made it considerably harder to for activists to build consensus around the need to dramatically cut GHG emissions to climate friendly levels. For eight years, the Bush administration's tight relationship with oil giants such as Exxon Mobil[190] and their

---

[185] Benedick, Richard E, 1991: 28.

[186] Maxwell, James H. & Sanford L. Weiner (1993): 33.

[187] From 1993 to 1999, The Southern Company, GE, ARCO, Chevron, Texaco and 121 other energy companies gave $39 million in campaign donations and received $7.3 billion in federal energy subsidy programs and grants – a 186:1 return on their investment. Dauncey, Guy, Patrick Mazza, & Ross Gelbspan. *Stormy Weather*. (Canada: New Society Publishers), 2001.

[188] Commoner, Barry. *The Politics of Energy*. (NY: Knopf), 1979: 70–4; Berman, Daniel & John O'Connor. *Who Owns the Sun?* (White River, VT: Chelsea Green), 1996; Reece, Ray. *The Sun Betrayed*. (Boston, MA: South End), 1979.

[189] By 1998, the U.S. was subsidizing the oil, coal and nuclear industries to the tune of $25 billion per year. See: Lovins, Amory & Imran Sheikh. "The Nuclear Illusion," *AMBIO* (November 8, 2008). http://www.rmi.org/images/PDFs/Energy/E08–01_AmbioNucIllusion.pdf; Gelbspan, Ross, 2004. Commoner, Barry, 1979: 70–4.

[190] One example of many: President Bush named Lee Raymond, the retired chief of Exxon-Mobil who chaired the National Petroleum Council (one of the most powerful lobbies in Washington), to head a key study to help America chart a cleaner energy course. "Bush Names Exxon Chief to Chart America's Energy Future," *Green Watch Today* (November 2, 2006). http://www.bush-greenwatch.org/mt_archives/000323.php.

policy mouthpieces such as the American Enterprise Institute[191] stonewalled every effort to move the United States away from a die-hard blocking position.[192]

Nevertheless, the blocking coalition's intransigence around the cost issue is being continually eroded by worldwide climate disturbances of increasing severity and frequency. As scientists, activists and the media draw attention to the connections being established between these climate calamities and GHG emissions,[193] a crisis atmosphere may galvanize public concern, draw the insurance and banking sectors of the global economy into the activist coalition and compel national policymakers to fundamentally reassess their interest calculations.

In addition, substantial advances in alternative energy technologies may lower the cost of solar energy and significantly alter the interest assessments of many businesses and countries in the near future. Some influential portions of the multinational business community are actively promoting these developments. The European and American Business Council for Sustainable Development (BCSD) maintained a high profile in Kyoto, supporting a viable treaty and calling for governments to encourage energy efficiency and renewable energy technologies. Multilateral agencies and private investors have begun integrating renewable energy into their portfolios, attracting the interest of the largest global companies. In 2007, global wind generating capacity increased 28 percent, while grid-connected solar photovoltaic capacity rose 52 percent.[194] Activist energy policies in Japan, Denmark and Germany have allowed these countries to seize leadership in the development of clean energy technologies.[195]

Nevertheless, it is highly unlikely that the major coal- and oil-producing sectors and the governments most under their influence will make the kind of radical about-face made by CFC producers. Fossil fuel producers are far more reliant on coal and

---

[191] Greenpeace. *Factsheet: American Enterprise Institute for Public Policy Research.* http://www. exxonsecrets.org/html/orgfactsheet.php?id=9. On February 26, 2003 President Bush's key-note speech at the American Enterprise Institute enthused that, at AEI, "Some of the finest minds of our nation are at work on some of the greatest challenges to our nation. You do such good work that my administration has borrowed 20 such minds. I want to thank them for their service." AEI has been an avid opponent of the Kyoto protocol and its in house climate science skeptics include James K. Glassman, also of Exxon-Mobil-funded Tech Central Station. Exxon-Mobil CEO Lee Raymond is on the AEI board of trustees and Exxon-Mobil gave AEI approximately $925,000 between 1998 and 2003.

[192] Ian Sample. "Scientists Offered Cash to Dispute Climate Study" (February 2, 2007) *guardian.co. uk* http://www.guardian.co.uk/environment/2007/feb/02/frontpagenews.climatechange.

[193] Minimal media coverage has been given to the probable link between the duration and frequency of recent El Niños and climate change. Some notable exceptions are: Davidson, Keay. "Global Warming Menaces the West," *San Francisco Chronicle* (April 12, 1998): A-1; Mazza, Patrick. *El Niño's Growing Ferocity: Ocean in the Greenhouse?* Atmosphere Alliance (March 1998); Mazza, Partick. *Global Warming and the Pacific Northwest: Perpetual El Niño.* Atmosphere Alliance (December 1997).

[194] *Renewables 21: Global Status Report 2007.* "Renewable Energy Accelerates Meteoric Rise" (February 2008). http://www.ren21.net/globalstatusreport/default.asp.

[195] Evans-Prichard, Ambrose. "Cheap Solar Power Poised to Undercut Oil and Gas by Half," *Telegraph Co, UK* (February 18, 2007). http://www.telegraph.co.uk/money/main.jhtml? xml=/money/2007/02/19/ccview19.xml.

petroleum than the chemical industry was on CFCs; in addition, fossil fuel producers are far less capable of profiting by switching to climate-safe alternatives. Thus, despite strong public support and a growing interest among some sectors of the business establishment for renewable energy, solar power provided less than 0.01 percent of America's electricity supply in 2006. Meanwhile, coal-burning power plants, the primary source of increasing global carbon emissions, are being built around the world at a rate of more than one per week.[196]

In sum, the growing demand for action is confronting stiff resistance from powerful entrenched interests. The BCSD's move toward the activist camp, the insurance and banking industries' budding alliance with Greenpeace, and the rising popularity of climate-friendly policies at the state and local levels are all signs that this obstacle may be eroding. After enjoying eight years of steadfast support from the Bush White House, the fossil fuel industry may soon face a more affluent and influential activist lobby as major industries with a vested interest in alternative energy and/or limiting their exposure to climate disruption begin to flex their political muscle.

In 2008, both U.S. presidential candidates criticized Bush's blocking position and supported the Kyoto Protocol, although McCain's support was largely due to his advocacy of nuclear power.[197] A new administration will surely amend U.S. climate policy, but it is highly unlikely that the fossil fuel industry or OPEC will experience the rapid conversion to activism made by DuPont and other CFC producers. Instead, they will use their substantial influence to keep the United States from playing an activist leadership role in the negotiations and retard any dramatic movement toward an effective climate treaty.

Christopher Flavin, president of the Worldwatch Institute, predicts that "Technologies such as solar cells, fuel cells, biorefineries and wind turbines are in about the same place today that the internal combustion engine and electromagnetic generator occupied in 1905. These key enabling technologies have already been developed and commercialized, but they are just now entering the world's largest energy markets."[198] If oil prices continue to rise; future climate negotiations produce increasingly more stringent GHG controls; U.S., European, Japanese and Chinese consumers convert to more energy efficient technologies; and an untapped market of more than two billion people without electricity in the developing world plug in to solar power; these technologies will take-off rapidly.

These developments could have an especially powerful impact on the interest assessment calculations of the developing countries in the equity coalition. Climate change is likely to be most devastating for these countries; and because most of the two billion people living in the developing world have little or no access to electricity, renewable energy technologies have the potential to be more attractive and affordable

[196] Revkin, Andrew C. & Matthew L. Wald. "Solar Power Wins Enthusiasts But Not Money," *New York Times* (July 16, 2007). http://www.nytimes.com/2007/07/16/business/16solar.html.

[197] Corn, David. "McCain's Nuclear Waste," *Mother Jones* (March 4, 2008). http://www.mother-jones.com/washington_dispatch/2008/03/john-mccain-nuclear-waste.html.

[198] Ullrich, Christy. "When Will the Peak Hit?" *National Geographic* (June 3, 2008). http://ngm.nationalgeographic.com/geopedia/World_Oil.

than fossil fuels. Unlike carboniferous energy, the sun and wind are widely distributed in the developing world; and renewables are free of the radioactive waste, deadly air pollution and environmental devastation associated with petroleum and nuclear energy.

A final aspect of interest assessment is closely linked to the equity dilemma and presents climate negotiators with some unique challenges. This is the issue of winners and losers. The damages resulting from ozone depletion are relatively straightforward and universal (although more intense in the southern hemisphere and nearer the poles). Most important, no country stands to benefit from overexposure to UV radiation. However, some climate modelers think global warming could temporarily improve life in some areas of the world (Scandinavia, Siberia, Canada) while making it much harder in others. This poorly understood differential impact will magnify the difficulty of creating a strong climate treaty if some national leaders come to believe global warming could possibly benefit their country – or even do "acceptable" levels damage – particularly if it appears that their traditional rivals might suffer far more.

So far, persisting uncertainties have prevented blockers from credibly claiming that some countries will benefit from global warming. Atmospheric science cannot predict whether climate change, if left unaddressed, will produce any "winners." Ultimately, this depends on the regional impacts of climate warming in combination with the rate and ultimate extent of overall change. Most studies indicate that climate disruption will harm all countries, but the worst calamities may strike the very regions where countries are least able to adapt. However, climate models lack the resolution to predict regional climate variations with much precision. In addition, no one can say how fast or how far climate disruption will go. Finally, the potential for "surprises" in the climate system, including the danger of a runaway greenhouse effect, is a major wild card that stifles any notion that global warming might benefit a particular country or region of the planet.[199]

The fact that all these factors remain veiled in uncertainty reinforces the perception of a serious universal threat. This perception is vital for building consensus around an effective agreement. Consequently, this "veil of uncertainty" may be essential to successful negotiations.[200] Even at the current level of climate knowledge, countries such as Russia are considerably less concerned about global warming than low-lying areas such as the Netherlands or the Maldives. If countries become convinced they can accurately predict how climate change will affect them, they may abandon the search for an agreement altogether or become motivated by the desire to achieve an outcome most favorable to their own particular interests rather than one

[199] Glantz, Michael H., Martin F. Price, & Maria E. Krenz. *Report of the Workshop* "On Assessing Winners & Losers in the Context of Global Warming". National Center for Atmospheric Research, Environmental & Societal Impacts Group (June 18–21, 1990); Meyer-Abich, Klaus M. "Winners & Losers in Climate Change," *Global Ecology: A New Arena of Political Conflict*. Wolfgang Sachs, ed. (London: Zed Books), 1993; Tunali, Odil. "Climate Models Growing More Accurate," *World Watch* (June 1995): 6.

[200] Rawls, John. *A Theory of Justice*. (Cambridge, MA: Harvard University Press), 1971; Young, Oran R. "The Politics of International Regime Formation," *International Organization*, v. 43 (Summer 1989): 363–4.

considered fair for all.[201] Such a change in perception would scuttle all hope for a consensual agreement. For example, if most rich nations concluded that climate change was harmless or might even bestow some potential benefits, their support for an effective agreement would dissipate, no matter how seriously poor nations stood to suffer.

SHARING THE BURDEN – WHAT'S FAIR?

Overcoming the equity roadblock requires crafting an agreement that addresses the specific fairness concerns of the developing nations to the satisfaction of all essential parties. While ozone negotiators eventually agreed upon mechanisms to promote fairness in the Montreal Protocol, equity issues have yet to be resolved by climate negotiators. Nevertheless, equity has already been the subject of considerable discussion and debate.[202]

During both atmospheric negotiations, the Asian, African and Latin American countries of the South raised specific equity concerns and insisted that their participation depended on the willingness of the wealthy nations of the North to address them. In both cases these concerns are similar. First, rich countries must assume the initial and primary responsibility for overcoming atmospheric disruptions because, until recently, they were the only countries that benefited from these polluting technologies. Second, regulatory commitments made by developing countries are contingent upon the provision of adequate financial and technical assistance from the North. And finally, the South should have as much control as possible over the management of these financial and technology transfers.

These concerns arise from the structural inequities in the international system and the South's ongoing struggle to reduce them. This inequity began with colonialism and is perpetuated by a global economy still designed to favor the powerful nations of the North. International cooperation is hampered unless this unjust relationship is recognized and efforts are made to offset rather than perpetuate it.

Equity concerns surface in nearly every international venue, and developed countries have very reluctantly and partially acknowledged them. In recent decades, addressing these inequities has become even more pressing for Southern political leaders. After the collapse of the Soviet Union, the world's geopolitical axis shifted. During the cold war, the third world was often a battleground for wars of proxy between the United States and the USSR. However, East-West rivalry produced some side benefits for nonaligned Southern leaders who learned to improve their situation by playing the superpowers off against each another.

---

[201] For more detailed discussion see: Coase, R. H. "The Problem of Social Cost," *Journal of Law and Economics*, v. 3 (October 1960): 1–44; Rawls, J. *A Theory of Justice*. (Cambridge, MA: Harvard University Press), 1976; Walton, Richard, & Robert B. McKersie. *A Behavioral Theory of Negotiations*. (NY: McGraw-Hill), 1965; Schelling, Thomas C. *The Strategy of Conflict*. (Cambridge, MA: Harvard University Press), 1960.

[202] Burtraw, Dallas & Michael A. Toman. *Equity and International Agreements for CO_2 Containment*. (Washington, DC: Resources for the Future, Discussion Paper ENR91–07), 1991. One website dedicated to this issue is *Eco Equity*: http://www.ecoequity.org/.

With the collapse of its superpower rival, the United States was no longer compelled to outmatch Soviet aid to the South, and many Eastern European countries eagerly sought Western development assistance. For the South, this problematic realignment coincided with a global economic recession, massive debt accumulation, extreme trade imbalances and a net negative flow of resources. In this new unipolar world, the size of the "aid pie" was shrinking while the number of countries that wanted a piece of it had grown.

Under these circumstances, Southern leaders took full advantage of the latent opportunities in a world without East-West tensions. One such opportunity was the possibility of tying the South's primary concern – development – to the North's growing apprehension about the global environment. If Northern leaders concluded that (1) solving the planet's dire ecological problems required Southern cooperation; and (2) cooperation was impossible without increased assistance, Southern governments would possess the leverage necessary to revive Northern aid flows and possibly their troubled economies. Thus, after an initial period of skepticism and indifference, by 1990 the South became a serious participant in both ozone and climate change negotiations and a major force behind the Earth Summit's quest for sustainable development.

However, the longstanding inequities between North and South generate serious obstacles to cooperation. First, poor nations don't trust rich nations, with their history of grabbing the benefits of development while shifting the burdens onto the South. They resent being told to make sacrifices to fix problems they neither created nor benefited from, and lack the resources to address. Conversely, rich nations resist giving substantial environmental aid and assistance to poor nations, especially if it undermines their wealth and power.

Despite these underlying tensions, the South hopes to integrate its equity concerns into the global environmental agenda. Southern leaders insist that environmental issues cannot be used as an excuse by the North to pull the development ladder up behind it. They aim to convince the North that major environmental threats are closely linked to North-South inequity, global poverty and unsustainable development schemes. Therefore, the North cannot hope to overcome global environmental threats without helping the South achieve environmentally sustainable development. Tariq Hyder, a negotiator and spokesperson for the G77,[203] captured the essence of the South's new position:

> The industrialized countries must realize that the rules of the game in the North-South dialog have changed. In the past ... the Southern world was seen in terms of "lifeboat" and "triage" theories where the weak might have to be left behind. It is now clear that in terms of the global atmosphere and environment, we are all in the same lifeboat. If the developing countries are not given the trade opportunities, debt

---

[203] The Group of 77 at the United Nations is a loose coalition of developing nations, designed to promote its members' collective interests and create an enhanced joint negotiating capacity in the United Nations. There were 77 founding members of the organization, but the organization has since expanded to 130 member countries.

relief, credit facilities, financial assistance and the technology flows that they require for their development, we will all eventually pay the price.[204]

With respect to ozone depletion and climate change, the extent to which the South's equity demands are actually met by the North is a function of the bargaining leverage the South commands in each setting. This leverage depends upon (1) how serious the atmospheric threat is perceived *throughout* the North; (2) Northern perceptions of how essential Southern participation is to an effective treaty; (3) the credibility of the equity coalition's willingness to abandon negotiations if their concerns are not addressed; and (4) the North's willingness to assume the estimated costs of securing Southern participation.[205] Compared to global warming, the ozone issue generated far more bargaining leverage for the South in most of these areas.

Even though ozone depletion is a truly global issue, with potentially dire consequences for all nations and peoples, very few developing nations were represented in the initial stages of negotiation. At the 1985 Vienna Conference, there were only 12 delegates from the South. The reasons for this limited participation arose from both the perceived causes and effects of ozone depletion. With regard to causes, because nearly all CFC production was in the North, third world countries were responsible for very little ozone depletion. In 1986, the South consumed no more than 15 percent of all CFCs and produced almost none.[206] Thus, developing nations did not appear to be part of the problem, so there was no need for them to alter their behavior significantly. With regard to effects, in the early phases of negotiations many thought that ozone depletion would not significantly affect the developing nations.

---

[204] Hyder, Teriq. "Climate Negotiations: The North/South Perspective," *Confronting Climate Change*. Irving Mintzer, ed. (Cambridge, MA: Cambridge University Press), 1992: 336.

[205] Burtraw, Dallas & Michael A. Toman, 1991; FoE. "Developing Nations Press for Ozone Fund," *Atmosphere*, v. 2, n. 3 (1989): 2; FoE, UK. *Funding Change: Developing Countries & the Montreal Protocol*. Friends of the Earth: International (June 1990); IFIAS/ISSC/UNU/UNESCO. *Climate Change and Energy Policy in Developing Countries: Report of an International Workshop in Montebello, Québec*. Human Dimension of Global Change (July 29–August 1, 1990); Kasperson, Roger E. & Kirstin M. Dow. "Developmental & Geographical Equity in Global Environmental Change: A Framework for Analysis," *Evaluation Review*, v. 15, n. 1 (1991): 149–69; MacDonald, Gordon J. "Technology Transfer: The Climate Change Challenge," *Journal of Environment & Development*, v. 1, n. 1 (1992): 1–40; Najam, Adil. "An Environmental Negotiation Strategy for the South," *International Environmental Affairs*, v. 7, n. 3 (1995): 249–87; Sell, Susan. "North-South Environmental Bargaining: Ozone, Climate Change & Biodiversity," *Global Governance*, v. 2, n. 1 (1996): 97–118; Speth, James Gustave. "Coming to Terms: Toward a North-South Compact for the Environment," *Environment* (June 1990): 16; TATA/Energy Research Institute/The Woods Hole Research Center/UNEP/World Resources Institute. *Conference Statement on Global Warming and Climate Change: Perspectives from Developing Countries*. International Conference on Global Warming and Climate Change: Perspectives from Developing Countries. (New Delhi, India/ February 21–23, 1989); Tripp, James T.B., Daniel J. Dudek, & Michael Oppenheimer. "Equity & Ozone Protection," *Environment* (July-August 1987): 43; U.N. Centre for Science & Technology for Development. *Report on the International Conference on Energy in Climate & Development: Policy Issues and Technological Options*. International Conference on Energy in Climate & Development (Saarücken/KongreBhalle: 1990).

[206] Rowlands, Ian H, 1995:165.

At this stage, truly global environmental threats were new and not readily imaginable. Southern political leaders saw ozone depletion as a problem for the light-skinned populations near the poles.

Consequently, most poor countries took little interest in ozone negotiations and conflicts over rival interpretations of North-South equity surrounding this issue remained nearly dormant. Although Article 4.2 of the Vienna Convention mentions the necessity to take "into account ... the needs of developing countries, in promoting, directly or through competent international bodies, the development and transfer of technology and knowledge," there was little pressure to make such general statements more precise. North-South issues did not begin to generate substantial political debate until after the Vienna Convention.

During the intersession deliberations leading up to the 1987 Montreal Protocol, this changed. By the time the parties reconvened in Montreal, half of the 60 participating governments were from the South. The change was based on altered perceptions of the causes and effects of ozone depletion. The use of ODSs was increasing dramatically in the developing world. For example, China's CFC consumption rose 20 percent during the 1980s.[207] Even though Southern CFC use remained relatively modest compared to rich nation standards, the potential for future growth elicited serious concern in the North and, in the South, a growing awareness of their latent bargaining leverage.

CFC production plants were typically small, easily constructed and paid for themselves in a short time span. Even relatively poor countries could become CFC manufacturers fairly rapidly. China was planning a massive increase in refrigerator production; and, unless alternatives were provided, the refrigerant used would be CFCs. Thus, even though the developing world's contribution to ozone depletion was perceived as modest, future possibilities generated apprehension that any agreement that did not include these countries could be rendered worthless over the ensuing decades.

With regard to effect, the discovery of the breach in the Antarctic ozone shield demonstrated the seriousness of this global problem and its potentially disastrous impact on all nations. UNEP alerted developing nation officials to ongoing research revealing the ominous threat to immune systems, agriculture and fisheries posed by increased UVB radiation.[208] The potential implications for health and food security got the attention of government officials in the South. Thus, by 1986 both Northern and Southern policymakers were becoming aware of the need for developing nations to participate in ozone negotiations.

---

[207] Shea, Cynthia Pollock. "Disarming Refrigerators," *World Watch* (May/June 1991): 36; Shea, Cynthia Pollock. *Protecting Life on Earth: Steps to Save the Ozone Layer.* (Washington, DC: Worldwatch Institute), 1988. FoE. "Are Flammable Refrigerants Worth the Risk?" *Atmosphere*, v. 2, n. 4 (1990): 6.

[208] Shea, Cynthia Pollock. "Sunburned Soybeans," *World Watch* (May/June 1989): 9, 10; Stetson, Marnie. "Who'll Pay to Protect the Ozone Layer?" *World Watch* (July–August 1990): 36, 37; UNEP. *Action on Ozone.* (NY: United Nations), 1990; UNEP Panel Report. *The Environmental Effects of Ozone Depletion: 1991 Update.* United Nations Environment Programme (November 1991).

Once developing nations entered ozone negotiations, North-South disagreements produced debilitating equity conflicts that threatened the quest for a strong treaty. Developed nations were reluctant to phase out CFCs at home if their efforts were going to be negated by the expansion of halocarbon production in the developing world. But leaders of developing countries were opposed to denying their growing populations the benefits of refrigeration and air conditioning, which had been enjoyed for so long in the industrial world, to prevent a problem the developed nations created. While Northern representatives insisted that Southern countries should curtail their growing use of CFCs, Southern representatives pointed out that rich nations were currently responsible for about 72 percent of global CFC emissions and their historical responsibility was closer to 90 percent, because it was Northern CFC use, from the 1930s on, that was threatening stratospheric ozone.[209]

For the South, because the rich nations of the North had created the problem, they were responsible for fixing it. Southern representatives realized that, if the North was serious about protecting the ozone layer, the South's future CFC production potential gave it the bargaining leverage necessary to compel rich nations to assume their historic responsibility. An equity coalition led by several key Southern states adopted a common position: Unless it received some sort of compensatory treatment, it would not become party to the ozone treaty. Faced with the possibility of unrestricted CFC use by developing nations outside the ozone treaty, rich nations began to take the South's equity concerns seriously.

The first substantive proposal to provide for compensatory treatment for developing countries came in the April 1987 meeting in Geneva. The Canadian delegation suggested that developing nations should be exempt from the provisions of any agreement for five years or until their annual CFC use reached 0.1 kg per capita. Although the proposal drew criticism, it proved to be a constructive starting point for confronting North-South issues. By the conclusion of the Montreal negotiations, two special provisions were made for Southern states. One permitted developing nations to delay compliance with measures restricting CFC production and consumption for ten years, providing that their annual level of consumption did not exceed 0.3 kg per capita. The other recognized, in principle, the need to facilitate the South's access to both the technology and financial resources to enable them to afford and use CFC alternatives more easily. However, the North made no concrete commitments to make this assistance a reality in Montreal.

The protocol's general commitments proved insufficient to induce participation from many large Southern states. Even those who signed on to the agreement became increasingly critical as they reassessed its impact on their interests. They argued that the protocol served to perpetuate Southern dependence on the North. The treaty prohibited developing countries from producing CFCs for export during their ten-year grace period, but it allowed Northern states to exceed their CFC production quotas by 10–15 percent if the excess was exported to the South. Therefore, the

---

[209] Rowlands, Ian H, 1995: 168.

Montreal agreement forced the South to buy CFCs only from Northern producers, not from each other.[210]

Northern negotiators soon realized that the equity coalition's concerns could not be taken lightly. If they chose to opt out of the agreement, developing nations with large domestic markets, such as China, India, South Korea and Brazil, could easily undermine the treaty by building CFC industries to fill their growing domestic demand for affordable refrigeration and air conditioning. These countries could then export CFCs to other countries not committed to the Montreal Protocol. Widespread free riding could seriously weaken any Northern effort to protect the ozone layer and drastically reduce the global market for CFC alternatives.

By the time the protocol was in force in January 1989, North-South equity had moved center stage. In March 1989, the U.K. and UNEP sponsored an international conference with the primary purpose of encouraging Southern states to ratify the Montreal Protocol. The British organizers of the conference still believed this could be achieved quite easily by showing Southern delegates that it was in their interests to use the substitute chemicals now available. However, from the outset of the conference, it was obvious that a strategy of information and education was entirely inadequate.

The basic problem was that the South was less enthusiastic about the goal of preventing ozone depletion than the North. First, the developing nations perceived the costs of controlling future CFC emissions to be higher than the developed nations; second, they did not see as many benefits from doing so; and third, they did not feel they had the resources or technology to import or develop CFC alternatives. Finally, because the North was the major source of the current problem and had benefited from CFC use for 60 years, the South felt the North had an ethical obligation to assume responsibility for addressing the problem.

The South was in a position to thwart the North's urgent desire for an effective ozone agreement, which gave the South considerable bargaining power to press its concerns. Chinese and Indian officials called for the creation of an "Ozone Layer Protection Fund." Paid for by the Northern states, this fund would sponsor research into CFC-free technologies and methods of transferring these alternatives, free of charge, to those Southern countries that agreed to phase out their CFC use. The Indian delegation reminded Northern negotiators that: "Lest someone think of this [fund] as charity, I would like to remind them of the excellent principle of 'polluter pays,' adopted in the developed world."[211] Southern states backed this proposal and refused to sign any treaty until the North made firm commitments to provide the South with financial and technical assistance.

Next, the equity coalition put forward its proposal for a new institution to manage the transfer of the financial resources necessary to allow developing nations to adopt

[210] Collins, Craig. *Interview: John Topping, Jr., Climate Institute President* (August 25, 1991); Collins, Craig. *Interview: Navroz Durbash (EDF) and Annie Roncerel (CAN Coordinator-Europe)* (January 21, 1992).
[211] Quoted in: Rowlands, Ian H, 1995: 173.

CFC alternatives without undergoing major hardships or setbacks in their development plans. It called for the following:

- A discrete multilateral trust fund established within UNEP to meet all incremental costs to developing countries of complying with the protocol;
- The fund should have "legally enforceable obligations" from the industrialized countries;
- All contributions to the fund should be additional to, rather than a diversion from, existing aid flows; and
- The fund should guarantee free access and nonprofit transfer to developing countries of safe alternative technologies.[212]

At this point, activist NGOs from the North and South coordinated a campaign to reduce the differences between their governments by pressing for an agreement that protects the ozone layer and addresses the equity concerns of poor nations. At the core of this North-South NGO alliance were Friends of the Earth (International) and Greenpeace (International). In addition to working with their traditional allies in the North (such as the NRDC and the Sierra Club), these two transnational NGOs with chapters in the North and the South began to link up with Southern NGOs such as the Kenyan Consumers Association, the Asian Pacific People's Environment Network, the Caribbean Environmental Health Institute (CEHI), WALHI-Indonesia and the Green Forum in the Philippines.

Ninety-three NGOs and several Northern countries soon backed the equity coalition's demand for an Ozone Layer Protection Fund to ensure their participation in the agreement.[213] However, major players such as the United States, Japan, the U.K., West Germany and France resisted this idea and insisted on using existing institutions – such as the International Monetary Fund (IMF) or the World Bank – to address the funding needs of the developing world.[214] Northern officials insisted that any new funding mechanism was redundant and would surely become an inefficient, unaccountable and bureaucratic nightmare.[215] But these were largely spurious protestations. The real issue was the possibility that a newly created institution might undermine Northern wealth and power by allowing the South to gain control over the dispersal and use of ozone funds from donor nations. However, most Southern states (and nearly all environmental NGOs) mistrusted the IMF and the World Bank because they had poor environmental records and were dominated by Northern

---

[212] Benedick, Richard E, 1991: 153.
[213] FoE (1989): 2; FoE. "Initial Talks on Protocol Amendments Grim," *Atmosphere*, v. 2, n. 3 (1989): 3.
[214] FoE (1989): 3.
[215] FoE, UK. (June 1990); Makhijani, Arjun. "Still Working on the Ozone Hole," *Technology Review* (May-June 1990): 53–9; Oppenheimer, Michael. *Global Lessons from the Ozone Hole.* (NY: Environmental Defense Fund), 1988; Rajan, Mukund Govind. "Bargaining with the Environment: A New Weapon for the South?" *South Asia Research*, v. 12, n. 2 (1992); Sell, Susan (1996): 97–118.

donor countries. Instead, developing nations sought a new institution more tailored to their needs and responsive to their will.

As the negotiations continued, Northern opposition to an ozone fund steadily waned under the threat of potential free riding. Northern delegates were concerned about the capability of large developing nations to undermine the agreement. In addition to China's plans for refrigerator production, India bought CFC technology from U.S. firms before the Montreal Protocol negotiations began. By 1989, there were at least four CFC plants in India, two of which were built after the protocol was signed. Since India's current domestic demand did not justify this available capacity, Indian businessmen were seeking foreign markets and had reportedly sold CFC production technology to Iraq.[216]

The potential for countries such as India, China, Brazil and South Korea to establish a CFC "black market" – possibly exporting CFCs and CFC facilities to the many third world countries that had yet to ratify the ozone treaty – proved critical to securing their equity demands. Eventually, UNEP's diplomatic leadership, the domestic political pressure mounted by activist NGOs and the South's substantial bargaining leverage won most Northern nations over to the need for a Multilateral Ozone Fund.[217]

However, there was one final obstacle: the United States. Although EPA chief, William Reilly and top State Department officials such as Richard Benedick and William Nitze saw the need for an ozone fund, chief of staff Sununu and OMB director Richard Darman were opposed. Their objections were based on ideological hostility toward "anti-growth, command-and-control, centralist environmentalism" aimed at "global management" and a fear that any ozone layer fund might set a precedent for subsequent negotiations on global warming.[218]

By the second meeting of the parties in London, White House resistance collapsed under intense domestic and international pressure. Domestically, Congress and the mainstream press criticized the administration's recalcitrance[219] while environmental activists and their newfound industry allies pressed the White House to agree to an ozone fund. Environmentalists argued that the fund was justified on the basis of equity and ozone protection; industry officials pointed out to Sununu that if poor nations lacked the funds to buy CFC-free technologies and products, U.S. chemical companies would be denied potentially lucrative markets.[220]

---

[216] Benedick, Richard E, 1991: 100, 101.

[217] This fund was governed by and executive committee composed of an equal number of representatives from North and South; it remained the subject of debate and contention between North and South for years.

[218] Darman, Richard. *Keeping America First: American Romanticism and the Global Economy.* Second Annual Albert H. Gordon Lecture, Harvard University (Washington, DC: Office of Management & Budget), 1990.

[219] Passell, Peter. "Penny Wise on Ozone?" *New York Times* (May 16, 1990): C2; Pell, Claiborne. "CFC Fund Decision Showed Flaws in US Policymaking," *Christian Science Monitor* (June 22, 1990): 20; Shabecoff, Philip. "U.S. Urged to Ease Ozone-Aid Stand," *New York Times* (June 13, 1990); Benedick, Richard E, 1991: 160.

[220] Rowlands, Ian H, 1995: 174; Passell, Peter (May 16, 1990): C2.

International pressure came from many Northern leaders as well, especially Prime Minister Margaret Thatcher who did not want the London conference to fail and warned the White House that U.S. obstinacy could scuttle ozone negotiations completely. The Bush I administration responded by reluctantly agreeing to a funding mechanism with increased Southern participation while making it clear that it was "without prejudice to any future arrangements that may be developed with respect to other environmental issues."[221]

Although there were continuing minor skirmishes over funding and technology transfer, this was the last major battle over equity. For the developing countries, the advantages of becoming a party to the agreement were substantial. In addition to contributing to the protection of the ozone layer, Southern nations could continue to produce CFCs for ten years and receive financial and technical assistance to adopt CFC-free substitutes. Those who refused to sign the treaty had no access to the financial resources or technology transfers granted to member nations; and could not buy or sell CFCs, or technologies that used them, to any treaty member. Overall, these carrots and sticks proved very successful in removing the equity roadblock and securing the participation of developing nations.

The successful removal of the equity obstacles barring consensus around an effective ozone treaty contrasts sharply with climate change negotiations. During ozone negotiations, equity coalition leaders utilized an effective holdout strategy, biding their time until it was clear that all Northern policymakers recognized the seriousness of ozone depletion and the need for Southern participation in any effective response. In addition to maximizing the North's desire for Southern involvement, holding out lent credibility to the possibility that the South might remain uninvolved unless the North helped finance its ozone protection efforts. By not signing the Montreal Protocol until the 1990 negotiating session in London, the leaders of the equity coalition maximized their bargaining leverage to restructure the ozone agreement to their liking.[222]

Like ozone negotiations, Northern negotiators realize that Southern participation is absolutely essential to an effective global warming agreement. In fact, Northern politicians often exaggerate the South's potential climate impact while minimizing their own. Yet, compared with ozone negotiations, the South's holdout strategy has been much less effective in leveraging equity concessions from the North. This is true for several reasons.

First, without a unanimous sense of urgency in the North for a strong climate agreement, Southern nations have found it far more difficult to advance their equity concerns. Northern climate negotiators are still divided into rival activist and blocking camps and have yet to reach the universally high level of concern the North displayed after the discovery of the ozone hole. Especially notable here is the powerful influence of the fossil fuel industry over American politics and public opinion.

---

[221] Pell, Claiborne (June 22, 1990): 20; Shabecoff, Philip (June 13, 1990); Stetson, Marnie (July–August 1990): 36, 37.

[222] This included the $240 million fund created by developed nations to underwrite the potential extra costs the South would incur in switching to CFC alternatives.

This power has been skillfully employed to maintain the divide between the United States and the rest of developed nations.[223]

Second, the effectiveness of the holdout strategy has declined because, unlike ozone depletion, the South needs to prevent global warming even more than the North. This reality has damaged the solidarity and diluted the resolve of the equity coalition while weakening the credibility of their threat to hold out. Especially in the early stages of ozone negotiations, the light-skinned, cancer-prone nations nearer the poles were considerably more worried about ozone depletion than the darker-skinned, equatorial populations of the South.[224] For climate change, the situation is reversed. Climate scientists predict drastic consequences for poor nations that lack the resources to protect themselves from the ravages of climate disruption. No countries will suffer more than the small island nations of the tropics and the low-lying coastal states of the South. The urgency of their situation has caused them to abandon the equity coalition's holdout strategy and become the most committed elements of the activist coalition.[225] In addition, oil-producing nations have spurned the equity coalition in favor of a hard line blocking position. Ultimately, the equity coalition's threat to abstain from a climate treaty is based on their willingness to suffer the consequences of undermining its effectiveness. As the escalating ravages of climate disruption continue to fall disproportionately on the South, this holdout strategy becomes less and less credible.

During ozone negotiations, the South's holdout strategy worked because free riding could have seriously harmed the market for CFC replacements developed by Northern chemical manufacturers. These chemical industries encouraged their governments to bring the South into the treaty by providing them with the financial assistance needed purchase the more expensive CFC alternatives instead of building CFC industries of their own. But for climate change, the holdout strategy is weakened because Northern fossil fuel companies are not trying to draw the South into a global market for their alternatives. The fossil fuel industry does not control the clean renewable alternatives to coal and oil. Therefore, it does not stand to profit from an equity fund to subsidize the South's purchase of renewable energy alternatives. True, some oil companies have small investments in renewables, but an equity fund designed to subsidize the purchase carbon-free alternatives would foster unwanted competition and undermine the fossil fuel industry's hegemony over the global energy market. In addition, because the petroleum industry is far more profitable and heavily subsidized than renewables, it has no interest in encouraging countries to adopt these less-profitable alternatives even if it has made some marginal investments in them.

Thus, although the North's chemical industries feared Southern abstention and supported an ozone fund to help them purchase their alternatives, this is not the case

---

[223] The power of the coal industry in Australia has kept it out of the activist camp as well.

[224] Ozone depletion remained a greater concern for the North even after studies showed that UV radiation could seriously weaken immune systems, harm fishing and damage crops in poor nations.

[225] From the opposite side, the OPEC nations have abandoned the equity coalition to become the most die-hard members of the blocking coalition.

for Northern fossil fuel producers. Instead of accommodating the South's equity concerns, these die-hard blockers have adopted the position that:

- Any serious effort to assist the South in leapfrogging fossil fuel–driven development will be enormously expensive; and
- The South's insistence that the North should go first is "free loading," their holdout strategy is "blackmail," and the demand for a climate fund is "charity."

This blocking strategy is designed to make the equity roadblock impossible to overcome. Beginning in Kyoto, blockers successfully employed these criticisms to aggravate North-South tensions and stall negotiations indefinitely. Before negotiations commenced, the U.S. fossil fuel lobby and its allies in Congress insisted that the Clinton administration not commit the United States to any GHG cuts unless the South made commitments as well.[226] However, the administration joined the

---

[226] The U.S. has consistently implied that developing countries are not acting to slow their greenhouse gas emissions. This is inconsistent with growing evidence that developing countries and countries in transition are undertaking more aggressive approaches to emissions reduction than many industrial countries have – including the U.S.

A few examples: Thailand: A 1991 national electricity conservation master plan requires all large buildings and factories to improve energy efficiency. Two separate funds totaling U.S.$250 million were established to finance the effort. India: Policy reforms opened the power market to independent generators and foreign investors and introduced strong tax incentives for renewable energy. Solar and wind development have grown explosively. Argentina, Brazil and Chile: These countries are jointly developing natural gas resources that will offset growth in oil and coal use and reduce projected carbon dioxide emissions. Mexico: FIDE, a nationwide NGO launched by the Federal Electricity Commission and a large electric utility in 1990 promotes efficient electric use. Savings from completed projects total over 5 percent of national electricity consumption. FIDE met its goal of 12 percent for the year 2000. The Czech Republic: By 2001, atmospheric protection legislation enacted in 1991 had reduced emissions by about 8 percent in large power and heating plants. Tax breaks are awarded for alternative energy and financial support is provided for residential conservation. Countries borrowing from the World Bank for energy service expansion have been forced to reduce subsidies and increase energy prices. Price reform is primarily an economic measure, but it also reduces the growth of GHG emissions. Even though it is socially and politically painful, it has been undertaken in many developing countries, including Argentina, Chile, Malaysia, China, Pakistan, Morocco, India, Indonesia and Cote d'Ivoire. The biggest surprise in 2006 was the dramatic growth in photovoltaic production in China. Last year, China passed the United States, which first developed modern solar cell technology at Bell Labs in New Jersey in the 1950s, to become the world's third largest producer of the PV cells, trailing only Germany and Japan.

What measures have the U.S. implemented that can compare with the progress made by developing countries? The U.S. still has the cheapest gasoline in the industrialized world, exacerbating emissions and huge U.S. trade deficits. U.S. auto fuel standards are the lowest in the industrial world (35 mpg. by 2020) while China set its standard at 43 mpg by 2008. Clinton's first climate action plan consisted mainly of under-funded voluntary programs the Administration admitted would not achieve the target for 2000, while Bush did worse. See: Flavin, Christopher & Odil Tunali. "Getting Warmer: Looking for a Way Out of the Climate Impasse," *World Watch* (March/April 1995): 10; IHASA/ISSC/UNU/UNESCO. *Climate Change and Energy Policy in Developing Countries: Report of an International Workshop in Montebello, Québec.* Human Dimension of Global Change (July 29–August 1, 1990); Lerner,

other Northern states in formally acknowledging the "common but differentiated responsibilities" of rich and poor nations to confront climate change. But when U.S. negotiators agreed to make minimal GHG reductions without similar commitments from developing countries, both Republican and Democratic Senators pitched a fit. They told the press that the treaty was "dead on arrival" and voted 95–0 to sink any treaty that failed to make poor countries adopt the same GHG cuts as rich ones.[227] In retreat, Vice President Gore acknowledged that the administration would not submit the treaty for Senate ratification until it was assured that there would be "meaningful participation" from key developing nations.[228] This basic position became official U.S. policy for the eight years that George W. Bush occupied the White House.

Since the United States is responsible for about 25 percent of the world's GHG emissions, its withdrawal from Kyoto made significant progress on climate change virtually impossible. It took eight years for the protocol to gain enough signatures to enter into force; and, even though 181 nations finally ratified the treaty, these countries account for only 60 percent of global GHG emissions. Equity issues remain largely unsettled and stand in the way of consensus around a strong agreement.

Since Kyoto, the equity coalition has argued for GHG emission targets to be set on a per-capita basis, rather than merely percentage reductions over 1990 levels as required by the protocol. While this seems fair in the long run, if countries were required to equalize their per-capita GHG emissions immediately, the result would be economic havoc in the North. Since the typical American is responsible for 25 times more GHG emissions than the average Indian, this arrangement would decimate the U.S. economy.

Therefore, the aim would be for the per-capita emissions of every country to *eventually* converge around a level considered climate safe. Countries with per-capita GHG emissions already below the safe level could increase their per-capita emissions upward to this limit, while countries over this per-capita ceiling would have to reduce their GHG emissions down to this safe level by the required date. This basic plan, known as "contraction and convergence," has important advantages. It takes into account the differing circumstances and means of all countries (rich and poor), thereby meeting the developing countries' demands for fairness; at the same time, it eventually imposes the same climate-safe GHG limits on everyone.

This proposal, originally developed by the London-based Global Commons Institute (GCI), has gained the support of several African nations, China and India. It would require countries to tentatively agree upon (1) what constitutes a safe concentration of atmospheric GHGs; and (2) when this level will be reached. This target could be revised up or down periodically in the light of improved climate knowledge. In order to reduce GHG concentrations to the agreed ceiling by the

Steve. "North Meets South," *Amicus Journal*, v. 14, n. 1 (1992): 18–21; Stetson, Marnie. "People Who Live in Green Houses . . . ," *World Watch* (September/October 1991): 22.

[227] Ott, Herman E. "The Kyoto Protocol: Unfinished Business," *Environment* (July/August 1998): 17. http://www.nytimes.com/1990/06/13/world/us-urged-to-end-opposition-to-ozone-aid.html.

[228] Dunn, Seth. "After Kyoto: A Climate Treaty with No Teeth?" *World Watch* (March/April 1998): 33; Morgan, Jennifer. "The Kyoto Protocol: The Devil's in the Details," *US Climate Action Network Hotline* (April 1998): 1.

agreed date, countries would have to agree on a yearly global emissions budget. Then countries would allocate this annual GHG budget among each other with the goal of converging their per-capita emissions by a negotiated date. Thus, contraction and convergence commits countries to a negotiated but flexible program for equalizing per-capita GHG emissions at safe levels of concentration over a fixed time frame.

In general, it is easier and cheaper to avoid future emissions in developing countries where fossil fuels have not yet become a major source of energy than in industrialized countries where it will take a generation to reverse existing dependence on fossil fuels. But the South's ability to leapfrog fossil fuel dependency will depend on its capability to develop or purchase clean renewable technologies. Where will the money come from?

Some policymakers believe contraction and convergence could solve this problem by allowing countries whose actual emissions fall below its GHG budget to sell their extra emission rights to big fossil fuel users whose GHG emissions are over budget. These resource transfers could help fund the South's climate-friendly energy development. However, critics point out that "emissions trading" and "carbon offset" schemes have tremendous potential for abuse, cheating and corruption. Emission markets would need to be carefully monitored and strictly regulated, but the difficulties and costs of oversight and regulation would be excessive.[229]

At first glance, emissions trading seems to provide market incentives for developed countries to reduce their GHG emissions while supplying the South with resources for clean development. However, the system's incentive structure encourages Northern companies to avoid paying for emission rights by moving their polluting, high-carbon technologies and factories to the South. Meanwhile, unscrupulous profiteers and corrupt government officials can easily scam the system with phony carbon reduction projects. Using creative accounting and elaborate shell games that make it nearly impossible to verify any genuine climate-protection benefits, these schemes often leave communities in the South saddled with phony carbon offset projects that may do more harm than good.[230]

The European Union (EU)'s Emissions Trading System (ETS) has already been tested and found wanting. A recent report on carbon trading by the *Financial Times* found:

- Widespread instances of people and organizations buying worthless credits that do not yield any reductions in carbon emissions;
- Industrial companies profiting from doing very little – or from gaining carbon credits on the basis of efficiency gains from which they have already benefited substantially; and

---

[229] Emissions trading can work relatively well within nations. Domestic cap-and-trade programs – like the U.S. trading program set up to reduce sulfur dioxide emissions – were relatively successful because they are easy to monitor and enforce. Most of the sulfur emissions came from about 2,000 smokestacks in the Midwest, a manageable number to monitor. The program, moreover, was subject to an enforceable system of national regulation.

[230] For excellent examples see the online video: *The Carbon Connection* by Carbon Trade Watch (2008). http://www.tni.org/detail_pub.phtml?&know_id=223&menu=11c.

- A shortage of verification, making it difficult for buyers to assess the true value of carbon credits.[231]

Sharp disagreements have surfaced between those who favor market mechanisms such as emission trading and carbon offsets and those who doubt that these schemes can possibly reduce GHGs and promote climate equity. Respected members of CAN, including the Sierra Club, the World Wildlife Federation and Environmental Defense; plus influential political leaders such as Al Gore and Senators Sanders, Kerry, Lieberman, McCain, Leahy, Feinstein, Bingaman, Snowe, Specter, Alexander and Carper have supported laws featuring emissions trading.[232]

Meanwhile, Friends of the Earth, Focus on the Global South, Carbon Trade Watch, the Center for Environmental Concerns, the Freedom from Debt Coalition (Philippines), the World Rainforest Movement and several other NGOs[233] have built an alliance called Climate Justice Now! that opposes carbon trading. Instead, Climate Justice Now! calls for:

> … reduced consumption; huge financial transfers from North to South based on historical responsibility and ecological debt for adaptation and mitigation costs paid for by redirecting military budgets; innovative taxes and debt cancellation; leaving fossil fuels in the ground and investing in appropriate energy-efficiency and safe, clean and community-led renewable energy; rights-based resource conservation that enforces indigenous land rights and promotes peoples' sovereignty over energy, forests, land and water; and sustainable family farming and peoples' food sovereignty.[234]

Unfortunately, these disputes create serious discord within and between the activist and equity coalitions.[235] This disunity undermines efforts to build the type of North-South NGO alliance among environmentalists and climate justice advocates that played such an instrumental role in overcoming the equity roadblock during ozone negotiations. The South's diminished bargaining position cannot benefit from this situation.

The South's bargaining leverage is already weakened by the assumption that the South needs a climate treaty even more than the North and the perception that funding their clean energy development will be extremely costly. By most accounts, the capital and technology needed to help poor nations leapfrog fossil fuel–based

---

[231] Gelbspan, Ross. "Global Carbon Trading Won't Work," *Innovation* (August/September 2008). http://www.innovation-america.org/index.php?articleID=455.

[232] Bond, Patrick. "From False to Real Solutions for Climate Change," *MR Zine* (June 1, 2008). http://www.monthlyreview.org/mrzine/bond060108.html.

[233] Including: Women for Climate Justice, the Global Forest Coalition, the Global Justice Ecology Project, the International Forum on Globalization, the Kalikasan-Peoples Network for the Environment, La Vía Campesina, the Durban Group for Climate Justice, Oilwatch, Pacific Indigenous Peoples Environment Coalition, Sustainable Energy and Economy Network (Institute for Policy Studies), the Indigenous Environmental Network, Third World Network, Indonesia Civil Society Organizations Forum on Climate Justice.

[234] Bond, Patrick (June 1, 2008).

[235] Bond, Patrick (June 1, 2008).

modernization will dwarf the funding involved in securing Southern participation in the Montreal Protocol.[236]

Unless the North becomes more (1) unified around the urgency of preventing climate disruption; (2) convinced that it must make significant equity allowances to garner Southern participation; and (3) willing to absorb the costs of assisting their transition to carbon-free development, the South will remain in a weak bargaining position, despite the strong ethical argument behind its equity demands.[237] Unlike ozone negotiations, time does not favor the South's holdout strategy because the ravages of climate disruption will be felt more in the South than the North. This means the South may have to settle for considerably less equity compensation than justice would demand in an ideal world.

Southern leverage is further weakened by the unpopularity of foreign assistance in the North and its poor track record in the South. Foreign assistance has a tragic legacy of enriching elite government and business interests in both the donor and recipient nations while leaving those who need it most out of the loop.[238] Corruption and abuse by recipients and donors can undermine and discredit the legitimacy of the entire process. Therefore, transparency, oversight and independent watchdogs are needed to ensure that climate equity mechanisms produce their intended effects. Activist NGOs may prove essential to this effort.

NGOs from the South and the North have been the most consistent champions of equitable, sustainable development. These NGOs have sought to create more permanent alliances between the activist and equity coalitions by circumventing governments and building direct people-to-people bonds between grassroots organizations in the North and South. These transnational NGO networks, such as CAN, can then be used to draft model agreements, show that cooperation between North and South is possible and pressure governments to emulate their example. Their stated goals are to:

(1) Increase Northern and Southern awareness of the inequitable and unsustainable nature of traditional notions of economic growth and modernization;

(2) Expose the fundamental connections between the plight of the developing world and global environmental degradation; and

---

[236] Hyder, Teriq, 1992; Sell, Susan (1996): 97–118.

[237] Many studies set the cost of funding clean energy to developing countries at between $300 and $350 billion a year for about ten years. The $350 billion figure was first identified by energy policy specialists and economists at the Tellus Institute and has been supported by experts from Tufts University, Harvard University, Boston University, Stockholm Environment, Woods Hole Research Organization and other institutions. There are a number of ways to raise that $350 billion. Three possibilities are: (1) a carbon tax on the countries of the North; (2) a tax on international air travel; (3) a very small tax of a quarter of a penny per dollar on international financial transactions (when countries and corporations exchange yen for euros and euros for dollars).

[238] Hayter, Teresa. *Aid as Imperialism.* (NY: Penguin), 1971; Lappe, Frances Moore, Joseph Collins, & David Kinley. *Aid as Obstacle.* (Oakland, CA: Institute for Food and Policy Development), 1975.

(3) Build broad alliances between the citizens of affluent and poor nations based on their common need for sustainable development.

It is also possible that these organizations could function as political watchdogs, creators and facilitators of bold new sustainable development programs.[239]

THE BOTTOM LINE

Analysis of these two atmospheric negotiations not only highlights the comparable coalitions and negotiating roadblocks involved but it also reveals the primary underlying differences that account for the ozone activists' relative success in overcoming them. Five critical differences stand out. Compared with climate change, ozone negotiations possessed:

(1) A deeper, more pervasive sense of immediate crisis and dread created by the discovery of the ozone hole. This increased the perceived costs of no agreement and lowered the threshold of scientific consensus necessary to take action;

(2) A much lower perception of the overall economic and political costs involved in responding to this crisis;

(3) A blocking coalition that became divided over, and finally abandoned, a strategy of uncompromising intransigence because, eventually, it recognized the possibility of profiting from an international agreement;

(4) A more unified equity coalition whose demands were accommodated with relatively modest institutional reforms and financial assistance; and

(5) An activist coalition with qualitatively superior levels of structural leadership and bargaining power, once the United States joined the coalition.

LEADERSHIP: THE FIFTH FACTOR

The fifth factor mentioned previously has yet to be discussed. The ratification of viable atmospheric agreements requires the fusion of activist, equity and blocking coalitions into a single winning coalition. Forging agreement demands leadership. The complex interplay between scientific research, public edification, political

---

[239] Barratt-Brown, Liz. "Watchdogs on the Convention," *ECO: Climate Talks NGO Newsletter* (February 26, 1992): 3; CAN. "Commitments, Equity and Mechanisms," *ECO: Climate Talks NGO Newsletter* (February 27, 1992): 3; CAN-US & Europe, 1995; Keohane, Robert O. & Joseph S. Nye, ed. *Transnational Relations and World Politics.* (Cambridge, MA: Harvard University Press), 1981; Livernash, Robert. "The Growing Influence of NGOs in the Developing World," *Environment* (June 1992): 12; Princen, Thomas, Matthias Finger, & Jack Manno. "Nongovernmental Organizations in World Environmental Politics," *International Environmental Affairs*, v. 7, n. 1 (1995): 42–58.

activism, institutional bargaining and power politics involved in generating consensus under adverse conditions places a premium on the exercise of leadership. The more complex and unfavorable the conditions, the more critical leadership becomes.

For negotiations to succeed, activist leadership has to convince rival coalitions that (1) the science is certain enough to take precautionary action; (2) action is less costly than doing nothing; and (3) there are equitable ways to share the burden of containing the atmospheric danger. Success or failure depends, in part, on the intransigence of rival coalitions around these three issues and on the effectiveness of activist leadership to overcome their resistance.

Ozone activists faced considerably less resistance around these issues than their climate change counterparts. Well ahead of climate change, stratospheric ozone depletion appeared more credible, immediate, menacing and uniform in its destructive potential, while at the same time less costly to address. The relatively high levels of public alarm generated by the discovery of the ozone hole lowered the threshold of certainty necessary to convince policymakers of the need for precautionary action. In addition, this "dread factor" altered the interest assessment concerns of the blocking coalition by increasing the perceived costs of a delayed, minimalist response. The consensus-building process also benefited from (1) a blocking coalition that fractured and collapsed when significant sectors of industry realized that they could salvage their corporate image and profit from an emerging market for CFC-substitutes; and (2) an equity coalition that was accommodated with relatively modest side payments.

However, in addition to critical differences in the magnitude of these three roadblock issues, the ability of leadership to traverse these roadblocks is a necessary, if not sufficient, condition for successfully building support for effective atmospheric treaties. By neutralizing efforts to block an agreement and crafting provisions all parties can support, activist leadership attempts to forge a winning coalition composed of *all* the essential negotiating parties.[240] To achieve this goal, activist leadership must pursue a strategy designed to (a) win the other two coalitions over to their perception of the problem and the appropriate response; or (b) satisfactorily accommodate their concerns without sacrificing the capacity of the final agreement to address the threat; or (c) impose enough political and/or economic pressure to secure their acquiescence.

Leadership is a multilevel, multifaceted endeavor requiring different combinations of individual, organizational and institutional assets at each phase of the consensus-building process.[241] For example, to surmount the uncertainty roadblock, scientists must offer plausible explanations for these atmospheric problems and credible

---

[240] This definition of leadership closely parallels those of Oran Young and Peter M. Haas. For Young, leaders are those "who endeavor to solve or circumvent the collective action problems that plague the efforts of parties seeking to reap the joint gains in processes of institutional bargaining." Young, Oran R. "Political Leadership and Regime Formation: On the Development of Institutions in International Society," *International Organization*, v. 45 (Fall 1991): 281–308.

[241] Oran Young defines leadership in this context as "the actions of individuals who endeavor to solve or circumvent the collective action problems that plague the efforts of parties seeking to reap joint gains in processes of institutional bargaining." While Young's definition is quite similar

assessments of the potential risks they pose. Drawing upon this work, policymakers and grassroots activists must build public support for a precautionary approach toward these potentially irreversible atmospheric threats.

Next, activist leaders must reconcile contending cost calculations and equity concerns. Forging consensus at these junctures requires leadership to develop convincing analyses of the benefits of an early, preventive response. Further, it demands judicious arbitration by respected intermediaries and shrewd intervention by astute deal brokers capable of crafting provisions all parties can live with. Finally, it calls for activists with significant clout to deploy the appropriate mix of pressures and inducements to overcome resistance.

Different members of the activist coalition are more suited to certain tasks, and more critical for surmounting particular roadblocks, than others. To compare the leadership capabilities of the ozone and climate change activists, it is useful to break down the concept of leadership into four basic components: grassroots, scientific-intellectual, entrepreneurial-diplomatic and structural.

Many analysts of atmospheric negotiations tend to overlook or ignore the influence of grassroots leadership.[242] *Grassroots leadership* refers to the efforts of local, national and transnational NGOs to increase public understanding, mobilize popular concern and generate political pressure for activist solutions. Activist NGOs have had a major impact on both negotiations by shaping world opinion and marshaling public pressure behind the call for climate protection.

Scientific-intellectual leadership refers to the ability to develop theoretical and empirical assessments of environmental problems that provide negotiators with an understanding of their causes and potential risks while orienting their thinking toward precautionary action. By and large, this leadership skill has been provided by transnational networks of key individual scientists; major atmospheric research institutions such as NOAA and NASA; UN-affiliated IGOs such as UNEP and WMO; and the assessments of broadly respected international scientific review panels such as the IPCC and the Ozone Trends Panel. The work of these expert organizations has been popularized through the efforts of well-known scientists such as James Hansen and influential public figures like Al Gore.

Entrepreneurial-diplomatic leadership facilitates the consensus-building process by establishing institutional settings and negotiating procedures conducive to learning, problem solving and protracted bargaining. These leaders are usually government diplomats or IGO officials tasked with organizing deliberations and promoting agreement by devising flexible, innovative solutions to bargaining impasses. Many

---

to the one employed herein, its key weakness is its singular focus on individual leadership. The complimentary and often cooperative leadership functions performed by activist NGOs, scientific panels, IGOs and nation-states at different points during these negotiations were often the product of their unique organizational roles, reputations, propensities and resources and can not be adequately understood or explained by Young's reductionist effort to focus entirely on the behavior of key individuals. Young, Oran R (Fall 1991): 281–308.

[242] For example, the most developed analysis of leadership under conditions of international institutional bargaining recognizes every form of leadership considered here except grassroots. See: Young, Oran R (Fall 1991): 281–308.

parties contributed their diplomatic skills to structuring and facilitating atmospheric negotiations, but one example stands out. UNEP's effort – led by its director Mostafa Tolba – on behalf of ozone negotiations was, by far, the most influential display of entrepreneurial leadership. In fact, the implementation of the framework-protocol approach was largely the work of Mostafa Tolba.[243]

Finally, structural leadership translates economic and political power into bargaining leverage in favor of consensus around an activist response. When public opinion, science and diplomacy fail, judiciously applied coercion may be necessary to convince holdouts to "step away from the dark side." In blunt language, structural leadership is the ability to promote cooperation through "arm-twisting and bribery."[244] This requires activists with substantial clout. Generally only influential governments, or groups of governments, can alter the structural power relations that shape international negotiations. For example, the United States was clearly the most influential structural leader during ozone negotiations because it was able to exert a convincing mix of economic carrots and sticks to induce European acquiescence to an effective ozone agreement.

Optimal activist leadership would possess full measures of all four of these leadership capabilities working in close harmony with one another. But clearly this has not always been the case. By comparing the leadership capacities of ozone and climate change activists, two significant contrasts emerge. First, grassroots activist leadership, while influential from the beginning, has steadily improved as NGOs applied the lessons drawn from ozone negotiations to climate change. Second, entrepreneurial and especially structural leadership have been much less effective throughout climate change negotiations.

GLOBAL GRASSROOTS LEADERSHIP CONTINUES TO GROW

Grassroots leadership takes science to the people and pressures policymakers to act on it. From the streets and the voting booths to the courtrooms and the airwaves, citizen activists employ every avenue available to educate and mobilize the public. Although few analysts have acknowledged the critical impact of grassroots activism upon the ozone issue, it had a major impact on the consensus-building process at several points.[245] Years before negotiations ensued, American grassroots activists – working with intellectual-scientific leaders such as Sherry Rowland – were responsible for organizing the first efforts to alert the public to the dangers of ozone depletion and the need to phase out CFCs. Their efforts paid off as consumption of aerosol products

[243] Haas, Peter M. *Saving the Mediterranean: The Politics of International Environmental Cooperation* (NY: Columbia University Press, 1990); Haas, Peter M (1992): 187–224. Tolba, M. K. "Building an Environmental Institutional Framework for the Future," *Environmental Conservation*, v. 17, n. 2 (Summer 1990).

[244] Kindleberger, Charles P. *The International Economic Order.* (Cambridge, MA: MIT Press), 1988: 186.

[245] An exception is: Cook, Elizabeth. "Global Environmental Advocacy: Citizen Activism in Protecting the Ozone Layer." *AMBIO*, v. 19 (1990): 334–8.

containing CFCs dropped dramatically and legislators were moved to ban CFCs in aerosols. Thus, grassroots activist leadership in the United States helped put ozone depletion on the national agenda.

Later, grassroots activism proved essential to reviving the Reagan administration's faltering efforts to protect the ozone layer and fracturing industry opposition to international CFC regulation. While environmental activists publicly shamed the administration into disavowing its "hats and sunglasses policy," the NRDC sued to compel the EPA to enforce CAA provisions capping CFC production.[246] By making the administration wary of further public embarrassment and court-ordered unilateral cuts, these tactics pushed U.S. negotiators toward favoring international efforts to phase out CFCs. Meanwhile, activist media campaigns by groups such as Greenpeace and Friends of the Earth tarnished the corporate image of CFC producers such as DuPont and encouraged them to abandon their blocking alliance with European producers, renew their search for alternatives and abandon their opposition an international accord. Finally, grassroots activists in Europe – especially Friends of the Earth (U.K.) and the Green Party in Germany – aroused public concern for ozone depletion and eroded the blocking alliance between industry and government in the EU.[247]

Building on their experience with ozone negotiations, climate change activists have dramatically expanded their grassroots leadership capabilities. Unlike the ozone issue – where the transnational activist alliance got off to a fitful, uneven start – climate change NGOs from all over the world created a broad, well organized, politically savvy alliance two years before the framework convention was adopted in Rio. Building on their previous experience, NGOs became adept at coordinating their grassroots efforts with scientific-intellectual and entrepreneurial leaders. They even developed affiliations with governments and corporations with significant structural clout.

In 1987, grassroots activists worked with scientific-intellectual leaders to organize an appeal for U.S. action on climate change by half the Nobel Prize winners in the United States and half of the members of NAS. Some NGOs, such as the World Wildlife Fund, the Union of Concerned Scientists and Greenpeace developed their own intellectual-scientific leadership capabilities. Greenpeace's foremost atmospheric expert, Jeremy Leggett, edited one of the first published assessments of the science of climate change.[248] In the mid-1990s, Leggett proved to be an effective entrepreneurial leader as well by brokering support for the activist agenda among an influential array of major insurance companies. Greenpeace even achieved a modicum of indirect structural leverage by offering its scientific, negotiating and legal services to the delegations of several small island nations.

---

[246] Nanda, Ved P. "Stratospheric Ozone Depletion: A Challenge for International Environmental Law & Policy," *Michigan Journal of International Law*, v. 10 (Spring 1989): 482–525; Nangle, Orval E. "Stratospheric Ozone: United States Regulation of Chlorofluorocarbons," *Boston College Environmental Affairs Law Review*, v. 18 (Spring 1989): 542–5.

[247] Cook, Elizabeth, v. 19 (1990): 334–8.

[248] Leggett, Jeremy, ed., 1990.

By forming CAN, NGOs from North America, Asia, Africa, Latin America and Europe (both East and West) used the Internet to coordinate their efforts and turn the spotlight of world opinion on climate negotiations. This made it harder for negotiators to ignore their pleas to (1) stabilize atmospheric concentrations of GHGs at levels that do not seriously disrupt the climate system;[249] and (2) recognize the primary responsibility of industrialized nations to address this problem without shifting the burden onto the developing nations.[250]

CAN's daily newsletter, *ECO* – which was distributed to climate negotiators on the morning of each negotiating session and appeared online by afternoon – was used to inform and mobilize concerned citizens worldwide and influence climate delegates at the same time. *ECO* increased the transparency of climate negotiations by raising trial balloons, amplifying corridor discussions, exploring potential directions and alternatives and providing an informal open forum for debate and discussion around key issues in a lively, humorous and timely manner. In addition, *ECO* facilitated consensus by critiquing obstructionist policies and putting blocking forces on notice that any efforts to stall or weaken the negotiations would not escape its sardonic spotlight.

Finally, many NGOs, especially in the South, gained access to government leaders and assisted their respective delegations in developing national policies and negotiating positions. In fact, last-minute deliberations between leaders of CAN, the U.S. delegation and Vice President Gore were rumored to be instrumental in moving the United States to accept stronger GHG controls in Kyoto.[251] In addition, activists have become very effective at popularizing and promoting climate-friendly policies in cities and states across America. The success of these efforts was dramatically illustrated in California, where popular support for climate action convinced Republican governor Arnold Schwarzenegger to challenge the Bush administration's legal right to prohibit the state from developing its own climate-friendly energy policies. Since the election of Barak Obama, climate activists have pushed hard to move the administration toward a more activist position on climate change, but the fossil fuel lobby still holds tremendous influence in Washington.

A defining moment in the struggle to prevent climate chaos will come in December 2009 when UN climate negotiations reconvene in Copenhagen to decide how to proceed once the Kyoto Protocol expires in 2012. These deliberations will alter the fate of climate negotiations for years to come and determine how serious the international community is about preventing a climate calamity. Consequently, the political clout of global grassroots activism to make a real difference will be seriously tested in Copenhagen. As usual, powerful governments and corporations with an abysmal history of GHG pollution will have a potentially

---

[249] Recognizing the importance of intellectual-scientific leadership CAN has made Alden Meyer, from the Union of Concerned Scientists, the chair of the coalition.

[250] Climate Action Network. *Everything You Ever Wanted to Know About Climate Change* . . . . (Brussels: C.A.N.), 1991.

[251] Hayes, Rich. "Sleepless in Kyoto," *Nucleus*, v. 20, n. 1 (1998): 8.

debilitating influence over the outcome. Grassroots activists will have to fight hard just to get their voices heard and prevent the blocking coalition from undermining any meaningful progress.

All these recent developments demonstrate the burgeoning leadership capabilities of the NGO component of the activist coalition. However, compared with ozone negotiations, the enhanced leadership of grassroots and scientific activists has been offset by serious deficiencies in the entrepreneurial and structural leadership displayed by IGO and governmental sectors of the climate activist coalition.

The climate change activist coalition has been unable to muster the structural leadership that was so critical to the success of ozone negotiations, which advanced dramatically after the Reagan administration finally threw its weight behind the activist coalition. The structural perks and pressures exerted by the United States decisively undermined opposition to the Montreal Protocol. But so far, no amount of scientific evidence and public pressure has been able to transform the United States into a structural leader of climate negotiations. Instead, the Clinton administration's halfhearted support for the Kyoto Protocol was merely a momentary interruption of Washington's unwavering opposition to an effective climate treaty. While the Obama administration has already moved away from Bush's deplorable record of blocking climate action, it has yet to demonstrate its ability to surpass the Clinton administration's halfhearted activism.

Throughout ozone negotiations the potential structural powers of the United States remained ubiquitous. Although the EC was well aware that the U.S. Congress had voted to impose trade sanctions against any nation that refused to negotiate a viable ozone treaty, U.S. negotiators did not make overt use of this threat until DuPont deserted the transnational blocking coalition. At this point, Washington's candid warning of possible trade sanctions helped convince Europe to accept across-the-board cuts in CFC production and consumption in Montreal. Compare this effective use of structural arm-twisting with the EC's refusal (or inability) to employ structural leverage to induce American acquiescence to an effective climate agreement.

In addition, ozone negotiations benefited from the skillful entrepreneurial leadership of UNEP's Mostafa Tolba. Time and time again, Tolba placed UNEP squarely behind tough international CFC regulations, assumed a central role in the negotiations, and exerted his considerable personal influence and authority (as a developing nation scientist and the head of a UN organization) to facilitate discussion, broker deals and break deadlocks. Many have endeavored to mediate disagreements in the course of climate change negotiations. Yet, compared with UNEP's efforts under Tolba, the diplomatic leadership displayed throughout climate negotiations has been described as slow, uninspired and ineffectual.[252]

---

[252] Kjellen, Bo. "A Personal Assessment," *Negotiating Climate Change*. Irving Mintzer & J. A. Leonard, eds. (Cambridge, MA: Cambridge University Press), 1994. 149–74.

At the regional and domestic levels, diplomatic and structural leadership has been lacking as well. European policymakers have had considerable trouble brokering energy policies and carbon taxes capable of meeting their emission-reduction goals, while the Clinton administration failed to convince, finesse or leverage Congress into backing a BTU tax or any mandatory GHG reduction legislation.

The complex and divisive cost-benefit and equity issues still on the table compound these debilitating weaknesses in diplomatic and structural leadership. The minimal emission cuts agreed to by industrial countries in Kyoto barely make a dent in the 60–80 percent *global* reduction needed to head off potentially catastrophic climate disruption. Future leadership must convince all essential parties of the need to steadily and dramatically reduce GHG emissions. Without improved structural and diplomatic leadership, this will be nearly impossible.

The short-range economic and political costs of GHG reductions may be substantial. For the sectors of the global economy most dependent on fossil fuels, they may be painful indeed. Compared with CFC manufacturing, the fossil fuel industry and the world economy overall are much less capable of making a swift, smooth and profitable transition to climate-friendly technologies. This fact underlies the climate change blocking coalition's dogged resistance and its resonance with a broader-based fear that economic prosperity may be sacrificed to any agreement that drastically reduces the consumption of fossil fuels.

Overcoming the die-hard resistance of a powerful blocking coalition – while assuaging fears of economic hardship – by crafting an agreement that can abate climate change without seriously damaging the well-being of citizens North and South, demands visionary leadership of the highest caliber. To lay the groundwork for the "structural decarbonization" of the world economy, this leadership must be as inspirational and farsighted as it is level headed and pragmatic.

Careful comparison of ozone and climate negotiations reveals that successful agreements are most likely when *activist leadership can neutralize efforts to block consensus by (1) convincing policymakers that a serious problem requiring a precautionary response exists; and (2) brokering an agreement all essential parties consider more ecologically safe, cost effective and equitable than no agreement* (or other possible alternatives).

Despite the absence of a dramatic crisis like the discovery of the ozone hole, polls indicate that activist leadership is becoming increasingly effective at using the growing scientific consensus to build popular support for a strong climate treaty.[253] These

---

[253] According to a Mellman Group national survey of 800 registered voters commissioned by the World Wildlife Fund, "The American public believes global warming is real and represents a serious threat." Two-thirds of the voters said they now view global warming as a "very" or "somewhat serious threat," and almost as many, 61 percent, said they believe it will get worse in the future. Three-quarters agreed with the statement that, "the only scientists who do not believe global warming is happening are paid by big oil, coal and gasoline companies to find the results that will protect business interests." The voters were also asked if they would favor or oppose an international agreement to reduce carbon dioxide emissions by 20 percent by 2005: 72 percent said they would favor it, while only 9 percent said they would oppose it. Although Democrats were most supportive (82 percent), Republicans (68 percent) and independents

efforts appear to be having an impact on some policymakers and politicians by winning over major sectors of the business community to a more precautionary position, including large segments of the insurance industry and even British Petroleum, a former member of the Global Climate Coalition. However, the extremely modest commitments made in Kyoto and Bali reveal that the cost-benefit roadblock remains basically intact – the OECD nations are a long way from committing themselves to the 60–80 percent emission cuts necessary to stabilize global climate.[254] In addition, equity has yet to become the primary focus of negotiations. This is a serious problem because it leaves major players such as China, India and Brazil largely uncommitted to any obligatory climate protection process.

Strengthening the essentially cosmetic protocol drafted in Kyoto will require more effective leadership than has emerged so far. In addition to raising the level of public concern and the political pressure for an effective treaty, activist leadership must avoid promoting policies that solidify resistance and unify disparate blocking interests into a more cohesive alliance. Previously, activists made the mistake of proposing unpopular policies such as new energy taxes. These proposals made many enemies, especially in the United States, where they fostered broad alliances between Congressional conservatives, energy producers, automobile manufacturers and average citizens already fed up with high taxes.[255] To limit and divide their opposition, activists should propose tax shifts and reductions instead. By getting rid of subsidies and tax loopholes for fossil fuel production, taxes could be lowered.[256] And, if current tax policies were shifted from taxing labor to taxing carboniferous energy, fossil fuel use could be significantly reduced without raising taxes.[257] Some energy producers will still resist these policies, but tax reductions are popular with the public and much

(65 percent) also favored such a proposal. By more than a three-to-one margin (60–18 percent), voters rejected the view that reducing CO_2 emissions will "hurt the economy and cost jobs."

[254] Working Group I. *Scientific Assessment of Climate Change* (June 1990). This conclusion was also drawn by the EPA.

[255] Owen, James R. "Energy Tax Idea Pulls Unlikely Allies Together," *San Francisco Examiner* (March 7, 1993): A-10.

[256] In 1984, these taxpayer giveaways amounted to $44 billion. Brower, Michael. *Cool Energy* (Union of Concerned Scientists), 1995: 76–7. A 2008 report by Friends of the Earth's shows that even though the oil and gas industry is experiencing record profits, it is set to receive at least $33 billion in handouts from taxpayers over the next five years. These companies stand to gain at least $23.2 billion from tax loopholes, $3.8 billion in royalty rollbacks, $1.6 billion in direct subsidies for research and development and $4.3 billion through accounting gimmicks. The tax giveaways have increased dramatically since the passage of a Republican-drafted energy bill in 2005.

[257] There is lively, complex debate over the costs and benefits of various carbon tax schemes. See: (DoE) Department of Energy (Interagency Task Force). *Economics of Long-Term Global Climate Change: A Preliminary Assessment*. Department of Energy (September 1990); Barrett, Scott. "Pricing the Environment: The Economic and Environmental Consequences of a Carbon Tax," *Economic Outlook* (February 1990): 24–33; Miller, Allan, Irving Mintzer, & Peter G. Brown. "Rethinking the Economics of Global Warming," *Issues in Science & Technology* (Fall 1990); Congressional Budget Office (August 1990); EECC. "Europeans Debate Macroeconomic Effects of Energy/CO2 Tax," *Energy Economics and Climate Change 2.2* (1992): 2–5; Loske, Reinhard. "Ecological Taxes, Energy Policy & Greenhouse Gas Reductions: A German Perspective," *The Ecologist* (August 1991): 173; Milne, Janet E. "Book Review: The European Carbon Tax: An Economic Assessment [Carlo

harder for Republicans to oppose. Further, many analysts believe that removing the tax on labor would create more jobs and help maintain a healthy economy.[258]

The single greatest step toward consensus at this point would be a fundamental policy shift in Washington. Once united by their common desire for an effective agreement, the United States and the other developed nations would possess both the will and the resources to make significant GHG reductions at home while promoting climate-friendly development in the South and punishing potential free riders with enforceable sanctions for noncompliance.

THE THEORY AND PRACTICE OF ENVIRONMENTAL COOPERATION

What does this comparison of ozone and climate negotiations tell us about the theories of international relations outlined at the beginning of this chapter? Clearly, there are elements of truth to be found in each of them. For example, during ozone negotiations the decisive impact that America's hard-nosed structural leadership played in altering the cost-benefit calculus of European blockers appears to strengthen the neorealist position that cooperation is unlikely without the imposing presence and structural influence of a hegemonic power such as the United States. This conclusion is reinforced by the detrimental impact Washington's intransigence and ambivalence have had on climate negotiations.

However, the neorealists' central assumption that power relations and national security are the ultimate motivators of state behavior cannot be squared with the actual motivations that have shaped the positions of national policymakers during both atmospheric negotiations. For example, Washington's flip-flop from activist, to blocker, and back to activist during ozone negotiations was not motivated by concerns about national security or power relations between nations. Instead, policymakers were responding to alarming new discoveries in the upper atmosphere, domestic political pressures, the development of CFC alternatives and corporate strategy reversals in the global CFC market.

In fact, neoliberals could credibly argue that the success of ozone negotiations was a reflection of the fact that profitable CFC alternatives were developed by DuPont. This critical breakthrough helped draw the United States into the activist coalition and fostered the ratification of a treaty that encouraged the business community to respond quickly (and profitably) to the threat of ozone depletion. Thus, neoliberals can make a strong case that the profit motive and the EU's fear of potential U.S. trade

Carraro & Dominico Siniscalco]," *International Environmental Affairs*, v. 7, n. 1 (1995): 94; Muller, Frank. "Mitigating Climate Change: The Case for Energy Taxes," *Environment* (March 1996): 12; Cline, William R. *Global Warming: Estimating the Economic Benefits of Abatement.* (Paris: OECD), 1992; Krause, Floertin. *Energy Policy in the Greenhouse: Cutting Carbon Emissions, Burden or Benefit?* (El Cerrito, CA: Dutch Ministry of Housing, Physical Planning and Environment & The International Project for Sustainable Development), 1996; GECR. "NGO Study Finds US Could Save Trillions by Cutting CO2," *Global Environmental Change Report 3.21* (1991): 4.

[258] Moore, Curtis & Alan Miller. *Green Gold: Japan, Germany & the United States & the Race for Environmental Technology.* (Boston, MA: Beacon Press), 1994: 205–9.

sanctions were far more significant for explaining the success of the Montreal Protocol than any neorealist concerns about national power or security.

The neoliberal argument is further buttressed by the fact that economic motivations played a major role in addressing equity issues as well. By creating an ozone fund in London, negotiators subsidized and expanded the HCFC market in the developing world while discouraging a widespread black market for CFCs. Therefore, this fund benefited chemical manufacturers' bottom line just as much, if not more, than it satisfied the equity concerns of poor countries.

Instead of being an issue of power or security, when it comes to climate change neoliberals can plausibly assert that the primary impediment to a viable agreement is the persisting paucity of profitable alternatives to carboniferous energy. Clearly, the cohesion and intransigence of the climate change blocking coalition rests on their determination that GHG reductions threaten the economic interests of the powerful fossil fuel industry far more than they threaten national security. In fact, Pentagon analysts have concluded that America's dependence on foreign oil undermines national security and that within 20 years, escalating GHG emissions could produce a climate catastrophe that foments wars, political unrest and widespread famine.[259] Therefore, if U.S. policymakers were heeding the Pentagon's security concerns, the Bush administration would have been leading the world toward an effective climate agreement years ago.

In their desire to fashion a climate agreement that makes carbon reduction profitable, neoliberals promote faulty emission trading schemes and lucrative government incentives for a host of questionable programs that purport to reduce carbon emissions while making their advocates a lot of money. However, the prospects for profit in these schemes are far greater than their potential climate benefits. While Cargill and ADM may gorge themselves on ethanol subsidies, and the coal industry may collect millions in government largesse for carbon sequestration programs, there is little hope that these and other dubious carbon-reduction schemes will actually make a significant dent in GHG emissions.[260] Meanwhile, truly effective climate policies are often shunned or marginalized by neoliberals as "unrealistic," which is usually code for lacking powerful sponsors on Capitol Hill.[261]

Ultimately, green theory is the most useful theory for explaining the dynamics and ultimate prospects for international atmospheric cooperation. The negotiation of the Montreal Protocol clearly demonstrates the decisive impact that grassroots environmental NGOs and respected members of the scientific community had upon this successful outcome. Yet these influential actors are virtually ignored by neorealist,

---

[259] Schwartz, Peter & Doug Randal. *An Abrupt Climate Change Scenario and its Implications for United States National Security* (October 2003). http://www.edf.org/documents/3566_Abrupt ClimateChange.pdf.

[260] Lilley, Sasha. "Green Fuel's Dirty Secret," *CorpWatch* (June 1, 2006). http://www.corpwatch. org/article.php?id=13646.

[261] Carmichael, Annie & Jim Baak. "Solar Takes a Backseat in National Climate and Energy Bill," Renewable Energy World.com (May 21, 2009). http://www.renewableenergyworld. com/rea/news/article/2009/05/solar-takes-a-backseat-in-national-climate-and-energy-bill? cmpid=rss.

neoliberal and world systems theory. Only green theory acknowledges the significance of citizen-based activism arising from civil society.

While green theory is not optimistic about the prospects for effective international environmental cooperation, it clearly recognizes that any successful effort will be the result of widespread public concern and political pressure organized by nongovernmental grassroots activism. Green theory considers this pressure, emanating from civil society, to be the only force capable of compelling business and political elites to put the welfare of humanity and the planet over profit and power.

Ozone negotiations provide a clear example of the accuracy of this theoretical proposition. Nongovernmental forces informed and mobilized a concerned public, educated and pressured policymakers on the dangers of ozone depletion, and threatened to harm the bottom line and corporate reputation of CFC producers who refused to take these dangers seriously. Once the Antarctic hole was detected, citizen-based pressure for action was the force that turned the tide in favor of a strong ozone treaty in both the United States and Europe.

In the United States, grassroots pressure compelled the Reagan administration to reverse its blocking position and prompted DuPont to salvage its corporate reputation and strengthen its market position by developing alternatives to CFCs. Although the threat of U.S. trade sanctions received most of the credit for the final collapse of the EU blocking coalition, this was actually just the straw that broke the camel's back. Ever since the discovery of the ozone hole, public pressure for ozone action had been steadily eroding the unpopular blocking position of one European government after another. This made it nearly impossible for European policymakers to withstand external pressure from the United States.

The basic premises of green theory provide a clear perspective on why climate change negotiations have been unable to replicate the Montreal Protocol's success. Green theory explicitly recognizes the profound importance of fossil fuels to modern life and the global economic and political status quo. To put it simply, CFCs are not fossil fuels. Their energy has not provided millions of people with a lifestyle unimaginable to preindustrial societies. CFCs are not the lifeblood of capitalism's high-energy metabolism and the source of tremendous economic wealth and political power. In short, CFCs are easily replaced and relatively incidental to the functioning of global capitalism; fossil fuels are not.

For 200 years, carboniferous resources have been the energy base of industrial society. Today they supply 85 percent of the energy necessary to power the global economy. Many Greens consider them essential to the exponential growth imperative of modern capitalism because no other known source of energy can be exploited at the rapid pace (and with the extreme versatility) of fossil fuels.[262] They contend that capitalism requires cheap, abundant sources of energy that can be used at a rate commensurate with the demands of exponential economic growth. Thus fossil fuels are uniquely suited to capitalism because their rate of exploitation is limited only by the pace that they can be

---

[262] Heinberg, Richard. *The Party's Over: Oil, War and the Fate of Industrial Societies*, 4th ed. (Canada: New Society Publishers), 2008: ch. 4.

extracted from the Earth and distributed to their users. This attribute has made coal, oil and natural gas the ideal energies to fuel capitalism's relentless growth.[263]

By contrast, solar energy is not well suited to meet the demands of exponential economic growth. Because the amount of solar energy that reaches the Earth is so enormous, some think it can easily replace fossil fuels as soon as the technologies to collect it are developed. It is definitely true that solar energy has tremendous untapped potential that could significantly supplement fossil fuels as they become scarcer. But because the sun's energy reaches the Earth at a constant pace, solar power cannot sustain capitalism's ever-increasing demand for energy. There are definite limits on how much direct and indirect solar energy can be taken for human use at any time without disrupting the planetary life-support systems powered by the sun.[264]

Green theory considers the expansionist metabolism of global capitalism unsustainable for two reasons. First, capitalism's limitless growth cannot be sustained by either solar energy or the finite, dwindling supply of fossil fuels that supply 85 percent of its current energy budget. Second, relentless economic growth not only depletes the economy's energy base but it also wreaks havoc with the ecological life-support systems that sustain human survival. Climate change provides a powerful example of this second premise. By burning fossil fuels and overloading the atmosphere with GHGs, our economic activity will wreak environmental havoc of increasing and unknown proportions.

Green theory clearly recognizes that global capitalism is caught on the horns of a dilemma. If it continues along its present course of economic expansion powered by fossil fuels, it will face environmental calamities of increasing magnitude, from climate change to ocean acidification and plummeting biodiversity. Ultimately, somewhere down this perilous dead-end road, it will deplete its most essential energy source: fossil fuels. However, breaking the economy's addiction to fossil fuels threatens the economic and political power of the world's largest, most profitable corporations and undermines the entire system's capacity to keep growing.

Some liberal economists and environmentalists believe the global economy can phase out fossil fuels and adopt renewable sources of clean energy with minimal political, social and economic dislocation.[265] However, most green theorists believe this outlook is naïve and overly optimistic because carboniferous energy is the source

---

[263] Nuclear is a less useful and more expensive alternative. About 12 percent of the world's power comes from nuclear power. It is far more expensive than fossil fuels (once the immense expenditures for plant construction and safety, reactor decommissioning and waste storage are taken into account) and much less versatile. There a major technical obstacles to using nuclear power for transportation and agriculture.

[264] Humans already appropriate for themselves about 40 percent of the terrestrial plant energy produced by photosynthesis, leaving all other life forms on land to live on the remainder. Vitousek, Peter, Paul R. Ehrlich, Anne H. Ehrlich & Pamela Matson. "Human Appropriation of the Products of Photosynthesis" *BioScience* (June 1986): 368–73. http://www.biology.duke.edu/wilson/EcoSysServices/papers/VitousekEtal 1986.pdf.

[265] Hawken, Paul. *The Ecology of Commerce.* (NY: Harper Collins), 1994; Hawken, Paul, Amory Lovins & L. Hunter Lovins. *Natural Capitalism.* (Boston, MA: Back Bay Books), 2008; Odum, Howard & Elizabeth C. Odum. *A Prosperous Way Down.* (Boulder, CO: University Press of Colorado), 2001.

of immense profits for a handful of tremendously powerful mega-corporations and it is essential for the continual expansion of the world economy. Thus, green theorists are skeptical that planetary threats such as climate change, which require drastic restrictions on the combustion of fossil fuels, can be tackled without facing intense resistance from the petro-industrial complex at the core of global capitalism. Thus, unlike ozone depletion, there is no politically expedient and economically profitable solution to climate change or other core environmental crises that cannot be overcome without transforming the very nature of industrial capitalism.

CONCLUSION

A Glimmer of Hope

Without environmental laws, the quality of our air, land and water would be frightening to imagine. This does not alter the fact that the Environmental Protection Agency (EPA) has never lived up to its name. Instead, its performance has ranged from feckless and feeble to crooked and criminal. Forty years after Congress enacted tough-talking ecological edicts and the president authorized the EPA to enforce them, nature remains in critical condition. Our environmental laws are riddled with loopholes, exceptions and exclusions, and the pollution police scarcely bother to enforce them. Worse yet, the established approach to environmental protection is fundamentally flawed and ineffectual because it relies on control and cleanup, rather than precaution and prevention.

Powerful forces, emanating from the very nature of our political economy, confound the basic intent of the law and undermine the entire environmental protection process. Even under the most ecologically inclined administrations, the EPA functions within a capitalist milieu where profit-driven polluters externalize their ecological costs whenever possible, while their political accomplices (in both parties) enact toothless laws and appoint ineffective enforcers. The EPA's regulatory efforts are completely incapable of avoiding an escalating ecological calamity. The established approach to environmental protection resembles paddling against the current in a leaky rowboat with a treacherous waterfall behind us.

Since the legal and institutional failures of the prevailing system stem from dysfunctions in the surrounding political economy, it is no accident that the EPA's pathetic record as a regulatory agency is hardly unique. From the Department of the Interior and the Food and Drug Administration to the Securities and Exchange Commission, profit trumps the public interest with grim consistency whenever corporate lobbying, campaign cash and the revolving door between regulators and industry corrode good governance. As long as corporate revenues and economic growth override all other concerns, even earnest efforts to protect our planet will be undermined and overwhelmed by these powerful prerogatives. Conversely, once the long-range health of our species and our planet become paramount, reforming our institutional and legal systems will no longer resemble rowing upstream.

Does this mean that, until we completely transform society, all efforts to improve the established system of environmental protection should be abandoned? Absolutely not. With our backs to the waterfall, we must not ignore the need to plug the leaks in our boat while paddling away from disaster. Repairing and rowing are both essential and, mutually complimentary tasks.

What types of reform are most necessary to improve the current system of environmental protection? The most effective political, legal and institutional reforms must be built upon the recognition that presidents, lawmakers and regulators are predisposed to favor the most powerful actors in society. As long as money remains "the mother's milk of politics," corporate polluters will hold tremendous leverage over the electoral, lawmaking, regulatory and enforcement processes. The only force capable of counteracting this corrupting influence is broad-based grassroots activism: an aware, outraged, mobilized public. Thus, genuine reform efforts must fortify and expand public influence over the political system in general and the environmental protection process in particular, while minimizing the machinations of corporate scofflaws and their government cohorts.

One potent weapon in the battle to enhance public power over polluters is the precautionary principle. This principle must become central to the entire process of environmental protection because it forces potential polluters to bear the burden of proof that their activities are safe in an open, informed, democratic policymaking process.[1] One commonly recognized description of this principle is that precautionary measures should be taken:

> ... when an activity raises threats of harm to human health or the environment, even if some cause and effect relationships are not fully established scientifically. In this context the proponent of an activity, rather than the public, should bear the burden of proof. The process of applying the precautionary principle must be open, informed and democratic and must include potentially affected parties. It must also involve an examination of the full range of alternatives, including no action.[2]

Environmental activists have fought for the acceptance of the precautionary principle since it emerged from the German environmental movement in the 1970s. The first international endorsement of the principle came in 1982 when the UN General Assembly adopted the World Charter for Nature. In 1998, an international group of scientists, government officials, lawyers and labor and grassroots environmental activists met in Wisconsin to define and discuss the precautionary principle. They adopted the definition quoted above and issued the *Wingspread Statement on the Precautionary Principle*, which stated that:

> The release and use of toxic substances, the exploitation of resources, and physical alterations of the environment have had substantial unintended consequences affecting human health and the environment. Some of these concerns are high rates of learning deficiencies, asthma, cancer, birth defects and species extinctions,

---

[1] Myers, Nancy and Carolyn Raffensperger, eds. *Precautionary Tools for Reshaping Environmental Policy*. (Cambridge, MA: MIT Press), 2006.

[2] *Wingspread Statement on the Precautionary Principle* (January 1998). http://www.sehn.org/pre1 caution.html

along with global climate change, stratospheric ozone depletion and worldwide contamination with toxic substances and nuclear materials.

We believe existing environmental regulations and other decisions, particularly those based on risk assessment, have failed to protect adequately human health and the environment – the larger system of which humans are but a part. We believe there is compelling evidence that damage to humans and the worldwide environment is of such magnitude and seriousness that new principles for conducting human activities are necessary. While we realize that human activities may involve hazards, people must proceed more carefully than has been the case in recent history. Corporations, government entities, organizations, communities, scientists and other individuals must adopt a precautionary approach to all human endeavors.[3]

Today the precautionary approach is a general, compulsory principle of law in the European Union.[4] However, in the United States, the precautionary principle has been distorted and attacked by the flacks of industry because it places the burden of proof on potential polluters and engages the public in an open, informed decision-making procedure.[5]

Despite stiff opposition, the precautionary principle has gained support and credibility.[6] In December 2001, the *New York Times Magazine* listed the principle as one of the most influential ideas of the year.[7] In June 2003, the Board of Supervisors of the City and County of San Francisco became the first government body in the United States to make the precautionary principle the basis for all its environmental policies. But it has yet to achieve official acceptance at higher levels of government.

In addition to making the precautionary approach the guiding principle of environmental policymaking, further institutional and legal reforms must widen the channels of public power over environmental protection while blocking polluter interference and intrigue. Within the EPA and other agencies with ecological

[3] Quoted in: "The Precautionary Principle," *Rachel's Environmental & Health News #586*, (February 18, 1998). http://www.rachel.org/en/node/3850.

[4] *The European Union's Communication on Precautionary Principle* (Brussels: February 2, 2000). http://www.gdrc.org/u-gov/precaution-4.html.

[5] Dezenhall Resources, a PR firm dubbed "the pit bull of public relations" by the editor of O'Dwyer's PR Report, offered to launch a smear campaign against the precautionary principle for the American Chemistry Council. See SourceWatch: http://www.sourcewatch.org/index.php?title=Nichols-Dezenhall#Opposing_the_Precautionary_Principle.

[6] Michaels, David & Celeste Monforton. "Scientific Evidence in the Regulatory System: Manufacturing Uncertainty and The Demise of the Formal Regulatory System," *Journal of Law and Policy*, v. 12, n. 1 (2005); Michaels, David. "Doubt is Their Product: Industry Groups are Fighting Government Regulation by Fomenting Scientific Uncertainty," *Scientific American* (June, 2005). http://www.scientificamerican.com/article.cfm?id=doubt-is-their-product. For a libertarian critique of the precautionary principle see: Sunstein, Cass. *Laws of Fear, Beyond the Precautionary Principle*. (NY: Cambridge University Press), 2005. For a response to common criticisms of this principle see: Montague, Peter, Ph.D. "Answering the Critics of Precaution," *Rachel's Democracy & Health News #790* (April 15, 2004). http://www.rachel.org/en/node/6464.

[7] Pollan, Michael. "Precautionary Principal," in *The New York Times Magazine*, "The Year in Ideas: An Encyclopedia of Innovations, Conceptual Leaps, Harebrained Schemes, Cultural Tremors and Hindsight Reckonings that made a difference in 2001" (December 9, 2001): 92.

responsibilities, the revolving door with regulated industries must be slammed shut and locked. Any expertise gained through these cozy collaborations is completely offset and compromised by the conflicts of interest they propagate. Common sense and the long, sordid record of corporate malfeasance clearly demonstrate that the fox cannot be trusted to guard the henhouse. This same principle applies to fixing laws that allow polluters to verify the safety of their own products or monitor and self-report their toxic releases.

Anyone engaged in defending their community from toxic wastes, polluted air and contaminated water knows that the law provides very limited protections. Environmental laws officially tolerate an enormous amount of pollution as an accepted cost of doing business. Laws that try to establish safe levels of pollution are incapable of ascertaining within any modicum of scientific certainty what "safe" means. The Clean Air Act is notoriously incapable of accurately determining what concentrations of any particular air contaminant are safe to breathe. Worse yet, the combined effect of these noxious wastes is virtually unknown. The Clean Water Act's technology-based limits don't even bother to use safety as the primary standard for controlling water pollution. Instead, the permitted level of water contaminants is based on the treatment technologies polluters can afford to install.

But these regulatory failures apply only to the toxins that already have been legally designated dangerous. From fire retardants and solvents to plasticizers and petrochemicals, industry inundates our environment with thousands of new chemicals every year. Most of them go virtually untested and unregulated.[8] Scientists readily admit they have little information about their toxic potential and absolutely no idea what their synergistic and cumulative impacts will be on human health and the environment. Therefore, even if the most egregious loopholes, exclusions and exceptions were removed from our current environmental laws, and the EPA made a serious effort to enforce them, these statutes would remain pitifully deficient and fundamentally flawed.

A prime defect in U.S. environmental law derives from its pervasive reliance on elaborate rules and regulations that control pollution instead of preventing it. Laws that target end-of-the-pipe releases of specified pollutants or attempt to control their concentrations in a particular medium (air, land or water) are extremely costly and complex to oversee, hard to obey, easy to defy and do not sufficiently protect people or the environment. Instead of preventing pollution in the first place, this approach generates an onerous regulatory regime with few actual benefits to show for it.[9] Ineffective legal labyrinths only intensify public frustration and validate polluter allegations that environmental laws are more trouble than they're worth.

---

[8] One example: polybrominated diphenyl ethers (PBDEs) are compounds used as flame retardants in plastic and foam consumer products like pillows even though they are known neurotoxins and suspected endocrine disruptors. *Chemical Encyclopedia.* http://healthychild.org/issues/chemical-pop/polybrominated_diphenyl_ethers/

[9] For abundant evidence of this failed approach see: Commoner, Barry. *Making Peace with the Planet.* (NY: Pantheon) 1990: ch. 4.

Genuine environmental improvement requires combining the precautionary principle's "better safe than sorry" approach with its two complementary corollaries: the "ounce of prevention is worth a pound of cure" and "waste not, want not" maxims underlying the policies of *source reduction* and *zero waste*.[10]

Even though industry complains bitterly about complying with a maze of environmental controls and restrictions, it has stubbornly resisted efforts to simplify the process by preventing pollution instead. In 1990, when Congress made a tentative step toward source reduction by enacting the Pollution Prevention Act (PPA), its directives were never taken seriously. The law authorized the EPA to make source reduction an essential objective. But even though participation in the PPA's underfunded, poorly monitored programs was entirely voluntary, the business community was suspicious and unenthusiastic.[11] Critics claimed to fear the "unanticipated rapid evolution of an intrusive regulatory system."[12]

Although some cities have tried to reduce their waste disposal burden by developing zero waste programs, commercial refuse has made actual reductions of more than 30 percent extremely rare. The main obstacle is industry; 94 percent of the materials used in the manufacture of the average U.S. commodity are thrown away before the product even reaches the shelves.[13] Unless American industries completely transform their operations to eliminate toxics and unnecessary energy and material use at every phase of the extraction and production process, residential recycling programs will make no more than a minor dent in the waste stream.

Zero waste, source reduction and the precautionary principle are extremely difficult to apply in a capitalist economy in which industry vehemently opposes any government restrictions on the resources it uses or the products it fabricates. The sanctity of private enterprise limits society's authority to prevent industry from pillaging ecosystems, wasting resources, using hazardous chemicals and marketing unsafe products. Further, the goal of building a zero waste economy – where the residues of one activity become resources for another – will never be fulfilled as long as the planet's wealth can be extracted more profitably than it can be recycled.

The multiple defects in America's system of environmental protection are magnified a thousandfold at the international level, where a fragmented and fractious system of nation states must address the most ominous perils generated by global

---

[10] The GrassRoots Recycling Network (GRRN) has identified 11 policies and actions that it believes are required to achieve zero waste. See: Leroux, Kivi "Clearing the Way for Zero Waste," *Resource Recycling* (March 15, 2001). http://www.precaution.org/lib/05/rpr16.htm#Clearing_the_Way_for_Zero_Waste

[11] Vig, Norman J. & Michael Kraft. *Environmental Policy: New Directions for the 21st Century*, 6th ed. (Washington, DC: CQ Press): 270–8; *Toxic Substances: Status of EPA's Efforts to Reduce Toxic Releases* GAO/RCED-94–207 (September 22, 1994). http://www.mapcruzin.com/scruztri/docs/ga094207.htm

[12] Anderson, Frederick R. "From Voluntary to Regulatory Pollution Prevention," *The Greening of Industrial Ecosystems*. (Washington, DC: National Academy Press), 1994. http://books.nap.edu/openbook.php?record_id=2129&page=98

[13] Motavalli, Jim. "Zero Waste: No Longer Content to Just Recycle Waste, Environmentalists Want Us to Reduce it to Nothing," *E Magazine* (April 1, 2001).

capitalism. At this level, the stakes are incredibly high because failure jeopardizes the long-range survival of humanity. Can we create a society that meets our needs without compromising the ability of future generations to do the same? History is littered with civilizations that decayed and collapsed after depleting and despoiling their ecosystems.[14] These civilizations were not global in magnitude, and neither were the environmental catastrophes they succumbed to. But today, our globalized society is provoking multiple ecological crises of planetary proportions simultaneously, from dying ocean ecosystems and fresh water scarcity to deforestation, plummeting biodiversity and global climate disruption.

The devastating potential of these converging calamities is compounded by our limited capacity to address them. The international community cannot mount a full-scale, unified response because it is deeply divided and propelled by internal dynamics that perpetuate self-destructive behavior. Society's major economic units are highly competitive, profit-driven corporations and financial institutions bent on maximizing their return on invested capital by transforming cheap labor, resources and energy into a vast array of commodities. Our major political units are rivalrous nation-states ruled by politicians, government officials and generals whose primary preoccupation is power. In the competitive pursuit of power and profit the environment seldom wins.

Beneath the politicians, generals, bankers and corporate executives, everyday people are separated by cultural differences and conflicting allegiances (national, class, ethnic, political, religious, etc.). Our daily lives are fragmented into numerous functions: as workers, consumers, citizens and family members. This makes it extremely difficult for us to recognize and act on the common environmental threats we face as a species. In fact, given the economic system we live in, our immediate individual goals and desires as consumers and workers often contradict our long-range interests as members of the human race.

The media have the potential to raise environmental awareness and encourage common action. But their basic purpose is not promoting education and awareness, or even providing information and entertainment. Corporate media's business is to deliver huge audiences of potential consumers to the advertisers who sponsor their programs. Advertising is the cash cow of the entertainment and information industry. Advertising is designed to promote consumption, which is both the father of economic growth and the mother of most environmental problems. Of course, astute advertisers try to resolve this conflict by selling us on the idea that we can promote economic growth *and* solve our environmental problems by purchasing green products. Buying green is not a bad idea, as long as we're not just buying green hype. Yet ultimately an economy addicted to greater consumption and unlimited growth is incompatible with the planet's ecological limits. Therefore, the greenest consumers are those that consume the least – a proposition that sends shivers down an advertiser's spine and tremors throughout the economy.

Galvanizing green awareness and global action under these adverse conditions may seem nearly hopeless. But the process has begun. Over the past few decades, a

---

[14] Diamond, Jared. *Collapse*. (NY: Viking), 2005.

grassroots movement of incredible scope and diversity has sprouted in every corner of the planet. This emerging challenge to the status quo has a political and a techno-logical side. The technological challenge comes from the groundswell of enthusiasm and innovation directed at developing renewable energy; zero waste; and sustainable farming, transportation and manufacturing alternatives to the dead end, petroleum-based edifice of industrial capitalism. The political side of the movement is dedicated to environmental protection and social justice. The primary antagonists are com-monly identified as the fossil-fuel industry, corporate globalization and militarism.

This eclectic movement is the general expression of hundreds of smaller move-ments, each one a product of its own particular history and most pressing concerns.[15] It includes an amazing conglomeration of activists, from alternative technology innovators, climate scientists, ecologists and organic growers to inner-city environ-mental justice advocates, landless peasants, labor organizers, farm workers and indigenous communities resisting resource exploitation and ecological destruction. It connects battles against water privatization, mega-dams, biopiracy, genetically modified crops and pesticide poisoning with fights for workers' rights, labor justice and corporate reform; it links campaigns to prevent climate chaos and adopt renew-able energy with demonstrations against war, militarism, repression and human rights abuses. Despite their disparate starting points, these multiple movements are con-verging to resist the juggernaut of global capitalism.

The Internet has had an immense impact on the ability of these previously distinct and disconnected struggles to communicate, coalesce and recognize themselves as part of a global battlefront. It began in the mountain jungles of Chiapas, where the Zapatista insurgency resisted the NAFTA-inspired effort to transform Mayan farming commun-ities into landless Mexican laborers. The Zapatistas were the first to use the World Wide web to seek global support and declare their intention "to make a collective network of all our particular struggles and resistances – an intercontinental network of resistance against neo-liberalism, an intercontinental network of resistance for humanity."[16]

Since then, a vast amalgam of popular movements, nongovernment organizations (NGOs) and community-based organizations have communicated and coordinated their efforts to protect people and the planet from corporate globalization.[17] To offer a counterpoint to the business elite's yearly gathering at the World Economic Forum in Switzerland, they have rallied their forces at annual World Social Forums, beginning in Porto Alegre, Brazil. While this intercontinental resistance movement remains rooted in efforts to protect particular habitats and communities, it has coalesced to demand action on climate change and environmental justice from Kyoto to Copenhagen; and to demonstrate its opposition to the World Bank, the International Monetary Fund and the World Trade Organization in Seattle, Genoa, Barcelona and elsewhere.

[15] Mertes, Tom. *Movement of Movements*. (London: Verso) 2004.
[16] Read by Subcomandante Marcos at the closing session of the First International Encuentro, August 3, 1996. See: Ponce de León, Juana, ed. *Our Word Is Our Weapon: Selected Writings of Subcomandante Insurgente Marcos*. (NY: Seven Stories Press), 2003.
[17] Mertes, Tom, 2004.

This movement is very young. Worldwide, its level of popular support remains shallow and uneven, and its political vision is unclear. As a political force in the United States, its voice remains marginalized. Most Americans are hardly aware of its existence. Its message was magnified after Hurricane Katrina and other disturbing climate events increased public fear of global warming, and the 2008 economic crash plus rising energy prices stimulated interest in green jobs and renewable energy. But despite these advances and the more tolerant political climate the Obama presidency elicited in Washington, this network of green social activists has limited sway in American politics. For now, there is little chance that its influence will translate into significant improvements in environmental policy or widespread crackdowns on corporate polluters. However, as the ecological and economic hardships engulfing us become harder to ignore, these activists' message and their movement may gain momentum. If they do, they will face stiff opposition.

The corporate core of the American economy will not tolerate any basic shift away from the growth-gripped, energy-guzzling, consumption-crazed system that has made it so wealthy and powerful. Significant reforms will be made only when corporate power is confronted with substantial public resistance, and radical new alternatives will not gain popular support until a critical mass of Americans considers the established order so bankrupt and broken they are willing to rise up and replace it.

Bibliography

Abrahamson, Dean Edwin. "Global Warming: The Issue, Impacts, Responses," Dean Edwin Abrahamson, ed. *The Challenge of Global Warming*. (Washington, DC: Island Press), 1989.

Adam, David. "Royal Society Tells Exxon: Stop Funding Climate Change Denial," *The Guardian UK* (September 20, 2006). http://www.guardian.co.uk/environment/2008/may/28/climatechange.fossilfuels.

Adler, Robert W. "Cleaner Water, but Not Clean Enough," *Issues in Science & Technology* (December 22, 1993). HighBeam Research (November 11, 2009). http://www.highbeam.com/doc/1G1-15155692.html.

Adler, Robert W., Jessica Landman, & Diane Cameron. *The Clean Water Act 20 Years Later.* (Washington, DC: Island Press), 1993.

"Air Pollution Linked to Infant Death, Including SIDs, New Study Reports," *Doctors' Guide* (June 11, 1997). http://www.pslgroup.com/dg/2c4b2.htm.

Alaska Department of Fish & Game. *Why Save Endangered Species?* (August 11, 2008). http://www.adfg.state.ak.us/special/esa/why_save.php.

Albritton, Daniel L., et al. *Stratospheric Ozone: The State of the Science and NOAA's Current and Future Research.* (Washington, DC: National Oceanic & Atmospheric Administration), 1987.

Allen, Barbara. "Environmental Justice and Expert Knowledge in the Wake of a Disaster," *Social Studies of Science* (February 2007): 103–10.

American Lands Discussion Paper. *Broken Promises of Recovery: The Clinton Administration's 10-Prong Attack on Endangered Species* (January 2000). http://www.defenders.org/esa-9.html.

American Lung Association. *Diseases A-Z* (January 2005). http://74.125.155.132/search?q=cache:IXEYMkAFVREJ: www.lungusa.org/site/apps/nlnet/content3.aspx%3Fc%3DdvLUK9Oo E%26b%3D4294229%26ct%3D3052555+American+Lung+Association.+Diseases+A-Z&hl=en&gl=us&strip=1.

State of the Air: 2004 (April 29, 2004). http://www.lungusa.org/site/apps/nl/content3.asp?c=dvLUK9OoE&b=40676&ct=66972&notoc=1 http://lungaction.org/reports/stateoftheair2004.html.

American Museum of Natural History (press release). "National Survey Reveals Biodiversity Crisis – Scientific Experts Believe We Are in Midst of Fastest Mass Extinction in Earth's History" (April 20, 1998). http://www.amnh.org/museum/press/feature/biofact.html.

Anderson, Frederick R. "From Voluntary to Regulatory Pollution Prevention," Braden R. Allenby & Deanna J. Richards, eds. *The Greening of Industrial Ecosystems.* (Washington, DC: National Academy Press), 1994. http://books.nap.edu/openbook.php?record_id=2129&page=98.

Appel, Adrianne. "Tiny Town Demands Justice in Dioxin Poisoning," *Inter Press Service* (July 15, 2007). http://openjurist.org/852/f2d/324/arkansas-poultry-federation-v-united-states-environmental-protection-agency.

Arkansas Poultry Federation v. EPA, 852 F.2d **324** (8th Cir. 1998). http://openjurist.org/852/f2d/324/arkansas-poultry-federation-v-united-states-environmental-protection-agency.

Associated Press. "ExxonMobil Paid to Mislead Public," *USA Today* (May 5, 2007). http://www.usatoday.com/money/industries/energy/2007-01-03-global-warming_x.htm.

Atmosphere Alliance. *Life Support: A Citizens' Guide to Solving the Atmosphere Crisis.* (Olympia, WA: Earth Island Institute), 1995.

Bailey, Jeff. "Concerns Mount Over Operating Methods of Plants That Incinerate Toxic Waste," *Wall Street Journal* (March 20, 1992): B1, B5.

Baldwin, Pamela. *The Role of Designation of Critical Habitat Under the Endangered Species Act.* CRS Report to Congress [RS20263] (July 16, 1999).

Ballard, Tanya N. "Bill to Liberate EPA Ombudsman Languishes," Gov. Exec.com Daily Briefing (November 26, 2006). http://www.govexec.com/dailyfed/1102/112602t1.htm.

Ballenger, Josey. "Bush's Choice of EPA Advisers Signals Tilt Toward Industry," Center for Public Integrity. http://www.publicintegrity.org/articles/entry/475/.

Balling, Robert Jr. *Global Climactic Change: A New Vision for the 1990s.* [available from the author] (January 1991).

Barcott, Bruce. "Changing the Rules," *New York Times Magazine* (April 4, 2004): 43.

Barratt-Brown, Liz. "Watchdogs on the Convention," *ECO: Climate Talks* NGO *Newsletter* (February 26, 1992): 3.

Barrett, Scott. "Pricing the Environment: The Economic and Environmental Consequences of a Carbon Tax," *Economic Outlook* (February 1990): 24–33.

Barry, D. L., L. Haroun, & C. Halvorson. *For Conserving Listed Species, Talk is Cheaper Than We Think: The Consultation Process Under the Endangered Species Act.* (Washington, DC: World Wide Fund for Nature), 1992.

Basile, Jason M. "Still No Remedy After All These Years: Plugging the Hole in the Law of Leaking Underground Storage Tanks," Indiana Law Journal (Spring 1998). http://www.law.indiana.edu/ilj/volumes/v73/no2/basile.html.

Batts, Deborah A. United States District Judge. *Opinion Against Defendants Christine Todd Whitman, Marianne L. Horinko, Michael Leavitt and the United States Environmental Protection Agency in United States District Court Southern District of New York* (February 2, 2006). 04Civ1888.pdf (accessed at: http://www.nyenvirolaw.org/nyeljp-benzman.html).

Baue, William. "Hazardous Waste as Fuel: Conservation or Corporate Irresponsibility?" *Social Funds Newsroom* (September 11, 2002). http://www.socialfunds.com/news/article.cgi/924.html.

Bean, Michael J. "Endangered Species – Endangered Act?" *Environment* (January 1999). http://www.findarticles.com/p/articles/mi_m1076/is_1_41/ai_53709851.

Beardsly, Tim. "Profile: Political Engineer," *Scientific American* (April 1991): 26.

Beaudry, Kendall. "EPA Ombudsman Fights for His Job," *Environmental News Network* (March 15, 2002). http://www.enn.com/news/enn-stories/2002/03/03152002/s_46676.asp.

Benedick, Richard Elliot. "Lessons from 'the Ozone Hole'," World Resources Institute, ed. *Greenhouse Warming: Negotiating a Global Regime.* (Washington, DC: WRI), 1991.

Benedick, Richard E. *Ozone Diplomacy*. (Cambridge, MA: Harvard University Press), 1991.
"Perspectives of a Negotiation Practitioner," Gunnar Sjöstedt, ed. *International Environmental Negotiation*. (London: Sage), 1993.

Berman, Daniel & John O'Connor. *Who Owns the Sun?* (White River, VT: Chelsea Green), 1996.

Bertazzi, Pier Alberto & Others. "Cancer Incidence in a Population Accidentally Exposed to 2,3,7,8-Tetrachlorodibenzo-PARA-dioxin," *Epidemiology*, v. 4, n. 5 (September 1993): 398–406.

Bleifuss, Joel. "Nightmare Soil," *In These Times* (October 16, 1995): 12.

Block, Alan & Frank Scarpitti. *Poisoning for Profit*. (NY: William Morrow & Co.), 1985.

Bond, Patrick. "From False to Real Solutions for Climate Change," *MR Zine* (June 1, 2008). http://www.monthlyreview.org/mrzine/bond060108.html.

Brodeur, Paul. "Annals of Chemistry: In the Face of Doubt," *New Yorker* (June 1986): 86.

Brookes, W. T. "The Global Warming Panic," *Forbes* (December 1989): 96–102.

Bronski, Peter. "Muddy Waters: The Push for Better Clean Water Protection," E Magazine. com. http://www.emagazine.com/view/?4574.

Brower, Michael. *Cool Energy*. (Cambridge, MA: MIT Press), 1992.

Brown, Mary Ashby. "Litigation Update. Key Teflon Chemical: Center of Lawsuits and Debates," *Sustainable Development Law & Policy* (May 2006). http://vlex.com/vid/335529.

Brown, Rep. George E. Jr. "Environmental Science Under Siege," *Environment* (March 1997): 12.

Bryner, Gary C., ed. "Policy Options for Responding to the Threat of Global Warming," *global Warming and the Challenge of International Cooperation*. (Provo, UT: David M. Kennedy for International Studies, Brigham Young University), 1992.

Buck, Susan J. *The Global Commons: An Introduction*. (Washington, DC: Island Press), 1998.

Burford, Anne M. *Are You Tough Enough?* (NY: McGraw-Hill), 1986.

Burtraw, Dallas & Michael A. Toman. *Equity and International Agreements for CO2 Containment*. (Washington, DC: Resources for the Future), 1991.

"Bush Names Exxon Chief to Chart America's Energy Future," *Green Watch Today* (November 2, 2006). http://www.bushgreenwatch.org/mt_archives/000323.php.

Byerly, R.Jr. *Stratospheric Research and Protection Act of 1975*. Report to accompany H. R. 3118. [Report 94–575] U.S. House of Representatives (October 28, 1975).

Canadian Institute of Child Health. *Climate Change and Your Child's Health: Fact Sheet on Air Pollution* (April 30, 2003). http://www.cich.ca/EnvironmentHealth_ClimateFactSheets. html.

"Carbon Emissions Threaten 'Underwater Catastrophe', Scientists Warn," Guardian.co.uk (June 1, 2009). http://www.guardian.co.uk/environment/2009/jun/01/carbon-emissions-ocean-acidification.

Carbon Trade Watch. *The Carbon Connection* [documentary video] (2008). http://www.tni. org/detail_pub.phtml?&know_id=223&menu=11c.

Carmichael, Annie & Jim Baak. "Solar Takes a Backseat in National Climate and Energy Bill," Renewable Energy World.com (May 21, 2009). http://www.renewableenergyworld. com/rea/news/article/2009/05/solar-takes-a-backseat-in-national-climate-and-energy-bill? cmpid=rss.

Cart, Julie. "Interior Department Official Resigns," *Los Angeles Times* (May 2, 2002). http://www. sourcewatch.org/index.php?title=Julie_A._MacDonald.

Case, David. "Grumbling About Gore," TomPaine.com http://www.tompaine.com/feature2. cfm/ID/3845.

Center for Biological Diversity (press release). "Scientists, Congress, Government Auditors and the U.S. Fish & Wildlife Service's Own Biologists Repeatedly Confirm That Imperiled

Species Are Not Being Added to the Endangered Species List Fast Enough." http://www.sw-center.org/swcbd/activist/ESA/critique.html.

Reagan Redux: A Review of the Bush Critical Habitat Record (April 21, 2003). www.biologicaldiversity.org/swcbd/activist/Bushrecord.pdf.

U.S. Fish and Wildlife Service Reports Show That Critical Habitat Enhances Recovery of Endangered Species (October 2003). http://www.biologicaldiversity.org/swcbd/Programs/policy/ch/sub1.html.

"Lawsuit Filed to Protect Endangered Tidal Marsh Plants: Bush Administration Continues to Withhold Critical Habitat for Imperiled Species" (November 19, 2003). http://www.biologicaldiversity.org/swcbd/press/tidal11-19-03.html.

Cleaning Up the Bush Legacy. http://www.biologicaldiversity.org/campaigns/cleaning_up_the_bush_legacy/index.html.

Center for Health, Environment and Justice. *Behind Closed Doors* (April 2001). http://www.trwnews.net/Documents/Dioxin/CHEJ%20BCDreport.htm.

Center for Native Ecosystems (press release). "Colorado Groups to Join Mexican Spotted Owl Critical Habitat Suit" (March 28, 2001).

"Notice of Intent to Sue Over Spotted Owl" (March 28, 2001). http://www.nativeecosystems.org/mexicanspottedowl/010328_noi.htm.

Center for Responsive Politics. *PACs in Profile: Spending Patterns in 1992 Elections*. (Washington, DC: CRP), 1993.

Chalfan, Larry. "Industrial Ecology: The Path to Sustainability," *Zero Waste Alliance* (October 16, 1999). http://www.zerowaste.org/publications/ie_pres/index.html.

Chandler, William U., ed. *Carbon Emissions Control Strategies*. (Washington, DC: World Wildlife Fund & Conservation Foundation), 1990.

Cheever, Frederico. "The Road to Recovery: A New Way of Thinking About the Endangered Species Act," *Ecology Law Quarterly* (Winter 1996): 1–78.

Chemical Encyclopedia. "PBDEs: Polybrominated Diphenyl Ethers." http://healthychild.org/issues/chemical/.

Chemical Manufacturers Association. *Production, Sales, and Calculated Release of CFC-11, and CFC-12 Through 1987*. (Washington, DC: CMA), 1988.

(Special Programs Advisory Group). "Record of Meeting," *CMA Papers* (April 21, 1981).

Cherry, Sheila R. "Uproar at EPA," *Insight on the News* (May 6, 2002). http://www.insightmag.com/main.cfm/include/detail/storyid/249993.html.

Citizen Works. *Why Are We Going to War? A Fact Sheet* (January 2003). http://www.targetoil.com/downloads/oilandwarv128.pdf.

Clarke, Chris. "Groups Petition Bush to List 225 Species," *Faultline: California's Environmental Magazine* (May 5, 2004). http://www.faultline.org/archives/001331.html.

Clarren, Rebecca. "Inside the Secretive Plan to Gut the Endangered Species Act," Salon.com (March 27, 2007). http://salon.com/news/feature/2007/03/27/endangered_species/.

"Clean Air Axed," *Mother Jones* (August 29, 2003). http://www.motherjones.com/news/dailymojo/2003/08/we_536_05a.htm.

Clean Air Task Force Report. *Death, Disease and Dirty Power: Mortality and Health Disease Due to Air Pollution from Power Plants* (October 2000). http://www.cleartheair.org/fact/mortality/mortalitylowres.pdf.

Clean Air Task Force (press release). "The Power to Kill: Death & Disease from Power Plants Charged with Violating the Clean Air Act" (July 10, 2001). http://cta.policy.net/proactive/newsroom/release.vtml?id=20720.

Clean Air Task Force Report. *Dirty Air, Dirty Power: Mortality and Health Damage Due to Air Pollution from Power Plants* (June 2004). http://www.catf.us/publications/view/24.

Clean Air Trust. *Clean Air Villain of the Month* (March 2002). http://www.cleanairtrust.org/villain.0302.html.

Clean Production Action. *Zero Waste* (2009). http://www.cleanproduction.org/Steps.Closed.Zero.php.

Clean Water Act. [Federal Water Pollution Control Act] (February 10, 2009). http://cfpub.epa.gov/npdes/cwa.cfm?program_id=45.

Clean Water Authority Restoration Act of 2003 (H. R. 962 and S. 473). www.nwf.org/wildlife/pdfs/CleanWaterAuthorityAct2003.pdf.

Clifford, Mary. *Environmental Crime.* (Maryland: Aspen Publishers), 1998.

Climate Action Network (CAN). *Everything You Ever Wanted to Know About Climate Change.* (Brussels: CAN), 1991.

"Commitments, Equity and Mechanisms," *ECO: Climate Talks NGO Newsletter* (February 27, 1992): 3.

Independent NGO Evaluations of National Plans for Climate Change Mitigation. (Washington, DC: CAN), 1995.

"Will the World's Ministers of the Environment Respond to the Science?" *US-CAN Hotline* (June 1996): 6.

"Patrick Michaels: A Correction," *ECO: Climate Talks NGO Newsletter* (July 16, 1996): 3.

Cline, William R. *Global Warming: The Economic Stakes.* (Washington, DC: Institute for International Economics), 1992.

The Economics of Global Warming. (Washington, DC: Institute for International Economics), 1992.

Global Warming: Estimating the Economic Benefits of Abatement. (Paris: OECD), 1992.

Coalition for Clean Air. *What Every Californian Should Know About Air Pollution and Health* (2006). http://www.coalitionforcleanair.org/air-pollution-10facts.html.

Coase, R. H. "The Problem of Social Cost," *Journal of Law & Economics*, v. 3, n. 1 (Fall 1960): 1–44.

Coequyt, John, Richard Wiles, & Christopher Campbell. *Above the Law: How the Government Lets Major Air Polluters off the Hook.* Environmental Working Group Report (May 1999).

Colborn, Theo, Dianne Dumanoski, & John Peterson Myers. *Our Stolen Future.* (NY: Dutton), 1996.

Collins, Craig. *Interview with John Topping, Jr., Climate Institute President* (August 25, 1991).

Collins, Craig. *Interview with Navroz Durbash (EDF) and Annie Roncerel (CAN Coordinator-Europe)* (January 21, 1992).

Interview with Sherwood F. Rowland (May 10, 1991).

Coalitions to Consensus: A Comparative Analysis of Stratospheric Ozone and Climate Change Negotiations (PhD thesis: UC Davis), 2000.

"Comment Welcome on Mexican Spotted Owl Habitat Reports," *Environmental News Service* (March 29, 2004).

Committee on Scientific Issues & the Endangered Species Act, National Research Council. *Science and the Endangered Species Act.* (Washington, DC: National Academy Press), 1995. http://www.nap.edu/readingroom/books/esa/executive.html.

Commoner, Barry. *The Politics of Energy.* (NY: Knopf), 1979.

Making Peace with the Planet. (NY: Pantheon), 1990.

Congressional Budget Office. *Carbon Charges as a Response to Global Warming: The Effects of Taxing Fossil Fuels.* US Congress (August 1990).

"Congressional Ozone & Climate Hearings," EcoNet (December 25, 1995).

Congressional Research Service (CRS). *History of the Water Pollution Control Act Amendments of 1972*, ser 1, 93rd Congress, 1st session (1972).

Cook, Elizabeth. "Global Environmental Advocacy: Citizen Activism in Protecting the Ozone Layer," *AMBIO* **19** (1990): 334–8.

Coppolino, Eric. "Pandora's Poison," *Synthesis/Regeneration* (Summer 1995). http://www.greens.org/s-r/078/07-50.html.

Corn, David. "McCain's Nuclear Waste," *Mother Jones* (March 4, 2008). http://www.motherjones.com/washington_dispatch/2008/03/john-mccain-nuclear-waste.html.

Costner, Pat. *The Incineration of Dioxin in Jacksonville, Arkansas: A Review of Trial Burns and Related Air Monitoring at VERTAC Site Contractors Incinerator, Jacksonville AR.* (Washington, DC: Greenpeace Toxics Campaign), January 29, 1992.

Cottin, Heather. "EPA and City Ignore Dangers," *Workers' World News* (MaCrch 7, 2002). http://www.mail-archive.com/wwnews@wwpublish.com/msg01518.html.

Countryman, Carol. "Getting the Lead Out – West Dallas, TX, Lead Contamination," *The Progressive* (November 1993). HighBeam Research (November 11, 2009). http://www.highbeam.com/doc/1G1-14233497.html.

Crawford, Mark. "United States Floats Proposal to Prevent Global Ozone Depletion," *Science*, v. **46** (November 1986): 927.

Crean, Ellen. "Toxic Secret: Alabama Town Was Never Warned of Contamination," CBS: *60 Minutes* (August 31, 2003). http://www.cbsnews.com/stories/2002/11/07/60minutes/main528581.shtml.

Cronin, John & Robert F. Kennedy Jr. *The Riverkeepers.* (NY: Simon & Schuster), 1999.

CSPAN *Congressional Chronicle (Text from Congressional Record). omments of Rep. Dana Rohrabacher on the Omnibus Civilian Science Authorization Act of 1995.* http://www.c-spanarchives.org/congress/?q=node/77531&id=6957511.

Cushman, J. H. "Spending Bill Would Reverse Nation's Environmental Policy," *New York Times* (September 22, 1995): 1.

Daly, Herman. *Beyond Growth: the Economics of Sustainable Development.* (Boston, MA: Beacon Press), 1996.

Darman, Richard. *Keeping America First: American Romanticism and the Global Economy.* Second Annual Albert H. Gordon Lecture, Harvard University. (Washington, DC: Office of Management & Budget), 1990.

Darmstadter, Joel. *The Economic Cost of CO2 Mitigation: A Review of Estimates for Selected World Regions.* (Washington, DC: Resources for the Future, Discussion Paper ENR91–06), 1991.

Dauncey, Guy, Patrick Mazza, & Ross Gelbspan. *Stormy Weather.* (British Colombia: New Society Publishers), 2001.

Davidson, Bob & Jeff Curtis. "The Endangered Species Act: 30 Years on the Ark," *Open Spaces* (September 13, 2004). http://www.open-spaces.com/article-v5n3-davison.php.

Davidson, Keay. "Global Warming Menaces the West," *San Francisco Chronicle* (April 12, 1998): A-1.

Davis, Derva. *When Smoke Ran Like Water.* (NY: Basic Books), 2002.

Deal, Carl. *The Greenpeace Guide to Anti-Environmental Organizations.* (Berkeley, CA: Odonian Press), 1993.

"Death of Animals Laid to Chemical," *New York Times* (August 28, 1974): 36.

Department of Energy, Interagency Task Force. *Economics of Long-Term Global Climate Change: A Preliminary Assessment.* Department of Energy (September 1990).

U.S. Department of Energy, Deputy Undersecretary for Policy Planning & Analysis. *Limiting Net Greenhouse Gases in the United States.* (Washington, DC: US Department of Energy, Office of Environmental Analysis), 1991.

Department of the Interior/Fish & Wildlife Service. "Endangered and Threatened Wildlife and Plants; Final Designation of Critical Habitat for the Topeka Shiner," Final Rule (Part II), *Federal Register Rules & Regulations* **69** (143) (July 27, 2004). http://mountain-prairie. fws.gov/species/fish/shiner/FRtshinerfinalCH.pdf.

Department of Justice (press release). "U.S. Sues Electric Utilities in Unprecedented Action to Enforce the Clean Air Act: Complaints Filed After One of the Largest Enforcement Investigations in EPA History" (November 3, 1999). http://www.usdoj.gov/opa/pr/1999/November/524enr.htm.

Diamond, Jared. *Collapse*. (NY: Viking), 2005.

"Dioxin: The Orange Resource Book." *Synthesis/Regeneration* (Summer 1995). http://www. greens.org/s-r/07–8toc.html.

"Dioxin Puts Dow on the Spot," *Time/CNN OnLine* (May 2, 1983). http://www.time.com/time/magazine/article/0,9171,953860–1,00.html.

Doniger, David D. "The Politics of the Ozone Layer," *Issues in Science & Technology*, v. **4**, n. 3 (Spring 1988): 89.

Dornbusch, Rudiger & James M. Poterba, ed. *Global Warming: Economic Policy Responses*. (Cambridge, MA: MIT Press), 1991.

Dowd, Maureen. "Lonely at the EPA Top," *CNN/Time OnLine* (March 14, 1883). http://www. time.com/time/magazine/article/0,9171,951954,00.html.

Dubose, Louis. "Whacked by Whitman," *The Texas Observer* (May 24, 2002).

Dudek, Daniel J. & Alice LeBlanc. "Offsetting New CO2 Emissions: A Rational First Greenhouse Policy Step," *Contemporary Policy Issues*, v. **8** (July 1990): 29–42.

Duhigg, Charles. "Toxic Waters," *New York Times* (September 13, 2009). http://projects. nytimes.com/toxic-waters.

Dunn, Seth. "After Kyoto: A Climate Treaty with No Teeth?" *World Watch* (March/April 1998): 33.

Durant, Robert F. *The Administrative Presidency Revisited*. (Albany, NY: State University of New York Press), 1992.

Earth justice (press release). "Judge Orders Cattle off Mexican Spotted Owl Habitat" (December 12, 2002). http://www.earthjustice.org/accomplishments/display.html?ID=142.

   "Stopping the Rollback of New Source Review" (July 21, 2006). http://www.earthjustice.org/policy/rider/display.html?ID=12#one.

   "House Rejects Bush Administration's Misguided Water Policy" (August 11, 2006). http://www.earthjustice.org/our_work/victory/house-rejects-bush-administrations-misguided-water-policy.html.

Easterbrook, Gregg. "Another Overstated NY Times Magazine Story," *The New Republic Online* (Easterblogg: April 5, 2004). http://209.212.93.14/easterbrook.mhtml?week=2004–03-30.

Edwin L. Miller Jr. San Diego District Attorney. *Final Report, Waste Management, Inc.* (Citizen's Clearinghouse for Hazardous Waste, March 1992). http://www.stopwmx.org/miller.html.

"Endangered Species Act Endangered," *Green Earth Journal* (December 22, 2000).

Endangered Species Coalition. *In-depth Look: Endangered Species Act*. http://www.stopextinction. org/cgi-bin/giga.cgi?cmd=cause_dir_custom&page=indepth&cause_id=1704.

Engels, Freidrich. *The Condition of the Working Class in England: From Personal Observation and Authentic Sources*. (Moscow: Progress Publishers), 1973.

"Enviro Enforcement Under Obama," Enviro BLR.com (July 14, 2009). http://enviro.blr.com/news.aspx?id=106318.

Environmental Integrity Project (U.S. Newswire press release). "EIP Data: Pollution Enforcement Efforts Under Bush Administration's EPA Drop on Four Out of Five Key Fronts," Washington, DC (May 23, 2007).

Environmental Technology Council. "Hazardous Waste Incineration: Advanced Technology to Protect the Environment," *Hazardous Waste Resource Center.* http://amser.org/AMSER–ResourceFrame.php?resourceId=1193.

Environmental Working Group Report (EWG). *Power Plants Caught Cheating* (November 3, 1999). http://www.ewg.org/reports/powerplants/powerplants.html.

"The Most Poorly Tested Chemicals in the World," *The Chemical Industry Archives* (March 27, 2009). http://www.chemicalindustryarchives.org/factfiction/testing.asp.

"The Asbestos Epidemic in America," *Understanding Asbestos (section 1)*. http://reports.ewg.org/reports/asbestos/facts/fact1.php.

"Something in the Air: The Asbestos Document Story," *Understanding Asbestos (section 3)*. http://reports.ewg.org/reports/asbestos/facts/fact3.php.

Environmental Working Group/Friends of the Earth. *Clean Water Report Card: Falling Grades* (March 2000).

Environmental Working Group/PIRG Report. *Moneyed Waters: Political Contributions & the Attack on the Clean Water Act* (1995).

"EPA Affirms Health Dangers from Dioxin," *New York Times* (September 13, 1994). http://query.nytimes.com/gst/fullpage.html?sec=health&res=9C00E6DA143BF930A2575AC0A962958260.

Epstein, Samuel. *The Politics of Cancer.* (NY: East Ridge Press), 1998.

"Europeans Debate Macroeconomic Effects of Energy/CO2 Tax," *Energy Economics and Climate Change* 2 (2) (1992): 2–5.

Evans-Prichard, Ambrose. "Cheap Solar Power Poised to Undercut Oil and Gas by Half," *Telegraph Co, UK* (February 18, 2007). http://www.telegraph.co.uk/money/main.jhtml?xml=/money/2007/02/19/ccview19.xml.

Extended Producer Responsibility Working Group. *Extended Producer Responsibility: A Prescription for Clean Production, Pollution Prevention and Zero Waste* (July 2003). http://www.grrn.org/epr/epr_principles.html.

"Exxon Mobil Takes First Steps to Accept Climate Change Science and Cut Funding of the Denial Machine," *Climate Science Watch* (January 27, 2007). http://www.climatescience watch.org/index.php/csw/details/exxon-mobil-first-steps1/.

Fagin, Dan & Marianne Lavelle. *Toxic Deception.* (Monroe, MN: Common Courage), 1999.

Farman, Joseph, B. G. Gardiner, and J. D. Shanklin. "Large Loses of Total Ozone in Antarctica Reveal Seasonal ClOx/NOx Interaction," *Nature* 315 (June 1985): 207–10.

Fidis, Alex. *Empty Pockets: Facing Hurricane Katrina with a Bankrupt Superfund* (U.S. PIRG), December 2005.

Fiorino, Daniel J. *Making Environmental Policy.* (Berkeley, CA: University of California Press), 1995.

"First Ocean Acidification Lawsuit Filed Against EPA," *Environment News Service* (May 14, 2009). http://www.ens-newswire.com/ens/may2009/2009-05-14-091.asp.

Fischlowitz-Roberts, Bernie. "Air Pollution Fatalities Now Exceed Traffic Fatalities by 3 to 1," *Earth Policy Institute* (September 17, 2002). http://www.earth-policy.org/Updates/Update17.htm.

Flavin, Christopher & Nicholas Lenssen. "Saving the Climate Saves Money," *World Watch* (November/December 1990): 26.

Flavin, Christopher & Odil Tunali. "Getting Warmer: Looking for a Way Out of the Climate Impasse," *World Watch* (March/April 1995): 10.

Forrester, Keith E. & Richard W. Goodwin. "Engineering Management of MSW Ashes: Field Empirical Observations of Concrete-like Characteristics," Theodore G. Brna & Raymond Klicius, eds. *Proceedings International Conference on Municipal Waste Combustion (vol. 1)* (Hollywood, FL, April 11–14, 1989): 5–16.

Fortson, Danny. "Stern Warns That Climate Change is Far Worse Than 2006 Estimate," *The Independent* (April 17, 2008). http://www.independent.co.uk/news/business/news/stern-warns-that-climate-change-is-far-worse-than-2006-estimate-810488.html.

Friends of the Earth (FoE). "Developing Nations Press for Ozone Fund," *Atmosphere* 2 (3) (1989): 2.

"Initial Talks on Protocol Amendments Grim," *Atmosphere* 2 (3) (1989): 3.

"Are Flammable Refrigerants Worth the Risk?," *Atmosphere* 2 (4) (1990): 6.

Friends of the Earth-UK. "Funding Change: Developing Countries & the Montreal Protocol," *Friends of the Earth International* (June 1990).

Gelbspan, Ross. *Boiling Point: How Politicians, Big Oil and Coal, Journalist and Activists Have Fueled the Climate Crisis – and What We Can Do to Avert Disaster.* (NY: Basic Books), 2004.

"Global Carbon Trading Won't Work," *Innovation* (August/September 2008). http://www.innovation-america.org/index.php?articleID=455.

Gibb, Tom. "A Terrible Waste Gets a Long Look," *Post Gazette News* (June 11, 2000). http://www.post-gazette.com/healthscience/20000611sludge4.asp.

Gibbs, Lois Marie. *Love Canal: The Story Continues.* (British Colombia: New Society Publishers), 1998.

"Learning from Love Canal: A 20th Anniversary Retrospective," *Orion Afield* (Spring 1998). http://arts.envirolink.org/arts_and_activism/LoisGibbs.html.

Glantz, Michael H., Martin F. Price, & Maria E. Krenz. *Report of the Workshop 'On Assessing Winners & Losers in the Context of Global Warming'. National Center for Atmospheric Research.* Environmental & Societal Impacts Group (June 18–21, 1990).

Global Climate Coalition. *Comments of the Global Climate Coalition on the National Energy Strategy.* (Washington, DC: GCC), 1990.

A Reasoned Approach to Global Climate Change. (Washington, DC: GCC), 1991.

Greenhouse Gas Emissions: Trends and Policy Options. (Washington, DC: GCC), 1991.

G M Watch. "Monsanto's Campaign Against Rachel Carson" (May 27, 2007). http://www.gmwatch.org/latest-listing/1-news-items/4681-monsantos-campaign-against-rachel-carson-.

Goetze, Darren. "Geneva Breakthrough: World Leaders Endorse Stronger Climate Treaty," *No Sweat News* (Fall 1996): 1.

Goldfrank, Walter L., David Goodman, & Andrew Szasz, eds. *Ecology and the World-System.* (Westport, CT: Greenwood Press), 1999.

Gonzalez, Juan. *Fallout: The Environmental Consequences of the World Trade Center Collapse.* (NY: W. W. Norton & Co.), 2002.

Government Accounting Office. *Issues Raised by the Reorganization of EPA's Ombudsman Function.* Report to the Honorable Diana DeGette, House of Representatives (October 31, 2002).

Government Accountability Project (Press Release). "Whistleblower Group Calls for Congressional Probe of EPA Leadership: GAO Exposes False Statements in Court" (November 14, 2002). http://www.whistleblower.org/article.php?did=173&scid=108.

Graham, John D. & Jonathan B. Wiener. *Risk vs. Risk: Tradeoffs in Protecting Health and the Environment.* (Cambridge, MA: Harvard University Press), 1997.

Green, Bill. "Congress: Policies on Global Warming and Ozone Depletion," *Environment* (April 1987): 5.

Greenpeace (video). *Rush to Burn* (1988).

Greenpeace. *Fact Sheet: American Enterprise Institute for Public Policy Research*. http://www. exxonsecrets.org/html/orgfactsheet.php?id=9.

The Climate Time Bomb. (Amsterdam, The Netherlands: Stichting Greenpeace Council), 1994.

Types of Incineration. http://www.greenpeace.org/international/campaigns/toxics/incineration/types-of-incineration.

Greenpeace Report. *Oiling the Machine: Fossil Fuel Dollars Funneled into the US Political Process* (October 20, 1997). http://archive.greenpeace.org/climate/kindustry/government/machine.html.

Greenpeace. "Exxon Still Funding Climate Change Deniers," *Greenpeace News* (May 18, 2007). http://www.greenpeace.org/usa/news/exxonsecrets-2007.

"Exxon is Pumping Out Lies," *Greenpeace News* (May 18, 2007). http://www.greenpeace.org/usa/news/exxonsecrets-2007.

"Juggling the Greenhouse Numbers," *Greenpeace Magazine* (May/June 1991): 4.

Greenpeace European Unit (press release). "First REACH Hazardous Chemicals List is a Drop in the Ocean" (October 28, 2008). http://www.greenpeace.org/eu-unit/press-centre/press-releases2/First-REACH-hazardous-chemicals-list-is-a-drop-in-the-ocean.

Griffin, Ginger L. *The TSCA Compliance Handbook*, 3rd ed. (NY: Wiley), 1996.

Griscom, Amanda. "Jumping Ship at the EPA," *Grist Magazine* (January 7, 2004).

"The EPA's Revolving Door," Salon.com (April 30, 2004). http://dir.salon.com/story/opinion/feature/2004/04/30/muck_epa/print.html.

Grunwald, Michael. "Confidential: Read & Destroy," *Washington Post* (January 1, 2001). http://www.mindfully.org/Industry/Monsanto-PCBs-Anniston.htm.

Guerro, Peter. "House Subcommittee to Hear Debate Over Climate Models," *Global Change* (November 1995): 8.

Haas, Peter M. *Saving the Mediterranean: The Politics of International Environmental Cooperation*. (NY: Columbia University Press), 1990.

"Banning Chlorofluorocarbons: Epistemic Community Efforts to Protect Stratospheric Ozone," *International Organization*, v. 46 (Winter 1992): 187–224.

Hackett, Steven C. *Environmental and Natural Resources Economics: Theory, Policy, and the Sustainable Society*, 2nd ed. (Armonk, NY: M. E. Sharpe), 2001.

Hanes, Spencer G. Jr. "Is Toxic Sludge Good for You?" *Vermont Journal of Environmental Law* (October 30, 2003). http://www.vjel.org/editorials/ED10039.html.

Hansen, Brian. "Removal of EPA Investigator Called Political Revenge: Why Gore Really Lost Ohio," *Environmental News Service* (December 18, 2000). http://www.mapcruzin.com/news/news121900a.htm.

"Critics Say EPA Needs Independent Oversight," *Environmental News Service* (September 25, 2002). http://www.agrnews.org/issues/90/environment.html.

Hardin, Garrett. "The Tragedy of the Commons," *Science* 162 (September 1968): 1243–8.

"Political Requirements for Preserving Our Common Heritage," H. P. Bokaw, ed. *Wildlife in America*. (Washington, DC: Council on Environmental Quality), 1978.

Harremoes, Gee, et al., eds. *The Precautionary Principle in the 20th Century: Late Lessons from Early Warnings*. (London: Earthscan Publications Ltd.), 2002.

Harrison, E. Z., M. B. McBride, & D. R. Bouldin. "Land Application of Sewage Sludges: An Appraisal of the US Regulations," *International Journal on Environment & Pollution* 11 (1) (1999): 1–36. http://cwmi.css.cornell.edu/PDFS/LandApp.pdf.

Harrison, Oakes, Matthew Hysell, & Antony Hay. "Review: Organic Chemicals in Sewage Sludges," *Science of the Total Environment* 367 (2006): 481–97. http://cwmi.css.cornell.edu/Sludge.html.

Hattam, Jennifer. "No Habitat, No Problem," *Sierra* (July/August 2002). http://www.sierraclub.org/sierra/200207/lol.asp.

Hawken, Paul. *The Ecology of Commerce*. (NY: Harper/Collins), 1994.

Hawken, Paul, Amory Lovins, & L. Hunter Lovins. *Natural Capitalism*. (Boston, MA: Back Bay Books), 2008.

Hayes, Dennis. "Earth Day 2000: End Global Warming," *TIMELINE* (No. 50; March/April 2000 – email edition). http://www.globalcommunity.org/cgpub/50/50.htm.

Hayes, Rich. "Sleepless in Kyoto," *Nucleus* (January 1998): 8.

Hayter, Teresa. *Aid as Imperialism*. (NY: Penguin), 1971.

Heinberg, Richard. *The Party's Over: Oil, War and the Fate of Industrial Societies*, 4th ed. (Canada: New Society Publishers), 2008.

Helmy, Eric. "Teeth for a Paper Tiger: Redressing the Deficiencies of the Recovery Provisions of the Endangered Species Act," *Environmental Law* (September 22, 2000). http://www.accessmylibrary.com/article-1G1-70393144/teeth-paper-tiger-redressing.html.

Hertsgaard, Mark. "Conflict of Interest for Christie Todd Whitman?," Salon.com (January 14, 2002). http://www.salon.com/politics/feature/2002/01/14/whitman/print.html.

Hoban, Thomas More & Richard Oliver Brooks. *Green Justice: The Environment and the Courts*, 2nd ed. (Boulder, CO: Westview Press), 1996.

Hoffman, A. J. "An Uneasy Rebirth at Love Canal," *Environment* (March 1995): 4–31.

Hogue, Cheryl. "The Future of U.S. Chemical Regulation: Two Views on Whether Current Law Overseeing Commercial Chemicals in the U.S. is Tough Enough," *Chemical & Engineering News* (January 8, 2007). http://pubs.acs.org/cen/government/85/8502regulation.html.

"Change is Coming: Converging Forces Spur Modernization of U.S. Chemical Control Law," *Chemical & Engineering News* (March 16, 2009). http://pubs.acs.org/cen/government/87/8711gov3.html.

House Committee on Resources (Richard W. Pombo, Chairman). *The ESA at 30: A Mandate for Modernization* (April 2004).

"Hudson River PCBs," *Riverkeepers*. http://www.riverkeeper.org/campaigns/stop-polluters/contaminated-sites/pcbs/.

Hurley, Brad. "Skeptics on Climate Change," *Energy and Climate Information Exchange Digest* 2 (6) (1992): 3.

Hyder, Teriq. "Climate Negotiations: The North/South Perspective," Irving Mintzer, ed. *Confronting Climate Change*. (Cambridge, MA: Cambridge University Press), 1992.

IFIAS/ISSC/UNU/UNESCO. *Climate Change and Energy Policy in Developing Countries: Report of an International Workshop in Montebello*, Québec. Human Dimension of Global Change (July 29–August 1, 1990).

"Industrial Group Plans to Battle Climate Treaty," *The New York Times* (April 26, 1998). http://www.nytimes.com/1998/04/26/us/industrial-group-plans-to-battle-climate-treaty.html.

InfoPlease. *U.S. Population by State, 1790 to 2008* (2009). http://www.infoplease.com/ipa/A0004986.html.

InsideEPA.com. "Activists' Suits Successfully Target States' Title 5 Permit Delays," *Clean Air Report* (May 23, 2002). http://www.ocefoundation.org/completed.html#bayarea.

IPCC. *Intergovernmental Panel on Climate Change: First Assessment Report* (August 31, 1990).

IPCC (Working Group I). *Scientific Assessment of Climate Change* (June 1990).

IPCC (Working Group II). *Potential Impacts of Climate Change* (June 1990).

IPCC/WMO/UNEP. *Report of the First Session of the IPCC*. Geneva (1988).

Ivester, David. "Critical Habitat" Should Promote Recovery, Not Just Survival, of Endangered Species, Says Court," *Stoles Rives* (March 1, 2002). http://www.stoel.com/resources/articles/environment/news-mar01-2.shtm.

Jennings, Humphrey. *Pandemonium 1660–1886: The Coming of the Machine as Seen by Contemporary Observers.* (NY: The Free Press), 1985.

Johnson, Jeff. "EPA's Top Cops Resign," *Chemical & Engineering News* (January 12, 2004). http://pubs.acs.org/cen/topstory/8202/8202notw6.html.

Joshua, Frank. "The Pentagon is America's Biggest Polluter," *AlterNet* (May 12, 2008). http://www.alternet.org/healthwellness/85186/.

Kasperson, Roger E. & Kirstin M. Dow. "Developmental & Geographical Equity in Global Environmental Change: A Framework for Analysis," *Evaluation Review* (Winter 1991): 149–69.

Kennedy, Robert F. Jr. *Congressional Testimony on the Clean Water Act* (October 8, 2002).

Kennedy, Robert F. Jr. *Crimes Against Nature.* (NY: Harper/Collins), 2004.

Keohane, Robert O. & Joseph S. Nye, ed. *Transnational Relations and World Politics.* (Cambridge, MA: Harvard University Press), 1981.

    Power and Interdependence: World Politics in Transition, 2nd ed. (Boston, MA: Little-Brown), 1989.

Kindleberger, Charles P. *The International Economic Order.* (Cambridge, MA: MIT Press), 1988.

Kjellen, Bo. "A Personal Assessment," Irving Mintzer & J. A. Leonard, eds. *Negotiating Climate Change.* (Cambridge, MA: Cambridge University Press), 1994: 149–74.

Knoz, Kenneth A. (Asst. Inspector for Audit, Office of the Inspector General, EPA). *Memorandum to Linda J. Fischer, Asst. Administrator for Prevention, Pesticides, and Toxic Substances, EPA* (September 30, 1992).

Kopel, David B. "Burning Mad: The Controversy Over Treatment of Hazardous Waste in Incinerators, Boilers, and Industrial Furnaces," *Environmental Law Reporter* (April 1993): 10216–27. http://davekopel.org/env/ipincine.htm.

Kovalic, J. M. *The Clean Water Act of 1987,* 2nd ed. (Alexandria, VA: Water Environment Federation), 1987.

Kraft, Michael. *Environmental Policy and Politics,* 3rd ed. (NY: Pearson/Longman), 2004.

Krause, Floertin. *Energy Policy in the Greenhouse: Cutting Carbon Emissions, Burden or Benefit?* (El Cerrito, CA: Dutch Ministry of Housing, Physical Planning and Environment & the International Project for Sustainable Development), 1996.

Kubasek, Nancy & Gary Silverman. *Environmental Law,* 5th ed. (NY: Prentice Hall), 2005.

Kurpis, Lauren. "Facts About Endangered Species," EndangeredSpecie.com http://www.endangeredspecie.com/Interesting_Facts.htm.

Landy, Marc K., Marc Roberts, & Stephen R. Thomas. *The Environmental Protection Agency: Asking the Wrong Questions from Nixon to Clinton.* (NY: Oxford University Press), 1994.

Lapp, David. "Defenders of Dioxin: The Corporate Campaign to Rehabilitate Dioxin," *Multinational Monitor* (October 1991). http://multinationalmonitor.org/hyper/issues/1991/10/lapp.html.

Lappé, Frances Moore, Joseph Collins, & David Kinley. *Aid as Obstacle.* (Oakland, CA: Institute for Food and Policy Development), 1975.

Lashof, Daniel A. (NRDC). "Country Report: USA," CAN-US & Europe, ed. *Independent NGO Evaluations of National Plans for Climate Change Mitigation (OECD Countries).* (Washington, DC: Climate Action Network), 1995.

    "Country Report: USA," CAN-US & Europe, ed. "IPCC Second Assessment Report," *US Climate Action Network Hotline* (January 1996): 1–2.

Lavelle, Marianne. "EPA's Amnesty Has Become a Mixed Blessing," *The National Law Journal* (February 24, 1997): A1, A18.

Layton, Lyndsey. "Pentagon Fights EPA on Pollution Cleanup," *Washington Post* (June 30, 2008). http://www.truthout.org/article/pentagon-fights-epa-pollution-cleanup.

Lazarus, Richard. *The Making of Environmental Law*. (Chicago, IL: University of Chicago Press), 2004.

Leaky, Richard & Roger Lewin. *The Sixth Extinction*. (NY: Doubleday), 1995. http://www.well.com/user/davidu/sixthextinction.html.

Lee, Jennifer. "White House Sway is Seen in EPA Response to 9–11," *New York Times* (August 8, 2003). http://www.732-2m2m.com/tt/2003-05_articles.htm.

Leggett, Jeremy, ed. *Global Warming: The Greenpeace Report*. (NY: Oxford University Press), 1990.

Leggett, Jeremy. "Global Warming: The Worst Case," *Bulletin of the Atomic Scientists* **85** (1992): 28–32.

Lehr, Jay H., ed. *Rational Readings on Environmental Concerns*. (NY: Van Nostrand Reinhold), 1992.

Leistner, Marilyn. "The Times Beach Story," excerpted from: *Proceedings of the Third Annual Hazardous Materials Management Conference*. Philadelphia, PA (June 4–6, 1985). http://www.greens.org/s-r/078/07-09.html.

Lerner, Steve. "North Meets South," *Amicus Journal* (Winter 1992): 18–21.
    Earth Summit: Conversations with Architects of an Ecologically Sustainable Future. (Bolinas, CA: Common Knowledge Press), 1992.

Leroux, Kivi. "Clearing the Way for Zero Waste," *Resource Recycling* (March 15, 2001). http://www.precaution.org/lib/05/rpr16.htm#Clearing_the_Way_for_Zero_Waste.

Lester, Stephen U. "Industry's 'True Lies': The Politics Behind the Scientific Debate on Dioxin," *Consumer Law Page*. http://www.safe2use.com/pesticides/truelies.htm.

Lewis,, Barry. "Biodiversity: Why Should We Care? What Does it Mean?" *Academy of Natural Sciences* (January 1997). http://www.acnatsci.org/education/kye/nr/biodiv1.html.

Liane C. Casten. "EPA Collusion with Industry," *Synthesis/Regeneration* (Summer 1995). http://www.mindfully.org/Air/Dioxin-EPA-Industry-Collusion.htm.

Lilley, Sasha. "Green Fuel's Dirty Secret," *CorpWatch* (June 1, 2006). http://www.corpwatch.org/article.php?id=13646.

Lindzen, Richard S. *Reasons for Questioning Global Warming Predictions*. CATO Institute Conference on Global Environmental Crises: Science or Politics? (Washington, DC, June 5–6, 1991).

Lipschutz, Ronnie D. & Judith H. Mayer. *Global Civil Society and Global Environmental Governance: The Politics of Nature from Place to Planet*. (Albany, NY: SUNY Press), 1996.

Lipsett, Brian. "BFI: The Sludge of the Waste Industry," *Multinational Monitor* (June 1990). http://multinationalmonitor.org/hyper/issues/1990/06/lipset.html.

Lipsett, Brian & Ellen Connett. "Jackson Stephens – Father of WTI," *Free Republic. com a Conservative News Forum* (July 1, 1997). http://www.freerepublic.com/forum/a37d95a0809ce.htm.

Litfin, Karen. *Power & Knowledge in International Environmental Relations: The Case of Stratospheric Ozone Depletion* (PhD thesis: University of California, Los Angeles), 1991.
    Ozone Discourses: Science and Politics in Global Environmental Cooperation (NY: Columbia University Press), 1994.

Livernash, Robert. "The Growing Influence of NGOs in the Developing World," *Environment* (June 1992): 12.

Lombardi, Kristen. "Sick of Being Lied to by the EPA, 9–11 Plaintiffs Use the Courts to Force the Answers They Seek," *The Village Voice* (February 21, 2006). http://www.villagevoice.com/2006–02–14/news/truth-out/.

Loske, Reinhard. "Ecological Taxes, Energy Policy & Greenhouse Gas Reductions: A German Perspective," *The Ecologist* (August 1991): 173.

Love, Dennis. *My City Was Gone.* (NY: William Morrow), 2006.

Lovins, Amory. "The Role of Energy Efficiency," Jeremy Leggett, ed. *Global Warming: The Greenpeace Report.* (NY: Oxford University Press), 1990.

Lovins, Amory B., et al. *Winning the Oil End Game: Innovation for Profits, Jobs, and Security.* (London, Colorado: Rocky Mountain Institute, Earthscan), 2005. www.oilendgame.org.

Lovins, Amory & Imran Sheikh. "The Nuclear Illusion," *AMBIO* (November 8, 2008). http://www.rmi.org/images/PDFs/Energy/E08-01_AmbioNucIllusion.pdf.

Lowell Center for Sustainable Production. "The Promise and Limits of the United States Toxic Substances Control Act," University of Massachusetts (October 10, 2003). http://www.chemicalspolicy.org/downloads/Chemicals_Policy_TSCA.doc.

MacDonald, Gordon J. "Technology Transfer: The Climate Change Challenge," *Journal of Environment & Development,* v. 1 (Winter 1992): 1–40.

Machta, Lester. "Ozone and its Enemies," *NOAA Magazine* (January 1976): 5.

Makhijani, Arjun. "Still Working on the Ozone Hole," *Technology Review* (May–June 1990): 53–9.

Makhijani, Arjun & Kevin R. Gurney. *Mending the Ozone Hole.* (Cambridge, MA: MIT Press), 1995.

Manne, Anne S. & R. G. Richels. *Global CO2 Emissions Reductions – Impacts of Rising Energy Costs.* (Menlo Park, CA: Electric Power Research Institute), 1990.

Buying Greenhouse Insurance: The Economic Costs of Carbon Dioxide Emission Limits. (Cambridge, MA: MIT Press), 1992.

Marcus, Adam. "Scientists Modify Plants to Remove Environmental Toxins," *Genome News Network* (October 18, 2002). http://www.genomenewsnetwork.org/articles/10_02/plant_arsenic.php.

Markowitz, Gerald & David Rosner. *Deceit and Denial: The Deadly Politics of Industrial Pollution.* (Berkeley, CA: University of California Press), 2002.

Martin, Robert J. *Statement of Robert J. Martin Before the US Senate Committee on Environment and Public Works* (June 25, 2002). http://epw.senate.gov/107th/Martin_062502.htm.

Maxwell, James H. & Sanford L. Weiner. "Green Consciousness or Dollar Diplomacy? The British Response to the Threat of Ozone Depletion," *International Environmental Affairs,* v. 5 (Winter 1993): 19–41.

Mazza, Partick. "Global Warming and the Pacific Northwest: Perpetual El Niño," *Atmosphere Alliance* (December 1997).

"El Niño's Growing Ferocity: Ocean in the Greenhouse?" *Atmosphere Alliance* (March 1998).

McGregor, Douglas B. & others. "An IARC Evaluation of Polychlorinated Dibenzo-P-dioxins and Polychlorinated Dibenzofurans as Risk Factors in Human Carcinogenesis," *Environmental Health Perspectives,* v. 106, suppl. 2 (April 1998): 755–60.

McHugh, Josh. "Chemicals," *Forbes* (January 13, 1991): 118.

Mertes, Tom. *Movement of Movements.* (London: Verso), 2004.

Meyer-Abich, Klaus M. "Winners & Losers in Climate Change," Wolfgang Sachs, ed. *Global Ecology: A New Arena of Political Conflict.* (London: Zed Books), 1993.

Michaels, David. "Doubt is Their Product: Industry Groups Are Fighting Government Regulation by Fomenting Scientific Uncertainty," *Scientific American* (June 2005). http://www.scientificamerican.com/article.cfm?id=doubt-is-their-product.

Michaels, David & Celeste Monforton. "Scientific Evidence in the Regulatory System: Manufacturing Uncertainty and the Demise of the Formal Regulatory System," *Journal of Law and Policy*, v. **13**, n. 1 (February 7, 2005): 17–41.

Michaels, Patricia. "Clean Air Act Performance Statistics," Greennature.com (2007). http://green nature.com/article247.html.

Michaels, Patrick J. *The Political Science of Global Warming*. CATO Institute Conference on Global Environmental Crises: Science or Politics? (Washington, DC, June 5–6, 1991).

    Sound and Fury: The Science and Politics of Global Warming. (Washington, DC: CATO Institute), 1992.

Miller, Allan, Irving Mintzer, & Peter G. Brown. "Rethinking the Economics of Global Warming," *Issues in Science & Technology*, v. **7** (Fall 1990): 70–3.

Miller, Anthony B. & others. *Environmental Epidemiology, Volume 1: Public Health and Hazardous Wastes*. (Washington, DC: National Academy Press), 1991.

Millichamp, Gordon G. "Is Our Water Safe to Drink?" *NOHA News* (Fall 1995): 3–8. http://www.nutrition4health.org/nohanews/NNF95WaterSafeToDrink.htm.

Milne, Janet E. "Book Review: The European Carbon Tax: An Economic Assessment [Carlo Carraro & Dominico Siniscalco]," *International Environmental Affairs*, v. **94** (Winter 1995): 94.

Mintz, Joel A. *Enforcement at the EPA: High Stakes and Hard Choices*. (Austin, TX: University of Texas Press), 1995.

    "Treading Water: A Preliminary Assessment of EPA Enforcement During the Bush II Administration," *Environmental Law Review* **34** (October 2004): 10933–53.

Molina, Mario & F. Sherwood Rowland. "Stratospheric Sink for Chlorofluoromethanes: Chlorine Atom – Catalyzed Destruction of Ozone," *Nature* **249** (June 1974): 810–12.

Monforton, Celeste. "Public Health Calls for TSCA Reform," *The Pump Handle* (November 13, 2007). http://thepumphandle.wordpress.com/2007/11/13/public-health-calls-for-tsca-reform/.

Montague, Peter. "What We Must Do – Part 4: A License to Pollute," *Rachel's Hazardous Waste News* **91** (August 22, 1988). http://www.ejnet.org/rachel/rhwn091.htm.

    "What We Must Do – Part 5: Winning Corporate Strategies," *Rachel's Hazardous Waste News* **93** (September 5, 1988). http://www.ejnet.org/rachel/rhwn093.htm.

    "What We Must Do – Part 7: Toxics in Your Drinking Water – When Did People Know It Was Bad?" *Rachel's Hazardous Waste News* **97** (October 3, 1988). http://www.ejnet.org/rachel/rhwn097.htm.

    "Dioxin Part 2: Gauging the Toxicity," *Rachel's Environmental & Health Weekly* **173** (March 21, 1990). http://www.ejnet.org/rachel/rhwn173.htm.

    "Hazardous Waste Incineration in Cement Kilns: 'Recycler's' Paradise," *Rachel's Democracy & Health News* **174** (March 1990). http://www.rachel.org/en/node/4465.

    "Incinerator Ash – Part 2: All Wastes Must Go Somewhere Forever," *Rachel's Democracy and Health News* **190** (July 18, 1990). http://www.rachel.org/bulletin/bulletin.cfm?Issue_ID=1547.

    "Incinerator Ash – Part 4: Dump Now, Let the Children Pay Later," *Rachel's Democracy and Health Weekly* **192** (August 1, 1990). http://www.rachel.org/bulletin/bulletin.cfm?Issue_ID=943.

    "Citizens Slow Growth of Incineration," *Rachel's Democracy & Health News* **206** (November 1990). http://www.rachel.org/en/node/4246.

"EPA Chief Harassing Whistleblowers," *Rachel's Hazardous Waste News* **254** (October 9, 1991). http://www.ejnet.org/rachel/rhwn254.htm.

"EPA's New Landfill Rules Protect Only the Largest Garbage Haulers," *Rachel's Hazardous Waste News* **268** (January 15, 1992). http://www.ejnet.org/rachel/rhwn268.htm.

"All Hazardous Waste Incinerators Fail to Meet EPA Regulations, EPA Says," *Rachel's Hazardous Waste News* **280** (April 7, 1992). http://www.ejnet.org/rachel/rhwn280.htm.

"Hazardous Waste Incinerators: A Technology Out of Control?" *Rachel's Hazardous Waste News* **281** (April 15, 1992). http://www.ejnet.org/rachel/rhwn281.htm.

"The Recent History of Solid Waste: Good Alternatives Are Now Available," *Rachel's Hazardous Waste News* **289** (June 10, 1992). http://www.ejnet.org/rachel/rhwn289.htm.

"What Has Gone Wrong? Part 1: Congress Creates a Monster – the ATSDR," *Rachel's Hazardous Waste News* **292** (July 1, 1992). http://www.ejnet.org/rachel/rhwn292.htm.

"Corruption Out of Control in Arkansas," *Rachel's Democracy and Health News* **311** (November 12, 1992) & **345** (July 8, 1993). http://www.ejnet.org/rachel/rhwn345.htm; http://www.ejnet.org/rachel/rhwn311.htm.

"A Sea of Troubles Engulfs Incineration," *Rachel's Democracy and Health News* **325** (February 17, 1993). http://www.rachel.org/bulletin/index.cfm?issue_ID=804.

"Killing Science," *Rachel's Environment & Health Weekly* **462** (October 5, 1995). http://www.ejnet.org/rachel/rehw462.htm.

"On Regulation," *Rachel's Democracy & Health News* **538** (March 19, 1997). http://www.rachel.org/en/node/3903.

"WMI: A Culture of Fraud and Dishonesty," *Rachel's Democracy & Health News* **556** (July 24, 1997). http://www.rachel.org/bulletin/bulletin.cfm?Issue_ID=567.

"Why is EPA Ignoring Monsanto?" *Rachel's Environment & Health News* **563** (September 10, 1997). http://www.rachel.org/en/node/3878.

"The Precautionary Principle," *Rachel's Environmental & Health News* **586** (February 18, 1998). http://www.rachel.org/en/node/3850.

"Incinerator News," *Rachel's Democracy and Health News* **592** (April 2, 1998). http://www.rachel.org/BULLETIN/index.cfm?St=4.

"Answering the Critics of Precaution," *Rachel's Democracy & Health News* **790** (April 15, 2004). http://www.rachel.org/en/node/6464.

Moore, Curtis & Alan Miller. *Green Gold: Japan, Germany & the United States & the Race for Environmental Technology.* (Boston, MA: Beacon Press), 1994.

Morgan, Jennifer. "The Kyoto Protocol: The Devil's in the Details," *US Climate Action Network Hotline* (April 1998): 1.

Morreale, David J. *A Survey of Current Great Lakes Research.* University of Buffalo (July 2002). http://www.eng.buffalo.edu/glp/articles/review.htm.

Morrisette, Peter M. "The Evolution of Policy Responses to Stratospheric Ozone," *Natural Resources Journal,* v. **29** (Summer 1989): 794–820.

Motavalli, Jim. "Zero Waste: No Longer Content to Just Recycle Waste, Environmentalists Want Us to Reduce it to Nothing," *E Magazine* (April 1, 2001). http://www.emagazine.com/view/?506&printview&imagesoff.

Moyers, Bill. "Justice for Sale," *Frontline* (PBS: November 23, 1999). transcripts available: http://www.pbs.org/wgbh/pages/frontline/shows/justice/etc/script.html http://www.pbs.org/wgbh/pages/frontline/shows/justice/interviews/cook.html.

Trade Secrets: A Moyers Report (PBS: 2005). http://www.pbs.org/tradesecrets/.

Muller, Frank. "Mitigating Climate Change: The Case for Energy Taxes," *Environment* (March 1996): 12.

Mullins, Richard & Joaquin Sapien. "EPA Diverts Money from Shared Superfund Pool," *Center for Public Integrity* (May 10, 2007). http://www.publicintegrity.org/Superfund/report.aspx?aid=871.

Murray, James. "Exxon Shareholder Revolt Highlights Investor Climate Risks," *Business Green* (May 19, 2008). http://www.businessgreen.com/business-green/news/2216960/exxon-shareholder-revolt.

Myers, Nancy & Carolyn Raffensperger, eds. *Precautionary Tools for Reshaping Environmental Policy.* (Cambridge, MA: MIT Press), 2006.

"Nader on Water," *TIME* (April 26, 1971). http://www.yachtingnet.com/time/magazine/article/0,9171,902895,00.html.

Nadler, Jerrold (press release). "Nadler Blasts EPA on Firefighter Snub Demands Answers" (March 13, 2003). http://www.house.gov/nadler/archive108/FirefighterEPA_031203.htm.

Nadler, Jerrold & the NRDC (press release). "EPA's Earth Day Sham" (April 22, 2003). http://www.house.gov/nadler/archive108/EPAEarthDay_042203.htm.

(press release). "EPA's Earth Day Sham" (April 22, (press release). "Rep. Nadler Offers Assessment of Federal Response to 9–11 in Front of National Commission" (May 22, 2003).

Najam, Adil. "An Environmental Negotiation Strategy for the South," *International Environmental Affairs,* v. 7 (Summer 1995): 249–87.

Nanda, Ved P. "Stratospheric Ozone Depletion: A Challenge for International Environmental Law & Policy," *Michigan Journal of International Law,* v. 10 (Spring 1989): 482–525.

Nangle, Orval E. "Stratospheric Ozone: United States Regulation of Chlorofluorocarbons," *Boston College Environmental Affairs Law Review,* v. 16 (Spring 1989): 542–5.

Narayanswamy, Anupama. "Lobbying the EPA Takes Money – and Connections," *Center for Public Integrity* (April 26, 2007). http://www.publicintegrity.org/superfund/report.aspx?aid=852.

National Academy of Sciences. *Halocarbons: Effects on Stratospheric Ozone.* (Washington, DC: NAS), 1976.

Policy Implications of Greenhouse Warming. (Washington, DC: National Academy Press), 1991.

National Cement Kiln Coalition. *Myths and Facts About Protecting Human Health and the Environment: The Real Story About Burning Hazardous Waste in Cement Kilns.* http://www.downwindersatrisk.org/DARNCCKCMythsAndFactsAboutBurningHazardousWasteInCementKilns.htm.

National Environmental Trust. *Toxic Beginnings: Cancer Risks to Children from California's Air* (Executive Summary). http://www.mindfully.org/Air/2002/Cancer-Risks-Children-CA-AirSep02.htm.

National Research Council. *Stratospheric Ozone Depletion by Halocarbons: Chemistry & Transport.* (Washington, DC: National Academy Press), 1979.

Toxicity Testing. (Washington, DC: National Academy Press), 1984.

Waste Incineration and Public Health. (Washington, DC: National Academy Press), 2000.

National Whistleblower Center. "Political Science Prevails Over Sound Science at EPA." http://www.whistleblowers.org/epawhistleblowers.htm.

Natural Resources Defense Council (NRDC). *Breath-taking Premature Mortality Due to Particulate Air Pollution in 239 American Cities* (May 1996). http://www.nrdc.org/air/pollution/bt/btinx.asp.

"Bush Administration Policy Makes America's Waters Vulnerable to Development, Pollution, Says New Report" (August 12, 2004). http://www.nrdc.org/media/pressreleases/ 040812.asp.

Testing the Waters 2005: A Guide to Vacation Beaches (August 2005).

(in collaboration with: American Lung Association, Clean Air Task Force, Clean Water Action, Clear the Air, League of Conservation Voters, National Environmental Trust, National Parks

Conservation Association, National Wildlife Federation, Natural Resources Defense Council, Physicians for Social Responsibility, Environmental Integrity Project, Sierra Club, Union of Concerned Scientists, U.S. Public Interest Research Group, World Wildlife Federation). *NRDC Backgrounder: The Bush Administration's Air Pollution Plan Hurts Public Health, Helps Big Polluters, Worsens Global Warming.* http://www.uwmc.uwc. edu/geography/350/clear-skies-NDRC%20analysis.htm.

Negroponte, John D. "Protecting the Ozone Layer: Testimony Before the Senate Subcommittee on Toxic Substances & Environmental Oversight," *Department of State Bulletin* (January 28, 1987): 59.

"New Evidence of Pollution Dangers," CNN.com Health (December 15, 2000). http://www. cnn.com/2000/HEALTH/mayo/12/15/pollution.dangers/.

New York State Attorney General (press release). "Spitzer to Sue Bush Administration for Gutting Clean Air Act" (November 22, 2002). http://www.oag.state.ny.us/press/2002/nov/ nov22b_02.html.

Newman, David. *NYCOSH Testimony at the EPA Ombudsman Investigative Hearing on the Environmental & Public Health Impact of the WTC Attack* (February 23, 2003). http://911 digitalarchive.org/webcontent/nycosh/UPDATES/EPAOmbudsHearingFeb23.html.

"NGO Study Finds US Could Save Trillions by Cutting CO2," *Global Environmental Change Report* 3 (21) (1991): 4.

Nightline. "Is Environmental Science for Sale?" *ABC* (February 23, 1994).

Nixon, Richard M. *Statement on Signing the Endangered Species Act of 1973* (December 28, 1973). The American Presidency Project. http://www.presidency.ucsb.edu/site/docs/ pppus.php?admin=037&year=1973&id=374.

Nordhaus, W. D. "Greenhouse Economics: Count Before You Leap," *The Economist* (July 7, 1990): 21.

Norman, Colin. "Greenhouse Policy: A Bargain?" *Science*, v. 12 (April 12, 1991): 204.

O'Donnell, Jennifer. "Gore & Bush Tied to WTI Incinerator," *Ohio Citizen Action* (Fall/ Winter 1999–2000). http://www.ohiocitizen.org/campaigns/prevention/wti/jennl.html.

Odum, Howard & Elizabeth C. Odum. *A Prosperous Way Down.* (Boulder, CO: University Press of Colorado), 2001.

OECD. *Convention on Climate Change: Economic Aspects of Negotiations.* (Paris: OECD), 1992.

Office of Planning & Research for Governor Gray Davis. *Environmental Justice in California State Government* (October 2003). http://www.opr.ca.gov/planning/publications/ OPR_EJ_Report_Oct2003.pdf.

"Oil: Exxon Chairman's $400 Million Parachute," *ABC News* (April 14, 2006). http://www. abcnews.go.com/GMA/story?id=1841989.

Olson, Erik & Diane Cameron. *Dirty Little Secret About Our Drinking Water.* (Washington, DC: NRDC), 1995.

Oppenheimer, Michael & Robert Boyle. *Dead Heat: The Race Against the Greenhouse Effect.* (NY: New Republic), 1991.

Orlando, Laura. "Toxic Avengers," *In These Times* (February 1999): 12.

Ott, Herman E. "The Kyoto Protocol: Unfinished Business," *Environment* (July/August 1998): 17.

Owen, James R. "Energy Tax Idea Pulls Unlikely Allies Together," *San Francisco Examiner* (March 7, 1993): A-10.

Oxford University Press Blog. "Rachel Carson: Saint or Sinner?" (March 2007). http://blog. oup.com/2007/03/rachel_carson_s/.

Paarlberg, Robert L. "A Domestic Dispute: Clinton, Congress and International Environmental Policy," *Environment* (October 1996): 16.

Parker, Larry. "Stratospheric Ozone Depletion: Implementation Issues," *CRS Issue Brief for Congress* (July 12, 2000). http://www.ncseonline.org/nle/crsreports/stratospheric/strat-5.cfm.

Parson, Edward A. "Protecting the Ozone Layer," Peter M. Haas, Robert O. Keohane & Marc A. Levy, eds. *Institutions for the Earth.* (Cambridge, MA: MIT Press), 1993.

Passell, Peter. "Penny Wise on Ozone?" *New York Times* (May 16, 1990): C2.

Pell, Claiborne. "CFC Fund Decision Showed Flaws in US Policymaking," *Christian Science Monitor* (June 22, 1990): 20.

Percival, Miller & Leape Schroeder. *Environmental Regulation: Law, Science & Policy.* (Boston, MA: Little Brown), 1992.

Pianin, Eric. "Dioxin Report by EPA on Hold Industries Oppose Finding of Cancer Link, Urge Delay," *Washington Post* (April 12, 2001). http://www.mindfully.org/Pesticide/ Dioxin-Industries-Oppose.htm.

Pianin, Eric. "Ex-EPA Officials Question Clean Air Suits; Assistant Administrator Disputes That He Misled Congress About Effect of Rules," *Washington Post* (October 10, 2003).

Piney Run Preservation Association v. Carroll County, MD, 523 F.3d **453** (4th Cir. 2008).

Pollan, Michael. "Precautionary Principal," *The New York Times Magazine.* "The Year in Ideas: An Encyclopedia of Innovations, Conceptual Leaps, Harebrained Schemes, Cultural Tremors and Hindsight Reckonings that Made a Difference in 2001" (December 9, 2001): 92.

Ponce de León, Juana, ed. *Our Word is Our Weapon: Selected Writings of Subcomandante Insurgente Marcos.* (NY: Seven Stories Press), 2003.

Pope, Carl. *Strategic Ignorance.* (San Francisco, CA: Sierra Club Books), 2004.

President's Committee of Advisers on Science and Technology (Panel on Biodiversity and Ecosystems). *Teaming with Life: Investing in Science to Understand and Use America's Living Capital* (March 1998) http://clinton4.nara.gov/WH/EOP/OSTP/Environment/ html/teamingsec2.html.

Princen, Thomas, Matthias Finger, & Jack Manno. "Nongovernmental Organizations in World Environmental Politics," *International Environmental Affairs*, v. 7 (Winter 1995): 42–58.

Project on Government Oversight (POGO). Comments on the "Draft Guidance for the National Hazardous Waste and Superfund Ombudsman and Regional Superfund Ombudsmen Program," *Federal Register* **66** (2) (January 3, 2001). http://www.pogo.org/ p/environment/eo-010112-epa.htm.

Project on Government Oversight (POGO). *Written Statements of Community Members Participating in the Citizens' Briefing on the EPA Ombudsman Issue* (January 14, 2003). http://www.pogo.org/pogo-files/testimony/natural-resources/nr-epa-20030114.html.

Public Citizen. "Bush Appointees Gut Air Quality Rule and Give Congress False Information About the Consequence," *The Baltimore Chronicle* (November 3, 2003). http://baltimore chronicle.com/nov03_choke-on-it.html.

"Bush Appointees Gut Air Quality Rule and Give Congress False Information About the Consequence," "Study: Top U.S. Air Polluters Are Closely Tied to Bush Fundraising, Pollution Policymaking Process" (May 5, 2004). http://www.citizen.org/pressroom/ release.cfm?ID=1706.

Public Employees for Environmental Responsibility (PEER-Texas). "Polluters Bet Big on Bush on the Campaign Money Trail," *The Toxic Texas Tour* (November 1995). http://www.txpeer. org/Bush/Polluters_Bet_On_Bush.html.

Murky Waters: An Inside Look at the EPA's Implementation of the Clean Water Act (May 1999).

"One-Third of Major US Air Polluters Still Lack Pollution Permits" (March 11, 2002). http://www.peer.org/press/217.html.

"Environmental Enforcement Continues Decline Under Bush," *Truthout* (September 5, 2006). http://www.truthout.org/article/environmental-enforcement-continues-decline-under-bush.

Qingsong Ji & Bo Yan. "EPA's New Chemicals Program Under TSCA: The Basics," Chem Alliance.org http://www.chemalliance.org/topics/?subsec=27&id=689.

Rajan, Mukund Govind. "Bargaining with the Environment: A New Weapon for the South?" *South Asia Research*, v. 12 (November 1992): 135–47.

Rawls, J. *A Theory of Justice*. (Cambridge, MA: Harvard University Press), 1976.

Reece, Ray. *The Sun Betrayed*. (Boston, MA: South End Press), 1979.

Reinhardt, Forest. *DuPont and Freon Products*. (Washington, DC: National Wildlife Federation), 1989.

Reinhold, Robert. "Missouri Now Fears 100 Sites Could Be Tainted by Dioxin," *New York Times* (January 18, 1983): A1, A23.

"Renewable Energy Accelerates Meteoric Rise," *Renewables 21: Global Status Report 2007* (February 28, 2008). http://www.ren21.net/globalstatusreport/default.asp.

Research/Strategy/Management Inc. *Global Warming and Energy Priorities: A National Perspective* [A Study for the Union of Concerned Scientists] (November 1989).

Resource Conservation and Recovery Act (RCRA) (2008). http://www.epa.gov/epawaste/inforesources/online/index.htm.

Reuters. "L. A. Babies Get Lifetime's Toxic Air in 2 Weeks, Says Study" (September 17, 2002). http://www.enn.com/news/wire-stories/2002/09/09172002/reu_48435.asp.

Revkin, Andrew C. "U.S. Curbs Use of Species Act in Protecting Polar Bear," *New York Times* (May 8, 2009). http://www.nytimes.com/2009/05/09/science/earth/09bear.html.

Revkin, Andrew C. & Matthew L. Wald. "Solar Power Wins Enthusiasts but Not Money," *New York Times* (July 16, 2007). http://www.nytimes.com/2007/07/16/business/16solar.html.

Richardson, J. D. & Mark A. *Recycling or Disposal? Hazardous Waste Combustion in Cement Kilns: An Introduction to Policy and Legal Issues Associated with Burning Hazardous Waste in Cement Kilns* (A Briefing Paper of the American Lung Association Hazardous Waste Incineration Project), April 1995.

Rind, D., et al. "Positive Water Vapour Feedback in Climate Models Confirmed by Satellite Data," *Nature* 349 (February 1993): 500–3.

Roan, Sharon. *Ozone Crisis*. (NY: Wiley Science Editions), 1989.

Roberts, J. Timmons & Melissa M. Toffolon-Weiss. *Chronicles from the Environmental Justice Frontline*. (NY: Cambridge University Press), 2001.

Roe, David & others. *Toxic Ignorance: The Continuing Absence of Basic Health Testing for Top-Selling Chemicals in the United States*. (NY: Environmental Defense Fund), 1997.

Rosenberg, Norman J., et al., ed. *Greenhouse Warming: Abatement and Adaptation*. (Washington, DC: Resources for the Future), 1989.

Rothenberg, Jerome. "Economic Perspective on Time Comparisons: Evaluation of Time Discounting," Nazli Choucri, ed. *Global Accord: Environmental Challenges and International Responses*. (Cambridge, MA: MIT Press), 1993.

Rowlands, Ian H. *The Politics of Global Atmospheric Change*. (Manchester: Manchester University Press), 1995.

Royte, Elizabeth. *Garbage Land*. (NY: Little, Brown & Co.), 2003.

Rutger's Biodiversity Center. *What is Biodiversity?*.

Sachs, Wolfgang, ed. *Global Ecology: A New Area of Political Conflict*. (London: Zed Books), 1993.

Sand, Peter. "Protecting the Ozone Layer," *Environment* (June 1985): 18.

Sample, Ian. "Scientists Offered Cash to Dispute Climate Study," guardian.co.uk (February 2, 2007). http://www.guardian.co.uk/environment/2007/feb/02/frontpagenews.climatechange.

Sanjour, William (EPA Chief Technology Branch). "Policy Implications of Sewage Sludge on Hazardous Waste Regulation," *United States Environmental Protection Agency Office of Solid Waste Management Programs* (October 17, 1975). http://pwp.lincs.net/sanjour/Sludge1. htm.

"In Name Only," *Sierra Magazine* (September/October 1992). http://pwp.lincs.net/sanjour/ Sierra.htm#hammer.

Santer, Benjamin D. "A Chilling Reaction to Warnings of Global Warming," *San Francisco Examiner, Sunday Magazine* (July 3, 1996): 2.

Sapien, Joaquin. "Human Exposure 'Uncontrolled' at 114 Superfund Sites EPA Secrecy About Sites' Toxic Dangers Extends Even to Senators' Inquiries," *Center for Public Integrity* (May 18, 2007). http://projects.publicintegrity.org/superfund/report.aspx? aid=870.

Sawyer, Kathy. "Experts Agree Humans Have 'Discernible' Effect on Climate," *Washington Post* (December 1, 1995): A1.

Scarpello, Robert J. "Statutory Redundancy: Why Congress Should Overhaul the Endangered Species Act to Exclude Critical Habitat Designation," *Boston College Environmental Affairs Law Review* (2003): 299–341. http://www.bc.edu/schools/law/lawreviews/meta-elements/journals/bcealr/30_2/04_TXT.htm.

Schaeffer, Eric. *Letter of Resignation from Eric Schaeffer*. Washington, DC (2004). http://ohio. sierraclub.org/tecumseh/EPAresignfeb02.htm.

Schelling, Thomas C. *The Strategy of Conflict*. (Cambridge, MA: Harvard University Press), 1960.

Schmidheiny, Stephan. *Changing Course: A Global Business Perspective on Development and the Environment*. (Boston, MA: MIT Press), 1992.

Schneider, Kenneth. "Faking it: The Case Against IBT Laboratories," *Amicus Journal* (Spring 1983). http://planetwaves.net/contents/faking_it.html.

Schwartz, Peter & Doug Randal. *An Abrupt Climate Change Scenario and Its Implications for United States National Security*. California Institute of Technology (October 2003). http://www.edf.org/documents/3566_AbruptClimateChange.pdf.

Seitz, Dr.Fredrick. "Renowned Scientist Finds 'Disturbing' Fault with IPCC Climate Change Report," *Wall Street Journal* (June 12, 1996): 2.

Selim, Jocelyn. "Fetuses Take Air Pollution to Heart," *Discover* (April 2002). http://www. discover.com/apr_02/breakair.html.

Sell, Susan. "North-South Environmental Bargaining: Ozone, Climate Change & Biodiversity," *Global Governance*, v. 2, n. 1 (Winter 1996): 97–118.

Shabecoff, Philip. "A Wrangle Over Ozone Policy," *New York Times* (June 23, 1987): A1.

"A Wrangle Over Ozone Policy," "U.S. Urged to Ease Ozone-Aid Stand," *New York Times* (June 13, 1990). //www.nytimes.com/1990/06/13/world/us-urged-to-end-opposition-to-ozone-aid.html.

"A Wrangle Over Ozone Policy," *Earth Rising*. (Washington, DC: Island Press), 2000.

Shanahan, John. *A Guide to Global Warming Theory (Backgrounder #896)*. (Washington, DC: The Heritage Foundation), May 21, 1992.

Shea, Cynthia Pollock. *Protecting Life on Earth: Steps to Save the Ozone Layer*. (Washington, DC: Worldwatch Institute), 1988.

"Sunburned Soybeans," *World Watch* (May/June 1989): 9.

"Disarming Refrigerators," *World Watch* (May/June 1991): 36.

Shimberg, Steven. "Stratospheric Ozone and Climate Protection: Domestic Legislation and the International Process," *Environmental Law*, v. 21 (Summer 1991): 2175.

Shin, Paul. "Health of 9–11 Heroes at Risk," *New York Daily News* (September 5, 2006). http://www.nydailynews.com/news/local/story/449817p-378596c.html.

Shogren, Elizabeth. "Bush Weighs Endangered Species Delay," *Los Angeles Times* (April 19, 2003). http://www.commondreams.org/headlines03/0419-06.htm.

"EPA Accused of Softpedaling 9–11 Data," *Los Angeles Times* (August 23, 2003).

Shulman, Seth. *The Threat at Home.* (NY: Beacon Press), 1992.

Siemaszko, Corky. "EPA's 9–11 'Secret' '02 Exec Order Let Agency Bury Info on Air Hazards," *New York Daily News* (July 28, 2006).

Sierra Club. "The Real Truth About the Rocky Mountain Arsenal" (July 1, 1999). http://www.rmc.sierraclub.org/emg/RMA.html.

"The Real Truth About the Rocky Mountain Arsenal" (July 1, *Species at Risk: The Pacific Yew.* http://www.sierraclub.org/lewisandclark/species/pacificyew.asp.

Sierra Club (press release). "Wisconsin: Worst in the Nation When it Comes to Issuing Air Permits" (December 16, 2002). 121602.pdf (available from: http://www.midwestadvocates.org).

Sierra Club, Greenpeace, Tri-State Environmental Council, Ohio PIRG, **et al**. "Letter to President Clinton with Concerns about WTI," *Greenlink* (December 6, 2000). http://www.greenlink.org/public/hotissues/wtipres.html.

Simon, Julian L. *The Ultimate Resource 2.* (Princeton, NJ: Princeton University Press), 1996.

Slovic, Fischhoff & Lichtenstein. "Facts and Fears: Understanding Perceived Risk," *Social Risk Assessment: How Much is Enough?* (Summer 1980): 168–94.

Small Wright, Machaelle. "Sewage Sludge/Biosolids: A Health and Environmental Crisis and Scandal," *Perelandra Health Watch* (September 12, 2002). http://www.perelandra-ltd.com/Sewage_3A_W288.cfm.

Snidal, Duncan. "The Limits of Hegemonic Stability Theory," *International Organization*, v. **39** (Fall 1985): 579–614.

Soraghan, Mike. "Ties to Shattuck's Owner Hike Scrutiny of EPA Chief," *The Denver Post* (January 21, 2002). http://www.denverpost.com.

SourceWatch. *Committee for a Constructive Tomorrow* (2009). http://www.sourcewatch.org/index.php?title=Committee_for_a_Constructive_Tomorrow.

Dezenhall Resources (2008). http://www.sourcewatch.org/index.php?title=Nichols-Dezenhall#Opposing_the_Precautionary_Principle.

Speth, James Gustave. "Coming to Terms: Toward a North-South Compact for the Environment," *Environment* (June 1990): 16–20.

St. Clair, Jeffrey & Alexander Cockburn. "Nature and Politics," *Eat the State* (January 2001). http://eatthestate.org/05-10/NaturePolitics.htm.

"Cancerous Air: Born Under a Bad Sky," *San Francisco Bay View* (January 2, 2009). http://www.sfbayview.com/2009/cancerous-air-born-under-a-bad-sky/.

"Going Critical: Bush's War on Endangered Species," *Dissident Voice* (June 9, 2003). http://www.dissidentvoice.org/Articles5/St.Clair_ESA.htm.

"Stalking the Mysterious Microbe," *Capital Times* (June 9, 2005). HighBeam Research (November 12, 2009). http://www.highbeam.com.

Stauber, John & Sheldon Rampton. *Toxic Sludge is Good for You!* (Monroe, MN: Common Courage Press), 1995.

Steiner, Achim. "The UN Role in Climate Change Action: Taking the Lead Towards a Global Response," *UN Chronicle* (February 7, 2007). http://www.un.org/Pubs/chronicle/2007/issue2/0207p24.htm.

Steinzon, Rena & Margaret Clune. *The Toll of Superfund Neglect.* (Washington, DC: Center for American Progress), 2006.

Stelzer, C. D. "Weak in Math," *Riverfront Times* (July 12, 1995). http://lists.essential.org/1996/dioxin-l/msg00784.html.

Stetson, Marnie. "Who'll Pay to Protect the Ozone Layer?" *World Watch* (July–August 1990): 36. "People Who Live in Green Houses . . . ," *World Watch* (September/October 1991): 22.

Stevens, William K. "Science Academy Disputes Attack on Global Warming," *New York Times* (May 22, 1998). http://query.nytimes.com/gst/fullpage.html?res=9A02EED71F3CF931A15757C0A96E958260.

Stossel, John. *Give Me a Break*. (NY: Harper/Collins), 2005.

"Studies Confirm Dirty Air May Cause Disease," CNN.com Health (March 6, 2002). http://www.cnn.com/2002/HEALTH/03/05/pollution.dangers/.

Sunstein, Cass. *Laws of Fear, Beyond the Precautionary Principle*. (NY: Cambridge University Press), 2005.

"Survey of Criminal Justice: Crime." *International Encyclopedia of Justice Studies (Chapter 4)* (2006). http://www.iejs.com/Survey_of_CJ/CH04.htm.

Suskind, Ron. *The Price of Loyalty*. (NY: Simon & Schuster), 2004.

Swearingen, Terri. *1997 Goldman Environmental Prize Acceptance Speech* (Greenpeace Website). (1997). http://www.greenpeaceusa.org/wti/terry.htm.

Szasz, Andrew. "The Process and Significance of Political Scandals: A Comparison of Watergate and the 'Sewergate' Episode at the Environmental Protection Agency," *Social Problems* (February 1986): 202–17.

Tapper, Jake. "The Town That Haunts Al Gore," Salon.com (April 26, 2000). http://archive.salon.com/politics2000/feature/2000/04/26/gore/index3.html.

TATA Energy Research Institute, The Woods Hole Research Center, UNEP, World Resources Institute. *Conference Statement on Global Warming and Climate Change: Perspectives from Developing Countries*. International Conference on Global Warming and Climate Change: Perspectives from Developing Countries (New Delhi, India/ February 21–23, 1989).

"The Dioxin Connection in Disposable Diapers," *Mothering* (Fall 1989). http://findarticles.com/p/articles/mi_m0838/is_n53/ai_8011827.

The Ecologist. *Whose Common Future?* (Philadelphia, PA: New Society Publishers), 1993.

The European Union's Communication on Precautionary Principle. Brussels (February 2, 2000). http://www.gdrc.org/u-gov/precaution-4.html.

"The President Must Decide – State Department Pushes Radical Ozone Treaty," (editorial) Human Events (June 10, 1987).

"The Superfund," *Mother Jones* (September 3, 2003). http://www.motherjones.com/news/featurex/2003/09/superfund.html.

"The Ties that Blind," *The Arizona Republic* (November 24, 1995): A2.

Titus, James G., ed. *Effects of Changes in Stratospheric Ozone and Global Climate*. (Washington, DC: EPA), 1986.

Tolba, M. K. "Building an Environmental Institutional Framework for the Future," *Environmental Conservation*, v. 17 (Summer 1990): 105–10.

Toon, John. "The Cost of Cleaning the Air: Study Shows Permit Application Costs Lower Than Expected – with Key Benefits to Industry," *Georgia Tech Research News* (September 21, 1999). http://gtresearchnews.gatech.edu/newsrelease/TITLEV.html.

"Tragedy in Hopewell," *Time* (February 2, 1976). http://www.time.com/time/magazine/article/0,9171,945509,00.html.

Trenholm, A. & others. *Performance Evaluation of Full-Scale Hazardous Waste Incinerators*. vol. I, Executive Summary. [EPA/600/2- 84/181A]. (Washington, DC: U.S. Environmental Protection Agency), 1984.

Tripp, James T. B., Daniel J. Dudek, & Michael Oppenheimer. "Equity & Ozone Protection," *Environment* (July–August 1987): 43.

Truell, Peter & Larry Gurwin. *False Profits. The Inside Story of BCCI, the World's Most Corrupt Financial Empire.* (NY: Houghton-Mifflin), 1992.

Tuohy, John. "2 Mothers, 2 Deaths Too Many Questions," *USA Today* (July 31, 2000). http://www.acereport.org/sludge52303.html.

Tunali, Odil. "Climate Models Growing More Accurate," *World Watch* (June 1995): 6.

Ullrich, Christy. "When Will the Peak Hit?" *National Geographic* (June 3, 2008). http://ngm. nationalgeographic.com/geopedia/World_Oil.

Union of Concerned Scientists. "Special Issue: The National Energy Strategy," *Nucleus* (Spring 1991): 3.

  Fighting Global Warming: A Profitable Solution. (Washington, DC: UCS), 1992.

  Smoke, Mirrors & Hot Air: How Exxon-Mobil Uses Big Tobacco's Tactics to Manufacture Uncertainty on Climate Science. (Washington, DC: UCS), 2007. http://www.ucsusa.org/ assets/documents/global_warming/exxon_report.pdf.

United Nations Centre for Science & Technology for Development. *Report on the International Conference on Energy in Climate & Development: Policy Issues and Technological Options.* International Conference on Energy in Climate & Development (Saarücken, KongreBhalle, 1990).

United Nations Environment Programme. *Action on Ozone.* (NY: United Nations), 1990.

  The Environmental Effects of Ozone Depletion: 1991 Update. UNEP (November 1991).

  [V. H. Heywood & R. T. Watson]. *Global Biodiversity Assessment: Summary for Policy-Makers.* (NY: Cambridge University Press), 1995.

United Nations. *General Assembly Resolution 43/53* (1988).

U.S. Department of Justice (press release). "U.S., Louisiana Secure $35 Million Settlement with Two Companies to Clean Up Hazardous Waste and Reopen Incinerator" (Friday, September 12, 1997). http://www.usdoj.gov/opa/pr/1997/September97/379enr.html.

  Superfund's 25th Anniversary: Capturing the Past, Charting the Future (2009). www.epa.gov/ superfund/25anniversary/.

  Fact Sheet on Love Canal. http://www.epa.gov/Region2/superfund/npl/0201290c.htm.

  EPA Organizational Structure. http://www.epa.gov/epapages/epahome/organization.htm.

  Air Quality Planning & Standards: Introduction. http://www.epa.gov/oar/oaqps/airtrans/intro. html.

  "U.S. Sues Hooker Chemical at Niagara Falls, New York" (December 20, 1979). www.epa. gov/history/topics/lovecanal/02.htm.

  Lining of Waste Impoundments and Disposal Facilities [Sw-870] (Springfield, VA: National Technical Information Service), March, 1983.

  An Assessment of the Risks of Stratospheric Modification (revised draft). (Washington, DC: EPA), 1987.

  Scope of the CERCLA Petroleum Exclusion Under Sections 101(14) and 104(a)(2) (July 3, 1987). http://www.epa.gov/compliance/resources/policies/cleanup/superfund/ petro-exclu-mem.pdf.

  Regulatory Impact Analysis: Protection of Stratospheric Ozone (3 vols.). (Washington, DC: unpublished report), 1988.

  Proceedings of the U.S. Environmental Protection Agency Workshop on Integrating Case Studies Carried Out Under the Montreal Protocol. (Washington, DC, 1990).

  Proceedings of the Superfund Relocation Roundtable Meeting (Pensacola, FL, May 2–4, 1996). http://www.epa.gov/oecaerth/resources/publications/ej/nejac/nejacmtg/ roundtable-relocation-0596.pdf.

Testimony by Lois Gibbs at the Proceedings of the Superfund Relocation Roundtable Meeting (Pensacola, FL, May 2–4, 1996). http://www.epa.gov/oecaerth/resources/publications/ej/nejac/nejacmtg/roundtable-relocation-0596.pdf.

U.S. Environmental Protection Agency (Office of Research and Development). *Exposure and Health Reassessment of 2,3,7,8-Tetrachlorodibenzo-p-Dioxin (TCDD) and Related Compounds, Part III Integrated Risk Summary and Risk Characterization for 2,3,7,8-Tetrachlorodibenzo-p-Dioxin (TCDD) and Related Compounds* [External Review Draft] (June 2000).

U.S. Environmental Protection Agency, Inspector General. *Water Enforcement: State Enforcement of Clean Water Act Dischargers Can Be More Effective* (August 2001).

U.S. Environmental Protection Agency, Office of Inspector General. *AIR: EPA & State Progress in Issuing Title V Permits* (March 29, 2002). www.epa.gov/oar/oaqps/permits/pdfs/oig-titlev.pdf.

U.S. Environmental Protection Agency Newsroom. "President Bush Announces Clear Skies & Global Climate Change Initiatives" (February 14, 2002). www.epa.gov/clearskies/clear_skies_factsheet.pdf.

U.S. Environmental Protection Agency. *Technical Addendum: Methodologies for the Benefit Analysis of the Clear Skies Act of 2003* (September 2003). http://www.epa.gov/air/clearskies/tech_addendum.pdf.

U.S. Environmental Protection Agency. *Toxics Relief Inventory* (2003). http://www.epa.gov/tri/tridata/tri03/index.htm.

U.S. Environmental Protection Agency. *National Listing of Fish & Wildlife Advisories* (2004). http://map1.epa.gov/.

U.S. Environmental Protection Agency. *Benefits & Costs of Clean Air Act: Study Design & Summary of Results* (March 6, 2007). http://www.epa.gov/air/sect812/design.html.

U.S. Environmental Protection Agency & The Government Accounting Office. *Water Quality: Inconsistent State Approaches Complicate Nation's Efforts to Identify Most Polluted Waters* (GAO-02–186), January 2002.

U.S. Fish & Wildlife Service. *Black-Capped Vireo Recovery Plan.* (Washington, DC: Government Printing Office), 1991.

U.S. Government Accountability Office. *Toxic Substances: Status of EPA's Efforts to Reduce Toxic Releases* (Washington, DC: GAO/RCED-94–207), September 22, 1994. http://www.mapcruzin.com/scruztri/docs/gao94207.htm.

U.S. House of Representatives. Hearing Series. *Scientific Integrity & the Public Trust: The Science Behind Federal Policies & Mandates*; Hearing #1: *Stratospheric Ozone: Myths & Realities* (Committee on Science, Subcommittee on Energy & Environment), September 20, 1995.

U.S.-PIRG Report. *Super Polluters: The Top 25 Superfund Polluters and their Toxic Waste Sites* (July 1998). http://www.pirg.org/reports/enviro/super25/index.htm.

U.S.-PIRG Report. *Troubled Waters: An Analysis of CWA Compliance (2003–4).* [Troubled_Waters.pdf] http://iowapirg.org/IA.asp?id2=23277.

U.S.-PIRG/CHEJ (press release). "Superfund 25th Anniversary Report Finds America's Safety Net is Weakest When Needed Most Groups Call on EPA Superfund to Lead Hurricane Katrina and Rita Pollution Cleanup with Special Appropriation" (September 29, 2005). www.besafenet.com/NarrativeSuperfundReport.pdf.

U.S. Senate. *Testimony of James Hansen Before the Senate Committee on Energy and Natural Resources: The Greenhouse Effect and Global Climate Change.* 100th Congress, 2nd Session 40 (June 1988).

Video Project. *Times Beach, Missouri.* Oakland, CA (1994).

Vig, Norman J. & Michael Kraft. *Environmental Policy: New Directions for the 21st Century*, 6th ed. (Washington, DC: CQ Press), 2006.

Vitousek, Peter, Paul R. Ehrlich, Anne H. Ehrlich, & Pamela Matson. "Human Appropriation of the Products of Photosynthesis" *BioScience* (June 1986): 368–73. http://www.biology.duke.edu/wilson/EcoSysServices/papers/VitousekEtal1986.pdf.

Vogel, Shawna. "Has Global Warming Begun?" Earth (December 1995): 25.

von Stackelberg, Peter. "White Wash: The Dioxin Cover-Up," *Greenpeace* (March/April 1989). http://www.planetwaves.net/contents/white_wash_dioxin_cover_up.html.

Wallerstein, Immanuel. *After Liberalism*. (NY: New Press), 1995.

World-Systems Analysis: An Introduction. (Durham, NC: Duke University Press), 2004.

Walters, Mark Jerome. *A Shadow and a Song: The Struggle to Save an Endangered Species*. (Post Mills, VT: Chelsea Green Publishing Co.), 1992.

Walton, Richard & Robert B. McKersie. *A Behavioral Theory of Negotiations*. (NY: McGraw-Hill), 1965.

"Water Pollution," *MSN Encarta Online Encyclopedia* (2009). http://encarta.msn.com/encyclopedia_761572857/Water_Pollution.html.

Waterman, Richard W. *Presidential Influence and the Administrative State*. (Knoxville, TN: University of Tennessee Press), 1989.

Watson, R. T., **et al**. *Present State of Knowledge of the Upper Atmosphere 1988: An Assessment Report*. National Aeronautics & Space Administration (August 1988).

Welch, Craig. "Bush Switches Nation's Tack on Protecting Species," *Seattle Times* (September 27, 2004). http://seattletimes.nwsource.com/html/nation-world/2002047271_bushesa27m.html.

Weisskopf, Michael. "Bush Says More Data on Warming Needed," *Washington Post* (April 18, 1990): A1.

White House, Office of the Press Secretary. *Remarks by the President in the Opening Address to the White House Conference on Science and Economics Research Related to Global Change* (Washington, DC, April 17, 1990).

White House (press release). "Executive Summary – the Clear Skies Initiative" (February 2002). http://www.whitehouse.gov/news/releases/2002/02/clearskies.html.

Williams, Gerald S. "Toxic Dumps: EPA's Hit List," *Newsweek* (January 3, 1983): 12.

Williams, R. H. *Low Cost Strategies for Coping with Carbon Dioxide Emissions Limits*. (Princeton, NJ: Center for Energy and Environmental Studies), 1989.

Wilson, Duff. "Wasteland," *Amicus Journal* (Spring 1998): 34–9.

Wingspread Statement on the Precautionary Principle (January 1998). http://www.sehn.org/precaution.html.

Woellert, Lorraine. "A Global-Warming Critic's Hot Stock," *Business Week* (June 5, 2000). http://www.businessweek.com/archives/2000/b3684066.arc.htm.

Wolk, Julie. *The Truth About Toxic Waste Cleanups*. (U.S. PIRG & Sierra Club), 2004. http://www.sierraclub.org/toxics/factsheets/cleanups.pdf.

Worland, Gayle. "Mr. Clean: Superfund Ombudsman is Either a White Knight or an EPA Whitewash," *The Denver Westword* (April 1, 1999). http://www.westword.com/issues/1999-04-01/feature2.html/1/index.html.

World Climate Report. http://www.worldclimatereport.com/.

World Meteorological Organization (WMO). *Atmospheric Ozone 1985: Assessment of Our Understanding of the Processes Controlling the Present Distribution and Change*. Geneva (1986).

World Meteorological Organization, Global Ozone Research & Monitoring Project. *Scientific Assessment of Stratospheric Ozone: 1989 (vol. 1)* (WMO: 1989).

World Meteorological Organization (WMO). "Key Points from the IPCC Second Assessment Report," *World Climate News* (January 1997): 5.

World Wildlife Fund. *Exposing Hormone Disrupting Chemicals* (February 25, 2005). http://www.panda.org/about_our_earth/teacher_resources/webfieldtrips/toxics/news/?18830.

Written Testimony of William A. Smedley for the Senate Environment and Public Works Committee Hearing regarding the EPA National Ombudsman Office [submitted on behalf of three nonprofit organizations: GreenWatch, the Pennsylvania Environmental Network (PEN) and Arrest the Incinerator Remediation (AIR)] (July 15, 2002). http://www.senate.gov/~epw/107th/Smedley_062502.htm.

Young, Oran R. "The Politics of International Regime Formation," *International Organization*, v. **43** (Summer 1989): 363–4.

"Political Leadership and Regime Formation: on the Development of Institutions in International Society," *International Organization*, v. **45** (Fall 1991): 281–308.

Zero Waste Alliance. *The Case for Zero Waste* (2001). http://www.zerowaste.org/case.htm.

Zuesse, Eric. "Love Canal: The Truth Seeps Out," *ReasonOnline* (February 1981). http://www.reason.com/news/show/29319.html.

Zweibel, Ken, James Mason, & Vasilis Fthenakis. "A Solar Grand Plan," *Scientific American* (January 2008). http://www.sciam.com/article.cfm?id=a-solar-grand-plan.

Index